by
Blaine Johnson & Brian Kamens

Tacoma Historical Society Press
Tacoma, Washington

Copyright 2017 by Blaine Johnson & Brian Kamens

Published by
Tacoma Historical Society Press,
Tacoma Washington

Printed in Tacoma, Washington
by LaserWriting

ISBN: 978-0-9846234-7-1

Library of Congress
Control Number 2017938569

Cover image "Theatre Row Circa 1930" courtesy
of Marshall L. Johnson

Portions of this material composed by Murray Morgan have previously been published and are printed here by permission of Lane Morgan, holder of all Murray Morgan copyrights.

Disclaimer: The materials contained in *Showtime in Tacoma* represent a compilation of the authors' research and compositions as well as contributions by other individuals and organizations. While diligent efforts have been made to ensure accuracy in the information and sources of this information, the authors are not able to assert the absolute accuracy represented in such a wide-ranging historical project.

Dedication

*This book is dedicated to all those who seek out
and support all forms of art and culture
Now Playing in your community.*

Table of Contents

"It's now Showtime. Shall we go in?" ⊙ TPL

CONSTANTI'S RIVIERA
R·C·A·
PHOTOPHONE
THEATER
9th and Pacific

THE LYRIC
1320 PACIFIC AVE.

PANTAGES
NINTH and BROADWAY

STRAND
DIRECTION JENSEN-VON HERBERG
H. T. MOORE GENERAL MANAGER

BEVERLY
THEATER

NINTH STREET THEATRE

RIALTO
TACOMA'S METROPOLITAN THEATRE

R. K. O.
Orpheum

APOLLO
L. A. DRINKWINE, OWNER.

LYCEUM THEATRE

CAMEO

11 A.M. to 11 P.M.
BLUE MOUSE
JOHN HAMRICK
25¢ ANYTIME

Empress Theatre

VICTORY

Introduction

This book is a labor of love with an agenda.

Labor, Love, Agenda – Each of these aspects is interwoven in the motivation for this book, how it has been developed, the elements it covers and the spirit in which the compositions were written. This is a book of historical perspective, but intended as an offering to promote communal experiences by informing the present and future.

As to the agenda – *Showtime in Tacoma* pulls back the curtain to reveal stories that begin with Tacoma's earliest entertainment venues, the raunchy to the regal, competing for, and ultimately helping to define, the character of a city. It continues with the drama of public events that established the Theater District as Tacoma's Gathering Place since the city's founding.

It covers the many dozens of downtown and neighborhood theaters, and a wide variety of other venues, as well as the performers and performance organizations that have attracted audiences to more than a century's worth of memorable experiences. This is the story of what we watched and where we watched, what was accomplished, what was lost and, most significantly, how these deep-seated roots anchor a dynamic new era in Tacoma's colorful cultural history.

More than 150 theater names have graced the identities of Tacoma theaters. The Pantages Theater is the gem that has not only survived, but starred as the catalyst for Downtown Tacoma's renaissance. Now it is poised to celebrate its 100th anniversary along with the Rialto Theater in 2018.

As to the love – *Showtime in Tacoma* is a non-profit project developed with Tacoma Historical Society Press in cooperation with the Broadway Center for the Performing Arts. These organizations are essential to Tacoma's culture, the former in telling its story, the latter, in leading its ongoing cultural engagement. In the Foreword, BCPA Executive Director David Fischer presents the dramatic next acts for the Pantages and Rialto Theaters as well as the Theatre on the Square.

This book is paired in spirit with the late Griselda "Babe" Lehrer, who began a biography of Alexander Pantages, concurrent with the launch of this project.

Just weeks before he was elected U.S. President, Franklin D. Roosevelt drew a huge crowd to 9th & Broadway on September 20, 1932. TPL

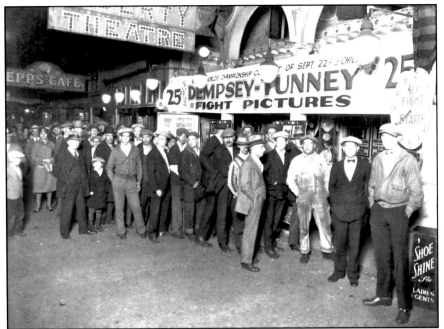
Boxing fans wait for the 1927 Dempsey-Tunney fight film at the Liberty Theater ⊙ TPL

Showtime in Tacoma features profiles of a dozen performance organizations that collectively have represented hundreds of years of distinguished live performances. As evidenced in these profiles, the passion and commitment by those who guide and support these organizations is crucial to their sustainability.

As a celebrated historian, Murray Morgan loved a good story and told many great ones. Before his passing in 2000, he had started a book about Tacoma's theaters. His daughter, Lane Morgan, generously contributed the various manuscript drafts and work-in-progress notes to this book project. A dozen of his stories about the influential personalities, theaters and colorful characters who operated them are showcased in this book.

After her passing in 2015, the book was completed under the direction of her family. Babe personified love of community with considerable support for the Broadway Center facilities and programs.

As Mayor Marilyn Strickland's Message asserts, the restoration of the Pantages Theater in the early 1980s came about through visionary passion and hard work. It was regarded as the key turnaround event when the downtown sector began its revitalization after decades of decline, and the project is considered a national model for the impact that can be provided by restoration of urban cultural centers.

Steph Farber and Phyllis Harrison, passionate supporters of the Theater District for decades, have authored a number of articles featured in the book, including the saga of the restoration of the Pantages Theater in early '80s. As they illustrate, love of community becomes an asset when talent is applied to action. Deborah Freedman's skills for genealogy and archival research led to several insightful articles in this book as well as an exhibit for *Showtime in Tacoma* at the Tacoma Historical Society Museum. Former Tacoma Mayor and current president of the Tacoma

On October 10, 1926, baseball fans swarm across St. Helens and Market streets to watch World Series results re-enacted on a display panel (far right).

Historical Society Bill Baarsma shares memories of sports gatherings in Tacoma's larger venues. Ron Karabaich's collection of historic photos has provided a number of the unique photographs shown here. And, thanks to Thomas R. Stenger's decades-long passion for collecting Tacoma memorabilia, we are able to display images of historic theater playbills, photographs and post cards.

Music has been woven through the entertainment fabric of Tacoma since the first honky tonk piano livened up the box-house theaters. We explore the role of the theater organists during the silent film era and the jazz legends who held forth in night clubs. Rock historian Peter Blecha provides insights into the Tacoma rock scene of the 50s and 60s and *Weekly Volcano* columnist Rev. Adam McKinney takes us into contemporary music venues.

Love of and belief in the value of story telling as a vehicle for community building inspired four entities to underwrite the production and printing costs for this book. They are McMenamins, Fred Roberson, Scott Warmuth and Ledger Square Law.

Acts of community love have played vital roles in protecting important Tacoma cinematic assets, including the discovery and restoration of the silent film *Eyes of the Totem,* produced by Tacoma's Weaver Studios. When a Proctor-based venue was at risk of being sold for a non-theater use, a group raised funds to buy the building and reclaim the Blue Mouse name. They later rallied again to raise funds for the necessary conversion to digital projection. Tacoma's Grand Cinema conquered an even bigger challenge when the non-profit independent theater successfully raised funds from the community to convert all four of its screens to digital. Executive Director Philip Cowan provides insights into the behind-the-screen film operations of the most loved independent theater in South Puget Sound.

As to the labor – At the convergence where passion for a community meets the hard work of enhancing it, the authors, Brian Kamens and Blaine Johnson, have donated their time and efforts in developing this book without expectation of personal compensation. They first collaborated in 2001 while doing research that led to the City of Tacoma designating the street section between South Seventh and St. Helens as Opera Alley, a tribute to the notorious corridor of gambling houses and brothels that had caused moral hand-wringing a hundred years earlier.

The foundation on which this project is built would not exist without an extra-ordinary research pursuit by Brian that began in 1983 as a hobby during lunch time in his position at the Tacoma Public Library. Over a span of more than three decades, Brian reviewed nearly every Tacoma newspaper from 1883 to 1966, creating the Tacoma-Pierce County Buildings Index to cover nearly 70,000 addresses – including coverage of every theater in Tacoma.

This research provided information for the stories by Murray Morgan, Steph Farber and Phyllis Harrison, as well as the composition and selection of images Brian and Blaine produced.

Babe Ruth, who played for the losing Yankees, appeared eight weeks later at the Pantages Theater. (See ad page 11.) ⊙ TPL

The Theater District has long been the city's gathering place, including this processional in 1908 for a fireman killed in the line of duty ⊙ TPL

Labor and passion for community have influenced Blaine's role in Tacoma. Among his projects, he directed the restoration of two historic buildings, one a structure that once housed the Savoy Theater on Broadway, and the other the former YMCA on Market Street. As founder of the Tacoma Theater District Association, Blaine led the development of Ben Gilbert Park on St. Helens, which features a 60-foot-long mural of a crowd gathered in 1926 to watch World Series results posted on a display board in front of the former *Tacoma Tribune* and *Ledger* building. This event is captured in the panorama image on pages 8 and 9. This photo was chosen for its portrayal of two important aspects that influence Tacoma's cultural history – the gathering for shared experiences and the impact of changing technology on how events are experienced.

On October 10, 1926, several thousand baseball fans swarmed across Ledger Square and everything surrounding the area to witness World Series results re-enacted on a large scoreboard mounted on the Tacoma News Tribune & Ledger Building. This event was the seventh and deciding game between the Babe

Ruth and Lou Gehrig-led New York Yankees and the St. Louis Cardinals. Ruth homered for the Yanks, but wound up being the goat, causing the last out by getting thrown out trying to steal second base. St. Louis won the game 3-2 and the World Series – much to the delight of the pro-Cardinals Tacoma crowd. Eight weeks later, Ruth performed his touring vaudeville act at the Pantages Theater, located one block away at 9th and Broadway.

On many occasions in the years before home radio broadcasts, let alone the emergence of television, throngs of locals gathered in front of the newspaper building at the intersection of St. Helens, Market and South 7th streets, awaiting transmitted news dispatches from the newspaper's teletype reports. Election results, major boxing events and the World Series were popular occasions for gatherings, creating social events. With the emergence of motion pictures, news information came from delayed film reports of major sporting events and news reels of far-off wars.

Many of the stories in this book reflect on the impact of changing technology, from a time when all enter-

A 1930 World Series game draws another crowd

tainment was provided as a "live" experience. There was a transition period when live vaudeville would share the evening's billing with movies. Eventually, sound came to cinema and it was a lot less expensive for theater operators to put rolls of film in a projector than to pay for traveling performers and house musicians. However, even as vaudeville was absorbed by cinema and as dozens of movie houses eventually surrendered to home television, there were still crowds lining streets for parades, political rallies, and celebrity events.

The technological evolution of individualized home entertainment has carried us from the radio to television to VCRs to the internet to social media to video games that seem to draw us ever inward. By comparison, the primitiveness in which information was conveyed to those baseball fans gathered in the street feels pleasantly nostalgic. The Pantages appearance of Ruth, who had been a focus of actions relayed from a baseball diamond thousands of miles away, dramatized the appeal of being able to see such a star figure in person. Imagine if you were to assemble that crowd today. Instead of the sea of hats and caps and suits and ties, envision everyone wearing virtual reality goggles that would put the viewer inside Babe Ruth's eyeballs as he waited for the next pitch.

TV sets for sale in 1950 in a Theater District storefront

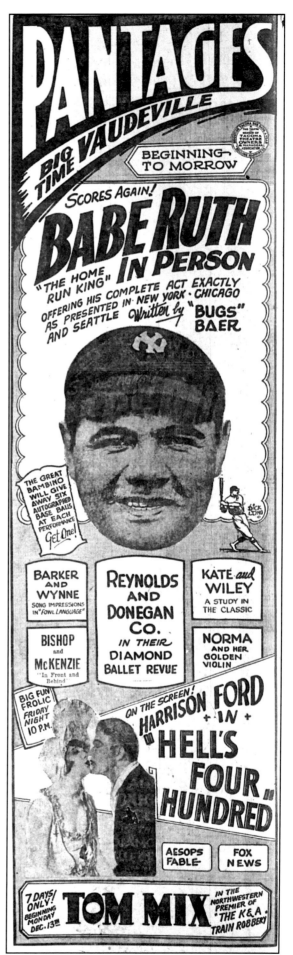

The parade moved up 9th and onto Broadway as a large crowd greeted the Cole Brothers-Clyde Beatty Circus in 1936

Yes, for those of us who look back fondly at events that drew the community together for shared experiences inside the venues or on the streets, there is the risk of melancholy over trends in entertainment. As this is written, the Ringling Bros. and Barnum & Bailey Circus is closing after 150 years of operation. In decades past, when the circus train pulled into town, a parade drew throngs to the streets. One of the reasons given for closing the big top was that "The Greatest Show on Earth" couldn't hold the attention span of kids anymore.

We lament the loss of architectural and cultural treasures such as the Tacoma Theater. However, it is not our intention to dwell in nostalgia for earlier eras, but to savor the stories about the journey that has brought us to the opportunities of today. Loss of any kind can make us that much more appreciative of the treasures that remain and are being enhanced as the centerpieces in our cultural and entertainment landscape. Aside from the theaters, these include per-formance venues being developed such as Fred Rober-son's Armory, the McMenamins' restoration of the Elks Temple and the variety of entertainment spots stirring the revival of the Theater District. Tacoma can be justifiably proud of its support for the performance organizations presenting live events on a broad spec-trum of art forms and for the nine distinctively regard-ed museums that encircle the Theater District.

As we value the past, we don't look upon the Pantages and Rialto Theaters celebrating their 100th anniversa-ries simply as iconic trophies, but as cherished vehi-cles to take us on to a new era of experiences. In show business, the desire is to always leave them wanting more. As to the agenda, we hope this book enhanc-es your appreciation for the drama that brought us across more than a century's adventures in entertain-ment and, most importantly, inspires you to step out and savor the offerings being presented in this era of revival for all aspects of *Showtime in Tacoma*.

NOW PLAYING

Mayor's Message

By Tacoma Mayor Marilyn Strickland

In 1978 the City of Tacoma decided to purchase the historic Pantages Theater, which had become a rundown movie house called the Roxy. It took five years to complete the restoration of the Pantages, but this proved to be instrumental to the revitalization of downtown Tacoma. Arts and culture are vital components of a cosmopolitan city and having a thriving Theater District that serves as the anchor for the performing arts has been crucial to reversing the trend of disinvestment and blight in the downtown core.

The Pantages Theater was built on the grand vision of a gathering space at the Palace of Versailles, and its unique, ornate beauty is a reminder that the performing arts are worthy of such spaces.

Today, our downtown is in the midst of tremendous improvement and economic growth. We are a center for creative and post-secondary education, we offer light rail transportation, and a diverse variety of businesses, from retail to breweries and professional services. The Broadway Center for the Performing Arts facilities play a major role in raising Tacoma's profile in the Puget Sound region. The people of Tacoma and our guests fully appreciate the beauty, detail and designs of theaters like the Pantages and Rialto, much like those who built them in the early part of the 20th century. Our city fully embraces the arts, which in turn drives the creative economy and strengthens our social capital.

The City of Tacoma strongly views these historic venues as assets that benefit the entire metropolitan region. Arts and culture shape our identity as a city, the value of which was expressed by nearly 3,000 participants during the City's recent Tacoma 2025 strategic visioning effort. We continue to look for ways to support and promote the arts to ensure community inclusion and equitable access to these beloved assets and experiences.

– Marilyn Strickland is a two-term Mayor of Tacoma (2010–2017)

The annual tree-lighting ceremony in front of the Pantages is a popular community tradition ⓘ BCPA/CVG

First Night

In 1992, the Pierce County Arts Commission brought a new celebration to the Theater District. First Night – a family-friendly, arts-focused, alcohol-free celebration of New Year's Eve – was created in Boston as an alternative to traditional New Year's Eve celebrations. Tacoma was the first city west of the Mississippi to adopt the festival. Pierce County ran First Night for several years until the license was obtained by the Theater District Associates. The TDA has run the event ever since, welcoming ever-growing, ever-more dedicated crowds. Over the years, First Night Tacoma/Pierce County – the Largest New Year's Eve Party in Washington – has won national awards for its posters, its buttons and its programming. Everything from fire dancers to the ever-popular Ice Walk, from Artis the Spoon Man to the Northwest Sinfonietta (playing Viennese Waltzes and Polkas!) from the World's Shortest Parade to the fire-infused Countdown at midnight – all this and more has continued to bring citizens and visitors – young and old – to the middle of Downtown Tacoma, in the middle of the night, in the middle of winter to celebrate as a community.

BJ

Foreword

By David Fischer

📷 BCPA/LM

We've come a long way from Tacoma's first downtown "theater," the opera house and pool hall! Through burgeoning and crashing economies, through wars and peace marches, through fires and new edifices, Tacoma's historic theater district has survived and, today, we can say, "thrives!"

For more than 100 years, our community has gathered at 9th and Broadway, and our social fabric has been strengthened. By that I mean, that we have congregated – rich and poor, black and white, LGBTQ and straight, Jew and gentile, and every other demographic – the whole of our community have convened, often with the help of a performing artist, author or politician. Through ideas that are big or intimate, our community has opened itself up, engaged empathy and connected as human beings.

As you will appreciate in your reading of this book, Tacoma's historic Theater District has hosted some remarkable people, including multiple Presidents and would-be Presidents, including F.D.R. who WALKED across the Pantages' stage when running for Vice President, Fred Astaire dancing with his sister Adele, W.C. Fields, Bill "Bojangles" Robinson, Babe Ruth, Steve Allen, Tony Bennett, Queen Latifah, Lyle Lovett, Buddy Guy, Garrison Keillor... oh, the list is too long to share!

Today, the Broadway Center, Tacoma's umbrella agency that "energizes community through live performance," proudly carries the more-than-century-old torch of gathering community in downtown Tacoma. Yet, because of the intrusion of media – big screen or palm-sized – the method by which we energize has become as important as the content. Live, non-medi-

ated, person-to-person connection is at the core of our work, and that's something we truly prize.

As of this writing, the South Sound community is embarking on a major philanthropic investment campaign to prepare the Pantages and other facilities to serve the next 100 years. Our goal is to improve "bricks and mortar," especially at the Pantages, one of the Northwest's most important buildings. It will get a much-needed facelift, seismic upgrades, and improvements to patron comfort, plus technical improvements to strengthen the business needs of the theaters. In addition, we are ensuring continued and deeper inclusion of the community by seeding a special program fund. Particularly exciting is the development of a new exhibit inside our newest theater which will tell the story of the South Sound's rise and development through civic engagement and citizen leadership.

Babe Lehrer

This new exhibit will honor two of the most stalwart civic leaders of Tacoma, two women who strengthened our social fabric, and who were instrumental in sustaining the performing arts. The new "Lehrer-Lucien Leadership Commons" is named in honor of Babe Lehrer and Dawn Lucien, who, despite each of their recent passing, are still forces of inspiration. These women were so active and engaged across a spectrum of community efforts, it is time we pay tribute to them both!

Dawn Lucien

You may ask, "why civic leadership"? From our emergence as an active rail, maritime and forest products community to a vital international seaport; from small savings and loans to large, regional banking business; from small health clinics to housing some of the nation's best medical facilities; from a small religious college to being the home of more than half a dozen venues for higher learning – it is civic leadership that made the difference. We have boomed in a way that leadership uniquely sculpted our community. There's no other place like the South Sound and we want to celebrate our unique nature by sharing the stories of those who have helped shape it.

Our contemporary Theater District has certainly benefited from the hard work of many citizen-leaders beyond Babe Lehrer and Dawn Lucien... as they say, "it takes a village." In 1979, a group of women with brooms (Virginia Shackelford, Barbara Baldwin, Josephine Heiman, Marcia Moe, Jan Dillon, and many others) pushed open the doors of the shuttered Roxy (Pantages) Theater and began a campaign to save it at a time when so many beautiful theaters around the country were being torn down. A young U.S. Congressman, Norm Dicks, stepped forward, to energize U.S Senator Magnuson, Tacoma City Council and a team of other leaders to save the Pantages and launch the Broadway Center. Since then, the City of Tacoma has been a remarkable partner with the Broadway Center in stewarding Tacoma's theaters.

This book helps place a marker in time that celebrates our successful past, and marks the next century that lies ahead when Tacoma's theaters will continue to bear witness and hold fast our community.

– David Fischer is the Executive Director of the Broadway Center for the Performing Arts

Big Birthdays for Broadway Center Theaters in 2018

100th Anniversaries for Pantages Theater and Rialto Theater
25th Anniversary for Theatre on the Square

The 1,169-seat Pantages Theater still showcases its original skylight

BCPA/CVGP

TPL

Architect B. Marcus Priteca's rendering of his design for the Pantages Theater led to the creation of an icon that, flanked by the Rialto and Theatre on the Square, represents the heart of Tacoma's cultural Gathering Place.

BLACK LIVES MATTER
A CONVERSATION
PANTAGES THEATER 5/3
TICKETS: $24
BROADWAY CENTER.ORG

Broadway Center
For the Performing Arts
™

BCPA/Act

The 738-seat Rialto Theater viewed from the stage

BCPA/CVGP

BJ

THEATRE ON THE SQUARE

The three Broadway Center performance venues will undergo significant renovations as they celebrate their respective milestone anniversaries in 2018 and beyond. Among these planned upgrades is the creation of the Lehrer-Lucien Leadership Commons at the Theatre on the Square. A project involving Pierce Transit, Broadway Center, City of Tacoma and private investment is being explored to convert the Theatre Square area into a prominent community gathering place and outdoor performance venue.

The 300-seat Theatre on the Square was built in 1993

BCPA/Act

NOW PLAYING

Prologue

The Enduring Vision

The ancient forest surrendered to the axe and saw so swiftly there wasn't time to pull the stumps before they carved out streets around them. They would come back later and dynamite them out, but, in the meantime, they painted the stumps white to keep humans and horses from running into them at night. "They" were the folks from the Tacoma Land Company, the division of the Northern Pacific Railroad with the mission to lay out a city with sites that were buildable – or more to point, with parcels that could be deeded and sold to the people who could be lured to the far western frontier on the newly laid northern transcontinental route.

When the Northern Pacific reached Tacoma as the Western terminus of the transcontinental in 1873, the connection to St. Paul, Minnesota required travel on a cobbled-together number of connections, including boat travel across the Columbia River. Still, the most primitive of rail connections took barely over a week, compared to the months that had been required to get this far west by covered wagon or by ship around South America. The journey had been shortened when

Circa 1913, Pacific Avenue is flanked by theaters, Old City Hall towers across from the Northern Pacific Railroad headquarters 	TSC

1

the first transcontinental rail connection opened to San Francisco in 1869. This provided a means to travel up the coast by ship, reducing months to weeks for travelers from the east.

Still, it is estimated that in 1874 Tacoma's mere population was 48 Caucasians and 175 Chinese, who had been involved with building the railroad. Charles B. Wright, president of the Tacoma Land Company, built the town's first masonry building at Ninth and Pacific in 1874 and rebuilt it following a fire in 1884. The 1880 census showed a modest population of 1,098, but in the next several years, architecturally dynamic multi-story buildings of brick and ornamental stone lined Pacific Avenue as the population surged. No streets were yet paved and domestic stock was vulnerable to attack by native wild animals.

2

Cor. 9th and C. Sts., Tacoma, Wash.

9

8

4

Port Waterfront, Tacoma, Washington.

5

3

6   7

In 1881, Tacoma Land Company (controlled by the Northern Pacific) began building the Tacoma Hotel. Designed by architect Stanford White, it was the largest hotel north of San Francisco. On January 7, 1884, old and new Tacoma united under a single government.

We can cringe to think of the quality and quantity of old growth timber that was used for sidewalks and planking under the dirt on main streets in an effort to keep man and beast from sinking in the mud. But, timber was coming out of the greatest forests that had been found in the two hundred years of logging that moved ever westward from Maine. Tacoma came to be called the "Lumber Capital of the World" and the economic impact was profound. There also was coal to be mined, grain to be shipped, fish to be harvested. This was an economy built on the extraction of resources.

The first electric light plant in the state was built in 1882 by the Tacoma Mill Company. Four years later, Tacoma Power & Light Company provided electricity for street lights. By the end of 1890 the first electric lights were provided to some 1,500 houses, but it would take until the turn of the century before every house in the city had electricity. In 1888 the first horse drawn carriage on rails ran from 7th to 13th on Pacific. The first electric street car line began operating in 1890 and the Interurban connecting Tacoma to Seattle through Kent and Auburn began in 1902. Statehood for Washington came in 1889.

An immigrant from Germany became mayor and led perhaps the most despicable event in Tacoma's history when the entire Chinese population was forcibly marched out of town on November 3, 1885.

In the spring of 1888 the first train passed through the Stampede Pass tunnel, providing the Northern Pacific with a direct route between the Great Lakes and Tacoma. The "boom" in boomtown was on as the town rushed to become a city. The Northern Pacific promoted Tacoma as far away as Europe and by the 1890 census there were 36,000 people calling Tacoma home. The headcount rose to over 52,000 by 1893. It is hard to imagine the drama of a city rising from barely 1,000 people in 1880 to a headcount of just over 52,000 by 1893. That's 50,000 people coming from somewhere else, as many as half foreign born, in essentially a dozen years.

As the population table shows, the momentum stopped abruptly. The Panic of '93 was crippling across the country, but perhaps no city took a greater hit than

Tacoma. It can be speculated that Tacoma's bid to be second only to San Francisco as a great city of the West perished as thousands retreated to where they came from or pushed on to greener pastures. Seattle drew some of the departing, but its surge came in 1898 as it became the primary jumping-off point for the Klondike Gold Rush.

Census population:

	Tacoma	*Seattle*
1870	78	1,151
1880	1,098	3,533
1890	36,006	42,830
1900	37,710	80,670
1910	83,740	237,100
1920	96,960	315,300

If trends can be seen as tides, Tacoma began with a tsunami and has ebbed and flowed with a lot of slack water ever since. Tacoma never again caught a wave of the magnitude of its birth and the downtown core was practically declared dead 100 years after its dynamic creation. The Panic of '93 had been a stunning blow to Tacoma's development, but the city regained its footing and built a vibrant downtown into the mid-60s. Then the tide swept out again. The Tacoma Mall opened in 1965, taking much of downtown retail with it. Fraternal organizations that had been gathering places for decades moved elsewhere or disbanded. Weyerhauser Co., the centerpiece of the timber empire on which Tacoma was built, moved to Federal Way. Tacomans and their regional neighbors engaged in a suburban lifestyle that did not show much interest in downtown. While the restoration of the Pantages in the early 80s is celebrated as the start of a downtown renaissance, it has only been since the turn of the 21st century that the currents of wider support for the urban core have flowed with increased growth in residential, business and entertainment.

Through it all, there has been a sense of orientation for Tacoma's cultural heritage that centers on Ninth and Broadway. This is the heart of the Theater District. Since we are addressing matters of the arts, we should be allowed to characterize this location as the home of Tacoma's cultural soul. We make that claim with the support of Murray Morgan's description of the vision Theodore Hosmer acted on more than 125 years ago. It is a vision that strongly influences us today.

Hosmer's Dream

By Murray Morgan

Before the beginning there was a young man with a dream. His name was Theodore Hosmer. He had come to Puget Sound in 1873 as a secretary for the party of Northern Pacific Railroad officials assigned to select the site of the western terminus of the first transcontinental railroad to reach the Pacific Northwest.

When they decided on the area at the head of Commencement Bay the bigwigs went back to headquarters in Philadelphia, leaving the 30-year-old Hosmer to get the ground cleared for what they expected to become the great city of the FarWest. He was city manager, city planner, city dreamer.

Hosmer spent his first months in a one-room shack with a privy out back in a swale of skunk cabbage. He hired men from Old Tacoma, Steilacoom and the surrounding farms to build a wharf at the foot of the slope running down from what is now Seventh and Pacific Avenue. He hired Chinese labors who had been imported to help lay the track between the Columbia River and Commencement Bay and set them to clearing the downtown area of trees and brush.

When the curvilinear city plan drawn up by the great landscape architect Frederick Law Omsted and sent west by the company failed to find favor with prospective buyers – merchants complained that the business district lacked corner lots where shoppers would be concentrated – Hosmer hired the unimaginative but competent engineer William Isaac Smith to impose a conventional grid pattern on Tacoma's bending waterfront and intermingled hillsides.

One result of Smith's efforts was a downtown site with five corners – the intersection of Ninth Street, St. Helens Avenue and Broadway (then called C Street.) Hosmer picked the southwest frontage of the intersection as the initial site for the Northern Pacific headquarters. He recalled later that while watching workmen frame up the headquarters he thought of the site, an area without sidewalks, on streets still filled with stumps, as the ideal location for a great theater, a source of community pride in the city he dreamed of building.

He made that dream come true with the building of the Tacoma Theatre in 1890. While the original great theater eventually met its demise, the intersection is the heart of Tacoma's cultural roots – now anchored by the Pantages Theater, flanked by the Theatre on the Square and the Rialto Theater.

Theodore Hosmer TPL

The Tacoma Theatre dedicated in 1890 with its original porte-cochere and turret defining the corner of 9th and Broadway TPL

Rudyard Kipling and Tacoma

By Murray Morgan

In the fall of 1889, twenty-four-year-old British journalist Rudyard Kipling, on a tour of America, came up from California to take a look at what he had been told was a classic example of town, a-booming. "*Tacoma was literally staggering under a boom of the boomiest*" Kipling reported in *Coast to Coast* his book on American travel:

"I do not quite remember what her natural resources were supposed to be, though every second man shrieked a selection in my ear. They included coal and iron, carrots, potatoes, lumber, shipping and a crop of thin newspapers all telling Portland that her days were numbered.

We struck the place at twilight. The crude boarded pavements of the main streets rumbled under the heels of hundreds of furious men all actively engaged in hunting drinks and eligible corner-lots. They sought the drinks first. The street itself alternated five-story business blocks of the later and more abominable forms of architecture with board shanties.

Overhead the drunken telegraph, telephone and electric-light wires tangled on tottering posts whose butts were half whittled through by the knife of the loafer. Down the muddy, grimy, unmetalied thoroughfare ran a horse-car line; the metals three inches above road level. Beyond this street rose many hills, and the town was thrown like a broken set of dominoes over all.

We passed down ungraded streets that ended abruptly in a fifteen foot drop and a nest of brambles; along pavements that beginning in pine-plank ended in the living tree; by hotels with Turkish mosque trinketry on their shameless tops and the pine stumps at their very doors; by a female seminary, tall, gaunt and red, which a native of the town bade us marvel at, and we marveled; by houses built in imitation of the ones on Nob Hill, San Francisco, after the Dutch fashion; by other houses plenteously befouled with jig-saw work, and others flaring with the castlemented, battlemented bosh of the wooden Gothic school.

The hotel walls bore a flaming panorama of Tacoma in which by the eye of faith I saw a faint resemblance to the real town. The hotel stationery advertised that Tacoma bore on its face all the advantages of the highest civilization, and the newspapers sang the same tune in a louder key.

The real estate agents were selling house-lots on unmade streets miles away for thousands of dollars. On the streets–the rude, crude streets, where the unshaded electric light was fighting with the gentle northern twilight–men were babbling of money, town-lots and again money.... I think it was the raw, new smell of fresh sawdust everywhere pervading the air that threw upon me a desolating homesickness."

Kipling's companion came back from a ramble, laughing noiselessly. He proclaimed the Tacomans mad, all mad. "Young feller" he warned, "don't you buy real estate here." Nor did he. Kipling took the Flyer to Seattle. It was a memorable trip, "*the water landlocked among a thousand islands, lay still as oil under our bows, and the wake of the screw broke up the unquivering reflections of pine and cliffs a mile away; 'twas as though we were trampling on glass."*

It brought Kipling to Seattle, which that summer had been swept by fire:
"*In the heart of the business quarters there was a horrible black smudge, as though a Hand had come down and rubbed the place smooth. I know now what being wiped out means."*

"Seattle, Seattle! Death rattle, death rattle!" chanted Tacoma school children. Businessmen, too, at luncheon meetings.

"Tacoma, a railroad promotion" sneered Seattle newspapers.

"Seattle, flea-town on the sawdust."

"Tacoma, village of destiny."

The high school tone of the jibes overlaid hatred. Antagonism lay deep. Fortunes were at stake. Men had bet their futures, and dominance in the region remained in doubt.

NOW PLAYING

First Theaters

Smith's Place

By Murray Morgan

A town's first theater seldom results from planning. The theaters just show up like dandelions. The folks in New Tacoma, as the railroad's community called itself to distinguish itself from the slightly older settlement to the north, held community get-togethers in the livery barn that Ira Cogswell built just north of Pacific Avenue on what became Seventh Street.

There are vague reports of a sleight-of-hand artist performing feats of legerdemain somewhere in New Tacoma for pay in 1874, but it was not until 1877 that the village had a theater.

Smith's Place, as it was called, opened on the east side of Pacific Avenue between South Seventh and Ninth. That two-block stretch – the first level ground reached by workmen and tourists plodding up from the Northern Pacific wharf on the waterfront, consisted of a dirt street flanked by board sidewalks in front of what a contemporary critic called "a crazy looking row of buildings of every conceivable size and shape in an architectural style classified under the all-embracing term of Pacific Coast modern."

Locally the street was called Whiskey Row. It was also the red light district. Smith's was the only place in town where men could go for live entertainment of the non-contact variety.

Smith's Place was on the upper floor of a narrow, two-story frame building grandly styled as Smith's Block. Entry was gained by climbing a narrow flight of stairs flanked at ground level by swinging door embellished with small porcelain signs – "PUSH." Such signage indicated the availability of liquor inside. No drinks were served in the theater upstairs, but intermissions were frequent and the only lavatories were in the saloons.

The Smith of Smith's Place was James W. Smith, a Kentuckian in his early fifties. He had come to Washington Territory about 1866 and was listed in both the 1870 and 1880 territorial census – as a general laborer, a categorization that failed to do justice to his entrepreneurial talents.

Early on he had attracted the attention of newspaper editor Thomas Prosch by running up a $300 bar bill in Steilacoom while selling to British buyers cattle that allegedly strayed from the Hudson's Bay Company herds.

As Tacoma's first impresario, he proved remarkably adept at culling low-priced talent from the motley cast of jugglers, acrobats, vocalists, fortune-tellers, necromancists, elocutionists, ventriloquists and puppeteers seeking performance space in the farthest corner of American show business.

His theater was a hall, about 20 by 60 feet in dimension. A low platform, perhaps 18-inches high and described as "about the size of a small hotel bedroom" stood at the far end. Calico curtains strung on wire served as drop curtain, the wire as proscenium. Along the side walls and across the upper end of the hall was an array of splintery benches that one visitor remembered as "sans paint, sans cushion, sans back, sans everything except a hard side." Lamps, redolent of coal oil, supplied and clouded the illumination.

Entertainers could count on the support of the house musical group, Tike Wood's Orchestra. The orchestra consisted of Tike, his fiddle and his vocal cords; they won favorable comparison, as to volume, with those of the train caller at the Northern Pacific siding.

Professor Carter's Great Musical Show made frequent appearances at Smith's. The Professor was an amiable African-American from the deep South, who served as advance man, bill poster, business manager, stage manager, property manager and sole performer for the company. He was acquainted with several languages and dialects, each delivered in a rich baritone. Fans of the Great Musical Show treasured memories of the Professor carrying on both sides of an argument between a heavily brogued Irish cop and an excitable Bavarian barkeep.

In 1880 the Cogswell family, which operated livery stables in both Old and New Tacoma, began building a hall on Eighth Street, just off Pacific Avenue. Smith shuttered his place and took the boat to Seattle to open a theater there. His Tacoma theater remained dark until it disappeared in the Pacific Avenue fire of 1884, a blaze that transformed "Whiskey Row" into the "Burned Blocks."

Cogswell's Hall had opened in 1881. The first theatrical performance seems to have been "Pike's Peak in Alaska," featuring a female troupe that advertised itself as "The Eleven Peak Sisters – or Ten Old Maids." The most dramatic performance at the hall, however, was not put on by an entertainer, but by the reigning financial wizard, Henry Villard.

Villard came to America from Germany after the collapse of the anti-monarchist uprisings in 1848. He learned English and transformed himself from journalist to financier after the Civil War. In the spring of 1881, in a maneuver that lives on in Wall Street legend as the Blind Pool, he borrowed enough money to buy a controlling interest in the partially completed Northern Pacific, with enough left over to give promise of completing the line.

That was the good news. For Tacoma the bad news was that Villard had major investments in Oregon and stood to benefit if Portland, rather than Tacoma, became the effective railroad terminus in the West. Tacoma's destiny seemed to rest on whether Villard would authorize construction of the Cascade Division, a direct route through the Cascades to Yakima and on to the Inland Empire, or abandon/indefinitely delay such construction, making it necessary for Tacoma freight, going or coming, to pass through Portland.

Prior to Villard's Blind Pool coup, Tacoma had made no secret of its distrust of the man. Local editorialists at their mildest characterized him as a foreign-born finagler. He was now coming to town with the city's fate in his hands. What would he do?

The Board of Trade, precursor to the Chamber of Commerce, decided against confrontation. The town band was at the platform of the NP wharf when the train from the Columbia River town of Kalama pulled in shortly after dark on the evening of October 4th. Kerosene lamps illuminated a banner bearing the message "Welcome to Villard and Party," which stretched across Pacific Avenue.

John W. Sprague, recently retired as superintendent of the western division of the NP and soon to be elected mayor of the united cities of New and Old Tacoma, put up a party in his mansion at the edge of the downtown cliff – a site later occupied by the Tacoma Hotel and later the Frank Russell headquarters. It was hoped the view of the tideflats and the bay would impress Villard with Tacoma's potential.

In the morning he was taken on tour of the town's industrial plants and at noon to the Cogswell for a confrontation that was a dramatist's dream.

The portly Elwood Evans, the town's most distinguished attorney, extended greetings. "In some parts of the world, countries build railroads, but you have reversed that doctrine. Here railroads build countries... Here abound coal, iron, lime and timber. Across yon mountain chain are wheat fields of unbounded area, of almost fabulous yield. We need the railroad to facilitate the profitable utilization of those products. From those eastern granaries, if you give us transportation to the sea, the world may be supplied with bread..."

Villard's response was cool. He pulled from his coat pocket some newspaper clippings, glanced at them, then reminded the audience that "efforts have been made in this town to abuse, slander and vilify me." He said he held no grudges, that such calumny "affects me no more than the wind which blows across your bay." His duty was to his shareholders. Since the Northern Pacific owned more property in Tacoma than any Tacoman did, he would be foolish to do the city harm. The Cascade Division would be built, eventually, but construction would be costly and he could not say when it would be done. Meanwhile, the connection between Tacoma and Portland would be improved.

This was not what Tacoma hoped to hear. The greatest drama yet staged in town trailed off in anti-climax. A cliff-hanger without resolution, it needed a sequel.

One came after six years. Before Villard returned he had completed the Northern Pacific track to the Columbia, linking them to existing tracks down river to Portland. Then he lost control of the Northern Pacific, which reverted to the Philadelphia group that favored Tacoma.

They started building the Cascade Division. Villard regained power, but did not attempt to stop construction. So his return engagement was a feel-good show, not confrontation, but celebration. Cogswell's Hall had gone dark in 1882, shortly after a touring troupe headed by the tragedian W.E. Sheridan put on a poorly attended Othello. Villard's Tacoma return engagement was at the Alpha Opera House.

Alpha Opera House

By Murray Morgan

In 1882 Seattle could boast of a number of theaters, if one included upscale honkytonks and saloons offering entertainment. Whatever the offerings, Tacoma felt its archrival had an unacceptable edge on the possibilities for culture and set out to build a real theater. The Tacoma Land Company offered adjoining 25-foot lots on the east side of Pacific Avenue between 10th and 11th for a theater site. A sawmill donated lumber, businessmen made contributions, and workers pledged a day's pay as a part of a civic campaign to build the Alpha Opera House.

If there was an architect for the Alpha, he never claimed credit. It was a modest frame building, almost square, its flat roof broken by a small arch. Below the arch, a wooden diamond framed what appeared to be a Masonic symbol. Below the symbol was an inset porch from which the house orchestra could serenade passers-by before a performance. Double doors, dead-center at street level, opened directly into the hall, which could seat 700 – about one-fourth of the town's estimated population in 1882.

With construction finished, the Alpha was turned over to the management of two well-connected young men. Charles Sprague was the son of General John W. Sprague, veteran of the Civil War and superintendent of the Northern Pacific Railroad Company construction during the building of the transcontinental line to Tacoma. Steven Baker was the son of A.J. Baker, who was president of the Bank of New Tacoma.

The grand opening drew people from Puyallup and Steilacoom. It was one of the few places of entertainment that was proper for women to attend and the competition to be in seen in style was intense. A touring company called "Muldoon's Picnic Party" came from San Francisco to present a minstrel show with four end-men and a farce about the misadventures of a Celtic bog-trotter fresh from the Old Sod.

The house was full when the Alpha's curtain rose for the first time. Revealed on the stage was an Irishman and his guests seated in a mule-drawn jaunting car – a two-wheeled open vehicle with the seats placed lengthwise, back to back. The actor cracked his whip, the mule turned its head, gave a malevolent look and began to kick. The cart disintegrated, scattering passengers and refreshments about the stage. Merriment

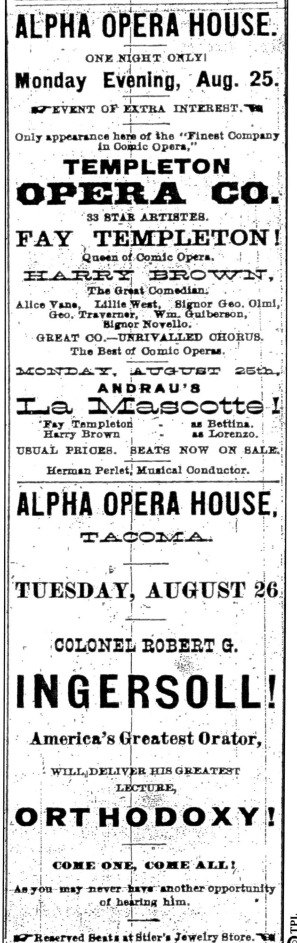

The Alpha Opera House (1877) was the main venue for entertainment and town meetings, then became a billiard hall in 1891　◎ TPL

reigned. Not art, but good theater. Tacoma thought the Opera House grand indeed.

There were complaints. The Alpha was poorly heated. During a cold snap in the winter of '84 the *Ledger* editorialized that "Comfort, which must take precedence over dramatic art, and health, to which nothing else should be sacrificed require that additional heating apparatus be placed in the opera house if it is to be used for public entertainments during the winters months."

When young Sprague and Baker printed a satirical handbill making fun of the *Ledger* and noting that their critic had attended the show on a pass, the *Ledger* sternly advised them to mend their ways. They should spend their money on coal, not handbills.

Sprague and Baker solved the heating problem temporarily, leasing the Opera House for use as a roller rink. Later they brought in an amiable postman named James M. Junett, as manager. He earned a reputa-

tion for dealing pleasantly with complaints without making changes that cost money. A Tacoma street is named for him.

Completion of the Northern Pacific's mainline track in 1883 released a flood of national and international theatrical roadshow companies upon the Pacific Northwest. Cultivated Tacomans could compare the Lady Macbeth interpretations by the stocky Czech actress Francesca Roman Magdalena Janauschek ("Fanny" to her admirers) with that of the slender, pensive Helena Modjeska, the wife of a Polish aristocrat whose radical views had forced the couple to flee to America. McKee Rankin, a matinee idol running to fat, came to town as the hero of Joaquin Miller's anti-Mormon melodrama, "The Danites." The lovely, unstable Margaret Mather appeared twice as the tragic Jewish heroine in the tear-jerker, "Leah, the Forsaken." The elegant James O'Neill, father of Eugene, was several times in town in his endless interpretation of "Edmond Dantes, the Count of Monte Cristo."...

Perhaps the most talked-about performer was John Lawrence Sullivan, last of the bareknuckle heavyweight prize fighting champs. He came to town heading "Sullivan's Combinations" – a troupe of pugs... To circumvent local ordinances outlawing prize fighting the shows were advertised as exhibitions, but they were so arranged that on occasion a local favorite might get into the ring to spar with the Boston Strong Boy, the notion being that should he kayo Sullivan the title would change hands.

Even with tickets priced at a then outrageous $1.50, $1 and 50 cents, Sullivan's appearance sold out the house. Sadly, no violence was committed. All the fighters did was spar. The *Ledger* devoted two incensed front-page columns to descriptions of the gentle activity and to complain. Its concluding judgment: "Every man in the combination may be a prodigy of strength, endurance, science and even 'good breeding' according to the Sullivan standard, but it was apparent that last night they played Tacoma's sporting public for what is popularly called a 'sucker' and they gave an unmistakable 'sucker' show."

Compounding his felony, Sullivan, in a Seattle appearance the next night, mixed it up convincingly for real with a lumberjack named James Lang, "showering him with sledge-hammer blows," knocking him down twice, splitting his lip, and knocking him out. All this in what a dispatch to the *Portland Oregonian* claimed was seven seconds. The *Ledger* picked up a rumor that on the steamer back to Tacoma members of the troupe staged an even livelier fight among themselves and continued the brawl at the Blackwell Hotel, though the great John L was too tipsy to take part.

As the novelty of being in the presence of such nationally known artists began to fade, complaints about the inadequacies of the Alpha mounted. "Grand" at its opening, the opera house by 1885 was hardly suitable for a community of 15,000. In its early days the Alpha

had only three sets: a kitchen scene, street scene, and a forest scene. If the script called for a drawing room or a throne room or an office, the contrast between dialogue and background could transform tragedy to farce.

New sets were added across the years, but the 1882 drop curtain remained a fixture. It was the work of a local artist whose identity remains uncertain, but whose amateur status was undeniable. Floating on a drab background variously remembered as "dim purple" and "dirty brown" were four somewhat human figures, each supposed to represent one of the races of mankind. The indicated race of each might be deduced from its coloring but all four shared the similarity of having two left hands and two left feet. These, according to one critic, "were appended to limbs awry and colossal, with charming disregard for symmetry and proportion." The four figures supported a disc representing the world. Tacoma business establishments had colonized the earth's surface with advertisements for their products. Brand names encircled the globe in a business-like halo. This remarkable drop unrolled before audiences so often that theater-goers learned every message by heart.

"You would be attending a tragedy," an old-timer recalled, "and after an act came to a moving climax, with your feelings having reached a high C, the drop would rattle down, the pulleys permitting, to confront you with humanity portrayed as all left-handed and left-footed, and the information that John Coffin was a first-class undertaker, and Haberdasher & Company kept the finest assortment of underwear. Even for the acclimated the transition was too sudden."

By 1888 the Alpha was old hat. A review of Wilson Barrett's "Hoodman Blind" began, "Considering the wretched facilities for mounting such a play in the opera house and the laborious disadvantages the members of the talented Levick company were compelled to combat, no better performance has been seen in this alleged theater."

THE OLD-FASHIONED **DEESTRICK SKULE.**

GROSS BROTHERS,
Dry Goods, Clothing, Boots and Shoes,
GENTS' FURNISHING GOODS,
CARPETS, CLOAKS AND DOLMANS.

A DEESTRICK SKULE
IN 1849
—AT—
ALPHA OPERA HOUSE,
Saturday, April 27 '89

THE LADIES OF THE
1st Methodist Church
Of Tacoma will give the
OLD FASHIONED DEESTRICK SKULE
SATURDAY EVENING.

This Entertainment has met with immense success in the Eastern and Central Cities.

Admission 75 Cts; Gallery 50 Cts.

Seats for sale at E. J. Stier's.

The London and Liverpool Clothing House
Leading Clothiers, Hatters and Gents' Furnishers,
902 and 904 Pacific Avenue, Cor. Ninth Street.
CHAS. REICHENBACH, Prop'r.

Forbes & Vose, the Leading Grocers, 914 Pac. Av.

TSC

The Germania

By Murray Morgan

Performance areas other than the Alpha Opera House became available. A Pacific Avenue saloon-keeper named Julius Kley built a hall "up the hill" on C Street (now Broadway) in 1885 for use by Tacoma's expanding German-American population. The Northern Pacific was advertising then in Northern Europe, especially in Germany and Scandinavia, about opportunities for industrious farmers, loggers and fishermen.

The response was such that Tacoma boasted a German-language weekly, German Lutheran and German Methodist churches, both holding services in German and a German-American Association with several hundred members and some political significance. The second mayor of the combined towns of New and Old Tacoma was a German merchant named Jacob Weisbach – who would lead perhaps the city's most infamous actions in the expulsion of the Chinese in 1885.

GERMANIA HALL.   KAHRELL & DAMMER ARCHITECTS

⊙ TPL

Julius Kley called his hall The Germania. It stood at 1331 C Street (Broadway) about where a movie house first known as the Apollo and later as Hamrick's Blue Mouse was located. A wood frame building, it does not seem to have gained popularity... In 1887 members of the German-American Association pledged $10,000 for a more elegant Germania Hall at the southwest corner of 13th and E Street (Fawcett Avenue).

Carl August Darmer was chosen as architect. He had studied architecture in Prussia and arrived in Tacoma in 1884 by way of England, Africa, Australia, San Francisco and Portland.

The new Germania had a distinctly northern German look. A handsome wood-frame building of three stories, it featured a grand open stairway under a high arch that led from the board sidewalk on Fawcett to the performance area. When it was dedicated in February 1889 there was newspaper speculation that it would supplant the old Alpha as the place to go if you wanted to be seen.

LAUNDRYMEN'S FIRST ANNUAL BALL GERMANIA HALL FEB. 24, 1900

⊙ TPL

John P. Howe came from Portland to manage the theater. He was by far the most experienced theater man to be associated with a Tacoma theater up to that time. To open the house, Howe brought back the aging Czech powerhouse Francesca Romana Magdalena Janauschek. On opening night the 59-year-old Janauschek appeared as the gypsy, the title role in "Meg Merrilies." The next evening she was Lady Macbeth. The reviews were enthusiastic. "At the close of the last act in the death scene, she appeared to rise above the occasion, for during the short time in which she struggles with death, once could almost hear the breathing of the audience."

Early audiences at the Germania were described as "composed of Tacoma's best citizens." For a time they filled the theater. But the theater failed to hold favor. During the winter of 1888–89 it proved to be as difficult to heat as the old Alpha. It was unfashionably far from downtown, high on the hill and on a street poorly drained and yet to be paved. (The building burned to the ground in 1921.)

Some of the church folk in town were outraged that the city council had given permission for beer to be served in the Germania, though not at the performances. And, Harry Morgan was offering a different kind of entertainment at the Theater Comique – also known as Morgan's Hell Hole – down on Pacific Avenue.

Theatre Comique

By Murray Morgan

Henry "Harry" Morgan drifted into town in 1884 from Maryland, or so he said, one of the flood of foot-loose men who followed the Northern Pacific tracks to the end of the line. He quickly established himself as Boss Sport, the fellow in charge of the community's illicit entertainment activities. He was in his mid-thirties, a compact, dark-haired man with a big dark mustache and ill-fitting dark suits, the prototype of the boomtown gambler: friendly, Republican (the Republicans were in local power), generous to the needy – especially to those he had helped become needy, provided they did not complain to authorities – and reputed to be a man of his word in business dealings, though this was hard to prove since he seldom signed papers. He seldom drank, but it was rumored he started the day, around noon, with morphine in his coffee.

Morgan rented a storefront, bought a license from the city council and opened a hole-in-the-wall saloon on Railroad Avenue, as Commerce Street was then called.

He soon found a bigger spot at 726 Pacific Avenue. He called his new joint the Board of Trade. Nice name, that, kind of a joke on the real Board of Trade, which was formed to promote commerce. What was good for Tacoma's business was good for Harry, and there were plenty of businessmen who felt that Harry's business was good for the town. (He also used the name Casino Theater at that site.)

By April of 1887 Morgan was able to buy a building of his own at 815 Pacific Avenue. It stood about where James Smith of Smith's Place had provided the town with its first professional entertainment a decade earlier and where the Olympus Hotel now stands. Morgan called his saloon Theatre Comique, the name deriving from Harrigan & Hart's pioneer variety showplace on lower Broadway in Manhattan.

Seen from across the muddied boards of Pacific Avenue it exemplified shabbiness: wood frame, two storied double-doors dead center at the street level, with two chairs on a raised platform for gents who needed a shoe shine and a chance to watch the girls go by. There was one unusual feature for a frontier town saloon – a narrow balcony, roofed, from which the Henry Morgan Band serenaded passers-by and standers-around from mid-afternoon to early evening when the band retired inside to play for the patrons. Morgan's band symbolized his commitment to the Three Principles: 1) All saloons offer similar drinks, though the water content may vary. 2) All gambling establishments use similar paraphernalia, though standards of honesty may vary. 3) A customer wanting to drink or gamble will go to the place that offers extra pleasure, such as entertainment. Las Vegas was built on the same three principles.

Live entertainment was the bait Morgan offered. Inside the swinging doors the visitors found themselves in a big room with a bar along one wall, He built a brick theater behind the saloon. Some accounts refer to it as a claptrap firetrap, but a picture in a newspaper supplement made it look elegant enough for a concert by the Philadelphia String Quartet. The photo shows a modest well-lit stage, adequate for small groups, a spacious main floor with chairs for perhaps 200 patrons, a horseshoe balcony with heavily curtained boxes from which theater lovers with a yen for privacy could watch the show without themselves being observed, and a gallery, or bum-box, for those who needed neither privacy nor libation while theater-going. Programs featured trick bicycle riding early in the evening and blowsy contraltos voicing double-entendre in the late evenings.

Waiters circulated on the main floor, selling beer at a nickel a glass. Drinks cost more in the boxes: $1 a bottle for beer, $5 a bottle for wine, $20 a bottle for champagne. These were delivered by barmaids of utmost accessibility. Sometimes they dallied. Morgan maintained that he did not know or care what the barmaids delivered besides drinks and none of the box hustlers claimed that he took a cut from their tips. But the threat that possible dalliance in the dimly lit boxes posed to Tacoma's reputation aroused the crusading instincts of the *Ledger*, which had been quiet since advocating for the expulsion of the Chinese four years earlier. Editorials exploded with condemnations of "Morgan's Hell-Hole!" The ministry, too, thundered and volleyed. Attendance increased as word of the danger got out.

The Boss Sport died unexpectedly on April 26, 1890, aged forty, to the relief of the *Ledger* and the benefit of the Pierce County legal profession. Morgan left no will. He was reputed wealthy, and court records showed him possessed of papers for considerable real estate, much of it gained on double-or-nothing bets lost by patrons who had blown their cash. Included in his inventory were a shingle mill at Buckley, a sawmill on Boise Creek in King County, and two thousand dollars in IOU's from Pierce County Sheriff Lewis Byrd, which might have come in handy.

But Morgan's list of creditors read like the city directory, and as word of his intestate state spread, heirs sprouted…. Litigation dragged on for more than a decade. By the time the estate was settled the lawyers had the money and the Tacoma Boom was hardly an echo. Morgan's property was auctioned at ten dollars a lot, the shingle mill for one hundred dollars, and the theater for fifteen hundred, including *Ledger* ill will. Dora Charlotta Morgan, whom the courts held to be Harry's one and only widow, was left with nothing except his bouncer, Frank "Jumbo" Cantwell, whom she had married.

The Comique went dark. H.H. Cline, who had been in charge of booking the acts for Morgan, opened a new variety house, the National, on the southwest corner of 12th and A Street, in the area where city authorities hoped to concentrate illicit, but tolerated, activity. In December 1890, Cline and a partner took over the old Alpha on Pacific and tried to reopen it as a variety house, the Tacoma Musee. Mayor George Kandle shut it down after one night, explaining that Cline ought to be satisfied with running the National without attempting to invade the respectable portions of the city with more theaters of the same style.

Opera Alley

Corridor of Corruption

By Murray Morgan

Tacoma had an open town tradition. There had been a "crazy house" on the hill above Old Town before the village was incorporated. New Tacoma was not far behind in providing commercial sex as an amenity. Harry Morgan gave gambling a good name. Prohibition brought the speakeasy. Night life in Tacoma meant bookie joints, slot machine and pinball routes, unlicensed drinking spots, and an abundance of brothels, most of them in Opera Alley, between Broadway and Market Street. They offered all the glamour of a fast food franchise, but the operators paid high rent. Reform advocates were assured that Seattle was worse and more prosperous. Control of night life in Tacoma centered on two local organizations that grew up during Prohibition. Sometimes they shared, more often they competed. There was little rough stuff, just politics and corruption. Each side financed one or more candidates in the quadrennial election of safety commissioner. The side that won the election got to run things without raids while its rival planned better precinct organization.

Police Report: Worst in the West

In the *History of Tacoma Police Department* the unsavory element of Tacoma's frontier entertainment in the early 1890s was characterized thusly:

"The city had been growing rapidly and the tough section of the city was then in the alley between South C and D streets, from Ninth to Seventeenth streets, and was known as Opera Alley. Perhaps no other city in the West with police protection at that time was as bad as Opera Alley. Dance halls and gambling rooms lined the alley from one end to the other, and numerous criminal characters made it their hangout."

MISS KITTY EVANS — No. 1143 D Street,
Telephone No. 434.

"THE JEWELL" as it is popularly known, is handsomely furnished throughout. The parlors, three in number, are uniquely and artistically arranged. Miss Kitty entertains with a charm that pleases all; it is needless to say everything is first-class.

COLORED.

MISS JENNIE CARR—No. 1127 Opera St.

Miss Jennie has excellent singers and dancers. One can visit this House in absolute safety.

MISS KATE CLARK—1147 D Street. Telephone, No. 110.

Miss Clark has an elegantly furnished house, and a more agreeable or pleasing hostess could not be found in any city. Experienced and up to the times. Her boarders, well, they are charming.

MISS RAY McROBERTS — No. 1143 Opera Street. Telephone 198.

The "CHICAGO HOUSE" is a fine spacious building, with many parlors, which are richly furnished throughout. Her boarders are all EASTERN ladies — every variety — blondes, brunettes, etc. Miss Ray is a graceful entertainer, The Chicago is one of the best houses in the city.

Showtime of a different flavor could be found in this pocket-sized booklet

The Daily Ledger devoted a full page of colorful prose in November of 1898, taking readers along as witnesses to a nighttime battle for Tacoma's moral character

TWO SIDES OF LIFE IN TACOMA

Under the lights on the street corner stand a little band of men and women surrounded by a curious crowd. Their clothes are blue and faded, they have hymn books in their hands and they are pleading with their hearers to turn from the world to the gentle Nazarene.

The night is cold and starlight and the frost crystals glitter under the glare of the electric light.

It is Saturday night and the hurrying throngs surge back and forth on the busy crossing. The cable car glides by with clamor of gongs, its glowing windows brightening as it passes up on the hill. The cabs dash past with their shining lamps and the horses' hooves ring keen on the frozen street.

Men and women saunter by, their throats muffled in furs and velvet, and they turn contemptuously from the singers to linger by the shop windows brilliant with lights and jewels…

… But, the little group under the electric light sing bravely on, although the blue uniforms are worn and thin, and when an eager gust whistles around the corner and the smoking torches trail away like flaming banners, they huddle closer to the lamps and sing the louder of the world which is all warmth and light…

… It is a pitiful little army. It needs all their bravery of drums and banners to keep up stout hearts beneath rebuffs and scorns. The airs they sing are jarring, their speech is crude and homely, and the cruel crowd jeers the maiden as she beseeches in His name. But for love of Him who was poor and lowly they suffer and are joyful. They have caught a glimpse of ineffable light and the vision is ever bright through all the wind and rain.

Aflare with light, the reeking overheated room is dim with smoke and steam from a hundred heated dancers. Reeling, staggering, they whirl madly by, some in a reckless rush, their burning passions carrying them faster and faster until they sink exhausted, some cirling languorously and silently in a stupor of weariness.

The sputtering lamps gleam yellow through the clouds of smoke and they dance and rattle as the building sways beneath the feet of the dancers. The fumes of alcohol and violent scents and the sickening odor of human perspiration grow more oppressive. The roar of shuffling feet and babble of voices rises and the snarling horns and violins are almost drowned. Now and then a brutal oath or drunken laugh rises above the tumult and the crowd turns eagerly toward the noises expectant for a fight.

The walls and ceilings are gay with ropes of tinsel and gaudy shameful pictures. In one end of the hall the bar glitters with mirrors and shining glasses. Along the walls on bare wooden benches are rows of men, ill-clad, low-browed brutes, with here and there a sallow, unwholesome looking boy, or a flashily dressed young tough, whose familiar air proclaims him a habitué. With them are women swearing and smoking…

… The Dancing goes ceaselessly on, although now and then they pause to drink. See that bedizened Delilah with her foot against her companion with one arm around his neck and a glass in the other hand. Her eyes are sunken and blue rings encircle them. Their lashes droop beneath their burden of charred cork. Her dress, once a gorgeous satin, is soiled and faded and she wears white slippers now streaked with dirt. A few long years of vice and carousal have done their work and what was once a woman is now a loathsome wreck…

… The dance goes on till morning. There is warmth and light. There is music and there is laughter and with it all there is not a happy face. Greed, misery and despair are in every feature and it to all they drink: drink until passion and sorrow are drowned; drink till the past and present are buried; drink until oblivion ends it all.

Tacoma Impresario, Writer, Public Servant

By Sydney Bernice Newell, Granddaughter

Bernice Newell

From 1904 until 1927, Bernice E. Newell brought world-class performing artists to Tacoma through her Artists' Course of Concerts, hosting up to eight performances per year during the fall-to-spring season. Under the auspices of the Artists' Course, the most renowned performing artists of that era came to Tacoma, including Rachmaninoff, Kreisler, Sousa, Schumann-Heink, Nijinsky and the Ballet Russe.

The Artists' Course of Concerts represented a milestone in the cultural life of Tacoma. Most of the concerts took place at the Tacoma Theater, but some were at the Heilig Theater and other venues, including the Tacoma Stadium.

Bernice lived in Tacoma from 1889 to 1927. She was born in New York, and in 1865 moved with her family to Iowa. In 1884, Bernice graduated from Iowa College, now called Grinnell College. After a two-year residence in California, she moved to Tacoma in 1889 and took a position with the *Tacoma Daily Ledger* as Society Editor and music critic. During Bernice Newell's life in Tacoma the family hosted lively home "musical evenings" at which assorted musicians performed, serving as a cultural gathering spot for the community. Her daughter, Doris, became an accomplished pianist.

Bernice made significant literary and civic contributions to Tacoma's history.
- In 1905 Bernice and her brother Ernest coauthored a book of poems entitled *The Mountain,* credited as the first book published in Tacoma.
- Bernice served as Superintendent of Fine Arts for the Washington State Building at the 1893 Chicago World's Fair.
- In addition to the *Tacoma Daily Ledger,* Bernice wrote for various other newspapers and magazines including *Sunset, Northwest Magazine* and *The Outing.* She was Associate Editor of *Western Woman's*

Outlook magazine.
- After meeting Mark Twain once at a reception, Bernice wrote an article "Story by Mark Twain" that was published in several newspapers across the country.
- During WWI Bernice helped arrange entertainment for the troops as the Tacoma representative of an organization of stage women for war relief work.

Sergei Rachmaninoff

Vaslav Nijinsky

Photos courtesy of Sydney Bernice Newell

The Temple of Drama & Opera

By Murray Morgan

Theodore Hosmer, the young man who, in 1874 amid the stumps and mud that constituted Tacoma, dreamed of a great theater that would dominate the five-corner intersection of Ninth Street, Broadway and St. Helens Avenue. In 1887 he took steps to transform that vision into brick, stone and mortar, box seats and gallery benches, house lights and stage lights.

Hosmer had already brought changes. As the Northern Pacific's man on the spot, he had arranged to have the town-site platted, a thousand acres cleared of timber, the first streets cleared, the wharf built. When the Tacoma Land Company was formed he was its first manager.

He helped form a de facto government. When New Tacoma was given a charter in 1882 he was elected to the council and his fellow councilmen elected him mayor. Soon after he became mayor, his wife's health began to fail. He resigned as manager of the land company and returned with her to Philadelphia, where she would have better medical care and attention from her sister, who was the wife of Northern Pacific president Charles Wright.

After her death in 1885, Hosmer returned to Tacoma as president of the Tacoma Light and Water Company, comptroller of the Tacoma Land Company, president of the Wilkeson Coal and Coke Company and trustee of Annie Wright Seminary. He at once began to work quietly to raise local money for construction of his dream theater.

While manager of the Tacoma Land Company, he had kept the property on the southwest side of the Ninth-Broadway-St. Helens intersection off the market except for lots 7–10 south of Ninth. These the land company offered free to Pierce County as site for a new county courthouse if voters approved the transfer of the county seat from Steilacoom to Tacoma. This they did in 1880.

After Hosmer had resigned in 1882, the new manager, Isaac Anderson, sold lot 6, adjoining the courthouse at the point where St. Helens merged with Broadway, to H.C. Davis, a local druggist and capitalist. Hosmer reached a tentative agreement with Davis for the re-purchase of the property if it were needed for theater purposes.

He then persuaded Northern Pacific vice president Thomas Oakes, who was in Tacoma in connection with the sale of 80,000 acres of NP timberland to the St. Paul & Tacoma Lumber Company, to offer the sale of the five-corner site at an exceptionally low price to a theater company that would guarantee a theater costing at least $75,000 be built on it.

The preliminaries over, Hosmer set out to find investors. He and Isaac Anderson agreed to go in for $10,000 each. They made up a list of Tacomans "whose other interests would allow them to spare the money, even should the returns on their investment not be large." He said that the first nine men he approached agreed, although some "demurred a little at first."

Hosmer set up a meeting to discuss the details of incorporation of the Tacoma Opera House Company. It is easy to imagine the

The main entrance to the theater was on the 9th Street side

⊙ TPL

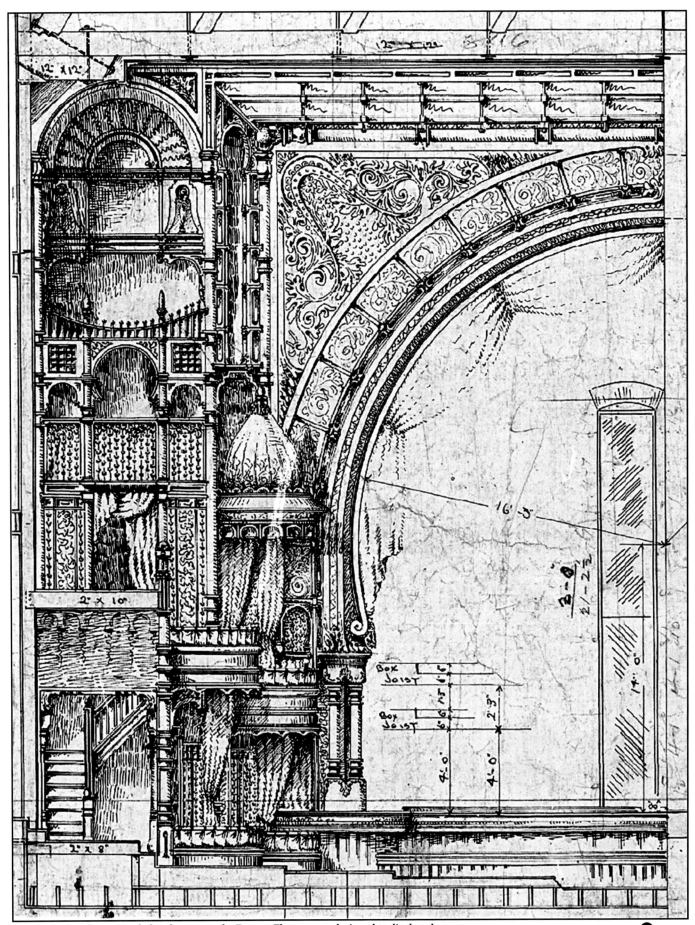

As exhibited in this original plan document, the Tacoma Theatre was designed to display elegance

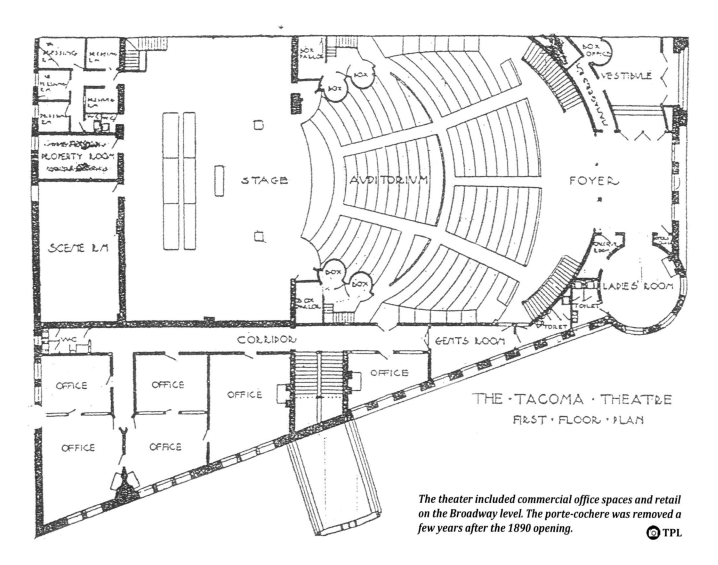

The theater included commercial office spaces and retail on the Broadway level. The porte-cochere was removed a few years after the 1890 opening. ⊙ TPL

sense of satisfaction that Hosmer felt when the men he had solicited individually gathered for the first time in early March 1888 in the soon to be dedicated Union Club that fronted the bluff on Broadway overlooking the bay.

From the verandah they looked down on what they believed to be the fastest growing city in the world, on a waterfront lined with new warehouses, on the bay dotted with sailing ships riding at anchor while waiting their turns to load lumber and wheat, and on Pacific Avenue graded and lined with newly built masonry buildings.

Could he have resisted reminding them that he had been there first, only 14 years before when the hillside was a vista of stumps, fireweed and nettles, the bay empty of anything but an occasional dugout?

"But, you, you men have brought the change," he told them. General Sprague built the railroad. Nelson Bennett was about to complete driving the 9,850-foot tunnel under Stampede Pass, giving Tacoma direct ac-

cess to the Inland Empire. S.M. Nolan, who arrived in Tacoma in 1878 to invest the fortune he had made in the California gold fields, had invested it well. Allen C. Mason arrived four years after Nolan with $2.85 to his name and was now estimated to be worth $10 million. William Blackwell came to town as manager of the little hotel NP built on the wharf and now he had a hotel of his own and was president of a bank.

William Fife had stayed in that little hotel his first night in town and the next day purchased the northwest corner of Ninth and Pacific. Now Fife was paying more property taxes than any individual in the county. C.P. Masterson was president of Pacific National Bank, and W.D. Tyler was vice president. George Browne, who retired young after making a fortune on Wall Street, had been drawn back into business as secretary of the St. Paul & Tacoma Lumber Company, which was building the largest mill in the world.

"You have done all this," Hosmer said. "You have created everything a great city will need – everything, that is, except a palace for the dissemination of culture and

Largest stage on the West Coast and exposed orchestra pit 📷 TPL

Original stage curtain, later donated to the Temple Theater 📷 TPL

the display of elegance – a great theater. It is up to you gentlemen to fill that need.

"Construction of a major theater will require considerable expense, but nothing that those assembled here cannot provide. Knowledgeable men estimate $150,000 would finance a theater worthy of the city you are creating, a theater incomparably better than anything in Portland or Seattle, equal to the best in San Francisco. I am making, on my personal account, the first commitment of $10,000. Mr. Anderson pledges another $10,000. Gentlemen?" They all subscribed.

📷 TPL

Articles of incorporation were agreed upon and signed. Capital stock was fixed first at $50,000. Hosmer, Anderson, Tyler, Masterson and Mason were designated as trustees and set the first meeting, required by territorial law, for April 5th.

At that session they chose Hosmer as president; Mason, secretary, and Masterson, treasurer. Bonds were issued for $60,000. The lot next to the county courthouse was purchased from H.C. Davis and paid for partly in stock. C.B. Zabriskie, the contractor in charge of dredging City Waterway (now Foss Waterway) and filling the tideflats, bought Hill's stock and became a member of the board, replacing Mason as secretary.

The Tacoma Opera House Company was now ready to build what they chose to call The Tacoma Theatre – the directors having decided the term "opera house" was somewhat provincial. They proudly promoted the new theater as the "Temple of Drama & Opera."

C.W. Wood was chosen to design the building. A native of Chicago, with architectural offices in Philadelphia and San Francisco, Wood was a disciple of Henry Hobson Richardson, an influential young American architect who had just died at the age of 48.

The Richardson Romanesque style, as it came to be called, with its relative simplicity and adaptability to varied materials, seemed especially suited to a theater building that would include commercial office space and had to be fitted onto the peculiar dimensions of the hillside at the Ninth and Broadway intersection.

The property extended 67 feet up Ninth from Broadway, 165 feet along Opera Court (Court C), then 125 feet back down to Broadway and 174 feet along Broadway back to Ninth.

HOW THE GREAT CHARIOT RACE IS OPERATED IN "BEN HUR."

This Great Drama Will Be Seen at the Tacoma Theater Monday, Tuesday and Wednesday

"BEN HUR," which will be presented at the Tacoma theater Monday, Tuesday and Wednesday nights and Wednesday matinee, brings out the bone and sinew of General Wallace's great story and holds the interest from the first to the last curtain, as it one were enthralled. The demands of dramatic sequence are strictly adhered to at all times, while the work of setting the story before the public gaze is so admirably done by the Klaw & Erlanger company that "Ben Hur," aside from its natural beauties, should live as an example of what vast possibilities the stage holds out when the rigid conjunction of author dramatist, producer and stage director is reached.

The story of "Ben Hur" is familiar to everybody. In the play, however, the main incidents of General Wallace's great novel are graphically and faithfully put forth, blending at times, and living up, as it were, at other times, those scenes of marvelous beauty of deep heart interest.

When General Wallace was first approached by Klaw & Erlanger in regard to the dramatization of his novel, Ben Hur, he said that the idea was useless, as they could never stage the chariot race, and "Ben Hur" without the race would be a case of "Hamlet" without the melancholy Dane. Klaw & Erlanger, however, had arranged to meet this contingency, and soon persuaded the unwilling general that they had a solution of the problem that would not only satisfy him, but the general public. Long before they submitted their proposition to General Wallace they had had the best theatrical mechanics of the country at work on this scene, and

Claude Higgins, who at that time was the chief of staff of the firm, invented the race as it stands today. But they expended something like $15,000 on the preliminary experiment.

The working model of the race, which appears herewith, gives a good, general idea of how the race is operated, but the detail is not shown. Each horse has a machine of his own. These machines, or treadmills, are twenty-seven inches wide and four of them are bolted together into a set. These sets are placed on rags and move forward or backward, at the will of the operator, carrying with them both horses and chariots. The machines, or treads, are of intricate mechanism and are adjusted by means of springs and other mechanical contrivances to the exact speed of the horse

operating them. The treads upon which the horses are run are twenty-seven inches wide and eight inches high. Each tread contains 225 ballbearing wheels. As these wheels are made to order and cost $2.25 each, an idea of the expense attached to the manufacture of these machines can be easily understood. The tread itself, or the floor upon which the horse runs, is made of hickory slats, each slat two inches wide. These slats are covered with a combination of rubber and canvas.

At the back of the stage is the panorama, the largest one ever built. It is forty-three feet between cylinders and contains 36,000 square yards of canvas. This panorama, by the way, is one of the most interesting features of the spectacle, as it caused more trouble to

the inventor of the scene than anything else connected with it. It was found that the weight of the canvas was so great that it would not stick to the cylinders without a support from the top, and then the groove was invented. This groove is forty-three feet long and is in reality a double groove. It contains a track on which ballbearing carriers travel at the rate of 500 revolutions per minute during the race scene. These carriers hold up the enormous spread of canvas used in the scene and which really makes the illusion of the race. The panorama moves in an opposite direction from the horses. In the cut which appears above, the mode of operating the panorama can be easily understood. Two 10-horsepower electric motors are used to move the horse machines and the panorama, while six one-quarter horsepower electric motors are installed in the machines to operate the dust blowing devices and to blow out the skirts of the drivers.

Tacoma Daily Ledger illustration of stage mechanics for presentation of Ben Hur in 1905

Clearing began in August. The three-story frame building that had served as the Tacoma headquarters for the Northern Pacific was rolled up St. Helens and settled onto the southeast corner of the intersection at Seventh. There it became the Florence Hotel. The theater site was graded down to the Broadway level. Colonel Woods' design called for an oblong theater space paralleling Opera Court. This left a five-story triangle along St. Helens that was divided into rental commercial spaces.

The main entrance to the theater was through a foyer on Ninth Street. An entrance on Broadway was covered by a three-arched porte-cochere that extended into the street, making it easy for the carriers of the fashionable to discharge their well-dressed passengers without risk to gowns or shoes, regardless of weather. It was said to be the only porte-co-chere west of Paris.

The five-story façade presented a turreted tower at the Ninth and Broadway corner with three lower towers jutting from the slate roof facing the bay. The ground floor was built of sandstone barged down from Bellingham. Sandstone arches enclosed the doors and display windows of the stores. Above the ground floor the building was brick made in local yards with terra cotta trim.

As the structure neared completion, the directors of the enterprise faced the problem of finding a suitable manager. The solution came by boat. John W. Hanna, who had managed theaters in the Midwest for more than twenty years, had been thinking of moving to the West Coast.

News of the great Seattle fire in June 1889 persuaded him to make the move: after such destruction there would surely be opportunity. But, Seattle proved to have more burned-out managers looking for new

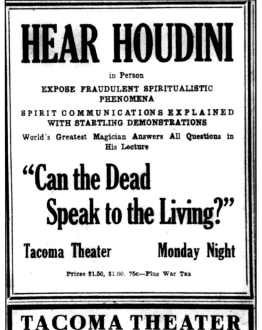

Famed magician appeared Nov. 2, 1924　　🔘 TPL

space than new theaters under construction. So he caught the *State of Washington* for the run down to Tacoma to look at the theater under construction, met Hosmer and signed on to book the shows for the first season.

Hanna's Midwest experience had acquainted him with the managers of touring companies operating out of New York and San Francisco, especially so with Al Hayman, who was establishing himself as the dominant figure in the western circuits. With the best theater in the Pacific Northwest as bait, Hanna booked a fine first season.

The Tacoma opened with the J.C. Duff Opera Company of New York in a week's stand beginning Monday, January 13, 1890 with the comic opera *Paola*. First-night prices were set at $20 for a five-seat box, $2.50 for seats in the Parquet and Parquet Circle, $2 for a balcony seat and $1.50 on the gallery benches.

Demand was so great that Hanna held an auction at the Tacoma Hotel with the highest bidder having the choice of the opening-night boxes and lower level seats, no bidder being allowed to take more than two boxes or 20 seats. Nearly $5,000 above the face value of the tickets was raised.

There were the usual last week emergencies. The gent's room toilets wouldn't flush. The great gas-jet chandelier refused to dim. Forty seats in the proscenium boxes were delayed and did not arrive until two days before opening night.

But, on Monday the 13th, all was ready, except the weather. It rained all morning, not a downpour, just a steady Puget Sound rain from a low gray sky. The festive bunting along Ninth and Broadway hung like seaweed at low tide. Gutters overflowed. But, the rain

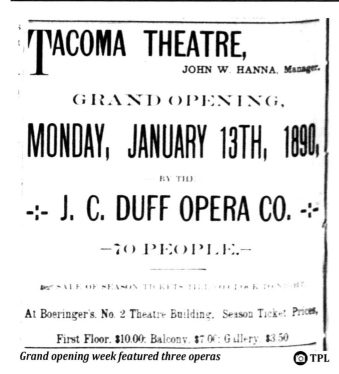

Grand opening week featured three operas TPL

faded to drizzle as the early darkness of January settled in, neither the sky nor manager Hanna wept.

First-nighters came early. There had been worry that horses might be skittish about going through the porte-cochere arches, but none bolted. Fashionable ladies, their gowns muffled under winter wraps, were helped to alight without need of umbrellas. Every carriage and hackney in town was kept busy in the two hours before curtain. Other ticket holders arrived by trolley.

Those who had dined in the Pacific Avenue oyster houses or at the hotels climbed the hill, sloshing in galoshes across Railroad Avenue (Commerce St.) and up to the main entrance on Ninth.

Beyond the pagoda-like ticket office, stained glass doors opened to the outer foyer, gas-lit, thick-carpeted, with blue and gold portiere hangings buffering the inner foyer and auditorium from the murmur of conversation. Compared to the old Alpha, this was grand indeed.

To check their wraps, the ladies retreated into the circular parlor in the tower overlooking the intersection. Their refuge was complete with chairs, settees, a fireplace and a lavatory "with all the latest accessories."

They reappeared "to the pleasure of the sterner sex" in outfits it had taken weeks to assemble and hours to fit into. The morning papers noted: "There is no social event among all the annals of balls, parties and the various forms of entertainments, so calculated to bring together the combined brilliancy of society, as the opening of a new theater."

Columns of front page space were devoted to the pageantry: "Mrs. C.W. Griggs, black silks and lace... Miss Julia Griggs, while silk and tulle, ornaments diamonds and pink hyacinths; Miss Anna Griggs, pearl gray cashmere skirt and pink surah silk waist; Mrs. Allen C. Mason, black lace, with diamonds... Miss Strong, red cashmere, décolleté, with white and silver embroidered front; Mrs. Dusenberne, red India silk with black lace, tulle bonnet; Mrs. Zabriskie, black lace net and green ribbons; Miss Fay Fuller, light blue cashmere with blue and white figured India silk... ." On and on, like box scores.

A feature writer spotted "half-hidden by the graceful fall of drapery from one of the circular boxes beside the proscenium a fair occupant. She is quite well aware that she is attracting comment and remark. She knows only too well that opera glasses are being leveled on her and that she is the principal point of observation. She triumphs in it. She has come for the particular purpose of being admired and, now that she has achieved her triumph, she doesn't trample upon it by wholly concealing her beautiful countenance behind the protecting curtain. And she is not to blame."

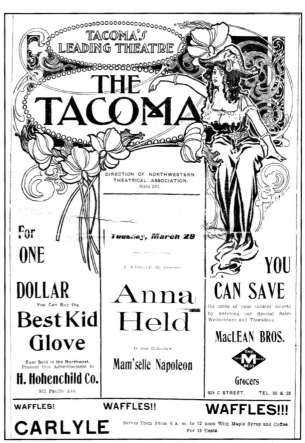

TPL

TULLY & BUCKLAND PRESENT

GUY BATES POST AS OMAR THE TENTMAKER

A PERSIAN LOVE ROMANCE

By Richard Walton Tully

Author of "THE BIRD OF PARADISE"

Poster for 1915 return engagement of Omar the Tentmaker

Ticket sheet for initial engagement on Aug. 17, 1914

Also attracting admiring attention in a proscenium box on the opposite side of the theatre were Colonel Wood, the architect; Moses Taylor, who had painted the curtain screen and sets; Frank Linden, the decorator who had chosen the cerise and blue color scheme, and Hanna's old friend Al Hayman.

There was admiring gush about the auditorium, though none of the reporters agreed about colors and shades. Here is how the *Globe* saw things:

"Entering the foyer proper the spectator gets a full view of the auditorium, which greets the vision with a wealth of soft color in rich tints of blue and gold,

which prove extremely pleasing under the effect of artificial light. The eye scans the large graceful proscenium arch, which is a gorgeous combination of plaster relief work, finished in sienna tints and illuminated with gold and bronze. So, too, in the general treatment of the auditorium the decorative design carries out the rich Indian or Oriental feeling, which is intensified by the graceful curves and picturesque appearance of the boxes, with their drooping canopies and golden ornamentation, above which rises a pretty finish of spindle work."

Taylor Moses's house curtain, mercifully without the grotesqueness of the old Alpha, was considered a

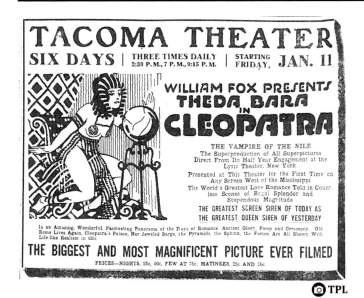

work of art. It was said to be a Roman street scene representing the Temple of Minerva.

Precisely at eight, and by Hanna's insistence without any dedicatory speechifying, the nine-piece orchestra went into the overture, the lighting master backstage dimmed the great gas-lit "sun-burner" chandelier and turned up the gas in the floorlights. The curtain rose on *Paola – The First of the Vendettas*, a comic opera with a Romeo and Juliet theme – but a happy ending.

There were some glitches. The announced leading lady, Georgine Von Janusehowsky, had (unannounced by the Duff Company) failed to make the trip to Tacoma. Her role was sung by a substitute whose voice was pronounced by critics "to be not what it used to be." Whoever had counted the chorus as numbering fifty had counted legs, not heads. The chorus girls were found "as a rule, not attractive to the eye." The opera was neither very operatic nor very comic. But the first-night audience, determined not to be disappointed, was not disappointed.

The audience went home happy. The playhouse, not the play, was the thing. During the rest of the week the company presented *The Queen's Mate* and *A Trip to Africa* in repertoire with *Paola*. No seat in the house was vacant.

One of the early bookings was Frederick Warde in *The Mountebank*. While in town, Warde, a personal friend of Hanna, invested in real estate. The first month of the shows concluded with a week's stand by Emma

Juch Opera Company, opening and closing with Faust, again every seat taken. Madame Juch did even better in real estate than Warde. She took a flier on a corner lot the day she arrived and sold it at the end of the week for 100 percent profit.

During the next season John Hanna resigned as manager to assume direction of the Seattle Opera House. Hanna, like several other theater men in the Northwest, saw that the wave of the future would be circuits of theaters that could offer national companies extended tours. He wanted a house of his own as a cornerstone for developing such an organization.

Hanna's place in Tacoma was taken by 29-year-old Calvin Heilig, who had come to Tacoma in 1890 from Reading, Pennsylvania, with his brother Irving, an attorney. Cal was working as secretary to Tacoma's mayor, Stuart Rice, when called to theater management. He was still managing a theater in Tacoma when he died fifty years later.

There were other changes. Property values in Tacoma were rising so rapidly that in 1892 the investors in the Tacoma Opera Theater Company recouped their investment at considerable profit by selling the theater to Prudential Trust and Savings. The theater company then leased the building back from the new owners.

One of the highlights of Heilig's first season as manager was the appearance of another heavyweight celebrity, James Corbett, who had won the title from John L. Sullivan. The most cerebral of early title holders, Corbett saw how Sullivan had made ten times more

LADIES WILL PLEASE REMOVE THEIR LARGE HATS.
They can be checked in Ladies' Parlor free of charge.

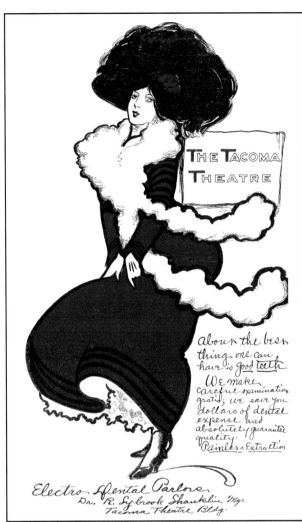

About the best thing one can have is good teeth. We make careful examination gratis; we save you dollars of dental expense and absolutely guarantee quality. Painless Extraction

Electro Dental Parlors.
Dr. R. Lybrook Shanklin, Mgr.
Tacoma Theatre Bldg.

money as an amateur thespian than as professional fighter. (The career figure was $1,101,050 on stage, $120,720 in the ring.)

So Gentleman Jim had a writer friend put together a play called *Gentleman Jack.* He had yet to master his lines, let alone stagecraft when the show came to Tacoma in May, 1893. His manager, Billy Brady, scheduled an afternoon rehearsal. Corbett not only blew some lines, he had trouble with clinches, failing to properly take his mother in his arms when called on to comfort her.

"Don't rush at her like you wanted to tie her up," Brady commanded, trying to break him of his boxing instincts.

"But that's how I did it last time in San Francisco."

Brady showed Corbett how he wanted the champ to circle slowly, gently toward her.

"But what's the use of a fellow walking all around the stage when he wants to put his arms around his mother." Corbett protested. "He'd just rush over and grab her. That comes natural. That's what I'd do."

"The stage effect is better. That's what we call staging in."

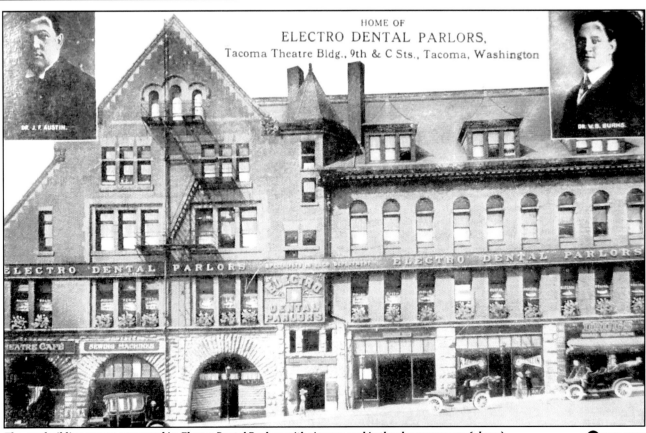

Theatre building tenant promoted its Electro Dental Parlors with signage and in the show program (above)

TPL/TSC

The rehearsal moved to a scene not involving the fighter. The champ sat down next to a reporter from the *Ledger*. "It kind of knocks me out when he makes me go over them things again and again. I lose confidence in myself. I want to do my best here, and now I'm upset. You know what I mean? It's easy enough, but kind of rattles a fellow, you know."

Corbett played to a full house with tickets at $1 lower floor, 50 cents gallery. The critics were kind. "Corbett makes a better actor and more pleasing one than the man whom he defeated for the championship," said the man from the *Evening News.* "He tries harder to act, and the fighter is lost sight of in the actor... As seen on stage Corbett does not look the fighter. He is pale, but does not show marks of great dissipation."

It was the economy that showed the effects of over-indulgence. Corbett's Tacoma appearance coincided with the worldwide collapse of farm prices, the flight of U.S. gold reserves abroad, a crash on Wall Street – the Panic of '93 ended the great Tacoma boom and the town's dream of becoming the dominant city of the Pacific Northwest.

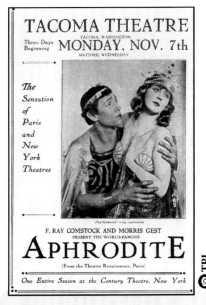

Tacoma Theater Timelines

- Opened January 13, 1890
- Spelling gradually changed from Theatre to Theater
- Remodeled and known as the Broadway Theater 1927–1933
- Known as the Music Box Theater 1933 until destroyed by fire in 1963

Tacoma to Broadway to Music Box to Ashes
By Murray Morgan

Henry A. Rhodes, who in 1892 had arrived in Tacoma from Wisconsin with his wife and about a thousand dollars, opened a tea and coffee store in a rented space in a former cracker factory at 932 Broadway. It prospered, as did Henry.

In 1925 he sold Rhodes Brothers department store at 11th and Broadway to B.F. Schlesinger & Sons to be operated in conjunction with stores he owned in Portland and Oakland. Henry, already a multi-millionaire with a 60-acre estate in the Lakes District, was 62 at the time and not ready for full retirement. In what was called the largest single real estate transaction in the city's history, Rhodes paid $450,000 to a group headed by Al Hearne, who with Cal Heilig had bought the Tacoma Theater from the ten original owners.

Rhodes was not planning a new career in show business. He was primarily interested in renting office and theater space. But, before space in the 35-year-old structure could be rented it needed updating. No man for half-measures, Henry gutted the entire building.

Everything was torn out inside plus half the roof. The sandstone and brick cavern hat remained and was sandblasted clean, inside and out. A new theater and tiers of modern offices were fitted into the hollowed-out interior.

For more than a year teams of workmen, 176 in all moved 335 tons of structural steel, 85 tons of reinforcing steel, 1,100 barrels of cement, 12,000 yards of metal lath, 900 yards of sand and gravel, 1,700 square feet of marble and uncounted miles of wire and pipe into the old enclosure.

When they finished in the late spring of 1927 Tacoma had a new and different theater, renamed The Broadway. Theater space had been enlarged. There was now seating for 1,575, 432 more than before. Stage space was deeper and the new proscenium, 36 feet across and 27 feet at the apex, met standards of most touring companies. Great attention had been paid to new possibilities in lighting the stage and in glorifying the effects achieved when the house lights were dimmed. It was hoped that lighting could be coordinated with the organ, but no reports on how this worked have survived.

The offices above the theater could be reached by the swiftest of Otis elevators. Henry Rhodes reserved prime space on the fourth floor of the tower for his office. The retail spaces on the street level had been provided more display windows, better lighting and higher rent.

The Tacoma reopened as The Broadway on February 4, 1927. Unlike the 1890 opening, the weatherman cooperated. This was a good thing since a crowd estimated at over 20,000 filled the streets adjacent to the theater under the glare of celebratory Klieg lights. Downtown businesses and the theatre had created a street festival, including four 26-piece bands. The Broadway marquee blazed to life and factory whistles let off a long blast at 6 p.m. to celebrate the grand opening.

To the 1,537 who gained entrance to the show were presented brilliantly colored programs emblazoned with The Broadway's slogan – "The Magic Sign of a Wonderful Time." Tightly uniformed usherettes, directed by the reigning Miss Tacoma, escorted them to their seats.

The lights dimmed and Felix the Cat appeared on the screen to improvised accompaniment of the house organ. A newsreel showed rioting in Vienna, Sacco and Vanzetti awaiting execution, Johnny Weismuller setting a swimming record. Then for the first time in Tacoma, the feature most old-timers remember about The Broadway, a Fanchon & Marco "Idea."

Ideas, as the dance numbers were called, were the creation of a Los Angeles woman named Fanny Wolff who, with her brother Mike, danced professionally under the name Fanchon and Marco. They were sometimes associated with a hoofer named Rodolfo Alfonza Raffaele Pierre Philibert Guglielmi, who became much better known as Rudolph Valentino.

When the Broadway opened on February 4, 1927, a massive crowd of over 20,000 celebrated with a lively street festival   ⊙ TPL

In the early 1920s Fanchon choreographed dance numbers to be performed before the movies at the Warfield Theater in San Francisco. The dance numbers were so popular that Fanchon formed a Pacific Coast Golden Gate Musical Revues Corporation to send troupes of dancers to major movie houses throughout the Far West. It was claimed that in the early 1930s that Fanchon employed nearly every professional dancer west of the Mississippi, enough at least to make her a figure of great influence in popular culture.

Fanchon's productions, deeply rooted in the lightness of adagio, which with its lyricism of lifting, balancing and turning, set the popular taste. The Fanchon lyric style helped prepare audiences for Fred Astair and Ginger Rogers after Astair overcame the handicap of his screen test report – "Can't act. Slightly bald. Can dance a little."

It was Fanchon and Marco dances, not Harold Lloyd's performance in *The Kid Brother* that fans were talking about when they left The Broadway. Fanchon and Marco prologues remained a big draw until the Depression crippled the economy. Prologues became a luxury movie managers could do without. The

troupes dissolved. Fanchon did some movie choreography, then dropped from sight.

As for The Broadway, it suffered through several closures during the Depression under the management of Fox Theaters. In early 1933, John Hamrick leased the theater and changed the name to John Hamrick's Music Box. He presented vaudeville, big-name orchestras and first-run movies.

On April 30, 1963, a team of consultants who had been hired by the City of Tacoma to draw a plan for revival of downtown Tacoma through urban renewal met with reporters at the Winthrop Hotel to discuss their proposal. During the informal press conference George Rockrise, the San Francisco architect who conceived the Ghirardelli Square redevelopment at Fisherman's Wharf, remarked that the building in Tacoma most worthy of preservation, perhaps the only one worthy of preservation, was the old Tacoma Theatre.

That evening, the Music Box was showing Alfred Hitchcock's horror film, *The Birds*. A little after six p.m. a fan under the balcony and projection room on the Ninth Street side of the building

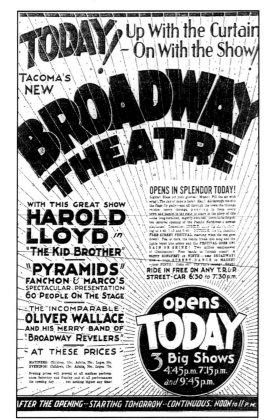

(Left) Grand opening ad; (Right) Line up to see Let Us Be Gay, *advertised above*

malfunctioned, starting a small fire. About twenty minutes later smoke was detected in the auditorium, not much, but enough for the doorman, Garry Ferrin, to go outside to see if something in the neighborhood was burning. All clear there.

He went back to the auditorium and could still smell smoke but could not locate the source. Checking the balcony he saw smoke rising through the projection light. He ran to a ladder that led from the men's room to the fan room. Looking in he saw sparks flying. The wall glowed. He managed to turn off the fan and empty a fire extinguisher against the wall, then climbed down to get another extinguisher. About this time somebody in management called the fire department.

Bill Jarmon, the 53-year-old projectionist who had been showing films at the theater for twenty years, reacted calmly. He turned up the house lights, but kept the film running, the recommended procedure for preventing a panic. "The birds were just beginning to fly out after the people," he recalled. Judy Jackstead, the head usher, quietly led the 100 or so in the audience onto Ninth Street, just as the first fire unit arrived. Before the night was over every unit in town, every off-duty fireman, was called out. But, nothing inside the theater was saved except the people, who escaped without any injuries.

Several firemen escaped death by inches when ceilings collapsed and a spectator on Ninth Street was knocked unconscious by a writhing fire hose. But The Broadway was a total loss, even the roof. Only the 1890 walls remained standing – the south wall is still visible today.

Henry Rhodes announced that a totally new structure would be built, but it would not include a theater.

Big-name performers and special events drew crowds to the Music Box with live shows and movies during the 1930s and 40s *All* ⦿ TPL

The fiery end came on April 30, 1963. (Above left) The last ad. (Above right) Roxy Theater ad the day after the fire

The Devine Sarah Bernhardt

By Murray Morgan

The triumph of the Tacoma Theatre's second season in 1891 was the visit by the most glamorous woman in the world, French actress Sarah Bernhardt. The Devine Sarah, as the less than divine Oscar Wilde was first to call her, might have been less famous than Queen Victoria, but Victoria was born to fame. Besides, the queen was 73 years old and never had been a beauty. Sarah was 26 years younger and beautiful, famous and scandalous. Besides that, at age 47, she was a great actress at the height of her powers.

She came to Tacoma by way of Australia and San Francisco, appearing in the title role of *Fedora*, a tragedy written for her by Victorien Sardou, the most popular lightweight dramatist of his day. *Fedora* is now remembered mostly because it lent its name to a style of soft-brimmed felt hat that Bernhardt wore in the title role.

Tickets went on sale a week before her appearance. Prices were outrageous for the 1890s: a box cost $30, a mayor's ransom. Parquet and parquet circle were $4, even the gallery benches were $1. All were sold out by nightfall.

Bernhardt arrived on the overcast morning of September 23. She came in a chartered 12-car train, which pulled onto a siding by the wooden shed at 17th and Pacific Avenue, which served as Tacoma's depot. While crowds gathered to watch the unloading of the sets and costumes, Sarah dined in one of the two salon cars she shared with her son Maurice, his wife – the Countess Terka, the countess' friend, Madame Seylor, a member of the acting company, and Sarah's manager. The French chef who travelled with the company prepared the five-course repast.

After being taken on a carriage ride through the business district, Sarah and her son and daughter-in-law slipped away for a stroll to Wright Park. It had recently been logged and replanted with deciduous trees brought from Europe by George Brown of the St. Paul and Tacoma Lumber Company.

On their way back, Sarah and her companions got lost and asked a policeman for directions to the theater. Perhaps there was a language barrier. Or perhaps it was the French clothing. The policemen escorted them not to the handsome Tacoma Theatre but to Morgan's saloon-fronted Theater Comique, which was offering *A Dollar for a Kiss*, fleshed out by "forty beautiful ladies." Sarah, when seventeen, had been turned down for employment by a French burlesque company, but had no current interest in performing at the Comique. She found her way up Ninth to the big theater in time for her performance.

Fedora may have been both more and less than Tacomans anticipated. Four acts long, with intermission it lasted almost four hours. Although Sardou had made his reputation with comedies so light that George Bernard Shaw dismissed them as "Sardooledom," this was a tragedy about nihilist terrorism in St. Petersburg and Paris. And it was entirely in French.

The *Ledger's* critic, writing against a hold-the-press deadline for the morning edition, declared Bernhardt "perfect," the play "brutal," then devoted the rest of his review to naming prominent Tacomans who had spent the evening with the Devine Sarah.

⬦⬦⬦⬦⬦⬦⬦⬦⬦⬦⬦⬦⬦⬦⬦⬦⬦⬦⬦⬦⬦⬦⬦⬦⬦⬦⬦⬦

The renowned actress returned to Tacoma at the Savoy Theater on May 10, 1906 on one of her "American Farewell" tours. It would be a similar promotion that brought her back to the Tacoma Theatre for three performances on June 14–15–16, 1918. She performed in three-hour productions of *La Dame aux Camelias (Camille)* before sold-out audiences at both theaters. Months before her appearance at the Savoy she had injured her leg while touring in South America and by the time she appeared in the Tacoma in 1918 her leg had been amputated. She continued to perform with a prosthetic leg. Her stage prowess translated to film and several months before her 1918 appearance at the Tacoma Theatre she was on screen at the Liberty Theater starring in *Mothers of France*, a drama set in World War I – which would not reach an armistice until November of that year.

LOC

It has been argued that Bernhardt is the most famous actress the world has ever known. Thus, it is easy to understand how sold-out audiences were willing to pay such expensive ticket prices to be able to see such a star in person. The bronze statue in Ledger Square, known affectionately among neighborhood residents as "The Spirit of Sarah Bernhardt," is located barely a block from the two venues in which she made local theater history a century ago.

Sarah Bernhardt appeared in Tacoma on three occasions over a period of nearly 30 years, the third occasion being a three-night stand at the Tacoma Theatre, five years before she passed away in Paris at the age of 78.

Tacoma Theatre – September 24, 1891 in *Fedora*

Savoy Theater – May 10, 1906 *in Camille*

Tacoma Theatre – June 14–15–16, 1918 in *Camille*

Prejudice

From virtually the first days of the city's existence, racial and ethnic prejudice played periodic, but villainous roles in Tacoma's theaters. Leading up to the November 3, 1885 expulsion of the Chinese, political leaders called people to the Alpha Opera House with posters reading: "The Chinese Must Go!" In 1902, factions were meeting at the Lyceum Theater advocating another round of anti-Chinese sentiment.

Racial stereotypes were at the foundation of minstrel shows dating back to the 1820s. As Deborah Freedman's sidebar "From Blackface to Burlesque" describes, the routines were performed by whites mocking characteristics of plantation blacks. Many prominent stage and screen entertainers performed in blackface into the 40s, the most famous perhaps, being the role played by Al Jolson in *The Jazz Singer* in 1927.

There were protests against blatantly racists films, but what debate there was in the community was dismissive. In April 1915, John Siefert defended showing a film called *The Nigger* at his new Liberty Theater.

The Tacoma Times, April 17, 1915:
**Siefert Refuses To Change
Name of Film – *The Nigger***

Caption: William Farnum, who acts the part of the "nigger-hating" governor who later learns that he has Negro blood in his veins, in *The Nigger* at the Liberty.

"*The Nigger,* a five-reel drama based on Edward Sheldon's famous story, caused an hour and one-half session of the Social Service Board yesterday afternoon. The board had met to consider a protest from the colored citizens of Tacoma, who asked that the film be barred from exhibition here. The picture starts a week's run at the Liberty tomorrow. At the end of the session, manager John Siefert was asked to change the title of the film to *The New Governor,* but Siefert today announced that he would not make the change. 'The film has made its big reputation partly because of its title,' said Siefert. 'I have leased the film for a week, and cannot afford to lose the benefit of the advertising by changing the name. If the movie censors want to arrest me, they can, but I will exhibit the picture just the same.'"

Then came *The Birth of a Nation*.

In answer to a segment in the March 2017 issue of *The Atlantic*, which asked "What was the most influential film in history?," Ty Burr, film critic for the *Boston Globe* answered:

"In American history, it has to be D.W. Griffith's *The Birth of a Nation* (1915) – the first cinematic blockbuster and a revisionist racist artifact that helped resurrect the Ku Klux Klan, led to a fresh wave of violence, bolstered myths about the antebellum South, and cemented the false image of the black male 'savage' in the white cultural mainstream. One hundred years on, the movie still has far too much to answer for."

On August 6, 1915, the Tacoma City Council held up the showing of the film at the Tacoma Theater "because of the fear of some that it might result in race riots." The next day it looked as though the right to show the film locally was headed to court. On August 12, *The Tacoma Times*, under the headline: "Lookee! Fem Debate is Declared a Draw." seemed to ridicule the protest, as representatives from women's clubs lined up against "six colored women in debate in Mayor Fawcett's private office." The film opened as scheduled on Sunday, August 20th and played to full houses for its two-week run. Nettie Asberry, secretary of Tacoma's NAACP chapter, followed with a lengthy letter to the editor of the *Tacoma Ledger*, pointing out many of the film's historical inaccuracies. The film returned to Tacoma in January of 1917, just before Griffith's follow-up film *Intolerance*, produced perhaps in answer to criticism of his earlier work.

All the major black characters in *Birth of a Nation* were played by white actors in blackface. This form of entertainment was popular even with local amateur productions, such as a 1928 event at the Scottish Rite Lodge in which a stage-full of performers were covered in blackface.

Racial segregation impacted where people gathered in Tacoma into mid-century. The United States military was still segregated during World War II, determining such activities as dances. In the accompanying photo, black servicemen turned out for dance night in the main auditorium of the USO club at 713-15 Commerce Street. Blacks and other minorities were denied service in a number of night clubs and bars into the 60s.

A wave of resentment against the Chinese had swept the West Coast after their work on the transcontinental railroad was done. Mass meetings in 1885 at the Alpha Opera House stirred the call that "The Chinese Must Go!" and Tacoma's mayor led the plans to expel the Chinese. The morning of November 3rd, gangs rounded up all the Chinese, over 200 in number, and force-marched them in driving rain to a train station south of town. Some bought tickets to Portland, a freight train picked up others at 3 a.m. the next morning. Some walked off into the night.

The above ad ran the morning of the expulsion. Seventeen years later, factions were meeting at the Lyceum Theatre to cast further threats against the Chinese who then had businesses and residences in Tacoma.

In 1994, the Chinese Reconciliation Project Foundation was established in alliance with the City of Tacoma to develop the Chinese Commemorative Park on the Ruston Way waterfront. The site is rich with cultural expression, including the Fuzhou Ting and annual Moon Festival.

All *TPL*

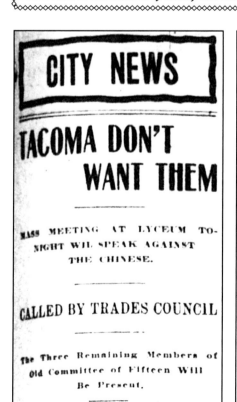

CITY NEWS

TACOMA DON'T WANT THEM

MASS MEETING AT LYCEUM TO-
NIGHT WILL SPEAK AGAINST
THE CHINESE.

CALLED BY TRADES COUNCIL

The Three Remaining Members of
Old Committee of Fifteen Will
Be Present.

VOLUME XX.   NUM

MUST KEEP OUT CHINESE

Mass Meeting of Tacoma
Citizens Passes Strong
Resolutions.

Urges Upon Congress Necessity of
Passage of Chinese Ex-
clusion Act.

Addresses Were Made by a Number
of Prominent Citizens, Including
United States Commissioner of
Immigration David Healy and
Labor Commissioner Blackman.

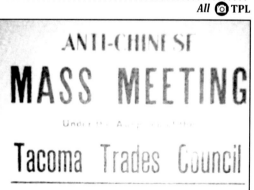

ANTI-CHINESE

MASS MEETING

Under the Au

Tacoma Trades Council

Wednesday Eve., March 26, 1902

At the Lyceum Theatre

The following speakers will address the meeting Im-
migration Inspector Healey State Labor Commissioner
William Blackman Rev. C. H. Little Rev. A. W. Martin
Col. W. J. Fife Col. J. J. Anderson and Frank R. Baker

Adler's Orchestra will furnish Music
during the evening

Everybody Invited   Seats Free

The USO club at 713 Commerce St. was segregated, as was the military, during World War II TPL

Circa 1930s, the cast in a blackface minstrel show at the Scottish Rite Lodge TPL

COURTS TO PASS ON "THE BIRTH OF A NATION" FIGHT

A legal fight will be necessary before "The Birth of a Nation," D. W. Griffith's massive production, can be exhibited at the Tacoma theater.

Commissioner Pettit has sent word to Herbert W. Glickauf, representing the film here, that the picture is a violation of an ordinance passed by the council last year, and that he would be forced to suppress its exhibition here.

Attorney W. P. Reynolds has been retained by Glickauf, and

LOOKEE! FEM DEBATE IS DECLARED A DRAW

Four club women representing four different women's clubs of Tacoma lined up against six colored women in debate in Mayor Fawcett's private office Saturday morning.

"The Birth of a Nation," a great film feature depicting the early history of the United States, which is booked for Tacoma this month and is declared prejudicial to the colored race, was the cause of the session.

The club women were present to insist that the film be shown here, and the colored women argued stoutly that the play was unmoral, untrue to history, and would ruin the efforts of the Ta-

coma colored population to elevate themselves and attempt to obtain equality.

Mayor Fawcett, Commissioners Pettit and Gronen, and Detective Capt. Fackler attended the session. At the end of an hour's debate the women withdrew, and the debate was declared a "draw."

The club women were Mrs. W. H. Johnston, Mrs. Inez Davis, Mrs. J. W. Brokaw and Mrs. Blanche Funk Miller. The colored women were Mrs. Henry Asbury, Mrs. W. H. Rees, Mrs. Mabel Davis, Mrs. W. N. Gaston, Mrs. I. M. Turner and Mrs. B. H. Parker.

LOCATIONS OF THEATERS

APOLLO, 1131-1133 Broadway
COLONIAL, 9th and Broadway
MELBOURNE, 916 Pacific Ave.
JEWELL, 1320 Pacific Ave.
SHELL, Pacific Ave. at 14th St.
VAUDETTE, 1112 South K St.
LIBERTY, 906 Pacific Ave.
PALACE, 12th St. and Pacific Ave.

Best Offerings
of the High Class
Photo-Play Houses

Watch This Page For All of the Latest Stories of What Is Going On at the Moving
➤ Picture Theaters ◄
The Best Reels In Town Will Be Advertised Every Saturday On This Page

Siefert Refuses To Change Name Of Film—"The Nigger"

William Farnum, who acts the part of the "nigger-hating" governor who later learns that he has negro blood in his veins, in "The Nigger," at the Liberty.

"The Nigger," a five reel drama, announced that he would make the change.

BACK TO MATTEAWAN

NEW YORK, April 17.—The supreme court has ordered Harry Thaw returned to Matteawan hospital for the criminally insane.

COLONIAL
Three Days Starting Tomorrow
THRILLS GALORE

VANDERBILT CUP RACE

Greatest Auto Race Pictures Ever Taken.

Taken at the Exposition Grounds, Frisco.

Thrilling accidents were the rule rather than an exception.

An auto overturns, another crashes into an iron post, another shoots through a wire fence; all running at the gentle rate of speed of 70 miles an hour.

BIG LAUGH COMEDY
C. O. D.

Four reels of sidesplitting laugh producing comedy that will drive away the blues. As funny as "Tillie's Punctured Romance."
Your Money Back If You Don't Laugh.

The COLONIAL
Never Disappoints.

'Most Beautiful 'Phone Girl' Comes to Tacoma

Irene Estelle Hough

Irene Estelle Hough, winner in the "Most Beautiful Telephone Girl" Contest.

ALL-STAR PROGRAM AT THE VAUDETTE

The Vaudette theater, 11th and K streets, has arranged an all-star program for its Sunday show.

THREE DAYS STARTING SATURDAY
World's Greatest Set Problem Play—Direct From New YORK HIPPODROME

Man and Woman
A Drama of Undeniable Truth.
Endorsed by Press and Pulpit Throughout the Universe

MELBOURNE
5c—First Time in America at—5c

Double and Triple Exposures On Film of "Satan Sanderson"

SCENE FROM THE FILM VERSION OF "SATAN SANDERSON"

"C. O. D.," Hilarious Comedy Opens at Colonial Tomorrow

'Man & Woman' at Melbourne

APOLLO THEATER
3—DAYS ONLY—3

Hallie Ermine Rives' Famous Book and Play

"Satan Sanderson"

—in 5 reels of thrills and heart interest—featuring the well known stars—

ORRIN JOHNSON
and
IRENE MARFIELD

EXTRA ATTRACTION
Stanford race winning the rowing match at the recent California meet.

APOLLO THEATER
1131-33 Broadway
Phone Main 2074

PALACE THEATER
SUNDAY ONLY
"AND THEY CALLED HIM HERO"

Two-reel Civil War Scenic Spectacle and Drama

Change of Program Monday

'Jitney Elopement' With Chaplin, Comes to Shell

LIBERTY THEATER

Commencing Sunday

William Farnum

America's Highest Paid and Most Popular Artist, in

THE NIGGER

By Edward Sheldon
America's Significant Young Dramatist.

In this play Mr. Sheldon handles unflinchingly and with unerring power a wonderful problem that must be faced fairly and squarely by the people of the United States.

A $100,000 Photo-play, 1000 People, 500 Scenes

10c Admission 10c

SEE THE LIBERTY FIRST
Ninth and Pac. Av.

Efforts to prevent the showing of the racists film Birth of a Nation *were dismissed by City of Tacoma officials, which led to capacity audiences viewing the film at the Tacoma Theater.*

All TPL

"BIRTH OF A NATION" IS FILLING TACOMA THEATER

Though attendance for "The Birth of a Nation" has approached very nearly capacity at every performance since the opening Sunday at the Tacoma theater, true to the traditions of the entertainment each day has been better than the preceding one, yesterday being the biggest of the engagement so far and it is evident that from now on empty seats will be very scarce at the Tacoma.

Fully half of those who see "The Birth of a Nation" see it a second and even a third time, and it is safe to say that this truly marvelous entertainment will long be remembered by all who see it.

From Blackface to Burlesque

By Deborah Freedman

When white actor Thomas D. Rice first put on blackface makeup in 1828 and sang and danced his "Jim Crow" routine, he sparked a form of entertainment that would become known as minstrel. Most-popular in the decades before the Civil War, the shows featured an entire cast in blackface pretending to be happy slaves, singing songs and speaking in exaggerated Southern dialects.

The minstrel performances followed fairly standard patterns. In the First Part, the entire cast would enter in a musical processional, mix in some jokes and songs, and finish with a cakewalk that gave each performer a brief chance to solo. The Second Part included several small acts performing in front of the curtain, typically including a "stump speech" of satirical monolog. (A tradition still carried on in late-night television.) The Third Part or After Piece featured a comic or melodramatic scene, often "burlesquing" or making fun of more serious theater. Despite their crude and racist humor, minstrel shows survived into the 1960s.

Eventually, any comic sketch was called a burlesque. Along came M. B. Leavitt, (Michael Bennett Levy, 1843–1935) who began as a performer in minstrel and worked his way up into management. In 1870 Leavitt cleverly replaced the blackface clowns with pretty girls in flesh-colored tights, while keeping the three basic parts of the minstrel show. Now widely recognized as the father of burlesque, Leavitt claimed in his memoirs to have also invented the term "All Star" and begun the American use of lithographic promotional posters (which occasionally tested local obscenity laws.) His Madame Rentz Female Minstrels traveling companies performed in small towns throughout America and in Canada and Mexico, and he managed theaters in San Francisco and Denver.

However, burlesque was fairly ribald for family audiences. A cleaner version of variety-style entertainment evolved, which performers dubbed the "Sunday School circuit." By the Gay '90s it was known as vaudeville. Entertainers were hired to perform at a series of theaters, booked as a circuit. Expanding from burlesque, a vaudeville show typically included nine acts and an intermission. The first act was usually a juggler or magician who could perform without speaking over the still-arriving audience, while the ninth act had to work to keep the crowd from leaving.

Beginning in 1896, short moving pictures were introduced into vaudeville. Initially they were just novel added attractions, designed to be tucked in between songs and sketches. As the popularity of motion pictures grew, so did the films. Eventually the roles were reversed, with live entertainment only before and after a feature film. Gradually theaters transitioned to showing just movies, and performers survived by moving on to radio and film, and later into television.

However, during the '20s and '30s the remaining burlesque shows became even raunchier, deteriorating into racy shows with skimpy costumes. According to one legend, in 1917 Mae Dix accidentally invented the striptease when she absent-mindedly started removing part of her costume as she left the stage at Minsky's in New York. The crowd started cheering and she returned to the stage to further undress, sparking the first of many police raids.

In April of 1892 Tacoma Theatre audiences were entertained by a well-known "Spider and Fly" traveling program produced by M.B. Leavitt, likely a blend of burlesque and vaudeville. Curiously, that month enumerators were engaged in taking a county census and included Mr. Leavitt as a resident of Tacoma. (Along with a woman named Isabel, although Leavitt's estranged wife Hattie was in New York at the time.) He was likely only in town briefly to make advance arrangements for his performers.

Tacoma Herald April 10, 1892

Six of Leavitt's burlesque stars, from his memoir *Fifty Years in Theatrical Management: 1859–1909.*

Sourced with permission by Wayne Keyser. His fun and informative website: **www.goodmagic.com/carny/vaud.htm**

NOW PLAYING

The Fifes

Old Bill Fife Played Song of Success in Early Tacoma

By Murray Morgan

The William Fifes, father and son, Old Bill and Young Billy, rode the rising tide of early Tacoma development to its crest in the early 1890s, then disappeared in the backwash of the financial Panic of '93. They left the family name imprinted on a Tacoma street, a Tacoma suburb and in Tacoma's theater history.

William H. Fife certainly deserved to have things named for him. He was one of the area's most enterprising characters. A Canadian, born in Ontario to Scottish immigrants, he was apprenticed at 17 to work in a general goods store for $5 a month. He owned his own store by the time he was 20. At 30 he took time off from store-keeping to join the rush to Caribou gold fields in British Columbia. Coming back three years later with a modest fortune, he moved his family to Michigan, then to Iowa, where he built a store at a river crossing east of Sioux City and watched the town of Cherokee grow up around it.

The idea of having the first store in a growing town appealed to him. In 1873, when Fife was 40, the *Northern Pacific Railroad* was about to decide where its western terminus would be on Puget Sound. Fife visited the area and happened to be on

Commencement Bay when the N.P. announced that New Tacoma was its choice. He hurried home, sold off his Cherokee holdings, and headed west with his wife, their five children and two servants.

They arrived at the Tacoma station on the wharf on the evening of April 14, 1874 – the day before the Tacoma Land Company officially put downtown lots on sale. After spending the night in the Blackwell Hotel, Fife sloshed up the dirt path to Pacific Avenue, climbed the hill to C street (now Broadway), and went to the headquarters of the *Tacoma Land Company*, a one-room shack in a patch of skunk cabbage at the southwest corner of Ninth and C. There, on the city plan sketched by William Isaac Smith, he selected the northwest corner of Ninth and Pacific Avenue as his first investment.

"We arrived on a Saturday," he recalled years later, "and on Tuesday we took dinner in our own house. You would hardly call it a house now, but it was somewhat of a mansion in those days, a shanty 18 by 24 feet. Nine of us sheltered beneath its roof until I could put up a large house, which I began without delay, a two-story frame directly in front of the shack. This I used as a store and dwelling combined. It was the first general merchandise store in Tacoma."

Two months after coming to town, Fife was appointed Tacoma's postmaster by President Grant. When the first sack of mail, containing six letters, arrived at New Tacoma, 17-year-old Billy Fife volunteered to hand deliver them. Young Billy (as he was called to differentiate him from his father, Old Bill) was curly haired, handsome, athletic and with a deep but flexible voice caught the town's attention in many ways. He also found time to play in Tacoma's first baseball game, an inter-squad match between members of the Tacoma Invincibles. It ended 28 to 29, both sides claiming victory.

Anyone wanting stamps or other postal service had to call at the Fife store. Old Bill thoughtfully put the counter in a far corner so

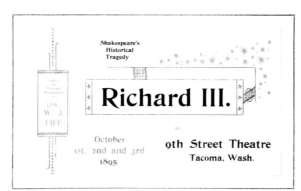

Aspiring actor "Young" Bill Fife starred in the 1895 play TSC

patrons had to thread their way past tempting barrels of molasses, pickles, flour, sauerkraut and fish. This encouraged conversation as well as sales. Fife became the best-informed man in town about business opportunities. He invested in timberland, mineral claims and nearby farmland, one section of which is now the City of Fife.

In an early venture, Fife bought the Southeast corner at Ninth and Market, where there was a free-running stream. (The whole Tacoma hill was so water-soaked that an Oregon editor joshed about the N.P. trying to build a city in the shallowest lake or steepest swamp known to man.) Fife built tanks, captured the spring water, piped it down Ninth in bored-out logs, and provided Pacific Avenue with its first tap water and a modicum of fire protection.

Young Bill graduated from a military academy in Oakland, California, but decided against a career in the peacetime army. He tried newspapering in California, but had no flair for writing or reporting. He studied law at Columbia law school, but never practiced. Returning to Tacoma at loose ends in the early 1880s, he helped old Bill in his various enterprises – the Hotel Fife which stood where the grocery had been, the Tacoma Coal Company, Exposition Hall, the Puget Sound Dry Dock Company.

Then, at a fund-raiser for the First Methodist Church, of which Old Bill was a trustee, young Bill recited *The Deathbed Scene of Benedict Arnold.* He was a sensation. He sensed destiny. That feeling was confirmed when he was given the lead in the Tacoma Dramatic Society's production of *Among the Breakers,* a melodrama of mistaken identity, at the Alpha in 1884. He revelled in the role of the heroic lighthouse tender. Although critical acclaim was tainted by reference to Hamlet's warning to the players against "O'er stepping the modesty of nature," Young Billy was hooked. He knew his fate was to be an actor, a great actor, the American tragedian.

To be in a burg a continent away from New York, half the world away from London, with only the old Alpha as a stage seemed real tragedy for an aspiring thespian. Old Bill might well have joined the other $10,000-apiece investors in the Tacoma Theatre even if his son's interests had not been in acting. After all Fife was one of the movers and shakers of the town. But his next move was almost certainly made with Young Billy's future in mind. Right across the alley (Court C/aka Opera Alley) from the Tacoma Theatre, on the site of the former waterworks which he had

transformed into a market, Old Bill in 1892 built a theater of his own.

Fife's showplace was built to a design introduced in the Pacific Northwest by John F. Cordray, a jeweler turned impresario. As a boy, Cordray did odd jobs at the Athenaeum Theater in Columbus, Ohio. His folks, who disapproved of show business, apprenticed him to a jeweler in New York City. Returning to Columbus, John ran a jewelry store with his brother. In their spare time they put together a performing clock that as it ticked off the seconds "told the story of the heavens, great events in sacred history and many other interesting things." They took the clock on tour, exhibiting it to wondering multitudes at fairs and expositions around the country." John found so much pleasure in entertaining that he never went back to the store.

For a time Cordray managed a theater in New Orleans. Then he moved to Denver and in the shadow of the Tabor Grand Opera House opened a storefront exhibition space he called a muse. To attract patrons to his display of oddities he hired jugglers, mimes and other itinerant artists to do casual turns. In 1888 he moved on to Portland where he set up a tent. It had a room for a stage as well as his performing clock, his stuffed platypus, his genuine mermaid and his Hawaiian grass skirts. The muse in the tent proved so popular that Cordray had the canvas replaced with an iron roof and wood walls without interrupting performances.

An impresario now, Cordray branched out. In 1890 he took over the Madison Street Theater in Seattle, remodeling it to house two separate performance areas: an intimate one for polite vaudeville at ten cents, and a larger area for legitimate theater. The idea was family theater, a place where a man could take the wife and kids without fear of corruption or embarrassment.

Seattle's Madison served as the architectural model for the Olympic, which was the original name of the theater Fife built. It had a small performance space for variety acts and a 900-seat auditorium with balcony for plays. Fife hired Mark Wilson to manage the theater and assemble a stock company of professionals. The Olympic was scheduled to open Christmas Day 1892, a Sunday. At the last moment the Tacoma Ministerial Alliance protested that this would be desecration of the Sabbath, compounded. The pastors asked that an ordinance be passed barring Sunday performances. Such an ordinance went through first reading but the chief of police refused to act unless ordered to do so by the mayor. As it turned out, the theater held its grand opening on Saturday, the 24th while running an ad that day proclaiming it would be presenting shows "every evening, including Sundays."

Thus, the show went on at 7 o'clock that Sunday as Mr. Sid J. Black did trick riding on a bicycle. Rita Wilson, the manger's wife, followed with a tender ballad. Russell, O'Dell & Russell did a comedy turn on the theme "A Fifteen Minute Recess." Professor Horman tried to live up to his billing as "The World's Greatest Magician and Illusionist." All this for ten cents.

At 8 o'clock, the house orchestra struck up a fanfare for the folks in the big auditorium and "the strongest stock company on the Pacific Coast" presented the West Coast premiere of *Michael Strogoff*, an adaptation of Jules Verne's novel about Russian military life. The house was full at prices ranging from $1 for a box seat to thirty-five cents in the gallery. The reviews were complimentary about the facility, praising the comfort of the seats, the sightlines and acoustics, the excellence of the lighting and the absence of drafts. About the performance there was an absence of enthusiasm.

The *Ledger* did attest that such a theater as the Olympic was needed and predicted that it would "unquestionably gain the clientele it seeks – that class of theater-goers who want a good performance at a moderate figure." Such moderate success was not to

be. Exactly three months after the Christmas opening, Wilson announced that the Olympic was going dark.

John Cordray came instantly to attempt a rescue. He leased the Olympic, changed the name to the Cordray, and reopened it in May as part of a Portland-Seattle-Tacoma circuit – just in time to go broke in the Panic of '93 that hit Wall Street in June. E.E. Keeley took charge, renamed the house The Ninth Street and, as manager, managed to keep it open in the worst years of the Gray Ninety depression.

Meanwhile, what of Young Billy? While the Olympic-Cordray-Ninth Street was being built and failing its early tests, he had been perfecting his tragic art. He studied in San Francisco and New York. He was tutored by professionals who came through Tacoma. He gave readings at benefits. Though still an amateur he played Dionysius in a 1891 professional production of *Damon and Dionysius*, winning local praise as better than the play-for-pay Damon. He visited California and interviewed actors about joining a stock company that would specialize in tragedies starring himself. He intimated to reporters that he had been sounded out about joining the touring company headed by Frederick Warde and Louis James. And, as the Panic of '93 sent the already stumbling Tacoma economy into a freefall, he confided to the *Evening News* that he was about "to begin a professional career that will take him starring through the country."

Billy said he preferred to say nothing about it. Then he said there was a proposal to form a first class company for him in New York, a company that would be rehearsed to perfection before he joined it. While it was rehearsing he would remain in Tacoma studying. When the company approached perfection, he would go east for his debut in one of the large theaters in the great metropolis.

"I should start from this city and practically step on stage," said the 34-year-old amateur. "Nothing like it has ever been done." That was the dream when the Fifes were rich, but then came the crash of 1893 and the setting in of reality. All of Old Bill's investments were in peril as eastern banks called in their loans, Tacoma banks closed their doors, property values collapsed, thousands of newcomers went back where they had come from. Broadway never beckoned Young Billy. The climax of his acting career was not a world-startling debut in Manhattan but a two-night stand in a now-forgotten play in June of 1894 as a benefit for a proposed Washington-Oregon-Idaho Interstate Trade Fair.

HOTEL◉FIFE.
EUROPEAN PLAN.

G. W. FIFE, Proprietor.

The stately Fife Hotel was on the corner of 9th and Pacific TSC

The vehicle was James Sheridan Knowles' five-act *Virginius*. It was set in early Rome and dealt with the uprising of the plebeians against the abuses of the patricians. Young Billy was manager, stage manager, director and, of course, the hero Virginius, defender of the Republic, and the fair Virginia, against the abuses of the tyrant Appius Claudius. As Virginia, Fife cast 24-year-old Eva Fay Fuller, the theater critic for her father's weekly paper, *Every Sunday*. Miss Fuller had gained fame, and considerable notoriety four years earlier by climbing Mount Rainier, the first woman to do so. The fact that she did it in bloomers was deplored by the established defenders of decency.

William Lightfoot Visscher, late of the *Morning Globe* and now employed by the *Evening News*, played Dentatus, and Visscher's daughter, Viva, was Servia. In all probability the profile of Young Billy, "The Coming Tragedian," was written by Visscher:

"Gifted as he is, with a physique as noble and manly as any antique Roman, with a face as clear cut as a medallion, and features mobile as Delsarte (Francois Delsarte, a French theorist on acting who formulated a system of coordinating the voice with physical gestures) and to crown all a voice whose deep and harmonious melody is as sonorous as an organ note…. The popular verdict has been that his present is good and his possibilities almost boundless. Those best qualified by education, culture and acquaintance with dramatic

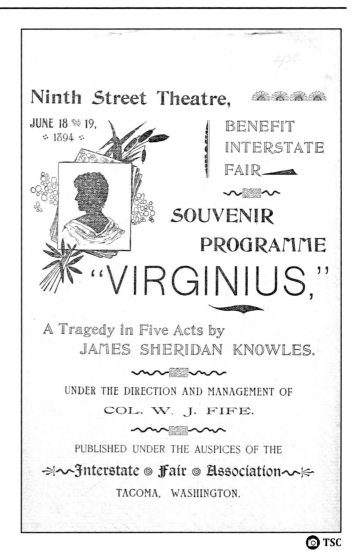

Ninth Street Theatre,

JUNE 18 & 19, 1894

BENEFIT INTERSTATE FAIR

SOUVENIR PROGRAMME

"VIRGINIUS,"

A Tragedy in Five Acts by JAMES SHERIDAN KNOWLES.

UNDER THE DIRECTION AND MANAGEMENT OF COL. W. J. FIFE.

PUBLISHED UNDER THE AUSPICES OF THE

Interstate Fair Association

TACOMA, WASHINGTON.

Young Bill was in his thespian glory in Virginius, presented in 1894 at the highly decorative Ninth Street Theatre

matters freely predict that he will write his name high up on the scroll of fame and fill the empty buskins dropped by Edwin Forrest." The reviews weren't bad either.

Young Billy took a curtain call on Thanksgiving, appearing with three professionals – Lawrence Hanley, McKee Rankin and Edith Lemmert, in a benefit production for the Knights of Pythias at the Tacoma Theatre, but that was his last hurrah. His next four years were spent in vain attempts to salvage Old Bill's varied enterprises, especially the Ninth Street Theater. He took over its management in 1897 and managed to keep the lights on, dimly.

A problem for theater management at the time was that the great Columbia Exposition in Chicago in 1893 stimulated American fascination with technology. The most popular shows were those involving machinery, usually as a threat to hero or heroine. Popular plots involving a damsel imperiled by a locomotive, a child to be rescued from a burning ship, a mother forced to leap with her baby between the opening gates of a lock on a dam. Such effects could be expensive. Fife got away with importing a cut-rate production of *Blue Jeans*, a melodrama of political and marital intrigue which leads to the villain locking up the heroine in a sawmill and tying her husband to a log being driven toward a great circular saw.

The United States went to war with Spain in April 1898 and young Billy immediately answered President McKinley's call for 125,000 volunteers to serve two years. Breveted lieutenant colonel, he led the first battalion of the Washington regiment as it marched down Pacific Avenue to the old Flyer dock on May 11. When all troops were aboard he appeared on the bridge to thank a cheering throng for their support, to express confidence in the triumph of right and to conclude:

"But should I never return, I leave you, citizens of my city, a sacred legacy – one dear to my heart. I leave in your care, friends, three motherless children (his wife had died four years before) and only ask that you can be to them fathers and mothers, both."

The battalion transferred to the troopship *Valencia* in San Francisco, but reached Manila long after Spain surrendered. They stayed on to fight the Filipino insurgents who wanted complete independence rather than an American protectorate.

During Young Billy's absences, Old Bill lost the theater to a mortgage foreclosure. Newspaper estimates in

1890 had put his wealth at between $1 million and $2 million. The crash of 1893 hit Tacoma harder than any other city in the country. The population fell from an estimated 53,000 in 1893 to a census confirmed 37,714 in 1900. The five-story Hotel Fife went too, and Old Bill moved from its best suite to a room in the rundown Hotel Bradley a block away. Friends marveled at his good humor and optimism. When word came of the gold strike on the Yukon, he rushed north but got no farther than Skagway. Returning to Tacoma as broke as when he left, he pulled up stakes and went to live with a daughter in California who had married a congressman. At 70 he went off to Nevada on news of another gold discovery. He returned to his daughter's house in Alameda just before his grandson and namesake, William Fife Knowland, was born in 1904. Old Bill died in January 1905.

When Young Billy got back to Tacoma from the Philippines in 1900 he stayed only long enough to close out what remained of the Fife businesses, then went to Los Angeles. He died suddenly of apoplexy in 1911 at the age of 51.

The Ninth Street Theater, which he had left under the management of C. Harry Graham, ran into censorship trouble. According to an *Evening News* account, "Graham was running a class of popular priced plays with a Sunday performance when certain good women in the city who believed that theaters were all bad and Sunday theaters particularly sinful, for the good of the cause made up a party and went to the show for the first time in their lives. When they saw the bright but abbreviated clothes of some of the girls and heard the songs and gags and stage talk they considered bordering on the ridiculous if not the absolutely wicked, they straightaway hauled the manager before the bar of justice for the violation of running a place of business on Sunday. He was convicted. The case is still hanging in the courts, somewhere, though the wicked manager has not yet been hanged."

In 1900, the formerly Fife-owned theater was purchased by John Donnelly, who had previously acquired the former Hotel Fife and renamed it Hotel Donnelly. He also bought the Tacoma Hotel, which he had the good taste not to rename.

Donnelly was an Eau Claire, Wisconsin businessman who joined the great migration of white pine lumbermen to the west after they had over-logged the Midwest forests. Arriving in 1888 at the height of the boom he specialized in real estate. He sold the Elks the site of their downtown temple, the Klopfensteins their Broadway site and the U.S. Postal Service the site of the post office at 11th and A Street. He was one of the organizers of the Country Club and helped lead the campaign that led to the building of the Five Mile Drive at Point Defiance, but his interest in theater was that of a real estate man. He let others manage the old Ninth Street. Its name was changed to the Lyceum, then to the Star before others would eventually build the Rialto on the site.

TACOMA KID

THE GREAT COWBOY LECTURER.

© TSC

Solve the mystery:
We like his name, we like his style, but, we don't know
what he lectured about or who he was, for that matter.

Jewish Bazaar at the Olympic
By Deborah Freedman

Jewish ladies held a three-day Christmas Bazaar in the new Olympic Theater before the seats were installed, courtesy of manager Mark Wilson. *Ledger* on Sunday, December 4th, 1892:

"Christmas Sales. The new Olympic theater will be opened December 15th, 16th and 17th by the Temple Aid society, who will hold a bazaar, which will be carried out on an extensive scale. The Jewish ladies of the city are energetically working that the entertainment may be successful in order to increase the fund for the erection of a Jewish temple. The merchants of this city and many leading houses in the east have donated with marked generosity, and handsome articles from their establishments will be placed on sale. Furniture, merchandise, jewelry, bric-a-brac and fancy work are among the valuable donations."

Tacoma Movie Quiz

Try matching the following movies with one of their Tacoma film locations.

1. Get Carter (1999)

2. 10 Things I Hate About You (1998)

3. Prefontaine (1996)

4. The Hand That Rocks the Cradle (1991)

5. I Love You to Death (1990)

6. Waiting for the Light (1989)

7. Come See the Paradise (1994)

8. Three Fugitives (1988)

9. Cinderella Liberty (1973)

10. Sweet Revenge (1976)

A. North "I" Street private home

B. Rialto Theater

C. Inside former Elks Temple

D. 3rd floor jail County-City Bldg.

E. Stadium High School

F. Chase scene down 15th Street hill

G. Spanish Steps

H. Greyhound Bus terminal

I. Bostwick Building

J. UPS Baker Field

Answers: 1-F, 2-E, 3-J, 4-A, 5-I, 6-B, 7-C, 8-G, 9-H, 10-D

NOW PLAYING
Eyes of the Totem

Rediscovering
Eyes of the Totem

By Lauren Hoogkamer

My role in the rediscovery of the *Eyes of the Totem* film began on June 23, 2014, when I was hired as the Historic Preservation Coordinator for the City of Tacoma. An important component of the City's historic preservation programming involves walking tours, workshops, lectures and others forms of community outreach. We are always looking for events that can draw interest for a large and diverse audience.

Years before, I interned at the Los Angeles Conservancy, an historic preservation nonprofit. As an advocacy intern I assisted with the highly popular Last Remaining Seats, a summer film series in which classic films are shown in Los Angeles' historic theaters for one night only. In 2011, I interned with Historic Tacoma, Tacoma's historic preservation nonprofit, so I was familiar with Tacoma's beautiful historic theaters and love of the arts. I was immediately interested in producing Tacoma's version of Last Remaining Seats.

At that time, JD Elquist, a Tacoma business owner, was on the Landmarks Preservation Commission as the liaison to the Arts Commission. He was also interested in outreach and mentioned that in the 1920s, Tacoma had a film production company called HC Weaver Productions. HC Weaver, he said, had produced three silent films – *Eyes of the Totem, Hearts and Fists,* and *Heart of the Yukon* – all of which had been lost since the Twenties. He thought it would be pretty cool if we could find those films – or at least part of one of them.

I met with former Mayor Bill Baarsma, President of Tacoma Historical Society, and prominent historian and historic preservationist Michael Sullivan to learn more about HC Weaver. They both confirmed that all three films were lost, a fact that had been proven by many hopeful researchers and historians, even famed historian Murray Morgan.

Like those before me, my research on HC Weaver kept leading to dead ends. I emailed national and

The Tacoma-made film provides many scenes of the city as it was in the 1920s

THS

international film archives. I contacted the companies that branched off from the companies that Weaver had used for film distribution. I searched for descendants. Finally, I stopped researching Weaver and began researching WS Van Dyke. Van Dyke became a famous film director during the 1920s and 1930s. He was nominated for an Academy Award for Best Director for *The Thin Man* (1934) and *San Francisco* (1934). He also directed *Eskimo* (1933), which won an Oscar for Best Film Editing.

I used his name as the keyword to redo my research and included ebay (you never know what historic ephemera will show up there), online blogs and film forums. One film forum mentioned seeing *Heart of the Yukon* in a private auction. *Eyes of the Totem,* it said, was in a catalog for a museum in New York City. This was confirmed by the National Film Preservation Foundation. It turns out that Van Dyke left his papers to this museum.

On July 1, 2014, the museum confirmed that it had a copy of *Eyes of the Totem* on seven nitrate reels, a highly combustible material. It would cost more than $30,000 for a preserved copy to be made, and it simply wasn't a priority. I immediately notified Bill Baarsma and Michael Sullivan – this was an historian's dream come true! Michael contacted the Tacoma Art Museum and the University of Washington and, somehow, managed to get the New York museum to agree to send a digital copy for less than $5,000, which he funded.

We all waited for the film to arrive – hoping that it would be at least partially viewable, but expecting it to be in poor condition. In early 2015, Michael announced that the film had arrived. For the first time in 90 years it would be watched in Tacoma. A small group related to the historic community met at the Blue Mouse Theater.

The movie started – if you've ever watched a silent film without sound you'll know how eerily quiet the theater was – we could hear each other shifting in our seats, chewing popcorn. We were all amazed to see that the film was in pristine condition, and this wasn't even a restored version! You could see the license plates on cars! The film was even complete, no parts missing! There it was, Tacoma in the 1920s, live on the silver screen!

There in the darkened theater, Team Totem was born. The team consisted of Michael Sullivan, Chairman; myself, John N. Miller, Production Coordinator for TV

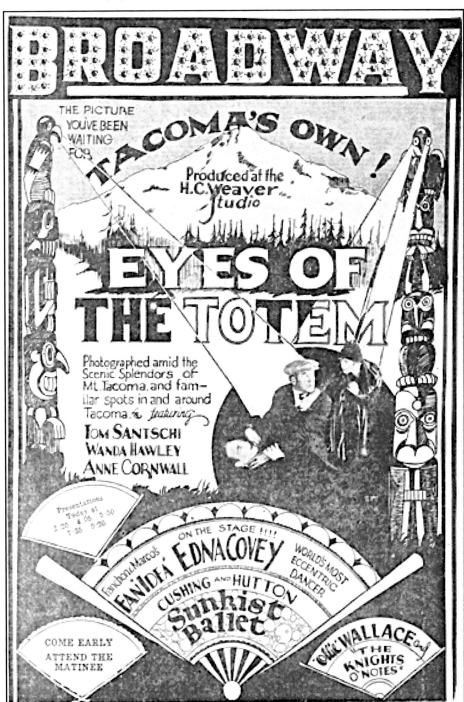

Original ad for 1927 release of "Eyes" at Broadway Theater

 THS

Tacoma; Mick Flaaen, Mariposa Productions; John Christopher Bayman, composer; John Carlton, multimedia producer; and Bill Baarsma of Tacoma Historical Society, the fiscal sponsor and keeper of the Eyes of the Totem project.

Team Totem was responsible for putting on a re-premiere event, letting the world know that *Eyes of the Totem* had been found and was back home in Tacoma, producing a new score (the original has never been located, if it even existed), and funding a complete restoration. We decided to plan a grand re-premiere in September of 2015, but we needed money for the event, and the score, and film cleanup. Composer John Christopher Bayman, who lives in Tacoma, agreed to produce a complete, multiple-instrument score.

As part of Historic Preservation Month, May 2015, a Kickstarter campaign was launched to raise $25,000. Team Totem was everywhere, giving talks, on TV and radio. More than 400 people contributed, raising just over $27,000 with enormous support from the community and local media outlets. *Eyes of the Totem* was originally produced and funded by community members, with the re-premiere it came full circle. Besides our donors, many other community members and organizations, including the City of Tacoma, Tacoma Public Library, Tacoma Art Museum, Washington State History Museum, Knights of Pythias, and the Broadway Center for Performing Arts, came together to make the re-premiere happen.

In preparation for the grand re-premiere we held lectures on film study and hosted book signings for authors who wrote about Tacoma's theater and film history. One in particular, Jamie Ford, author of *Songs of Willow Frost,* was there because of pure kismet. In 2013, Jamie, whose fictional books involve Pacific Northwest history, published *Songs of Willow Frost. Eyes of the Totem* is one of the main plot devices; Jamie did his research on the film based on historical articles and photos from the Tacoma Public Library's Northwest Room. He never imagined that anyone would actually find the film. When Michael Sullivan contacted him – they knew each other from research on Seattle's historic Panama Hotel, which plays a role in Jamie's other book – he was more than excited to fly to Tacoma for the re-premiere weekend.

In another strange twist, Joanne Ribaill came across the story of *Eyes of the Totem* and realized her mother, Peggy Ann Sessoms, was the young child in the beginning of the film. Peggy died 13 years ago and never once told her children that she starred in a 1920s film as a toddler. After her passing, her daughter, Joanne, found photos and an article about the child actor, the "Baby Peggy of the Northwest." Entranced and looking for more information, Joanne contacted Team Totem. Not only did she solve the mystery of who the child actor was, she found us in time to attend the re-premiere and watch her mother as a child on the big screen.

The Grand Re-Premiere was everything Team Totem had dreamed of over months of meetings and planning. We took Tacoma back in time to the 1920s, attendees and theater staff wore period clothes with flappers and men in zoot suits circulating around 1920s-era cars outside of the theater, the Pythian Temple opened up its historic speakeasy (password: "HC Weaver sent me") for an after-party complete with live piano music, a tintype photographer, and a gold rush exhibit.

Over the weekend of September 18, 2015, approximately 2,000 people came together to watch *Eyes of the Totem* in the historic Rialto Theater, where the film was first viewed in a private showing for producers, almost 90 years before. This was the first audience to see the film with the new score. Looking around the room, people's faces were full of excitement and emotion. There were tears in the eyes of longtime local historians who worked so many years to keep Tacoma's history alive. Here was their city, in all its Roaring Twenties glory.

That's what's remarkable about this film, you see Tacoma as it was in the 1920s, a boom city where people really did come to find their destiny. You see the Winthrop Hotel newly built. Thornewood Castle, Annie Wright School, downtown Tacoma with all the buildings we hadn't lost yet. You see Tacoma when Weaver Studios was located at 1600 Titlow Road and people really thought the city would be Hollywood by the Sea. Tacoma's richest citizens invested in HC Weaver; major movie stars came here to film. It was all very glamorous. When you see *Eyes of the Totem,* imagine how excited people would have been to see their city in a movie, at a time when film wasn't as common as it is now. That excitement continues to draw crowds in small theaters around the region.

– *Lauren Hoogkamer is the City of Tacoma Historic Preservation Coordinator. Her research uncovered the location of the only known remaining copy of HC Weaver's films, Eyes of the Totem. Before her discovery, the film had been lost to Tacoma for almost 90 years.*

Eyes of the Totem
– Synopsis

By Mick Flaaen

Eyes of the Totem tells the story of Mariam Hardy (Wanda Hawley), who persuades her husband Jim (Monte Wax) to sell his rich Alaska gold claim and return to civilization in order to properly raise their small child (Peggy Ann Sessoms) in a house with a white picket fence. On their passage to Tacoma, Washington aboard a steamer, a nefarious character with evil eyes named Phillip LaRue (Tom Santschi) kills Mariam's husband and steals the bankroll right in front of her fainting eyes. Arriving in Tacoma, she is without funds or friends until she meets Toby (Bert Woodruff) who convinces Mariam to disguise herself as a blind beggar in front of the landmark Totem pole, where she awaits the sight of the murderer's eyes.

With her humble earnings she makes the great maternal sacrifice and gives up her toddler child, sending her to live in a seminary to spare her the shame and hardships of her mother's existence as a street beggar. Years pass and young Betty Hardy (now Anne Cornwall) grows into a fetching young woman who attracts a young beau named Bruce Huston (Gareth Hughes), as well as the interest of the evil Phillip LaRue, now owner of the Golden Dragon, a cafe/speakeasy in town.

In rich melodramatic fashion all events culminate as Mariam recognizes Phillip LaRue in front of the Totem pole as her husband's killer and alerts the police chief (W.S. Van Dyke), as young Bruce races to the Golden Dragon to save Betty from the clutches of LaRue. LaRue is killed by the chief of police but not before a grand knockdown brawl with Bruce. Mariam reveals herself to her daughter Betty, and they are reunited as mother and daughter.

Weaver Studios

By Mick Flaaen

In the early 1920s, the City of Tacoma stood poised atop Commencement Bay for the arrival of something fantastical. When a larger-than-life motion picture promoter named Harvey Cook Weaver appeared, it rolled out the red carpet. Although Tacoma was more of a "rails meets the sails" town than the fictional River City of Meredith Willson's *Music Man*, it was a willing participant in the grandeur and excitement that this Weaver fellow was selling.

"H.C." Harvey Weaver's own dramatic arc had taken him from Spokane, where he grew up, to Salt Lake City, where he married, then to Hollywood, and later, to San Francisco. He came selling a dream of cinema, stardom, commerce, and global marketing to the City of Destiny.

Weaver began his career in motion pictures as a producer in the 'Teens (1917–1919). He went to work on Hollywood's Poverty Row, at the Christie Film Company on Sunset and Gower Street. There movies were made on the quick and cheap: stars were hired on Friday for one day of shooting, then their stand-ins were shot from behind on Saturday and Sunday, and the projects hurriedly wrapped by Monday morning. Working at what would become Sunset/Gower Studios, Weaver learned the ropes of film production while he built contacts in the business, most notably with a young actor/director named Woodbridge Strong Van Dyke, who was a protégé of D.W. Griffith. Van Dyke's decisive, often slapdash shooting methods would earn him the moniker of "One-take Woody."

In 1920 Weaver moved north to San Francisco to work for Paul Gerson Studios, producing the *Plum Center* comedies with character actors Dan Mason and the very tall Wilna Hervey. In San Francisco he also produced some of Frank Capra's early short films. Paul Gerson served as a mentor to the still green Weaver; he kept his studio afloat by selling common stock certificates to investors in the Bay Area. Weaver would emulate this strategy when he returned to the Pacific Northwest.

In 1923, the peripatetic Weaver moved still farther up the coast, landing in Seattle with the idea of exploiting this new area for filmmaking. On May 24th, 1924, H.C. Weaver Productions applied to the Washington Secretary of State's office for a Articles of Incorporation through the Seattle firm of Alexander, Bundy & Swale. Preferred and common stock certificates would be sold totaling $202,000 for the production, exhibition, sale, and distribution of motion pictures to be made in the Pacific Northwest. By October 23 of that same year the application for incorporation had been altered at the request of Tacoma attorney James M. Ashton. The amendment requested to move the principal place of business from Seattle to Tacoma. All the company's escrow and the common stock was transferred from

The Titlow Beach facility was the largest studio structure outside of Hollywood in the 1920s

the Metropolitan Bank of Seattle to the National Bank of Tacoma. Weaver put a board of directors in place, including attorney Ashton as treasurer, William R. Rust and Chester Thorne as vice presidents.

The Tacoma community embraced the ambitious venture. The new company received a donation of a five-acre parcel of land at Titlow Beach as well as lumber from a local mill. The construction of the movie studio's 105-by-180-foot building began with a cost of $50,000. It boasted a 52-foot-tall ceiling, which made it the second-largest film stage/studio in the United States at the time. A formal dedication, open to the public and attended by the state's governor (the Republican Louis Folwell Hart), was held on December 14th,1924. Local developers began to plan a subdivision around Weaver Studios that they envisioned would become the highest-priced real estate in Tacoma – "Hollywood by the Sea."

Excitement in Tacoma approached a fever pitch as the local newspapers posted daily articles in anticipation of arriving Hollywood movie stars and crew. This was no fluff: stars such as the veterans Alan Hale Sr. and Wanda Hawley were serious box office draws in the silent era. Hawley, for example, had starred opposite Rudolph Valentino in *The Young Rajah* (Paramount Pictures, 1922).

H.C. Weaver Productions was now a working studio about to begin production of its first feature. The not-so-young (43) upstart from Gower Street had managed to convince enough people in the City of Destiny not only to dream, but to dream big right in their own town. One of his main selling points was that motion pictures had become global commodities. Silent films were universal in translation, and the world's masses

were flocking to cinemas everywhere. What better way to promote Tacoma to the world? Weaver assured his backers that every film, every bit of print, advertising, or solicitation from Weaver Productions would bear the stamp MADE IN TACOMA.

Ultimately, Weaver succeeded in producing three films at the Tacoma studio before the advent of sound film brought an end to his grand plans: *Hearts and Fists* (1926, directed by Lloyd Ingram), *Eyes of the Totem* (1927, W.S. Van Dyke), and *Heart of the Yukon* (1927, Van Dyke). Having worked with Van Dyke on Gower Street in Hollywood, Weaver didn't have to ask the director more than once to come work with him in Tacoma. Van Dyke had grown up in Seattle. His wife, Tacoma girl Zina Ashford, was the youngest daughter of Pierce County settler W.A. Ashford, who had settled on land at the entrance to what would become Mount Rainier National Park. Nor was Van Dyke an exception: most of the cast and crew who worked on the three films had strong ties to the Pacific Northwest. Wanda Hawley spent her childhood in Seattle, and actors from local theatres were cast in the films. A local Renaissance man named Gaston Lance became the studio's art director and designed and built sets for the films. Some of his photos of the studio and the productions are archived at Tacoma Public Library today.

The board's early offices were located in the Rust Building. William R. Rust, former owner of the Tacoma Smelter, had donated the office space while also procuring a large amount of preferred stock in the movie company. Gen. James M. Ashton, attorney and treasurer for the studio, was probably its greatest proponent. His sense of adventure and calculated risk-taking was essential to this quixotic endeavor, and he helped string together the core members. The board of directors included Chester T. Thorne, the man who literally saved Tacoma: he kept the National Bank of Tacoma open during the Panic of 1893 by securing its loans and deposits with his own personal assets. Thorne had also built and developed Paradise Lodge at Mount Rainier – used as location in all three Weaver films. He was a key player in securing Annie Wright Seminary as a location for *Eyes of the Totem*; and for *Totem* he provided his own home too, the imposing Thornewood Castle.

By 1927 the distribution deals that had been informally agreed upon by American Distributors, Selznick Pictures, and others had not materialized. The $100,000 guarantees per picture that Weaver had proposed came to nothing. *Hearts & Fists* was sold to Pathé for $40,000. Production costs reached $1,000 a day at H.C. Weaver Productions and debts were adding up.

On October 6, Warner Brothers' *The Jazz Singer* premiered at Warner's flagship theater in New York City, and sound had come to motion pictures. But at what a cost: the major Hollywood studios had to align themselves with major banks in order to survive and continue production. Independent studios like Weaver's that had sprung up around the country had to face the harsh realization that they were no longer able to compete.

Nor should it be overlooked that on October 16, 1927, Chester Thorne died. If by some miracle H.C. Weaver Productions had been able to make the jump to the staggeringly more costly new medium of sound, it's unlikely the company could have thrived without the man who had saved Tacoma.

Precisely a year later on October 16, 1928, a handwritten letter was addressed to Washington's Secretary of State, J. Grant Hinkle, from Mr. N.A. Kopf, president of the Model Pickle Company and stockholder in H.C. Weaver Productions. Mr. Kopf inquired how many actual shares of stock Mr. Harvey Weaver had owned. At the last stockholders' meeting On October 2, 1928,

there seemed to be a discrepancy over how much stock the now absent president of the company held. One source showed him owning five shares of preferred stock, but other sources indicated that he had $18,000 of common stock in escrow. The shareholders were fuming, demanding information about the state of the company and the whereabouts of the suddenly elusive Mr. Weaver. On October 20th Hinkle replied to Kopf that Mr. Weaver did in fact have $19,797 in stock holdings at one time at the Metropolitan National Bank of Seattle, but that it had been transferred to the National Bank of Tacoma where it remained in escrow until such time as the escrow had terminated. At that time the stock was issued to H.C. Weaver as part interest for certain scenarios and good will.

So, as suddenly as he had appeared, Weaver seemed to have disappeared on the rails from the sails. The 1930 census shows him living in New York City working as a motion picture salesman; he apparently moved to St. Petersburg, Florida in 1940, where he and his wife Anna lived with his partner Joseph Siegel. Although the motivations and dedication of H.C. Weaver remain somewhat of a mystery, he did manage to pull off one of the greatest entrepreneurial feats in Tacoma's history. And he roused the community as the citizens rallied behind his ambitious enterprise. Three feature films were MADE IN TACOMA, and for a brief period during the Roaring Twenties the music man sang and the band really did march.

– Mick Flaan is a film maker and member of Team Totem

H.C. Weaver (far right) pastes ad; Rialto operator H.T. Moore, faces camera TPL

NOW PLAYING

Stage Meets Screen

The First Flickers of Film

By Murray Morgan

During the hard times that followed the Panic of 1893, two Tacoma brothers, John and Bill Shaw, met an itinerant French photographer who had gone broke in the City of Destiny. As John told the story some fifty years later, Pierre enlisted them for a venture in a kind of con game called the "House Beautiful Flim-flam."

Attracting as much attention as possible, they would set up the Frenchman's 12-by-12-inch glass plate camera on a tripod in front of one of the Victorian mansions that had mushroomed in Tacoma during the boom. Pierre would disappear under the black shroud that cut out the light while he focused, then he would emerge, shaking his head, and with broad Gallic gestures direct the brothers to carry the camera to a point offering a better angle. If their scheme worked, the homeowner would come out to ask what they were doing.

Why, they were taking pictures for a magazine article about America's most beautiful homes. Their hope was that the proud owner would ask to buy a print. If he did, Pierre would actually expose a plate; if not, he would click the shutter on an empty camera. The flim-flam flopped. During the mid-1890s in Tacoma even the owners of mansion – especially owners of mansions – had no money to spare.

Pierre had another idea. He knew a man in Seattle who had bought a gadget made in France that projected a series of images onto a screen in a manner that gave the illusion of moving pictures. The poor fellow had quickly tired of the toy. They could buy it real cheap, along with two films, one showing a bullfight in Mexico, the other capturing Loie Fuller dancing the Serpentine.

The Shaw brothers didn't know anything about Mexican matadors, but they knew all about Loie. She was a self-promoted scandal. As a child she had toured with the Buffalo Bill Cody Wild West Show. As a young actress she had played leading roles in New York and London. She spread, and coyly denied, the rumor that she posed nude for photographers. But it was as a dancer that she became an international celebrity. She had discovered that by wrapping herself in clouds of silk that reflected the new stage lighting made possible by electricity she could achieve intriguing effects. An enthralled critic rhapsodized about her signature dance, the Serpentine.

"At the back of the darkened stage, there appeared the indistinct form of a woman clothed in a confused mass of drapery. Suddenly a stream of light issued apparently from the woman herself, while around her the folds of gauze rose and fell in phosphorescent waves, which seem to have assumed, one knew not how, a subtle materiality, taking the form of a golden drinking cup, a magnificent lily, or a huge glistening moth, wandering in obscurity."

Who could resist? Not the Shaw boys. They bought the projector and film. They rented a storefront at 905-07 on the water side of Pacific Avenue. Bill and Pierre took turns cranking the reel that pulled the film between the carbon arc lights and the lens. There was no take-up reel, so the film dropped into a basket to be rewound after each showing. John served as barker, standing on the sidewalk outside, urging passers-by to spend a dime to watch a Spanish (promoted from Mexican) bullfight or the ravishing Loie.

They had been in business only a few days when the reel on the projector jammed. Before Bill could turn off the carbon lights, the film caught fire. The audience fled. Horse-drawn fire engines clanged to the scene from stations on A Street and St. Helens. The building was saved but the bull and matador went up in flames. Fire Chief Lellis declared movie houses a public nuisance, not to be tolerated in wooden buildings.

Again Pierre had an idea. Why not show the films outdoors? After dark. Free.

Oh great, how do we make money showing movies without charging for admission?

Easily. We have colored slides made picturing merchandise that is on sale in local stores. We charge the store owners for showing these along with the film. It sounded good to the Shaw brothers, and it sounded good to the Gross Brothers, who had the biggest store in town. They agreed to pay for commercials.

John, Bill and Pierre got permission to hang a screen on the south wall of the Fife Hotel and to put their projector in the second floor of the Gross Brothers store on the other side of Ninth. When darkness fell, they put Loie through her paces. Tacomans were transfixed. They crowded the board sidewalk to overflowing. They spilled into the street. Carriages couldn't get through. This time it was the police, not the firemen, who appeared. Loie was blocking traffic. They ordered the Shaws to cease and desist.

Pierre left town. Bill Shaw, too, disappears from records. Brother John studied pharmacy. Fifty years later his drugstore at Burton on Vashon Island was the only pharmacy in America with an 1892 movie projector on display beside the cash register.

Sally Sloan and The Searchlight

The Shaw boys were premature in their movie business by only a few years. On March 5, 1897, Tacoma saw and heard the opening of The Searchlight, a theater featuring motion pictures located at 744 Pacific Avenue in a store front in the Donnelly Building.

The theater opened, literally with a fanfare. Sally Chandler Sloan, the 39-year-old proprietress, stood at the front door beside her $350 Gramophone-Grand, one of only three talking machines in the state. Holding a silver lorgnette to her eyes, she carefully lowered the playing head of the apparatus to the turning celluloid. The music, pouring from a five-foot brass horn, could be heard inside the theater, but the horn was pointed across Pacific Avenue at the Theatre Comique from which Harry Morgan's band had long since departed. Folks complained Mrs. Sloan's signature tune, Stars and Stripes Forever, could be heard at Browns Point.

Inside the theater her operator turned the crank on the cinematropraphe. It was of the type developed by the Lumiere brothers in France. Shadowy pictures danced on a canvas screen hung well above the row of chairs set on a level floor. Mrs. Sloan later claimed that The Searchlight was the second permanent theater in the United States devoted exclusively to showing moving pictures. The films were mostly what came to be called newsreels or short commentaries.

For a dime – a nickel for children – Tacomans could marvel at seeing Queen Victoria reviewing a parade,

Sally Sloan

By Deborah Freedman

Sally Miles Chandler Sloan (1851–1937) was widowed in January of 1897, creating the opportunity – or perhaps the necessity – for her to become a businesswoman. (Her husband, Matthew M. Sloan, had organized the Tacoma Grocery Company a decade earlier.) Sally attended the 1893 Chicago World's Fair, where perhaps she witnessed Ottomar Anschutz' demonstration using a Geissler tube to project the illusion of moving pictures. City directories verify that Sally managed Searchlight Moving Pictures in Tacoma in 1901 and 1902.

Sally was not the only member of her family in the entertainment field. Her brother, Stephen A. Chandler, was a classical actor. Her eldest son, Chandler Sloan, married a concert singer. Her younger son, William, worked much of his life as a moving picture operator, initially described as an "electrician."

Sally's partner and film source was likely James McConahey (1864–1944) a California building contractor who taught himself to operate a moving picture camera. McConahey managed the Searchlight Advertising and Amusement Company in Seattle in 1898. A few years later he moved to Spokane, where he lived for nearly thirty years. There McConahey operated the Best Theater, among others, and traveled to demonstrate his camera work. In 1908 he was selected to provide moving pictures to the Alaska-Yukon-Pacific exposition. McConahey's sons Robert and James Jr. also learned to be operators, eventually living and working in Los Angeles.

Image
Tacoma Daily Ledger, March 5, 1928, page 1.

Pioneer Tacoma Woman Showed First Movies Here

Mrs. M. M. Sloan, pictured here, is one of America's pioneer theater owners. With a partner she opened Tacoma's first movie house, the second in the country, 31 years ago. Her generosity enabled many boys and girls to see their first picture shows in her theater in the old Donnelly hotel at 9th and Pacific

President McKinley being sworn in as the nation's 25th president, Zulus dancing, warships making waves, models modelling, Marconi sending wireless messages, hounds and gentlemen in mutual pursuit of an unseen fox. Other attractions were brief adaptations of Red Riding Hood, Sleeping Beauty and Cinderella. The favorite comedy was The Astor Tramp. It concerned the misadventure of a vagrant who blundered into the William Waldorf Astor mansion at Clivedon and was surprised by Lady Astor while sleeping in her bed chamber. Americans at that time considered the Astors, who had taken to life in Britain over that in New York, as especially ridiculous.

The Searchlight musical equipment was soon expanded to include a piano. The Gramophone-Grand went silent as the pianist thumped out tunes accompanying illustrated songs. (The bounding ball, which showed the musically illiterate what in the text they should be singing, did not make its debut for several years.) Invited to sing along, the audience seldom did.

Films could not be rented, only purchased at a cost from $300 to $500. Mrs. Sloan offered a new program every week. The subjects to be shown were announced on a handbill she hired boys to pass out along Pacific Avenue. The changes often amounted to nothing more than a shuffling of films familiar from previous showings. In 1902 she opened a second movie house in Seattle making it possible to rotate programs between the cities. It seems she thereby initiated the concept of a movie chain in Washington.

The Grand

John Considine was the Seattle version of Tacoma's Harry Morgan as the "Boss Sport," operator of the People's Theater, the most successful box house. He was a handsome man from Chicago, solidly built, well-spoken. Although he ran a saloon he never touched alcohol, even when making a toast. He never gambled but could deal a swift hand for other men's games. He seldom swore, but had a cold, furious temper. Considine prided himself on being a man of his word, and he killed a Seattle chief of police who had failed to do so. Charged with first-degree murder, he was found not guilty by a jury of his peers.

He sought respectability and saw moving pictures as a way to change his image by changing his business. Film would replace alcohol in his places of entertainment and would double the potential audience. Women didn't go to saloons, but they did watch films. Since the picture shows would be much the same in

most show places, customers would flow to those that offered the best live entertainment. As a box house operator Considine knew the booking agencies in New York and California, and he had confidence in his judgment of performers.

For $200 and a promise to help in the hiring of entertainers he bought half interest in Seattle's Edison Unique. Aware that talented performers demanded long engagements he set out to establish a circuit. He bought or leased existing theaters in Vancouver, Victoria, Bellingham, Everett, Yakima and Spokane. He built the Orpheum in Seattle to replace the Edison Unique.

The eight-theater circuit is credited with being the first popularly priced vaudeville chain in the world – ten cents general admission, twenty cents box. On a visit to New York to attend a national convention of the Eagles fraternal organization he met Big Tim Sullivan, the boss of Tammany Hall. The two Irishmen hit

TSC

The Grand was built at 9th and Pacific in 1905

TPL

it off famously. Considine contributed show business savvy and the circuit expanded to include 21 houses in the Pacific Northwest, agreements with 20 others in California and book arrangements in the Midwest.

In 1904 Sullivan & Considine bought two lots on the northeast corner of Ninth and Pacific for $42,000. They were directly across the avenue from the lots Old Bill Fife had purchased for $200 nearly 30 years earlier. The new owners announced their intention to build "the costliest home of ten-cent vaudeville in the country." And they did spend another $40,000 on a handsome three-story theater building faced with pressed brick and Tenino sandstone with terra cotta ornamentation. Aware they were coming into a town suspicious of Considine's Seattle connection, they made a point of using only Tacoma union labor and suppliers.

Publicity stressed family values – gentility, safety, comfort. The 1,100 seats were all cushioned. The stage had a sprinkler system as well as that new fire suppressant, an asbestos curtain. Sixteen exits offered quick egress. A 32-switch system for the theater's 800 electric lights "left no chance of the house ever going dark." A matron would be in constant attendance in the Baby Chamber for diapering that adjoined the "retiring area for the fair sex." Placards in the dozen dressing rooms beneath the stage reminded performers that profanity was impermissible anywhere at any time in The Grand. This was to be, indeed, Polite Vaudeville.

Opening night was sold out. A string of electric lights stretching across Pacific Avenue spelled out G-R-A-N-D. The show was preceded by speeches from assorted political and theatrical dignitaries. They were upstaged, said the gentle reviews the next day, by the performance of the star of the show, Princess Trixie, an educated horse. She was, said the News, "the wonder of the world."

"The Human Quadruped" was preceded by six other acts. Musical Bently, "The Xylophone King," hammered the boards "in a manner undreamed of." T.E. Box, "The London Coster," offered "a distinct novelty of dialect humor and fine whistling." The blackface team was pronounced "the best on the Coast." Christy and Willis did comic juggling. Danny Mann and Lola Haines "brought their own scenery and effects" for a playlet, subject undescribed. Francis J. Morrell, the song illustrator "had a sweet voice and took High C with ease." There was also a movie, The Nihilist, about terrorism in Czarist Russia. Reviews emphasized the presence

of women in evening dress in the box seats, and a delegation of 200 representatives of organized labor in the audience.

The Savoy

Four months after the lights came up in The Grand an even larger playhouse, 1,600 seats, opened at Seventh and Broadway. It was fitted into the former Grand Pacific Hotel in the Abbott Block building, which had been built just before the Panic of '93. T.O. Abbott was one of the white pine lumbermen who had migrated to Tacoma at the height of the boom, looking for investment opportunities. He teamed with G.W. Thompson to form the Tacoma & Steilacoom Railway which ran electric cars between the two communities – the first interurban service in the nation. It was started in May of 1891 and continued until 1915. The Grand Pacific Hotel, on the other hand, was in trouble before it opened.

The site, just west of a wooden stairway connecting Commerce and Broadway at Seventh (now the site of the Spanish Steps) was alongside an underground

Operated as the Savoy Theater 1905–1909 TPL

stream. The five-story ornate brick and sandstone structure was built at a cost of $90,000 in 1889. In rainy weather water flowed across the floor of the Abbott Block and into the basement. The roof leaked too. Abbott had persuaded the U.S. Postal Service to lease most of the Broadway level for use as the main Tacoma post office. His theory was that this would introduce the building to the public. That worked, but not as expected. Downtown business and professional people were accustomed to going to the station in the Mason Building, 10th and A streets, for postal service. The idea of having to "climb the hill to the outskirts" seemed bad in concept but when they got to the post office and had to wade through flowing water to reach the counter, outrage overflowed.

The *Ledger* ran a facetious story about Postmaster Hogue wearing rubber boots and a rain hat in his office and shielding his desk with an umbrella while trying to decipher rain-soaked letters of complaint. He felt something rubbing against his foot, but dismissed it as the office mud turtle. A sea serpent was gnawing barnacles from his shin.

Soggy hyperbole aside, postal authorities cancelled their lease and moved back downtown to the A Street level. Abbott sued for breach of contract and eventually won a small settlement. The Grand Pacific fared little better. It proved difficult to heat and Abbott eventually let the building go on a mortgage foreclosure. It was purchased in 1904 by William McGeorge of Philadelphia, who ordered its conversion into a theater.

The building was gutted, except for the top floor which was built out with luxury units and soon become the "swank residences" of a group of prominent bachelors, including George Francis Train, who would bring attention to Tacoma with his famous round-the-world trip.

The seldom used Grand Park auditorium was

Glimpse at the interior of the new Savoy theater, to be opened tonight, with the presentation of the "Kentucky Belles."

The Savoy seated 1,600 with two balconies

expanded to fill the rest of the building. Two balconies, each holding about 450 seats, were put above the 600 seats in the parquet circle and parquet. The 1,600-seat theater was described in advance stories as "cozy." Upholstery was "Northwest green," painted surfaces cream. There was a "prettily furnished parlor for women patrons." The new theater was called The Savoy, a name popularized by the success of D'Oyly Carte productions of Gilbert & Sullivan shows in the London theater of the same name.

Two Portland women, Wynn Coman and Lois Steers, leased the Savoy, making it the only theater on the West Coast under feminine management. They announced a policy of bringing in two touring shows each week, one from the eastern "big burlesque" wheel, which was emphasizing acts of comparative cleanliness, and the other melodrama, comedy or "similar high class attractions."

The Savoy opened August 31, 1905 with a troupe called The Kentucky Belles presenting Murphy's Mistakes, a show written by, directed by and starring Jack Reid. The plot involved an Irish city councilman running for re-election. Reid managed to involve in this municipal affair a comedy wire act, a male quartet, a couple who did dignified dances, a skit about the Russ-Japanese war and President Theodore Roosevelt. There was also a chorus line in flesh-colored tights.

Tacoma filled the house for that one and the audience was said to have included "a brilliant array of womanly beauty and grace and manly attractiveness." Full houses were rare, an exception being a performance of Camille on May 10, 1906, by the one and only Sarah Bernhardt, who came through on one of her many American farewell tours.

Coman and Steers decided after a season that Tacoma was not ready for refined burlesque. Desmond Kelly, a young Tacoma actress who had been selling out smaller venues, moved into the vast Savoy with her own company, achieved almost instant financial failure, and was heard of no more. Eventually competition diluted the crowds to such a point that Henry McRae, who was managing the rival Star Theater, tied up the Savoy on long-term lease, took all the scenery to his place and left the Savoy dark. Months later the scenery caught fire and the Star burned down.

After five years in which the seats mildewed and "tramps" took up residency, fire ravaged the vacant theater, prompting the city to condemn the building. Despite falling portions of the structure, an agent for the Philadelphia-based owner claimed the building was owned by a stock company in which "the money of widows and orphans is invested," and successfully lobbied Mayor Fawcett to save the building. After major remodeling, it became a dealership on what developed into "Auto Row." (It was restored as an office building known as the Passages Building in 2001.)

The Savoy had never seriously challenged Considine's Grand as the main venue for vaudeville in Tacoma. That threat to Considine's Tacoma house and his national circuit came from a Seattle neighbor and rival, Alexander Pantages.

Pantages Comes to Tacoma

(For a more expansive look at the Considine/Pantages rivalry, see the profile of Alexander in the Pantages Theater chapter.)

Shortly after opening his second Seattle theater, Pantages leased space at 910 Pacific Avenue, alongside Morris Gross of the former Gross Brothers department store, and opened his first Tacoma theater. He called it The Crystal. It had a stage 22 feet wide and could seat 200. Acts could be booked for runs up to two months. (Pantages arrived in town in 1904 as part of a coalition of businessmen who called themselves the Pacific Coast & Northwestern Vaudeville Circuit, with 37 vaudeville theaters in the West. Two years later, Pantages would buy out his partners.) At that time, Pantages expanded the circuit further, opening his third Seattle theater, much the largest on his circuit.

He named it after his wife – The Lois, much to the surprise of Klondike Kate, who was touring Texas at the time, doing her Klondike Kate routine to raise money, she thought, for the circuit. Alexander and Kate had not bothered to legalize their long relationship. He had found a new, and lasting, love – a young violinist

who was playing their circuit. Kate sued for breach of promise but settled out of court for what she said was less than $5,000. Pantages prospered.

He expanded his circuit southward into California, then eastward as far as Ohio and Pennsylvania. This brought him into further competition with Considine, with whom he was also competing in Seattle. When Considine and Sullivan built The Grand, Pantages responded by enlarging the Crystal. He leased the building just south of it on Pacific Avenue and instructed W.J. Timmons, who had been in charge of building his Spokane and Butte playhouses, to transform the miniature showplace into a mammoth.

Timmons literally raised the roofs, adding a third floor above Commerce Street to the west, enlarging seating capacity to what was variously claimed to be 1,100 or 1,200. He put in eight boxes, two upper, two lower to each side of the stage, which was larger to accommodate what it claimed would be "the most pretentious acts in the vaudeville line." A heating plant was installed under the stage, dressing rooms under the Commerce Street sidewalk and an elliptical awning 50-feet wide extended across the Pacific Avenue façade.

The New Pantages – not to be confused with the much larger Pantages to be built later at Ninth and Broadway – opened March 23, 1908. Mayor George Wright again hailed the addition to Tacoma culture, his headlined competition not being an educated horse, as at The Grand, but a quintet of "sensational European acrobats, five in number, four men and one woman, doing the highest type of finished acrobatic work." They were supported by Bamm, Bomm and Burr, an electrical musical act. Allen, Domain and Allen offered a comedy sketch called *A Tin Wedding.* The Kamm brothers did a burlesque routine, quite clean. Faust and Window sang opera, and Lester Shaw, a song illustrator, rendered *Nobody's Little Girl* in the deepest of baritones.

The battle between The Grand and the New Pantages was thus joined. Tacoma had recovered from the setbacks of the gray nineties and was in the midst of its first renaissance. It supported small theaters as well as large. At least ten small houses offered live entertainment along with film: monologists, jugglers, dancers, songsters, psychics, burlesque skits, performing mice and futurists, none of whom seem to have predicted the coming world war.

Every night in the years before World War I several hundred visiting theater professionals sheltered in

Tacoma. Luminaries of the national scene – the John Drews and Lillian Russells, the Al Jolsons and the Anne Helds – usually stayed at the Tacoma or Donnelly hotels. Lesser lights took rooms in the second-floor hotels along Pacific Avenue and Commerce, which were as abundant as saloons. There were showbiz boarding houses whose managers were accustomed to tenants of uncertain income, peculiar hours and alarming habits, such as practicing pratfalls on the stairs or pulling snakes from a stranger's ear. One of the more staid was at 918½ Broadway, where the management drew the line at Professor Stanskeld's request for permission to keep his trained seals in the establishment's only bathtub. He was informed that seals are saltwater animals and Tacoma had an extensive waterfront.

A boarding house on Pacific Avenue, variously called the Donavan and Donnalion, is said to have served lunch at 5 p.m., dinner at 11:30 and to keep an enameled coffee pot on the wood-fired range. So unvarying was the menu that travelling troupers often added "Hebrews 13–8" to their signatures on the register. Even the unbiblical recognized the reference: "Jesus Christ, the same yesterday, today and forever."

The menu of entertainment served Tacoma patrons changed with the climax of the national contest between Pantages and Considine. The latter controlled the most theaters, Pantages the larger ones in the biggest cities. Both men paid well. Pantages had a reputation for offering conditional contracts, cancelling when performers were far from home, then renegotiating for lower pay. Considine's contract was said to be the only one in show business you could borrow money against at a bank. Pantages had the surer instinct for what the public would like. The determining factor was Considine's partner. Big Tim Sullivan, the Tammany boss, became insane, then died.

Without Sullivan's political clout in the eastern reach of the circuit, Considine found the job of running the business too demanding. He made a conditional sale of his theaters and leases to Marcus Loew, who had parlayed a peep-show operation in Manhattan into a big time eastern circuit. Loew was slow to adjust to Midwestern tastes, insisting on continuous shows in towns where the custom was matinees and evening performances. Finding the circuit unprofitable, he turned it back to Considine. By then Pantages was dominant. Considine turned his attention to the business that eventually killed vaudeville – the movies.

The Grand in Tacoma had been one of the first houses to be cut from the Considine circuit. It went through a series of name and management changes, becoming successively the Majestic, the Empress, the Regent and finally the Hippodrome.

Its Majestic incarnation began when ties were cut with Considine. Manager W.W. Ely continued to present vaudeville, but without the affiliation with a major circuit found that the theater could not compete with its rival across Pacific Avenue. After a year of trying

Alexander Pantages' Crystal Theater sign marked his arrival on Pacific Avenue in 1904

x

WSHS

he surrendered his lease. Worthington J. Pickerill had just begun to present dramatic productions in a tiny performance hall called the Princess at 906 Pacific Avenue, adjoining the Pantages. When the Majestic became available in 1912 he moved in with the Princess Stock Company. Soon after he left for San Diego.

His former assistant, Charles Richards, took over running the theater, which was now named the Empress, as well as managing the troupe, which he called the Richards Stock Company, with C.L. Richards as manager.

Jane O'Roark at the Empress

Richards had operated theaters in Denver and Butte. He had the born showman's gift for calling attention to his attractions and was well aware that notoriety draws as well as talent. During the 1915 season he got the theater on the front page of Tacoma and Seattle papers. The Empress was putting on Jack Lait's melodrama *Help Wanted,* which dealt with sexual harassment in the workplace. Jane O'Roark, a diminutive sexpot from Los Angeles, played a double role as the poor stenographer who was being propositioned by her boss, a wealthy importer, and as the wife of the lecher.

Jane's real life was not without complications. She had first attracted attention when she began taking flying lessons in 1910. Her mother made her give up the idea of becoming an aviatrix when her instructor was killed in a crash. She made more news when she filed for bankruptcy and announced that her stage training had been financed by unsecured loans, amounts in the tens of thousands of dollars, from well-fixed Los Angeles businessmen, among them a past president of the prestigious Union League Club. Manfully they denied having loaned her anything at all. While divorce lawyers studied the bankruptcy petition, Jane found it expedient to rusticate on Puget Sound. She managed to run up such a bill at the New Washington Hotel that management threatened to sue her. She rented a house in Tacoma, brought her mother north to live with her, and signed for the season with the Richards Stock Company. Richards must have smiled when she began tooling around town in a red Maxwell racing car loaned by a local dealer, calling attention to herself and the Empress.

During the opening week of *Help Wanted,* Jane met Gustave Stromer, a Scandinavian aviator who was building what he called hydro-aeroplanes in a workshop on Day Island. Jane told him of her attempt to learn to fly. Stromer made her an offer she couldn't refuse: the opportunity to be the first woman to look down on Tacoma from the air. Would she? She would. When? Let's say Saturday.

At this point Richards let it be known that he objected to having his leading lady risk her pretty neck in a flying machine, especially on Saturday the thirteenth. Jane told reporters she wasn't afraid of the calendar or the air. Richards said she was under contract and he would get an injunction against her becoming airborne. Jane said she'd get aloft. Saturday arrived and actress and manager staged a dramatic tableau for reporters gathered in front of the Empress. Jane sat at the wheel of her borrowed Maxwell. Richards came down the street waving a legal-looking document. Jane ordered a stage hand to crank the starter. Richards handed her the paper. She tore it in two and handed him back the pieces, stating, "I'm sorry but this morning I can't read."

The motor coughed, then roared. "I'll be back for the matinee," she called. Richards threw himself across the hood. Accounts differ as to whether he slipped off or rode that way to the Middle Waterway on the

WEEK OF DECEMBER 13-19, 1914

JANE O'ROARK

TACOMA'S OWN THEATER
Home of the Empress Players.
This Program Sanctioned by Tacoma Ad Club

tideflats where Stromer was waiting with the plane. Jane and Gustave posed for the photographers, he imposing in leather jacket and leather helmet, she lovely in dark skirt, red sweater and wool cap. To the cheers of a considerable crowd the plane taxied down the channel, lifted off, climbed to 800 feet as it passed over Browns Point, then circled back over the city and touched down after a flight of fifteen minutes.

"Wonderful, simply wonderful – but I'm nearly frozen," Jane exclaimed to the reporters. "I've been up with a great many celebrities, but Mr. Stromer has them beaten to a pulp."

"Do?" asked Richards when queried about what he was going to do about his star's disobedience. "What's the use of doing anything after everything's done?" But Jane and Stromer and probably Richards were by no means done. Having made the front page of the Sunday papers, they connived a more newsworthy event or the following Saturday – the first delivery of mail by air in the Pacific Northwest.

Postmaster Fred Stocking agreed to commission Jane as a deputy postal clerk assigned to carry government mail to Seattle. He wrote a letter to the Seattle postmaster declaring that its delivery would "mark the beginning of daily (!) air service between the cities," and expressing the hope that "the conclusion of this flight will not be like that of Darius Green and his Flying Machine of 90 years ago, when Darius soliloquized that he liked flying well enough but they ain't such a thunderin' sight of fun in it when ye come to light."

Mayor Angelo Fawcett wrote a similar letter to Mayor Hiram Gill of Seattle. Jack Haswell, manager of the Tacoma Motor Company, added to the excitement by announcing that he would try to beat the plane to Seattle in the red Maxwell that Jane had been driving.

At 10 a.m. Saturday, February 20, 1915, Haswell started from the Tacoma post office in the racer while Stromer and Jane started down the Middle Waterway. The float plane lifted off in a light fog, crossed Browns Point, caught up with the steamer Indianapolis off Poverty Bay, skirted Three Tree Point, cut across West Seattle and came in for a landing in Elliott Bay off the Colman Dock at 10:24, only to be faced with a 134-foot complication. The steamship H.B. Kennedy, pulling away from the dock on its way to Victoria, was kicking up bigger waves than Stromer cared to risk. He made a wide circle of the bay before landing, but as he touched down a wave brought the plane to a shuddering halt, drenching Stromer and Jane, killing the motor.

The plane, Jane and the mail drifted for nearly a quarter of an hour before someone came out in a small boat and towed them to Pier One. Jane hitched a ride to town. She was just going up the post office steps when Haswell arrived in the Maxwell. They delivered the mail together. Haswell was credited with making it from post office to post office in 46 minutes, a new record. Stromer was credited with having made the longest heavier-than-air flight in Washington. Jane drove back to Tacoma in the Maxwell with Haswell in time to play wife and secretary at the Saturday matinee. Stromer's plan for regular Seattle-Tacoma flights never materialized. He left town in 1917 and wound up manufacturing boxes in Oregon. Jane returned to California and was last reported to be in Oakland playing the seductive vampire in A Fool There Was. Richards struggled to keep the Empress going in face of the ever-increasing competition from the movies.

Movies Take Over

Films were no longer a novelty. Projection equipment had improved. There were seldom pauses while reels were changed. Seldom did film break. Movie makers had learned how to tell stories, not just shoot scenery or record parades. Actors knew how to perform for the single eye of the camera, not an audience spread from parquet to peanut gallery. The film industry was shifting from New York to Hollywood, distancing itself from the Eastern trust that was trying to strangle independent producers. The new studios were promoting fresh stars whose dazzle would be greater than those of the Great White Way. In the year that Jane O'Roark carried the mail, Charlie Chaplin filmed The Tramp, Mary Pickford was crowned America's sweetheart, and Douglas Fairbanks formed the Douglas Fairbanks Film Corporation to make movies starring Douglas Fairbanks.

The Colonial

Most significant of all the theaters that were sprouting up as cinema screens pushed aside the actors on stage was the Colonial which opened October 14, 1914, alongside the Tacoma Theatre on Broadway. Built to be the showplace of a chain of movie houses operated by John Siefert of Tacoma and Eugene Levy of Seattle, it occupied 100 feet of frontage on the fashionable street. The papers called it a movie palace. It was also something of a fortress, with walls and floor of concrete (covered with soft carpeting) and the projection room sealed in steel: "Absolutely Fireproof" said the ads. There was, of course "a commodious and handsomely furnished retiring room with a maid in attendance, where babies and bundles may be left." And there was a $30,000 pipe organ "similar to but larger than the one now is use in the First Presbyterian church in Seattle…. This organ has the echo attachment, which consists of a series of sweetly toned pipes in the rear of the house to give the echo effect." Ladies wore evening gowns for the opening of *Tillie's Busted Romance* starring Charlie Chaplin and Macie Dressler.

The flickering shadows of Loie Fuller that the Shaw brothers had projected in a white hung sheet in a vacant store on Pacific Avenue 25 years earlier were now to be seen in a temple comparable to those used by live actors. Movies, plays and vaudeville competed on equal terms. America's entry into World War I in April of 1917 changed the odds. In a time of high wages and manpower shortages, movie houses could operate with only a projectionist and a ticket seller. Live shows required a far greater overhead. The Tacoma Theatre survived, but the Empress (which had changed it name to the Regent) went dark. The Richards Stock Company disbanded and most mem-

bers left town. A half century passed before Tacoma again would have a professional theater company in residence.

Mary Pickford at the Colonial in 1917

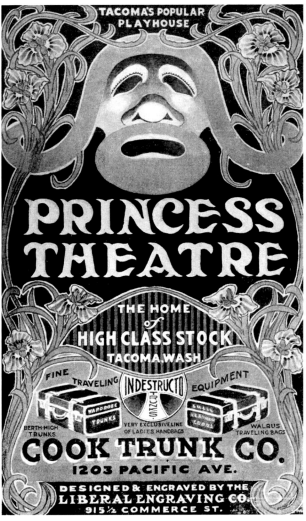

The Princess had decorative programs 1912–1914

NOW PLAYING
Pantages Theater

Alexander Pantages

By Murray Morgan

Pericles Pantages, who started calling himself Alexander after he had been told the story of Alexander the Great, was born on a Greek island. He ran away from his native village at the age of nine and shipped out as cabin boy on an undermanned schooner.

Three years later he was beached in Panama after contracting malaria; he stayed on the isthmus two years, swinging a pick and running a donkey engine in the ill-fated French attempt to dig a canal. He learned to speak "a sort of French," as a friend phrased it, and he got malaria again. A doctor told him he'd die if he stayed in Panama, so he shipped out on a brig bound for Puget Sound. Young Pantages made a memorable entry into the Sound. As the ship entered the harbor at Port Townsend, he fell off the yardarm into the chill water, a shock treatment that he later claimed cured his malaria.

The free-and-easy atmosphere of Seattle's Skid Road (where John Considine was in his first term as manager of the People's Theatre) appealed to Pantages; he talked about jumping ship and settling there, but a companion persuaded him it would be better to go on the beach in San Francisco.

Pantages spoke half a dozen languages, "English as bad as any," as an acquaintance put it. He found a job as waiter in a German restaurant on the San Francisco waterfront; the owner liked him because he could always find a language in which to communicate with a sailor. Though multilingual, he could read "very little much more than my very own name," but he was a meticulous man with figures.

When his boss decided to visit his homeland, he left Pantages in charge of the restaurant. Pantages seems

to have run it efficiently. For a time young Alexander thought that his future was in the prize ring. He appeared in some preliminary bouts in Vallejo, a booming fight center. Short – about five feet six inches – but husky, he fought as a natural welterweight, 144 pounds. Some experts soon decided that Mysterious Billy Smith, the reigning welter champion, had nothing to fear from Pantages, and though it took him longer to make up his mind, he came to the same conclusion and hung up his gloves.

He was still looking for a quick way to fame and riches when the *Excelsior* steamed into San Francisco on July 26, 1897, with more than a million dollars in Klondike gold. Pantages felt that fate had nudged him. He withdrew all his savings – more than a thousand dollars, for though his pay was not large he was frugal – and started north. But fate put him aboard a ship loaded with some of the world's most adroit cold-deck artists. When he reached Skagway, a boomtown where coffee cost a dollar a cup and ham and eggs five dollars a plate, he had twenty-five cents in his pocket.

He stopped worrying about getting rich and started worrying about getting food. He took the first job offered, as a waiter in the Pullen House, an establishment that had just been started by Harriet "Ma" Pullen, a 37-year-old widow who had arrived in Skagway from

Alexander Pantages   GBLC

Puget Sound with four children, seven dollars, and a knack of making wonderful pies out of dried apples.

Alexander failed to make anything like the money his employer did – his salary was board and room – but he did pick up enough information about the trail to the gold fields to be able to foist himself on a party of tenderfeet as a guide. The party made it over the White Pass Trail, escaping the dangers of the precipices and the infantile paralysis epidemic then raging. Pantages' role as guide had the advantage of permitting him to cross the Canadian border in spite of the fact that he had no grubstake or passage money to display to the Mounted Police, but the disguise also had its complications: a guide was expected to build a boat to take his charges down the Yukon to Dawson City.

Alexander bluffed it out. He wandered about a riverside camp, watching the experts whipsaw lumber from the trees, arguing with the experienced boat builders, telling them what they were doing wrong, soaking up information when they explained why their methods were right. He learned enough to build a boat that looked like a boat, but when he put it in the river it listed dangerously. Quickly he hauled it ashore, explained, "Well, the job's half done," and made another. He lashed the two boats together and ushered his uneasy companions aboard. They made it to Dawson. Pantages later confided to a friend in Seattle that his method of shooting the rapids was to close his eyes and trust that he was too young to die.

Pantages had a quick enough head for figures to realize that while prospectors might get very rich, they were more likely to die or go broke. He abandoned his dream of finding gold in the creek beds and concentrated on removing it from the men who had already found it. He found a job in Dawson tending bar. He had never mixed drinks, but a sign over Charlie Cole's Saloon read, "Wanted, One Expert Mixologist. Salary $45 per day." The money convinced him he was an expert, and he soon became one, not only at mixing drinks but in such specialties of the Alaskan bar keep as pressing his thumb on the bar to pick up stray grains of gold and spilling a little dust on the ingrain carpet under the scales when he weighed out payment for drinks. After a good day a shaky man could fluff an ounce from the carpet.

It was at Dawson that Pantages first became interested in the financial possibilities of entertainment. He realized that, the drinks being equal, men would patronize the saloon that offered the most amusement. He suggested that Charlie Cole turn his saloon

into something of a box-house, with a real stage and a regular orchestra. Cole did, and his place prospered.

When gold was found in the dark sands along the beach at Nome, Pantages rushed there with a group that has been described as "the liveliest, speediest, swiftest and most sporting Dawsonites, with everyone ready to do everyone else." Alexander was as greedy as the next sourdough "to do" a rival or, if there were enough money in it, a friend. He had been trained in a tough school; many of his friends were pugs and pimps; the most legitimate people he knew were gamblers; he asked no quarter and he gave none. In the town of white tents on the dark and treeless beach he expected to start his conquest of the world of entertainment.

He spent the first winter working in another bar. It was so cold that he could hear his breath snap when it left his mouth, but he burned with an inner fire. Finally he found what he was after: a theater in financial trouble. Though the costs of operation were fantastic

Klondike Kate

(a new violin string cost forty dollars), Pantages was sure the reason for the failure was bad management. He talked some entertainers into staking him and took over management of the enterprise. Pantages did well; his associates did well to get their money back.

Among those he was reported to have bilked was Kate Rockwell, Klondike Kate, the Queen of the Yukon. There were men who hated him until his dying day (in 1936) for playing fast and loose with the money lent him by Alaska's favorite dancing girl. Even if they hated him, they had to go to Pantages' Orpheum, where a seat cost twelve-fifty, if they wanted to see the best show in Nome.

The rush petered out before Pantages could make a millionaire's killing in Nome. What he gained was a grubstake and confidence that he knew what people wanted. In 1902 he sold the Orpheum and sailed for Seattle. He rented an 18-by-75-foot store on Second Street, fitted it out with hard benches, bought a movie projector and some film, hired a vaudeville act, and opened the Crystal Theater. He was his own manager, booking agent, ticket taker, and janitor.

Sometimes he ran the movie projector. Instead of twelve-fifty a ticket, Pantages set admission at ten cents. He based his hopes on keeping ticket costs down and turnover up. He was seeking a mass audience and he found one. "On Sundays there was no such thing as a performance schedule at the Crystal," a vaudeville fan has reported. "With people lined up at the box-office waiting to get in, Pantages would limit a vaudeville turn that usually was on stage twenty minutes to half that time, and the moving picture streaked across the screen so fast you could hardly recognize the scene. Turnover was all that mattered."

Pantages made enough from the Crystal to open a more pretentious establishment at Second and Seneca in 1904. He unblushingly named it The Pantages. Tickets still cost a dime and customers still lined up to wait for the next show. In 1907 Pantages opened a third theater in Seattle and began to expand his circuit southward along the coast.

Big John Considine became aware that in the little Greek from Alaska he had a rival who might run him out of business. The duel between Considine and Pantages was intense. Each man wanted to break the other, yet in the moments when they were not trying to steal each other's acts and customers they got along well. Each knew the other was an able operator in a difficult field.

In their battle for control of vaudeville, first in Seattle, then along the coast, and finally in all points west of the Alleghenies, Considine had the advantage of the political and financial connections of Tim Sullivan, the boss of Tammany Hall; Pantages had the advantage of genius. A man without roots, a man who knew six languages but could write in none of them, a man who had traveled widely and always among the lower classes, a man without illusions, tough with the cynicism that comes from rubbing elbows with pugs and pimps and gamblers, he had an unerring instinct for what would please most people. He judged any act by the act itself, not by the names of the performers.

On a trip to New York he saw outside a theater an enormous electric sign which said simply, "John Drew." "Who's he?" asked Pantages. "What kind of act does he do?" His rivals scornfully repeated the story. How could a theater man not know the great star of the day? But that was one secret of Pantages' success: he wouldn't have booked a Barrymore for his name's sake.

Pantages and Considine took great pleasure in stealing acts from each other. Pantages probably came out ahead; he worked at it full time, often putting in an eighteen-hour day at his booking office noon to six a.m. Whenever Considine announced a star attraction, a juggler for instance, Pantages would not rest until he could hire someone better, say W. C. Fields, and put him on stage the day before Considine's man arrived. Performers, aware of the rivalry between the two promoters, would make tentative agreements with each and wait until they arrived in Seattle to learn which promoter offered more.

Pantages fought fire with fire. While Considine's agents met the trains with a row of greenbacks, Pantages' man met them with a moving van. The actors might sign with Considine only to find their equipment at Pantages,' who of course wouldn't give it up. Eugene Elliott tells, as typical, the story of a xylophone trio that came to town. When Considine offered them twice the money, they argued with Pantages that their agreement with him was not airtight and they preferred the schedule at the other house. Pantages got his stage manager on the phone. "Are those xylophones down there?" he asked. The stage manager said they were. "Take them in the alley and burn them." The wood-block virtuoso tore his hair. "My life, my soul!" he cried. "For twenty years I've played those instruments. You couldn't do that to me." "Burn 'em," repeated Pantages into the phone. The trio appeared at his theater.

The two Seattle showmen fought each other in their hometown and across the nation. Considine had entered the national entertainment scene in 1906 when he allied himself with Sullivan; the same year Pantages had begun to expand by buying out a six-theater circuit that had lost its principal showplace in the San Francisco fire.

By 1911 the Sullivan-Considine Circuit had become the first transcontinental, popular-priced vaudeville chain in America and could offer performers seventy weeks' continuous work; Pantages, the same year, made agreements with three Middle Western chains that let him offer sixty straight weeks. Better booking procedures won the day for Pantages in Seattle, and nationally. He simply booked better acts. Nationally he never made the mistake of relying blindly on New York booking agents. The New Yorkers were likely to send out talent that had succeeded on Broadway with the attitude that if the hicks in the sticks didn't like the act, the hicks didn't know what was good for them. Pantages shuddered at such efforts to uplift the national taste. He wasn't out to improve the customers' minds; he just wanted their money. He gave them exactly what they wanted.

Ten years after their personal rivalry started in 1904, Pantages was clearly the victor. Considine was ready to quit. Sullivan had gone insane in 1913 and could no longer raise money or use his political influence to arrange for good theater sites. The circuit involved a great amount of real estate, but each new theater had been built by mortgaging one of the others. To keep things going, Considine had to travel a hundred thousand miles a year, and he wanted some home life. The Considine and Sullivan interests sold out to Marcus Loew and a Chicago syndicate in 1914; they were to receive a million and a half for good will and two and a half million for the real estate four hundred thousand in cash and the rest over a period of several years. Loew retained the right to call off the agreement on thirty days' notice.

World War I disrupted vaudeville business by shutting off the international circuit, and in 1915 Loew turned the chain back. Though Considine had Loew's down payment with which to finance operations, he was unable to get vaudeville going again. In 1915 he told the court he did not have cash on hand to meet a twenty-five-hundred-dollar judgment. The next year the New York Life Insurance Company foreclosed a mortgage on his most important property. The circuit fell apart and Pantages picked up the pieces.

Pantages in front of his Pacific Ave theater circa 1910   WSHS

TACOMA HAS A NEW VAUDEVILLE HOUSE

CRYSTAL THEATER WILL BE FORMALLY OPENED MONDAY.

Is One of Circuit of Thirty-Seven and Will Present High-Class Attractions—Has a Seating Capacity of 600 and Is Constructed on Most Modern Lines.

TPL

By the end of the war in Europe, Pantages had the strongest circuit in America. He kept adding to it. At the peak of his operations in 1926 he owned 30 playhouses and had control of 42 others. In 1929 just before the crash picked the pockets of the nation's audience and the talkies administered the coup de grace to vaudeville, Pantages sold his circuit to Radio Keith Orpheum for twenty-four million dollars. Throughout the struggle Considine and Pantages remained personal friends, not close friends, but amiable. Some years after Pantages had driven his rival to the wall, his daughter Carmen, who had been born in Seattle, married Considine's son, John Junior, in Los Angeles, where both families had moved after leaving the Puget Sound area. There the Considines, father and son, did very well indeed as motion picture producers.

The Jewel on Broadway

By Murray Morgan

Benjamin Marcus Priteca was a teenager in Edinburgh, Scotland, when he noticed a poster advertising something called the Alaska-Yukon-Pacific Exhibition, which was to be held in a place called Seattle. What fascinated Priteca was that the host-city was shown to have board sidewalks overhung by a tangle of telephone and electric wires.

As a would-be architect who had spent five years as an apprentice in a local firm, Priteca decided that Seattle, wherever it might be, needed an architect with vision. He was 19 years old when he arrived in 1909. The exposition was over before he found a job as a draftsman with E.W. Houghton, the architect who designed Seattle's Lippy Building, Majestic Theater and the Moore Theater and Hotel.

While delivering some drawings to another firm in 1911, Priteca fell into conversation with Alexander Pantages. The young Jew from Scotland so impressed the impresario from Greece that Pantages hired him to design a theater he was planning to fit into a building on Market Street in San Francisco. It was a complicated assignment: the playhouse had to be built without disturbing the tenants in the building through which it would be entered and the work had to be completed in time for New Year's 1912.

Pantages was pleased not only with the punctuality with which Priteca practiced his art but with his design, which the architect claimed derived from classic Greek. For the next quarter century every new theater in the expanding Pantages vaudeville circuit was designed by Priteca. The fellow immigrants never had a formal contract, just understandings and handshakes. Their bond was so close that when Pantages was imprisoned after being convicted of a sexual attack on a would-be performer (the conviction was later reversed) Priteca joined him for his first night in jail. Their association did not end until Pantages' unexpected death from a heart attack in 1936.

Priteca's first work in Tacoma was a relatively minor remodeling of the first Pantages, at 910-912 Pacific Avenue. He improved sightlines by rearranging the seating. He "clarified" (his term) the façade. Returning to Seattle, he created the Pantages (later called the Palomar) at Third and University. Late in his career he chose it as his favorite, "perfect for the clientele Pantages wanted to reach – those who were hungry for entertainment but who lacked money." Priteca maintained an office in it for 60 years and mourned its eventual demolition.

In 1916 Pantages assigned Priteca to design a major showplace in Tacoma, one that would symbolize his total triumph over John Considine and reflect the Pantages Circuit's status as dominant in the West. The Tacoma Pantages was to demonstrate who ruled the vaudeville roost. But it wasn't to cost too much. Priteca never forgot a lecture Pantages once gave to him: "Any damn fool can build a million-dollar theater with a million dollars. It takes a real architect to build one that looks like a million dollars, but costs half that much." No one knows how much Priteca spent on the Pan, but it looked like a million.

The site for Tacoma's "new" Pantages was the southeast corner at the intersection of Ninth, Broadway and St. Helens – the old

The New Pantages

Broadway at Ninth Street

Alexander Pantages, Lessee and Prop'r   Thos. J. Myers, Resident Manager

Formal Opening

Monday Night, Jan. 7 at 7 o'Clock

Doors Open at 6 p. m.   Box Office at 5 p. m.

PRESENTING AN UNEQUALED VAUDEVILLE PROGRAM OF 7 ALL STAR ACTS

Arrangement of Prices

Matinees	10c. 20c.	Nights—Upper Floor'Loges	55c
Boxes and Loges	30c	Nights—Reserved Section	35c
Nights—Entire Lower Floor	30c	Nights—Last Section	10c. 20c.
Nights—Boxes	55c	WHICH INCLUDES WAR TAX	

The NEW PANTAGES

Broadway at Ninth Street

Alexander Pantages, Lessee and Prop.   Thos. J. Myers, Res. Mgr.

Opening Performance

MONDAY EVENING, JANUARY 7, AT 7 O'CLOCK

Presenting an Unequaled Vaudeville Program of Seven All-Star Acts

Doors Open at 6 p. m.   Box Office at 5 p. m.

Alexander Pantages

THE opening of the New Pantages Theatre in Tacoma, marks another mile stone in the career of Alexander Pantages.

Mr. Pantages, whose career has been as meteoric as that of the Golden West itself, needs no eulogy of any layman.

He stands out boldly in the cold selfish business world as an absolute and positive business success.

In the theatrical sphere he is the genius of the century. Starting a few years ago in that greatest of all typical western towns, Seattle, in a remodeled frame building, on Second Avenue, he has by industry, thrift, and the greatest hard work built up the greatest individual vaudeville circuit in the world today.

No one man of today in the theatrical world outdoes or even rivals the great Alexander Pantages. Little by little he has planted his houses like little acorns in the various cities of the west in the United States and throughout the provinces of Canada to see them grow into big, strong oaks.

Now like the genius that he is you see him going back after ten or twelve years and building anew fine mammoth architectural paradises. They are rising in the places of the original playhouse sites of the few years back.

One sees first the rebuilding of his Seattle playhouse in the new up-to-date business district alongside the Seattle Postoffice. Then the erection of a beautiful Vancouver house; then followed the mammoth Minneapolis playhouse; now comes this beautiful Tacoma house. Next to follow is the new Spokane playhouse. And so it is to be until the original Pantages circuit will be rebuilt step by step; and then one wonders what will follow. Will it be the great and final drive right into the very heart of the greatest of all cities, the big New York of these United States? One can see no other end to such a career.

But above all stands that one stupendous fact, the Pantages Circuit by one individual.

Vaudeville circuits have come and gone—some are here now, some in the making; but where the great circuit by one individual and not by the collective effort of two or three, or by stock or partnership organizations?

With all this success comes perhaps the greatest satisfaction, as it must to Mr. Pantages, the knowledge that no one manager of all his various organizations, wishes him but well. Their zealous desire is only to give their best efforts that he may achieve even greater fame and untold wealth.

Mr. Pantages has a personality that has not changed with wealth or added influence in the business world. He is "Alec" to some, "Mr. Pantages" to others. To his old friends whom success has passed by he is not the one to give the "down-and out push" or the failing glance or recognition. Pantages would rather give up ten or fifteen minutes of his busy time any day to an old friend than any of his late millionaire acquaintances. His friendships are those of lasting time and not those of passing moments.

Mr. Pantages' success must in a measure be attributed to a powerful physique, for no man of less powerful vitality could stand the strain that must be undergone, to keep at his fingers end the detail and management of a string of vaudeville houses, working as he does from early morning to early morning.

It is a common occurrence for Mr. Pantages to leave the general offices of the Pantages building in Seattle at one or two or three o'clock in the morning, and then re-appear at nine, ten or eleven o'clock the same morning.

One rule Mr. Pantages seems to hold inviolate in his business office, and that is when he leaves the general offices of his Seattle building at night, every man under him is through work. With the din of long-distance phone calls, untold number of telegraph messages, messengers coming and going, the click of typewriters from mid-day until morning hours, the secretaries of the general circuit offices find relief when Mr. Pantages announces the day's work done.

As an added bit of information it might be said that Mr. Pantages spends enough in telephone and telegraph to build up a small size vaudeville circuit.

The public and the acts on the Pantages circuit are never accorded a deaf ear by Mr. Pantages. A peculiar characteristic of his is that he seems to take as much pleasure in listening to the criticism of an act by one of his ushers as by any one of the numerous experts called in to pass judgment.

Another characteristic—no act ever gets shut out without a hearing. Day after day Mr. Pantages will give up time that seemingly cannot be spared, that all may have a fair hearing.

Mr. Pantages has sixteen houses, besides bookings in twenty-two different houses between New York and Chicago, together with an interest in some and with revenue from bookings in others.

ALEXANDER PANTAGES

Program

WEEK BEGINNING MONDAY EVENING, JANUARY 7, 1918

Arrangement of Acts

—A—

NEW PANTAGES ORCHESTRA
Under direction of Edwin Michael.

—B—

ANIMATED PICTURES.

—C—

3 MARTLETTES MARIONETTES
Present
"Stars From Toyland."
The Quaint Comedienne

—D—

ALICE HAMILTON
Offering
"A Breath of Old Lace and Lavender"
With Songs and Stories.

—E—

TOM KYLE & CO.
In a Comedy Sketch.

—F—

Agnes——————Charley
FINLAY AND HILL
Presenting
Voila a la Mode.
First Tour in Vaudeville

—G—

JAN RUBINI
Wonderful Young Swedish Violinist
In Solos from His Extensive
Repertoire.

—H—

The Political Futurist
SENATOR FRANCIS MURPHY
Who Lifts the Mirthful Safety
Valve.

—I—

GEORGE PRIMROSE
and
His Seven All Star Minstrels
Earl Woods, Ned Silvers, John Goss,
Jack Rowland, Harvey Goodnow,
Cliff Berger, Albert Wilson.

Arrangement of Prices

Matinees 10c, 20c
Boxes and Loges 30c
Nights—Entire Lower Floor 30c
Nights—Boxes 55c
Nights—Last Section 10c, 20c
Nights—Reserved Section 25c
Nights—Upper Floor Loges 55c

Which Includes War Tax

After the show—Muehlenbruch's!
Every want satisfied. 917 Broadway

PANTAGES
NINTH and BROADWAY

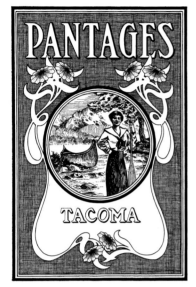

Buildings south of the Pantages were demolished in the 1980s, now site of Theatre on the Square

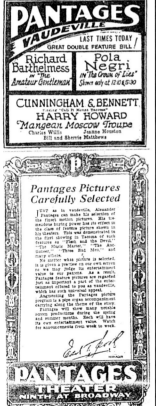

Elaborate display ads promote shows featuring a mix of vaudeville, cinema and theater orchestra and organ music

five corners that young Theodore Hosmer had thought of as a crossroads of civic culture. The presence of the Tacoma Theater was making Ninth and Broadway the most fashionable.

The southeast corner was owned by William Jones, a figure of importance in the business and social communities. Born in Stratford, Ontario, in 1855, Jones migrated to Walla Walla in the 1870s. He came to control a small empire of wheat land, rose to the presidency of the James Scott Company, international grain exporters, and after completion of the Northern Pacific's Stampede Pass tunnel through the Cascades, Jones chose to ship much of his wheat through Tacoma rather than Portland.

He bought the former Gross Brothers Mercantile Store at Ninth and Broadway after the department store business foundered with the Panic of '93 and after Abe Gross' suicide. Jones then moved to Tacoma, buying Paul Schulze's showplace residence at 601 North Yakima after Schulze, too, shot himself during the bad times.

Jones helped organize the Tacoma Golf and Country Club. He served as a director of the Pacific-Alaska Steamship Company and was elected five times as president of the Tacoma Chamber of Commerce. He was a leader in the drive to acquire property to give to the federal government as an inducement to create Camp Lewis and establish a military payroll in Pierce

The Candy Shops
By Deborah Freedman

In the Teens and Twenties, before electric household refrigerators were common, going to a soda fountain or ice cream parlor was a vibrant social activity. These shops were often operated by a local candy manufacturer, and were located next to or in the theater buildings. Tacoma's emerging Theater District on Broadway was no exception.

Charles T. Muehlenbruch opened the Puget Sound Candy Factory in Tacoma in 1892. A decade later, he moved to 1111 Tacoma Avenue, where across the street the new Tacoma Public Library was under construction. In 1908 Muehlenbruch opened a second location at 905 C Street in the Jones Block,

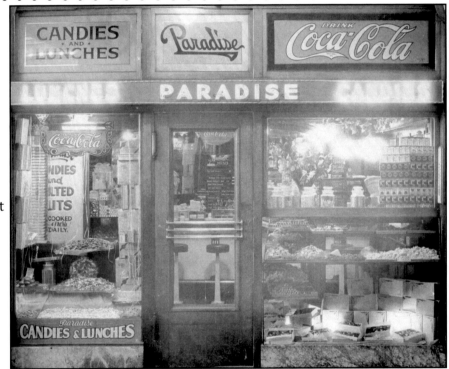
The confectionary opened with the Pantages Theater ⦿ TPL

formerly the Gross Brothers' "San Francisco Store," taking advantage of the existing elaborate fixtures and counters. In the spring of 1916 Muehlenbruch completed an extensive remodel, adding an upstairs seating area for the ice cream parlor. Unfortunately, just weeks later the building was slated for demolition in order to build the new Pantages Theater.

Muehlenbruch's competition across the street was run by W.E. Humphrey, at 908 Broadway in the Tacoma Theater. Initially begun in 1914 as a branch of the national Meadowmoor Dairy Company, the business soon added a soda fountain and a line of chocolates. Advertising in school yearbooks noted that the retail outlet stayed open until 11:30 p.m. to satisfy after-theater cravings. In 1920 Humphrey was able to move his factory to 2919 Alaska Street, a property that had been recently vacated by the bankrupt Frank Mars. Humphrey's Assorted Chocolates were manufactured in Tacoma through 1927.

When the new Pantages Theater opened in 1918, so did Paradise Confections. The confectionery and lunch counter, "Home of the Famous Toasted Sandwiches," was operated by Greek immigrant Thomas Makres for over 40 years.

Pantages Theatre

ALEXANDER PANTAGES, General Manager

WEEK BEGINNING MONDAY, OCTOBER 30, 1922

—A—

PANTAGES ORCHESTRA

Glenn Goff on the Robert Morton Organ

Playing the Following Selections

March—"The Whip" ....
"My Wild Irish Rose"..Ball
Selection No. 1—"Pagliacci".....................Leoncavallo
"Just An Old Love Song"......................Schertzinger
    (Theme of Robin Hood Photoplay)
Foxtrot—"Marcellonie" .... Hoffman

—B—

PANTAGESCOPE
Presenting
PATHE NEWS
"TOPICS OF THE DAY"
—and—
Comedy Feature
"TORCHY'S FEUD"

—C—

THE AVOLOS

Premier Xylophonists, Introducing the largest Xylo-

phone in the World

—D—

HANSON & BURTON SISTERS

The Magic Man and His Magical Maids

—E—

LeGROHS

Pantomimic Novelty

—F—

MR, ALEXANDER PANTAGES PRESENTS
Mack Sennett's Comedy Star

B E N T U R P I N

Supported By
KATHERYN McGUIRE and **BERT HADLEY**
In a Comedy Playlet"

"LOOK AT ME"

—G—

DeMICHELLE BROTHERS
—in—
"OFF KEY"

—H—

THE FOUR ORTONS

Comedy Wirests

Introducing That Awful Orton,

"THE DUKE OF DUCK"

Thompson Bakery & Delicatessen, Corner 7th and
Pike Street.

The 1922 program illustrates the mix of live and cinematic elements that were promoted on the theater's signage   TPL

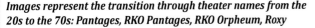

Images represent the transition through theater names from the 20s to the 70s: Pantages, RKO Pantages, RKO Orpheum, Roxy

All ⦿ TPL

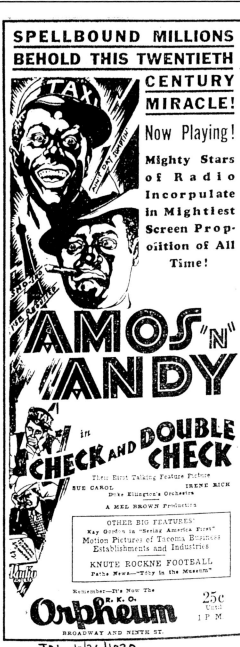

SPELLBOUND MILLIONS
BEHOLD THIS TWENTIETH
CENTURY
MIRACLE!

Now Playing!

Mighty Stars
of Radio
Incorpulate
in Mightiest
Screen Prop-
oiition of All
Time!

AMOS "N" ANDY

in
CHECK and DOUBLE CHECK

Their First Talking Feature Picture

SUE CAROL   IRENE RICH
Duke Ellington's Orchestra
A MEL BROWN Production

OTHER BIG FEATURES'
Kay Gordon in "Seeing America First"
Motion Pictures of Tacoma Business
Establishments and Industries

KNUTE ROCKNE FOOTBALL
Pathe News—"Toby in the Museum"

Remember—It's Now The
R. K. O.
Orpheum
BROADWAY AND NINTH ST.

25¢
Until
1 P.M.

TDL 10/26/1930

DIRECTION OF JENSEN and VON HERBERG
ROXY   BROADWAY AT NINTH
MAIN 4242

NOW! THE LAUGH CONVENTION IS ON!

A THOUSAND NEW LAUREL AND HARDY HOWLS IN THIS GRAND LODGE CONVENTION OF LAUGHTER!

HAL ROACH presents
Stan LAUREL
Oliver HARDY
in
SONS OF THE DESERT
with CHARLEY CHASE

ADDED LAUGHS!
TED HEALY & HIS STOOGES
in "HELLO POP"
OUR GANG COMEDY
"WILD POSES"
OHIO SALE in
"WHISPERING BILL"
ROXY NEWS

25¢ 11 A.M. TO 5 P.M.   35¢ After 5 P.M.

FREE PARKING
AFTER 5 P.M.
MOTORAMP

TDL 1/21/1934 p.A4

25c Till 6 P.M.   R.K.O. Orpheum   40c Till Close

TOMORROW
A BIG PICTURE
in every way . . . story . . . cast
. . . scenes . . . direction
tense, thrilling adventure . . .
exciting drama—

UNION DEPOT

with
DOUGLAS FAIRBANKS, JR.
JOAN BLONDELL
and a tremendous cast of
talented players

And for a Good Laugh
'WIDE OPEN SPACES'
Masquers' Comedy

"Swift Justice"   PATHE
Nick Harris Story   NEWS

COMING
FRIDAY Weaver Bros. & Elviry

R-K-O PANTAGES

Starts Saturday Oct. 5

DOUBLE THE SHOW!
COSTS YOU NO MORE!

"IT'S R-K-O LET'S GO!"

Starts Saturday Oct. 5

TACOMA'S
First Big
R-K-O
UNIT SHOW

"GOLF
FIENDS"

RAYMOND
WILBERT

DUNIGAN

COX & DOOL

DIXON & DIXON

8 - HONEY GIRLS - 8

ALMIRA SESSIONS

ROSE & ROBERTS

"A NIGHT
WITH THE STARS"
25—COMEDY
CHAMPIONS—25

VITAPHONE

Can Flaming Youth
get away with
MURDER?

BRINGS YO
FACE to FAC
WITH TH
FACTS

"FAST LIFE"

Page 91

County just before the United States entered World War I. It was entirely in character when he got together with Alexander Pantages in a complicated arrangement that brought the second major performance hall to Ninth and Broadway.

In return for Pantages' promise to sign a 49-year lease, Jones agreed to fit a theater designed to Priteca's specifications into the Jones Building which would rise on the site of the former Gross Brothers store. The Jones Building would extend 115 feet south from Ninth along Broadway and Commerce, with the theater on the corner, four stores fronting Broadway and 85 offices on the upper floors. The deal was announced on June 3, 1916.

Permits for demolition of the ornate former department store were granted the next day. Work was underway in mid-September with completion scheduled for February 1, 1918.

Watching the Pantages grow became Tacoma's favorite outdoor activity. A steam shovel scooped out the basement and sub-basement area in a few days. Sand and gravel bunkers were built on the Broadway side to supply a large concrete mixer. A narrow, six-story steel frame allowed three "mixologists" to feed liquid concrete into a hopper and direct the flow into the desired areas, the three men doing the work that had previously required 18 with wheelbarrows and shovels.

While the concrete walls rose and hardened on the Tacoma site, laborers at the Washington Brick, Lime & Sewer Pipe Company's plant on Loon Lake, northeast of Spokane, baked clay for the terra cotta exterior coating Pantages demanded on the outside walls of all his new theaters. By April 1917 interior steel supports were being installed to carry the ceiling and gallery in the auditorium.

By September from 65 to 100 men were spreading plaster inside while another 40 to 50 attached the terra cotta to the exterior walls. In October stage equipment was arriving by train and ship. Masons faced the rooftop water tank, which fed the interior sprinkler system, with brick. Some sidewalk superintendents thought the water house looked like a medieval bell tower; those of less romantic mind were reminded of a brick privy.

As in most theaters Priteca designed, the Tacoma Pantages featured Greco-Roman ornamentation on the proscenium and a triple-domed ceiling in which light

was cast on the main ceiling from the lower cove-lit domes. The stage stretched 60 feet wall to wall, with a proscenium 34-feet wide at floor level and a total stage depth of 30 feet. Backstage there were 50 set lines for moving scenery, more than in most Pantages houses, enabling the Tacoma Pantages to handle any show sent out on the circuit.

Another distinctive feature in nearly all Priteca's Pantages was that the balconies were entered from each side of the auditorium by a cross-aisle that separated the second and third sections. The loge seats were placed lower, a low wall separating them from the first section of balcony seats. These loges were entered from little stairways at the extreme sides of the auditorium behind the entrances to the upper stage boxes. The stairways gave Pantages special pleasure; when the house was sold out, they provided additional standing room.

The acoustics were wonderful. Priteca never explained his methods of handling sound, merely implying that they resulted from good sightlines. "Seeing is hearing," he would say, sometimes adding, "A good ear doesn't hurt." Some architects studying his work speculate that elaborate decorative plaster elements serve as sounding boards and a concave surface eliminated acoustical dead space by directing sound to the orchestra seats. Priteca responded to all such theorizing with a standard "Could be."

By November of 1917 the painters were tinting the interior walls in tones variously described as "French renaissance" and "Priteca Florentine." The exterior terra cotta gleamed white, rain or shine.

Early in December the light bulbs on the four-story vertical sign hanging from the northwest corner of the theater spelled out in yard-high letters PANTAGES. Tacomans were already calling it The Pan.

The Pan opened to a full house of 1,293 on Monday, January 7, 1918. Governor Ernest Lister of Tacoma was on hand for the dedicatory ceremony but with the war still going on in Europe (and the Germans worrisomely on the offensive) attention centered on General Foltz from Fort Lewis and Admiral Rogers from Bremerton. The curtain rose to reveal a replica of the Statue of Liberty. Applause was tumultuous.

Advance publicity said Pantages himself picked the bill for the opening of what he proclaimed "my finest theater." In fact, he seems simply to have added one act to a program making the regular swing around the western circuit – Chicago, Minneapolis, Winnipeg, Regina, Saskatoon, Edmonton, Calgary, Great Falls, Helena, Butte, Anaconda, Missoula, Spokane, Vancouver, Victoria, Seattle and Tacoma – before moving on to Portland and the California houses.

The added attraction, highlighting the show, was George Primrose, a veteran of more than 50 years in minstrel and vaudeville shows, who was said to have been the first practitioner of soft-shoe tap dancing. A special favorite of Pantages, he appeared in a tabloid minstrel show that climaxed the program.

Others on the bill included puppeteers, a pseudo-senator who explained the high cost of living, tumblers, trick bicyclists and vocalists. There was a walk-out showing of a Yellowstone Park travelogue. Lois Pantages did not play the violin as she usually did at Pantages theater openings (she performed later at the post-performance party at the Tacoma Hotel), but their eldest daughter, little Carmen Pantages, danced to the music of the house orchestra.

Through the early 1920s, the Pan dominated theater attendance in Tacoma, but with the coming of sound films Pantages saw the future of popular entertainment lay with the talkies. In a deal managed in part by Joseph P. Kennedy, father of the future president, Pantages sold his chain to Radio Keith Orpheum, a motion picture company that had grown out of the merger of the Orpheum and Keith vaudeville circuits. The usually shrewd Pantages lost millions when the RKO bonds he received in payment went into default during the Depression,

Under RKO management the name of the theater was changed to the Roxy. It featured movies. The townsfolk for years continued to call the building "The Pan."

Pantages Theater Timelines
- Opened January 7, 1918
- Known as the RKO Orpheum from August 1930 to August 1932
- Known as Roxy Theater in September 1932
- Added to Tacoma Historic Register by Resolution #23292, 4-1-1975
- Added to National Historic Register 11-7-1976
- Purchased by City of Tacoma 1979
- Rededicated as Pantages Theater following restoration 2-12-1983

When *Star Wars* Fought the Downward Trend

By the late 1970s, the downtown theaters had fallen on the hardest of hard times. The Blue Mouse had been torn down for an escalator, the Music Box had burned in 1963, the Pacific Avenue movie houses had closed and the Roxy and Rialto found their audience numbers dwindling. The crowds that used to fill the downtown theaters were now shoe-horned into sparse concrete multiplexes in the suburbs that contrasted sharply with the gracious movie palaces of the recent past. However, given the right attraction, the Roxy Theater proved it was still possible to draw audiences to the former Pantages vaudeville house. On June 16, 1978, the *Tacoma News Tribune* reported that the Roxy was celebrating the first full year of screenings of *Star Wars*. During that year, the film was shown over 1,200 times and brought in over 225,000 people. Of those, over 70% bought a $3.00 adult ticket. Alexander Pantages would have been proud.

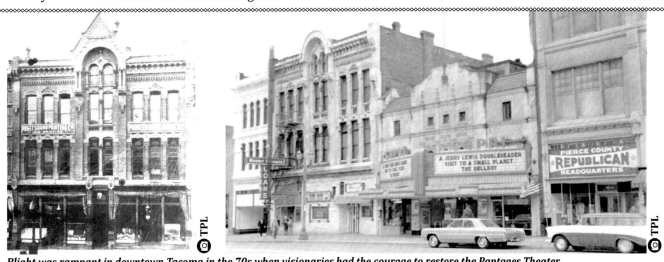

Blight was rampant in downtown Tacoma in the 70s when visionaries had the courage to restore the Pantages Theater.
(Left) Pantages' first theater in Tacoma in the 20s (after he built the current theater on Broadway in 1918.
(Right) The former Pantages and Capri Theaters were in dreary shape before demolition in 1969.

Source: TPL

Theater Organists Set the Tone

As an icon of the silent film era, Charlie Chaplin expressed this opinion of the arrival of talkies: "Movies need sound like Beethoven symphonies need lyrics." His opinion was informed by his talents that went beyond stardom as an actor and director, since he also composed the music for most of his films.

Those compositions might be performed by musicians in the orchestra pit. However, often it would be the theater organist filling the house with music evoking the moods and sound effects that augmented the action on the screen. The theater organists were sometimes given a score to follow, but were just as likely called upon to improvise in accompaniment of the film. Theaters often promoted the organist as a feature of the evening's entertainment.

The golden age of the theater organ spanned from early 20th century vaudeville until the arrival of the sound-era of motion pictures in the late 20s. Arnold Leverenz was a local star of that era, performing as the featured organist for over 10 years at the Pantages Theater. He started at the Colonial Theater in 1916 at the age of 20 and also performed at the Rialto Theater. He was acclaimed for his talents at improvising intricate scores for motion pictures, changing tempos and fast-playing. He might lead a sing-along to start the evening, accompany a vaudeville act, then a newsreel before playing in support of the feature film.

In early 1926, a reviewer in one newspaper had this to say about a portion of the Pantages bill: "Max Frolic with his augmented orchestra playing late hits, gives Tacomans pit music extraordinary. Then follows Arnold Leverenz with as fine a songalogue as he has yet staged. While Frolic and Leverenz are steady diet as house acts. they are showing this week what can be done in the way of really high-class entertainment."

Leverenz did a radio show from the theater in the 20s, and when talkies silenced the theater organs, he later was a regular performer at the Elks Temple, the Top of the Ocean restaurant and Steve's Gay 90's restaurant. He passed away in 1979.

– *Information provided courtesy of the Puget Sound Theatre Organ Society. For detailed information about the organs that were used in Tacoma theaters, readers are encouraged to explore the PSTOS website:* **www.pstos.org**

Leverenz with Pantages Robert-Morgan organ PSTOS

Robert Morton console at the Music Box Theater PSTOS

What is a Theater Pipe Organ?

A Theatre Pipe Organ differs from a traditional church or classical organ in that its special sound effects and orchestral voices were designed specifically to accompany silent movies of the 1920s. During the heyday of silent movies, most theatres of any size boasted a theatre pipe organ. The pipes were located in chambers high up in the front of the theatre, usually found on either side of the stage and covered with decorative screens. An immense blower produced the massive amounts of air required to cause the many pipes to "speak," and it was this large quantity of moving air that made listening to the booming theatre pipe organ in a large cavernous theatre an experience unmatched by even the most sophisticated speaker systems of today.

Tacoma Theater Organs:

Apollo (Blue Mouse) Theatre – 2/5 Wurlitzer
Colonial Theatre – 2/9 Wurlitzer
Heilig Theatre (1927) – 2/4 Robert Morton
K Street Theatre – 2/4 Wurlitzer
Music Box (Tacoma, Broadway) Theatre – 3/12 Robert Morton
Liberty (Riviera, Regent) Theatre – 2/5 Wurlitzer
Pantages (Roxy) Theatre – 3/10 Robert Morton
Park Theatre – 2/4 Wicks-Robert Morton
Perunke (Sunset) Theatre – 2/4 Wurlitzer
Regent Theatre (1916) – 2/7 Wurlitzer
Rex Theatre – Aeolian player w/pipes
Rialto Theatre – 3/15 Wurlitzer
Temple Theatre – 2/9 Kimball
Victory Theatre – 2/5 Smith

The Tugboat Annie Films

By Steph Farber & Phyllis Harrison

Perhaps nothing measures the excitement for motion pictures better than Tacoma's all-out response to the world-premiere of *Tugboat Annie Sails Again.* The star-studded film version of Norman Reilly Raine's short stories published in *The Saturday Evening Post* was inspired by Tacoma pioneer Thea Foss. Marjorie Rambeau, Alan Hale, Ronald Reagan and Donald Crisp arrived on "Tugboat Annie Day," Friday, Oct. 18, 1940, for a series of gala events beginning at 3:30 p.m. with a boat ride from Seattle on the *Arthur Foss* and an escort into Commencement Bay by a flotilla of 300 boats – commercial fishing boats, tugs and pleasure craft from the Tacoma Yacht Club.

Actress and radio commentator Hedda Hopper also joined the cast of honored guests. In an unprecedented move, the film premiered in three downtown movies houses simultaneously: The Roxy, the Music Box and the Blue Mouse. All three theaters concluded their current attractions by 6 p.m. on the 18th to ensure that final preparations were in place for the 8:30 p.m. premiere. The 85 cent admission included *Service with the Colors*, "dedicated to our 40,000 soldiers at Fort Lewis, Camp Murray, and McChord Field."

The 1940 film was a sequel to the 1933 original *Tugboat Annie* starring the popular screen team of Marie Dressler and Wallace Beery in the Depression era comedy. The film, which also featured Robert Young and Maureen O'Sullivan, was a big hit with box-office sales of over a million dollars for MGM. The film was set in the fictitious town of "Secoma," but the now historic tug *Arthur Foss* proudly played itself.

Promotional montage for 1933 Tugboat Annie   TPL

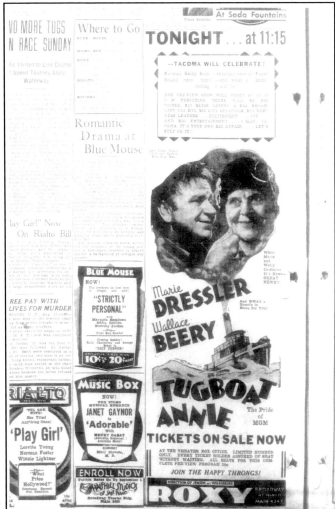

Henry Foss speaks as Ronald Reagan (coat) waits to install Tugboat Annie plaque in front of Roxy Theater

Skylight Rediscovered

By Steph Farber & Phyllis Harrison

The gracious splendor of the stained glass skylight in the Pantages auditorium staggered patrons when the Pantages reopened. One of the many original features brought back to life during the 1983 restoration, few even knew of its existence. But Virginia Shackelford knew it was there. She vividly remembered lying on the Pantages stage looking up at a gorgeous skylight while her father, vaudeville magician *The Great Lester*, carefully sawed her in two.

The skylight was one of the casualties when vaudeville gave way to motion pictures. Theater manager Will Conner found that the glass caused reflections

which interfered with the image on the screen, so the glass had to go. "But that skylight was beautiful, and I made sure that when we covered over it, we used a water-based paint that could be washed off later on if someone wanted to remove it." Despite Conner's meticulous care, Don Brown, operations manager at the time, reported that "The first coat may have been water based, but the next nineteen were not." The paint had to be scraped off slowly and carefully by hand.

TPL

It is actually a false skylight, illuminated first by gas light and now by electric light bulbs. Catwalks in the cove ceiling provide access for those daring souls who replace the burned-out bulbs.

BCPA

The Restoration

By Steph Farber & Phyllis Harrison

It started with a need and a vision.

The need was arts groups in Tacoma looking for a performance venue outside of high school auditoriums and a then-deteriorating Temple Theater. Many arts groups in Tacoma shared that need.

The vision to restore the Pantages Theater to its former glory was sparked by Virginia Shackelford and her drive was instrumental in pushing that vision into a wonderful, community-wide reality. As noted elsewhere in this book, the eventual restoration is credited with sparking the renaissance of downtown Tacoma. However, the restoration saga was filled with challenges.

As a member of the Tacoma/Pierce County Arts Commission, Virginia Shackelford pushed her fellow commissioners to take up the task of restoring the Roxy Theater for use as a community wide performing arts center. Finally, in order to go on to other matters, commission president Elida Kirk appointed Shackelford chairman of a Pantages Restoration Committee. With fellow commissioners Barbara (Corsi) Baldwin, Les Baskin and a cast of others in place, the job of restoring the old vaudeville house began in 1974.

Roxy as Civic Center?

Money for a feasibility study came from the first of an endless line of fund raising events. The committee rented the Temple Theater for a performance of the *Stars of the New York Ballet*. Suzanne Ferrell, Peter Martins and others appeared at the Temple for the outlandish price of $3.50 per ticket. The money raised paid consultants who found Richard McCann, a protege of the theater's architect B. Marcus Priteca, along with an original Priteca sketch of the Pantages.

In the meantime, Josephine Heiman contacted local arts groups from magicians to symphony musicians to see if they would use a restored Pantages. Affirmative answers led to the next step. Members of the Presidents' Council were invited to a meeting at the Roxy. But the Roxy, ignored for so many years, was in terrible condition. Working with brooms and sponges, with cleansers and vacuums Virginia Shackelford, Jo Heiman, Barbara Baldwin, Marsha Moe, Jan Dillon, Dawn Lucien and a handful of other early volunteers swept the stage and cleaned a section of seats. Fifty cleaned seats later, the Pantages restoration committee described their vision of the Pantages to the assembled group. Seeing the grandeur under the grime, the President's Council also bought into the project.

And then came more fund raisers, generating interest and income from every part of the community. Jo Heiman became a Brick, dressing up in a brick costume, and visiting any groups that might have money to give for the project. Carol Virak Sutherland made $175,000 worth of tiles with donors' names on them that now form the entry way of the restored Pantages.

A fund-raising party at Schoenfeld's furniture store brought 1,000 Tacomans together with the Gold Diggers, Tacoma Youth Symphony Wind Quintet, The Totemaires, Bill Ramsey's Big Band, magician John Rhea and Red Kelly's Roadhouse Jazz Band. Red Kelly and his family also organized the talent, provided food and generally managed the bash.

Tacoma School students took part in a district-wide competition to raise money for the Pantages by selling bricks, collecting aluminum, and organizing school breakfasts, penny drives, bake sales, popcorn sales and after-school cartoon shows. Kay Engleson, spokesperson for Tacoma Public Schools, told the *Tacoma News Tribune* in June 1982, "For years we have gone to the voters and asked for this or that for the schools. This was the schools' way of saying thanks to

Tacoma for the support." The students "Thanks" amounted to over $12,000.

A series of parties, performances and special appearances by artists like Buster Crabbe and Dorothy Lamour kept the Pantages in the public eye and helped keep pocketbooks open.

◉ TPL

By this time, the estimates for the restoration had reached millions of dollars. And through it all, Virginia Shackelford worked and talked and convinced and coerced, and others played key roles to drive the vision forward. One of those key players was Dawn Lucien and one of the key steps to the eventual success of the project was her role in securing a pledge of $1.5 million in federal funds from Senator Warren Magnuson. (That turned out to be an adventure in its own right. See sidebar.)

"Maggie's" promise was enough for most people and fund raising moved into a higher gear. The Pantages gained its first board of directors with Dave Williams

Dawn Lucien: Maggie plus Norm Dicks equals $1.5 million

Dawn Lucien recalled the saga of securing the vital $1.5 million in federal funds which involved United States Senator Warren Magnuson, a powerhouse who served 36 years before being ousted by Slade Gorton in 1980 and United States Congressman Norm Dicks, who served 34 years in Congress before retiring in 2013.

"Norm had worked for Maggie and came to me in 1975 asking for support as he first ran for Congress. I asked him one question: 'How do you feel about the restoration of the Pantages Theater?'

"He asked: 'What's that?'

"I told him what we were trying to do and it was important for Tacoma. He quickly got on board and that helped him with voters as he beat six other candidates."

Magnuson was chairman of the Senate Appropriations Committee and signaled the $1.5 million would be provided. The process dragged on, causing some challenges for the local fund-raising process. One day, Magnuson and Dicks were meeting in Washington D.C. with an administrator who told them the funds were moving forward. Dicks, sitting next to Magnuson, slipped the Senator a note, which Maggie read out loud: "The man sitting across the table from you is lying." Within hours the funds were released.

Lucien, who would become head of the 35-member Pantages Board of Directors at the completion of the project, was saluted by Pantages House Manager Josephine Heiman: "Without Dawn, the project would have been in trouble. She knows how to get things done, beautifully and diplomatically."

The same could be said of Senator Magnuson and Congressman Dicks.

as its president. Bob King and Archie McLean agreed to head the major fund drives, and continued to do so, far past opening night. A request for $100,000 from the Weyerhaueser company came with money for another feasibility study. The researchers, skeptical at first as to the possible success of such a project in Tacoma, became converts. Their enthusiasm spilled over to other parts of the Weyerhaueser Corporation, and its development entity Cornerstone decided to become active in the redevelopment of downtown Tacoma. Directly and indirectly, the arts were affecting growth in Downtown Tacoma.

The Partnership

City Councilman Phil Shroeder played a significant role in the Pantages story. Shroeder joined the project in its early stages and was among the first members of the theater's original board of directors. He brought a visible member of Tacoma's city government to the restoration. In years past, he had found himself constantly on the opposite side of the political fence from Virginia Shackelford. At one time, Shackelford had sued Shroeder and his fellow councilmembers. But following a meeting with City Manager Erling Mork, the councilman found himself walking out with his former adversary. Virginia Shackelford placed her arm through his, turned to him and said, "Isn't it wonderful to be on the same side?" The Pantages project brought together former adversaries, just as it brought together the Gold Diggers and the Youth Symphony, school students and the Weyerhaueser Company, and a new and creative public/private partnership for a community-wide effort.

Shroeder first promoted the idea of the City buying the Jones Building from its bankrupt owners, in part because of several Federal funding programs which depended upon public ownership of the facility. His participation proved vital to the City's acceptance of a pioneering partnership that preserved the Pantages.

April 13, 1977

Nothing like the Pantages restoration had been done before, either in terms of the architectural challenges or the public/private partnership that administered the restored facility. According to theater consultant Richard McCann, "The Pantages is known throughout the U.S., in hundreds of cities, as one place that led the way. It was one of the reasons other projects have had the nerve to try." It was also the first major restoration project ever undertaken in or by the City of Tacoma.

The City purchased the building in 1974. After much deliberation and much more fund raising, restoration on the Pantages began in December of 1981.

A Few Key Players

Restoration architect Richard McCann recalled fondly his work on the theater. As a devoted student of Priteca, McCann did not want to change the Pantages. Rather, he saw this effort as a tribute to his mentor and as an opportunity to "explore, enjoy, almost celebrate his work. I knew this was the last bit of training he would impart to me."

Both McCann and Patty Sias, the first Historic Preservation Officer for the City of Tacoma, agreed that actual restoration took at least a year's worth of meetings and deliberations. "When you have a vision, if you're convinced you're right, you fight for completion of the job... . If we were able to convince others and we all gained the vision, this would be worth the struggle," said McCann.

Sias remembered tremendous cooperation between City departments as a key factor in the success of the project. In fact, she described the effort as a stage with a multitude of players, each playing a vital role in the production, and each stepping back from the spotlight when that particular role was through.

One of the major actors on that stage was Steve Rothman, professional theater consultant. Starting in 1979, Rothman helped guide the Pantages as "... advisor, troubleshooter and chief cheerleader for the project during its transition from Approved Idea to Nascent Reality... . He submitted detailed, step-by-step plans for how the Pantages Board and City Department of Community Development should go about restoring the old theater. He also helped shepherd the project through federal funding hearings, a half-million-dollar fund raising drive... and squabbles among local arts groups, aiding the board and city fathers along in a project completely new and different to almost all of them." (*News Tribune* 1/4/81) Rothman's experience with four similar projects made him far and away the most experienced player of the Pantages' cast. One of Rothman's contributions was his insistence that no more money be spent on his consulting. By January of 1981 the time had come, he said, for the Pantages to move on to its next act, a full-time managing director.

Early in 1982, with one year to go until opening night, Tom Tomlinson became the first managing director of the Pantages Centre.

Construction

The first step in construction involved destruction of buildings adjacent to the Jones Building to make way for the three-story annex that would house rehearsal space, scene shops, dressing rooms and the enlarged stage. Theater seats were removed for refurbishing. The back wall of the theater was knocked out, the columns supporting the proscenium arch were removed and ancient plumbing, heating and wiring systems were all carted away. At the same time, the classical carvings and decorations surrounding the stage were carefully preserved. A new lobby extended some 15 feet beyond the original facade.

Though the stage and the skylight provided two of the more dramatic features of the restoration process, McCann found his biggest challenge in the balcony – adjusting the slope and the sight lines, then fitting the seats. The original balcony used shallow, two-foot platforms which the restoration increased to three feet. Then the new rake was "snuggled in" to the old

No Opposition

Dawn Lucien and Elodie Vandervert took time for lunch one day in 1980. Sitting down, Lucien remarked that there never was a project in Tacoma that had no opposition. It seemed that the Pantages restoration project was the exception to that rule. This was a grass-roots project that so many people had joined, so many had agreed with the vision of a performing arts center. Finally the city was working as one behind a community wide project!

At that moment, a woman rose from a table near by and approached them. "You are working on that Pantages project, aren't you?" she asked. "Well, I wanted you to know that I think it is a bad idea, and I am against it."

Twas always thus, in Tacoma.

space. One result is that the first row is six inches higher than the original first row – the extended rail on the balcony front wall is tangible evidence of the work. Taking out the old storefronts was also a challenge, as was adding the mezzanine lobby upstairs, where no lobby had ever been before.

The Stage Controversy

The original Pantages proscenium arch was built high and narrow – an ideal size for vaudeville. The dimensions allowed aerialists to perform above the stage, swinging out over the audience, often nearly reaching the balcony seats.

As planned, the renovated Pantages stage would remain at the original 34-foot width, some 10-feet smaller than the Temple Theater stage most performing arts groups had used comfortably in the past. That 10-foot difference would prevent accommodations for larger dance companies, more complex theater sets, and a full orchestra of 115. Opponents of a wider stage cited historical accuracy, architectural integrity and cost. Proponents of a wider stage feared that a smaller stage opening would compromise the versatility and economic viability of the new theater.

Shirley Getzin of the Tacoma Youth Symphony proposed a trial concert using her group to test the present stage. The question was, just how flexible, how usable would the restored Pantages be? Would the community get the best possible facility from its restoration efforts? The answer: enlarge the stage.

Richard McCann, already one-third of the way through the construction documents, agreed to look at different ways to widen the stage, though he was not sure the finished product would be worth the cost. He worked with several possible solutions to the proscenium problem, including developing revolutionary, movable columns that would widen or narrow the stage opening as needed by the particular shows. He finally proposed moving each of the original columns five feet further apart, thus giving the Pantages a stage width two-feet wider than the Temple Theater's ample stage. His solution also gained an additional 30 seats for the house.

In a post-project interview, McCann observed that actually moving the huge columns was not as major a problem as it first appeared. The process required building a framework to support the original arch, removing the columns, replacing the columns 10 feet farther from one another, and then removing the temporary supports. He did acknowledge, however, that all of the reconstruction work was experimental. Once again the Pantages project broke new ground to overcome new obstacles. Many years after the restoration other communities reference the finished Pantages project and its experienced architect, Dick McCann. In those days, the builders were creating the model.

After some 14 months of work, the Old Pantages had been restored and was ready once again for opening night.

Opening Night

Saturday, February 12, 1983, at 8:00 p.m., the curtain went up at The Pantages Centre. After all the meetings, all the crises, all the planning, all the fund raising, all the conflict and all the cooperation, all the work was finally done. Tacoma stepped out in its finery to celebrate the success of years of work and to bask in the glow of the brilliant Pantages Theater and a job well done. The opening night audience looked splendid, although at least one patron declared that this would be the first – and the last – time he would ever be seen alive in a tuxedo.

Steve Allen topped the bill that evening, commenting that he, too, had a special connection to the old hall. As a child, he had traveled with his vaudeville trooper parents on the Pantages circuit. Also performing that night were the Joffrey Ballet, which had spent several summers in residency at Pacific Luthern University, and Pat Finley, who was backed by the ever-present Red Kelly.

Continuing the tradition of odd partners cooperating in this community collaboration, the night saw Governor John Spellman as he saluted the arts-funding work of his predecessor, Dixy Lee Ray, and they both smiled as if they meant it. It was the sort of night where U.S. Sen. Slade Gorton paid tribute to his predecessor, Warren G. Magnuson. It was the sort of night where Gorton and Congressman Norm Dicks – one a Republican and the other a Democrat – stood side-by-side before the assembled media and couldn't find enough kind words to say about each other." (*Seattle Times* 2/14/83)

It was a night of celebration, and many in the audience had had a hand in the success of the venture. Along with the political dignitaries were many of the hundreds of donors, volunteers and workers, the people who bought bricks, and the people who poured concrete, the committee members who had been with the Pantages project for years, and those who had come to its support only recently. Perhaps no other under-

taking in Tacoma's history had generated this kind of community wide involvement, and Tacoma turned out to celebrate.

75th Anniversary Celebration
An Afternoon with
Marvin Hamlisch

*Mother's Day Gala to Celebrate the
75th Anniversary of the Pantages
and Rialto Theaters and the 10th
Anniversary of the Pantages Restoration*

Special Anniversary Season Sponsors:
Ben B. Cheney Foundation
The Boeing Company

Broadway
THEATER DISTRICT CAMPAIGN

Pantages Centre

901 BROADWAY
TACOMA
WASHINGTON 98402

The Pantages Brings Broadway Back to Life

Nearly a decade after visionaries sparked the bold idea to restore the Pantages, the city celebrated the achievement with a gala event on February 12, 1983. Northwest media chronicled this as a pivot point, where downtown would turn around from decades of decline – a prophesy that has been proven valid.

All *TPL*

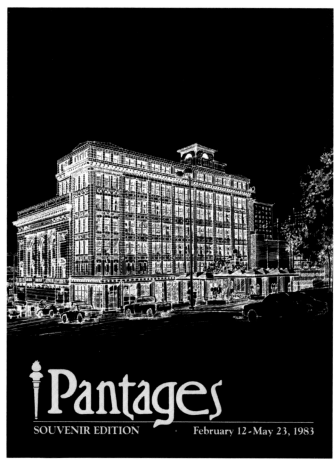

Pantages

SOUVENIR EDITION · February 12 - May 23, 1983

Pantages Centre

Saturday, February 12, 1983, at 8 p.m.

Gala First Night Celebration

Steve Allen

The Joffrey Ballet

Pat Finley

Vaudeville Performers Guide

In 1919, *Herbert Lloyd's Pantages Guide* provided insights for performers touring the Pantages and other circuits. Drawing on his own experiences as a vaudeville performer (a comedy juggling act), Lloyd profiled details about the theaters and services in each city as well as general information for those navigating the circuits. He spoke well of the treatment performers experienced on the Pantages Circuit and included these notes about Tacoma:

"Great town for hard shell crabs. Fine markets on Broadway and Market St. ... Splendid specimen of a 'Totem Pole' at 10th and A Sts. ... McLean Bros. grocers on Broadway make the finest chocolate eclairs the author has ever eaten.... On account of the U.S. Military Camp at American Lake the town is badly crippled for hotel accommodations, so reserve in advance or you stand a good chance of walking the streets all night... ." His geography was a bit misplaced in noting "the wonderful view of the Columbia River" that could be seen from the garden of the Tacoma Hotel. But, Lloyd thought so highly of Regal Cleaner & Dyers, located at 728-1/2 St. Helens Ave., that he sent his costumes all the way from Philadelphia to be cleaned every summer.

Lloyd profiled Tacoma's three vaudeville circuit theaters, the Pantages, the Hippodrome (originally the Grand), and Tacoma Theater (operating at that time as part of the Orpheum Circuit). This included baggage handlers for each theater, stage specifications, weekly schedule and number of shows per day, rehearsal times, and instruments in each orchestra so performers would know what music books they needed to provide. There was a listing of train schedules to the next city on the circuit. When possible, performers would take a sleeper and avoid the cost of a hotel for a night. He acknowledged the remoteness of the West

with this suggestion: "When crossing the mountains or desert and you pass any isolated farms or ranches, throw out any old newspapers or magazines that you are finished with. They will be greatly appreciated by those who live off the beaten path." One can imagine publications containing bad reviews were the first to fly out the train window.

Lloyd's Theater Profiles:

Pantages

TACOMA, WASHINGTON.	PANTAGES' THEATRE.
Mgr.—Geo. A. Calvert.	Conductor—Billy Small.
Stage Mgr.—Carl O. Ellis.	Operator—Clyde Ellis.
Carpenter—Stage Manager.	Flyman—Royal Baker.
"Props."—Ben Mennick.	Grip—Ben Minnick.
Electr.—Jerald Crow.	No. Days Engaged—7.
Current—110 Volts A. C., D. C.	Opening Day—Monday.
Proscenium Opening—33 feet.	Shows Daily—3.
Wall to Wall—60 feet.	Shows Saturday—3.
Height of Grid—68 feet.	Shows Sunday—3.
Depth of Stage—30 feet.	Matinee—2:30 P. M.
Depth of "One"—8 feet.	First Night Show—7 P. M.
Sets of Lines—50.	Rehearsal—11 A. M.
Stage Open—10 A. M.	Salary Paid—Between Shows.
Mail Back—11 A. M.	Where Salary Paid—Back Stage.

Theatre Baggageman—Auto Trans. Co. Trunks $1.00 (round trip). Have hotel trunks ready at 7 P. M.
Theatre has shower baths.
Number in Orchestra—Seven.
Instruments in Orchestra—Piano, Violin, Cornet, Trombone, Drums, Clarionette, Organ.
Next usual stand is **Portland, Ore.**
Nor. Pac. R. R.—Leave 1:40 A. M.; Arrive 7 A. M.
Cost of Sleeper—Upper, $1.76; Lower, $2.20.
Reserve your sleeper berths for **Portland** early in the week at the Nor. Pac. City Office on Pacific St., corner of 10th (see local map). Sleeper ready after 10 P. M.
This theatre claims to have the best lighted stage in the west, having 22-1000 watt globes in addition to the usual ordinary lighting on the stage. The stage manager, Carl O. Ellis, has his own patent medium of colored lights, in which he uses a series of glasses in place of gelatine, making a great saving to the management.

Hippodrome

TACOMA, WASHINGTON.	HIPPODROME (A. & H.).
	Local Manager here goes to Hip., Portland, in September.
Mgr.—H. W. Pierong.	Conductor—Geo. Rugers.
Stage Mgr.—Arthur Avery.	Treas.—Mr. Barry.
Carpenter—Stage Manager.	Press Rep't.—Mr. Quinlan.
"Props."—Jas. McDonald.	Operator—Howard Lila.
Electr.—J. L. Page.	Flyman—Harry Thompson.
Current—110 Volts A. C.	Grip—Chas. Glocker.
Proscenium Opening—24 feet.	No. Dressing Rooms—8.
Wall to Wall—46 feet.	No. Days Engaged—4 and 3.
Height of Grid—46 feet.	Opening Day—Sun. and Thurs.
Depth of Stage—20 feet.	Shows Daily—3.
Depth of "One"—7 feet.	Shows Saturday—5.
Sets of Lines—32.	Shows Sunday—5.
Stage Open—10 A. M.	First Night Show—7:30 P. M.
Mail Back—11 A. M.	Rehearsal—11 A. M.
Matinee—3 P. M.	Salary Paid—Last Show.
	Where Salary Paid—Back Stage.

Theatre Laundry—Olympic Laundry.
Theatre Baggageman—Auto Trans. Co. Trunks 75c (round trip). Have hotel trunks ready at 7 P. M.
Theatre has shower baths.
Number in Orchestra—Six.
Instruments in Orchestra—Piano, Violin, Cornet, Trombone, Drums, Clarionette.
Next usual stand is Seattle.
Puget Sound Nav. Co.—Leave 7:15 A. M.
See **Seattle Hippodrome** (page —) before arriving there as to the disposition of your baggage checks.

Tacoma (Orpheum Circuit)

TACOMA, WASHINGTON.	TACOMA THEATRE. (ORPHEUM.)
Mgr.—Glen Sutter.	Conductor—D. N. Nason.
Treas.—Manager.	Press Rep't.—Chas. McKee.
Stage Mgr.—Dave Lindsay.	Flyman—Andy Dunn.
Carpenter—Stage Manager.	Grip—Chester Baker.
"Props."—Tom Dunn.	No. Dressing Rooms—12.
Electr.—Paul Vallely.	No. Days Engaged—3.
Operator—John Manning.	Opening Day—Friday. (No. Mat.)
Proscenium Opening—32 feet.	Shows Daily—2.
Wall to Wall—67 feet.	Shows Saturday—2.
Height of Grid—75 feet.	Shows Sunday—2.
Depth of Stage—42 feet.	Matinee—2:30 P. M.
Depth of "One"—7 feet.	Night Show—8:15 P. M.
Sets of Lines—60.	Rehearsal—11 A. M.
Stage Open—10 A. M.	Salary Paid—Sunday Night.
Mail Back—11 A. M.	Where Salary Paid—Back Stage.

Theatre Laundry—Olympic Laundry.
Theatre Baggageman—Tacoma Baggage & Trans. Co. Trunks 75c (round trip). Theatre has shower baths.
Number in Orchestra—Eleven.
Instruments in Orchestra—Piano, Violin, Cornet, Trombone, Drums, Clarionette, Bass, Flute, Second Violin, Cello.
At time of going to press with this book this theatre had discontinued vaudeville. It may be renewed.

HERBERT LLOYD'S "PANTAGES GUIDE"

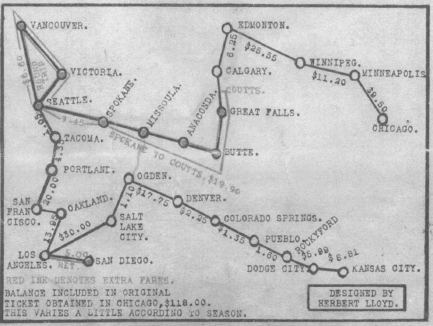

"Off with the old,
On with the new,
Is a saying ancient
Wise and true;
But no other Guide Book
Either old or new;
Will keep you posted
As this book will do."

"I sit and smoke and Puff and Ponder,
Near the old grate fire and wonder
Why, when man's "THINKER"
Has done such marvels galore
A "Pantages Guide" was not thought of before."

RED INK DENOTES EXTRA FARES.
BALANCE INCLUDED IN ORIGINAL
TICKET OBTAINED IN CHICAGO, $118.00.
THIS VARIES A LITTLE ACCORDING TO SEASON.

DESIGNED BY HERBERT LLOYD.

FARES COVERING THE PANTAGES TOUR.

G. B. PANTAGES.

PRICE 15¢

"ALL WHAT IS" ALEX. PANTAGES.

J. C. MATTHEWS, MGR. CHICAGO OFFICE.

This Booklet is not

"PANNING The PAN TIME"

Being a Compilation
of Information appertaining
to the

PANTAGES CIRCUIT
"COOKED UP BY"
HERBERT LLOYD
"Chef de Claque"
3640 N. 21ST St. PHILA. PA.

"INTRODUCTION" (forte)

IN presenting this little booklet, descriptive of the Pantages Circuit, the author has endeavored to cover every item of interest to performers playing this tour which we think will be of value to both old as well as new acts on the Circuit.

While a portion of the information may seem superfluous, it will be acceptable, we hope, to many.

To those who are playing the Circuit for the first time, the author can say that it is a wonderful tour and the treatment accorded the performers is all that they could wish themselves, provided they give the same generous treatment in exchange to the managements along the line. Performers who have played the tour before, with a grain of fairness in them, will substantiate this statement.

A spirit of friendliness will be found on the Pantages Circuit, from the manager down to the last member of his staff, unexcelled by any other circuit in the world. This applies to most of the affiliated houses as well

The undersigned is indebted to the managers, jointly, in the compilation of this book and sincerely thanks them for their very great courtesy and assistance.

While there is a price placed on this book, it was not written for the purpose of making a profit, as the price just about covers the cost of paper used, but with the one idea of furnishing fellow artistes with information that will be of benefit and to further advertise the name of

Herbert Lloyd.

THIS BOOK FOR SALE BY:
HERBERT LLOYD, 3640 N. 21st St. Phila., Pa.
MR. BARKMAN, c. o. Pantages Offices, Chicago.
SPRINGER HOUSE, Edmonton, Alberta, Canada.

GENERAL INFORMATION

THE author holds no brief for any of the hotels incorporated in this book but simply mentions the one that he stops at himself and where he would stop again. The cities on the Pantages Circuit are blessed with many first class hotels.

No Sunday shows in Canada though this Circuit pays full weekly salaries.

Sleeper rates are given for lower berths only.

Traveling "Tourist" is good if the company reserves the entire car as it allows one to sleep late, dress comfortably and prepare a light meal, if wanted. Exclusive "Tourists" can be obtained between Winnipeg-Edmonton, Spokane-Seattle and Portland-San Francisco.

Special day coaches can be had on all journeys between Edmonton and Spokane by making polite request of the different station masters.

Excess is usually covered after Calgary, except between Denver and Kansas City. (See Denver page)

All the Pantages managers do their utmost to save excess for the acts. Time lost in traveling is reduced to a minimum on this circuit.

Two days are open between Missoula and Spokane and sometimes a portion, or the entire bill, can arrange a night at Sand Point, Mont. on percentage. It being on the direct line between these two towns. Add. Mgr. Rink Opera House.

A number of Pantages houses pay salaries at noon of the last day but this may be abolished as the courtesy has been badly abused.

Nurse your voice when playing cities of high altitude. Do not cut your act but take it easy and do not strain.

Avoid petty arguments with other acts and the stage crews as it injures both your act and your dignity and lessens your value to the tour, which when you finish, you will be glad to play again, with slim chance if you create the reputation of an agitator.

It is Mr. Pantages' prerogative to select his headliner and arrange his bills. If the "other fellow" is billed more prominently than you; do not blame the "other fellow" as it is beyond him. The error (?) is made in Seattle.

Profane language is rarely heard back of a "Pantages" stage.

Verify the railroad time of leaving and arrival, as possible changes may have been made.

 TPL

A full-page newspaper ad promoting the Rialto as a motion picture theater in 1918

NOW PLAYING

Rialto Theater

Rialto Prevails on Historic Site

By Steph Farber & Phyllis Harrison

The site of the 1870s Fife Water Works at South Ninth Street between C and D Streets (now Broadway and Market) proved a favorite spot for theaters. Just over 40 feet from the entrance to the Tacoma Theater stood the entrances to a series of theaters which preceded the Rialto.

As mentioned earlier, the Olympic Theater opened its doors in 1892, with a performance of *Michael Strogoff.*

The 1,200-seat theater was praised for it pleasing décor, 35-by-50-foot stage and a 45-foot fly gallery. Within the first year of opening, the Olympic was renamed the Cordray Theater for a very brief stint and then the Ninth Street Theater. By August of 1901, the playhouse had become the Lyceum Theater, in which "extensive improvements" had "transformed one of the most handsome playhouses in the Northwest… The improvements at the Lyceum have cost $6,500, or enough to have erected an ordinary building." The improvements included excavation of the auditorium, new furniture, new paint and fresco work, a new drop curtain ("one of the most handsome ever lowered in a Tacoma house"), and absolute safety in case of fire. (*Ledger* 8/4/1901, p.4)

By September of 1904, the Star Theater had replaced the Lyceum. Though noted for its revolutionary use of oil heaters, the Star seems to have suffered a brief and troubled fate. It burned to the ground in May of 1909. The *Ledger* described the fire as "one of the most spectacular downtown fires of late years," observing that the flames from "the ancient pile" jeopardized "the fine structure occupied by the Tacoma Theater" as well as the First Baptist Church across the street. The bulk of the estimated $20,000–30,000 loss was in uninsured costumes and props belonging to lessee

The Star Theatre, which burned down in 1909, was the fourth theater on the future Rialto site

TPL

Henry McRae, manager of the McRae Stock Company. The building was valued at $5,000. The *Ledger* predicted that "It is very likely... that a deal will be carried through whereby a modern theater will be built on the site, which is considered one of the best in the city for theatrical purposes." (5/9/1909, pp. 1, 47)

The lot sat vacant for nearly 10 years, but eventually the fourth theater to be established on the site was the one with staying power as the Rialto, which opened to genuine fanfare on September 7, 1918, now approaches its 100th anniversary.

The Beaux-Arts-style movie house seated nearly 1,500 patrons in its elaborate Florentine-Italian Renaissance auditorium. The Rialto was designed by Roland E. Borhek, who had previously been the architect for the Colonial Theater. A series of loges, furnished with upholstered wicker rocking chairs and upholstered banisters and hand rails, spanned the balcony and the rear floor of the main level. Each loge could seat a private party of four to ten movie-goers.

Hearts of the World, a critically acclaimed love story set in war-torn France and directed by David Wark Griffith, was the featured film on opening night. Sharply critical of the German armed forces, this film is credited by many historians with contributing

significantly to the United States' decision to join World War I.

Built as one of a national chain of movie houses, the Rialto was designed primarily for motion pictures and perhaps an occasional one-or-two-artist act between movies. The stage space, orchestra pit and dressing rooms occupied minimum space, as did the single men's restroom stall and the two stalls for women.

These vaudeville-era theater architects concentrated on the auditorium, seeking acoustically successful theaters and concert halls as models for the theaters they designed. Tacoma's Rialto was built to resemble Vienna's 1631 Redoutensaal, the first "shoe box" shaped orchestral hall.

Kids line up in 1927 to see Strongheart, a movie starring a German Shepard named Etzel von Oeringen

A special section on September 7, 1918 celebrated the opening of the Rialto

Tacoma native Bing Crosby, along with Dorothy Lamour and Bob Hope, was playing in Road to Utopia in 1946 when local students cruised by ◉ TPL

The Fox Rialto sign was in place 1929–1933 ◉ TPL

Clara Bow starred in this 1929 talkie ◉ TPL

The Rialto's interior and exterior detailing was luxurious and traditional. Much of the original ornate plaster decoration – including replicas of Cupids and patriotic eagles – remains in good shape today. The color scheme emphasized grays, yellows, peacock blue and mauve. Blue and gold damask wall hangings and a plaid gray and blue carpet added to the splendor. Technical accomplishments included a pipe organ that replicated the largest in the country at that time and a highly touted ventilation system which doubled as a vacuum cleaner after hours.

The 9th Street side of the theater originally housed four storefronts. Many a Rialto patron remembers buying candy at the Rialto Candy Store near the box office. Murray Morgan remembers using the candy store as part of a scheme to see a free movie. "We'd go in with a group of guys. One guy would buy a ticket, then pick a seat on the aisle, near a door. The rest of us would go into the candy store and buy some candy. Then the guy inside would sneak over to the side door and prop it open. We'd all get in to see the movie on one ticket!"

A Transformative Train Ride for the Theater District
By Steph Farber & Phyllis Harrison

The Pantages Centre made great changes in the cultural and economic life of Tacoma with the theater's restoration in 1983. A permanent home for music, drama and dance allowed local arts groups to play to larger, more consistent audiences. The Pantages served as an anchor for the rehabilitation efforts of downtown Tacoma. By 1988, cultural life in Tacoma was secure enough for local arts supporters to look for a new project: a new home for the Tacoma Actors Guild.

David Allen, Executive Director of the Executive Council, arranged a train trip to Portland which proved an expedition into the future.

Members of the boards of directors from the Pantages, TAG, and other arts groups, City of Tacoma officials, Pierce Transit officials, and members of the business and funding communities traveled to Portland to see that city's performing arts center. Situated in Portland's central business district Portland's Performing Arts Center used several renovated theaters. After the tour, the enthusiastic group discussed options, described a home for TAG in the neighborhood of the Pantages, and planted the seeds for the Broadway Center for the Performing Arts by adding the old Rialto Theater into the formula.

By now, people in Tacoma were more experienced in the field of theater building. The Broadway Theater District Task Force brought together members of the arts community, the Greater Tacoma Foundation, officials from Pierce Transit, the City of Tacoma and Pierce County. Led by Frank Underwood, the Task Force developed the concepts for the Theater District, and a funding drive led by Bill Weyerhaeuser proved amazingly successful in raising $12 million.

This set the stage for the City of Tacoma's acquisition and restoration/renovation of the Rialto Theater in 1991. Two years later brought the opening of the new, state-of-the-art Theatre on the Square, an intimate 300-seat home for the Tacoma Actors Guild. The City of Tacoma purchased Air Rights from Pierce Transit, allowing the new structure to be built atop the new Transit facility. Once again, funds from the private and public sectors secured this next step in the vision of a revitalized Theater District.

Rialto Rebirth
By Steph Farber & Phyllis Harrison

The City of Tacoma, through the generosity of an anonymous donor, acquired the Rialto in 1990. In October of 1991, Tacomans gathered to open the newly renovated Rialto, adapted to serve a multitude of community needs. Designed as the primary home for the Tacoma Youth Symphony, one of the major adaptations replaced the narrow, ten-foot stage with a fifty-foot thrust stage which could accommodate the entire symphony corps. The Rialto's lively acoustics proved perfect for the symphony's needs.

Restoration workers made a number of interesting discoveries during their eight months of work. The Rialto was built of unreinforced brick, surprising even for construction in the early 1900s. To bring the building up to current standards, architect Jim Merritt and builder Randy Rushforth literally built a box within a box, adding steel reinforcing beams to the Court C and Market Street sides and hiding them under new walls which duplicate the original walls exactly. Workers lifted the roof off the brick walls and set it back down on the new steel structure, so the old brick building is completely enclosed.

The balcony also held a major surprise. During excavation of the lobby area, workers found that the Rialto rested on a very uncertain foundation. Between the renovations of previous theaters and debris from the fire which destroyed the earlier Star Theater structure, the "foundation" consisted of dirt, bricks, old theater seats and rubble. As restoration supervisor Bill Wood observed, "You don't have to be a structural engineer to figure out that's not going to work... . The balcony is concrete, and it sank at the corners and began to raise up slightly in the middle. Of the four columns holding up the balcony, the two inside were acting like a pivot on a teeter totter... . Workers were digging down, trying to get to the base of the columns and finding all this junk, and one day we heard this big 'thwoooosh.' The whole building felt it. One of the columns had dropped six inches into the excavation hole!" When workers finally dug to the bottom of the column, "We found an empty gin bottle, so maybe that explains it." The restored balcony rests on an eight-foot by four-foot concrete beam that is tied to the now-solid building foundations.

The old storefronts on South 9th Street fell victim to modern patrons' needs for restrooms and performers' needs for rehearsal space. Wood remembers the deci-

Actors in Ziegfeld Follies skits pose with pipes in 1925 TPL

sion to save several thousand dollars by omitting floor drains from the star dressing rooms back stage. When a plumbing backup created an opening-night flood that reached within inches of the stage, the thousands did not seem such a high price. "It was interesting to see a star sitting on a dressing room counter so her dress wouldn't get wet. It was even more interesting to see the facilities manager in his tuxedo managing a mop!"

Replacing the refurbished theater seats had proven just as interesting somewhat earlier in the day. All the seats were removed from the auditorium to be recovered for a sparkling new Rialto. Assuming all seats were the same size, workers began replacing them with no particular concern for their previous order. When installers reached the last few rows in the balcony, they found they had more space than seats to fill it. The Rialto seats had come in three widths – small, medium and large; the smalls and the mediums proved almost but not quite interchangeable. Fittingly, late in the afternoon of opening night, the workers played musical chairs in the auditorium, removing, replacing and recounting seats. "We finished at five," recalls Wood, "And the doors opened at six."

All this makes the small fire caused by an exploding gel at the restored Pantages' Opening Night, 1983, seem rather small potatoes.

Rialto Theater Timelines
- Opened January 7, 1918
- Remodeled in 1958
- Acquired by City of Tacoma 1990
- Added to Tacoma Historic Register (Resolution #31055) September 18, 1990
- Restored/renovated 1991

Two Roads to the Rialto

Two men who had found success essentially across the street from each other on Broadway, took their respective aspirations to make it big in the theater business up half a block and joined forces in the creation of the Rialto Theater. Murray Morgan tracks Henry T. Moore from the projectionist's booth at the Colonial Theater to management of the Rialto. In Deborah Freedman's coverage of Dave Gross, we follow the path from the days when he and his brothers established themselves as Tacoma's foremost merchants from Pacific Avenue to their architecturally dramatic store on Broadway to ownership of the Rialto site. That store was demolished to make way for the Pantages Theater – but not before Gross and Moore thought they had a deal to build Pantages vaudeville house on their Ninth and Market Street site.

The Migration of Dave Gross up the Hill
By Deborah Freedman

From the first wood structures built in the 1870s, Tacoma's retail business district was centered near Pacific Avenue and Ninth Street. However, a fire early on Easter morning in 1884 created a spark of an idea that eventually expanded the city's shopping area two blocks uphill to what was then C Street (now Broadway).

As fire swept the west side of Pacific Avenue, citizens helped take rescued merchandise across the street to the Alpha Opera house. Gross Brothers' San Francisco Store, owned by brothers Ellis, Dave, Morris and Abe Gross, was destroyed. Within a week the brothers re-opened in a hastily-built shanty on Ninth and C Streets on the hill above. There they held Tacoma's first fire sale, and operated a temporary clothing and dry goods store while they rebuilt with brick on Pacific Avenue.

But they had fallen in love with their temporary site and vowed to return. In February of 1888 the Gross brothers purchased four adjoining lots on the southeast corner of Ninth and C Streets, declaring they would build the largest store on the Pacific Coast. The new building would have 115 feet of frontage on Railroad and C Streets, and 100 feet of frontage on Ninth Street. Three months later word came that a grand opera house, to be called the Tacoma Theater, would be built across the street on the southwest corner.

Both opened in the spring of 1890.

Others followed suit and the intersection became a center of activity and a transportation hub. Eventually so many shops and theaters were clustered in the area that the name of the street was changed to Broadway.

However, the story doesn't end there. Although the brothers eventually went their separate ways, Dave Gross continued to own and develop property in Tacoma. In the summer of 1909 Dave purchased the burned Star Theater parcel on Ninth and Market, just west of the Tacoma Theater. He held onto the lot until 1916, then entered into negotiations with Alexander Pantages to build a vaudeville theater on the site. Instead, Pantages chose to build on the southeast corner of Ninth and Broadway, demolishing the Gross brothers' 1890 brick building in the process. (Then known as the Jones Block.) In 1918 Dave Gross opened the Rialto Theater on his Ninth and Market property as a moving picture house rather than vaudeville.

H.T. Moore Ruled the Rialto

By Murray Morgan

The projectionist at the Colonial for the first show when it opened on October 14, 1914, was Henry T. Moore, a skinny young Midwesterner who had just arrived in Tacoma by way of California. He had made some money showing movies in small towns in Iowa but was looking for a growing town. Seattle seemed a bit too established, but Tacoma "just naturally looked good to him. It housed a population made up of normal-minded, amusement-loving individuals ready to patronize clean, wholesome, first-class entertainment."

He bought an interest in the Colonial. In 1918 he found backing for a larger, more pretentious showplace at Ninth and Market, the long vacant site of the Fife Water Works and the Olympic-Ninth Street-Lyceum-Star theaters.

Under Moore's management, the Rialto opened on September 7, 1918, ahead of schedule and way over budget. It was a handsome building, the exterior gleaming with white terra cotta, the interior seating 1,450. Governor Ernest Lister, a native of Tacoma, spoke at the open-ing-night screening of the war-time propaganda film *Hearts of the World* starring Lillian and Dorothy Gish. The governor thanked Moore for his confidence in Tacoma and expressed hope that as the Ponte di Rialto bridging the Grand Canal in Venice had become a symbol of culture and commerce the Italianate motion picture palace on Ninth would symbolize Tacoma's dedication to the arts.

Moore almost immediately went into partnership with Jensen & Von Herberg to operate a chain of movie houses that included the Victory on Pacific Avenue, the Camp Lewis and the Strand. He later acquired an interest in the Sunset and built and operated the Kay Street. By then Moore was employing more than a hundred Tacomans, most of whom he introduced to show business. Then a group of California and Washington capitalists put together the Pacific Northwest Theaters Association in 1927. They took over Moore's interests in booking and operations, but he remained as general manager and retained ownership in the Rialto. He remained a key figure in the local rivalry between the talking screen and the live stage as represented by the Tacoma Theater and the new Pantages Theater, which had opened on the southeast corner of Broadway and Ninth just nine months earlier than the Rialto.

Philip Whitt and the Projectionist

A conversation with Philip Whitt about movies, the movie industry, theaters and cinematic history can make time disappear both in the present and into the past. What is particularly intriguing is how his experiences in Tacoma provide what could be characterized as insights behind the scene of what was seen.

His links to film tap into some obscure roots of cinema in Tacoma. From 1993–1998, he operated the Rialto Film Guild under a contract with the Broadway Center for the Performing Arts. This was a program designed to show independent and classic films on dates that wrapped around the major bookings for the theater. Although the Rialto had been built in 1918 as a silent movie house, it had subsequently been remodeled to suit live performances.

He brought in what was called a "Voice of the Theater" speaker – a big box at least four feet wide by six or seven feet high. This speaker dated back to what was used with the beginning of sound in movies in the late 20s. This is the type the Blue Mouse Theater used when the era of the "talkies" came in. Eventually they were able to install a stereo system at the Rialto.

In 1999 Whitt became manager of The Grand Cinema. The theater at 606 Fawcett Avenue had just been transformed from a failed for-profit endeavor to a non-profit, community based pursuit that has become a Tacoma cinematic treasure. This was a role he performed until 2004.

Whitt learned from a maestro of the projection room. Jim Burke missed his high school graduation because he had a job to show a movie, a silent film in those days. Much of a century later, he was teaching Whitt how to run a projector. "A movie came in five to seven reels. There would be two projectors with the first reel starting in projector one; the second reel threaded into the second projector. Little dots would appear on the side of the screen to indicate it was time to change. A little bell would sound if the projectionist needed to be awakened. He would then switch on the second projector and put the third reel on projector one for the next change. Each reel was 15–25 minutes in length, but it varied since they wanted to make the switch when the screen was momentarily black between scenes, rather than in the middle of dialogue.

"The studios didn't make a lot of prints and oftentimes there would be only one copy of a film in town to be shown at multiple theaters. Jim talked about when he would start a film at say the Music Box and after the first two reels had run, he would jump in his old Volkswagen and race over to the Star-Lite Drive-In to start the movie there. Then race back, get the next two reels and race off again to the drive-in. The projectionist union required one of its own handle the films.

"Bob McCrae was managing a number of the theaters and he changed over to an automated system where all the reels would be taped end to end and loaded on a huge three-tiered platter. The 35mm film would run through the projector and end up in the top platter. For the next showing it would be rethreaded and run back down. Jim was so mad when he no longer was changing reels between projectors. He still had to go to the different theaters to start each movie – which involved proper threading, focus, sound, things that a craftsman projectionist like Jim took pride in doing right.

"When the multiplexes came along in the 80s and 90s the journeymen projectionists were being replaced by the kid selling popcorn. They might be able to flip on

the film, but didn't have the knowledge to adjust sound and focus or fix things if something broke. Many times theaters were forced to refund tickets over quality issues. Eventually everything went digital."

And, with that, there would be no more incidents like the time a dropped film canister rolled down South 9th from the Rialto all the way across Pacific Avenue.

Burke, who shaved his head for the rest of his life after seeing Yul Brynner in "The King and I" in the 50s, was working well into his 80s. When he died in 1996 the Star-Lite Drive-In closed down and became a swap meet. Burke would have fit right in with his passion for collecting and restoring Volkswagens.

"Before the Rialto was restored, the balcony was in such bad shape it was closed off," Whitt related. "I was told when they went down under the supports they found old VW trunk lids propping up the columns." He paused a bit, then continued. "I should share something else. A few months after Jim passed away, we were closing up things after a show at the Rialto. I was up in the projection booth and a stage hand was dealing with the screen and speakers down below. As we were going out she asked, 'Who was that bald-headed man you were talking to up in the booth?' I told her there wasn't anyone else up there. She insisted she had seen the other man. I didn't tell her whose spirit I knew it must have been."

Owners of The What? Shoppe located at 749 Broadway, Philip and his wife, Charlotte, have operated their store selling pop culture and movie memorabilia in the 700 block of Broadway for 37 years. They started when there was one antique shop on what is now known as Antique Row. Their shop is believed to be the second oldest operating small business in Tacoma behind the 75 years of LeRoy Jewelers. In that timeframe they have seen the downtown sector climb out of the blight that infested downtown in the 70s and 80s – and the endeavors (some successful, some missteps) to resurrect the area. The most dynamic was the restoration of the Pantages Theater in the early 80s. As the Pantages and Rialto theaters undergo upgrades as they celebrate their 100th anniversaries, it is good to know there are the likes of Whitt to explain any possible sightings of bald-headed ghosts in the projectionist booth.

NOW PLAYING

Downtown Theaters

84 Downtown Theaters in Review

Theater names have come and gone in Tacoma over the past 140 years, some reappearing at different locations with the same operator, some adopted by new operators after going dark elsewhere. Many playhouses were set up in buildings constructed for other uses, the theater operation sandwiched between functions ranging from bars to retail to restaurants. Some were built as theaters, often at considerable investment. Pictures, if available at all, do not do justice in convey-

ing the often elaborate interior designs. Many marquee names lasted only a year or two, some a matter of months – The Pantages and Rialto are the precious two names that have prevailed for a century. Here is a quick review of the 83 names that have adorned marquees and newspaper references in downtown Tacoma.

In the First Theaters chapter, Murray Morgan related stories about **Smith's Place** located at 704 Pacific Avenue (1877–1882), **Cogswell's Hall,** located at 8th and Pacific (1881–1882), the **Alpha Opera House** at 1011-13 Pacific Avenue (1882–1890), the **Theatre Comique** at 815 Pacific Avenue (1887–1892) and the **Germania Hall** at 1308-10 South Fawcett Avenue (1888–1921). The Germania became the Moose Lodge in 1911 and was known as **Tahoma Hall** when the building burned in 1921.

In the **Tacoma Theater** chapter, the vital role that venue played at 902-914 Broadway is related in detail by Murray Morgan. The founders wanted a "palace for the dissemination of culture and the display of elegance – a great theater." They formed as the Tacoma Opera House Company, but decided that was perhaps a little too elitist (as if the Alpha hadn't already disabused that notion) and the signage on opening

The Colonial Theater was a popular movie house on Broadway from 1914 to 1930

night January 13, 1890 proclaimed **Tacoma Theatre.** The "r" and "e" swapped places along the way before the show house proceeded as the **Broadway Theater** (1927–1933, with a short-lived **Fox Broadway** in 1930) to its era as the **Music Box** which ended when fire destroyed the icon in 1963.

In his chapter on the transition period when vaudeville competed with the arrival of movies, Murray took us into a storefront at 905-907 Pacific Avenue where, in 1893, the **Shaw Brothers Movies** hand-cranked two short reels for curious customers . The curiosity turned to flight when one of the reels caught fire, forcing closure after only a few days – making it the shortest theater operation in city history, but providing the Shaws the opportunity to show the city's first outdoor movie on a white sheet hanging on the south wall of the Fife Hotel.

In 1897 Sally Sloan's **Searchlight Movie Palace** (742-50 Pacific Ave.) operated inside what had been the Fife, then renamed the Donnelly Hotel. The **Savoy Theater** (708-12 Broadway) operated 1905–1909, almost concurrent with the battle between John Considine's **Grand Theater** (821-23 Pacific) from 1905 to 1910 and the arrival in 1904 of Alexander Pantages with the **Crystal Theater,** then the first **Pantages Theater** at 910-912 Pacific. Murray Morgan also led us through the escapades of Mary O'Roark at the **Empress Theater,** which succeeded the Grand from 1913–1914, and introduced us to the **Colonial Theater** (916-18 Broadway), the first Tacoma theater

built specifically as a movie house in 1914 and lasting until 1930.

In Murray Morgan's chapter on the Fife's we learned about their devotion to the stage when they built the **Olympic Theater** at 312 South 9th St. in 1892. That had been the site of their Fife Water Works and would become the **Cordray Theater** for a few months, then **Ninth Street Theater** (1893), the **Lyceum Theater** (1901) and the **Star Theater** (1905–1909) at which point it burned down. Nine years later the **Rialto Theater** would rise on the site to become a Tacoma cultural and architectural icon that will celebrate its Centennial anniversary in 2018. The Fox West Coast Theaters chain operated the venue in 1929 with a marquee name **Fox Rialto.** The theater was dark through much of the Depression years of 1932 and 1933, but re-emerged after bankruptcy proceedings as the Rialto – which is the longest, sustained theater name in Tacoma's history.

In the chapter on the **Pantages Theater,** Murray Morgan profiles the man Alexander Pantages and the theater he built at 901 Broadway in 1918. Steph Farber and Phyllis Harrison take us through the saga of the theater's restoration in the early Eighties after its marquee presented the names **RKO Pantages** (August 1929 to July 1930), **RKO Orpheum** (August 1930 to August 1932) and the **Roxy Theater** (September 1932 to February 1983) before the Pantages sign was restored to its rightful place on the corner of Ninth and Broadway.

Members of the Theater Manager's Association of Tacoma representing more than 25 theaters posed in 1926   ⊙ TPL

Virtually all the downtown theaters were stretched along Pacific Avenue and Broadway. The **National Theater** was an exception, operating at 1316-18 A Street from 1889 to 1895 in the C.A. Darmer-designed Pincus Block Building, which, at that time, was the largest block.

Along Pacific Avenue

Concurrent with his opening of the Theatre Comique, the notorious Harry Morgan operated the **Casino Theater** for one year (1888) at 726 Pacific, an ornate building that still stands as a reminder of the architectural treasures that lined Tacoma's first main street. Morgan had operated the Board of Trade and Billiard Hall on the east side of Pacific between 7th and 8th for a year or two beginning in 1885.

Almost next door, the Fife Hotel – called "the finest structure on the North Pacific Coast" when it was constructed in 1887 – was called the Donnelly Hotel when the Searchlight operated there in 1897. The building was demolished in 1925 to make way for the Motoramp Garage.

In a 17-year span no site wore more theater signs than the northeast corner of 9th and Pacific (821-23), beginning with Considine's Grand Theater (1905–1910), followed by the **Majestic Theater** (1911–1912, the **Empress Theater** (1913–1914), the **Hippodrome Theater** (1915), the **Regent Theater** (1916–1917), back to the **Hippodrome Theater** (1918–1920) and the **American Theater** (1921). In 1922 the first floor became a market, the second floor a dance hall and the third floor lodge rooms, followed by used car dealerships in the Thirties, a place of church services for G.I.s during World War II, then a bowling alley on the third floor before the top two floors were removed in the Sixties, and that's the way it sits today with a café on the remaining first floor.

Half a year after a fire destroyed their wood-frame store at 906-908 Pacific Avenue, the Gross Brothers opened a brick store on the site in 1884. After they relocated to their new ornate department store at 9th and Broadway, the Pacific Avenue site became the **Princess Theater** from 1912 to 1914. In 1915 John Siefert sold his interest in the Circuit and Palace theaters and invested $30,000 on what was called a "gorgeous" interior remodel by acclaimed architect C.A. Darmer to create the **Liberty Theater.** A new organ, described as "a great instrument" was installed in 1918 and in October 1927 crowds lined up to see a film of the Tunney-Dempsey heavyweight title fight.

The theater closed in 1928 to make way for a new $60,000 movie house with a stylishly designed interior called the **Riviera Theater.**

The ornate interior of the Riviera Theater　　　　　⦿ TPL

The Riviera opened in 1929 and had action on and off the screen before closing in 1950. The newspaper accounts of a 1940 robbery read like a movie pitch. A 21-year-old small brunette North Dakota farm girl robbed the cashier at the Riviera last night. She had come to Tacoma to see her sweetheart off to military service and lost her only $10 to get home. Her stickup weapon was a 25-cent toy G-man revolver she had bought to take home for the young son of the family where she was employed as a maid. She was arrested in her hotel room two blocks away. We are in the dark as to her fate, but we can tell you that week's feature was Boris Karloff in *Before I Hang.*

In 1964 still another theater opened on the site, this one named the **Capri Theater,** which would last until 1968 before the building was torn down the next year as part of an urban renewal project that would result in the cavernous Park Plaza North Garage.

Next door at 910-12 Pacific Ave., in an 1884 building that had been a club for the Tacoma Wheelmen during the bicycle craze of that era, Pantages opened the Crystal Theater in 1904. Following a remodel in 1906, the first Pantages marquee went up. In 1913, Pantages needed more space and had architect B. Marcus Priteca remodel the theater again. That still wasn't enough to accommodate his popular vaudeville programs, so he set Priteca on the mission to design the Pantages theater that still occupies its site on 9th and Broadway.

The day (January 7, 1918) Pantages moved into his new vaudeville palace, the **Oak Theater** opened in the old theater space. A week later, in what must be a record for theater turnover, the **Columbia Theater** was announced, along with plans for another remodel. By December of that year the **Victory Theater** was in the new space with a new organ. Show business finally gave way as the Veterans of Foreign Wars occupied the building in 1923, but action continued on the site as the Turf Smoke Shop was often raided as bookies were rounded up in several police raids during the Forties.

Just two doors farther south at 916-18 Pacific, the **Nicolodeum Theater** opened in 1908 after a remodel

In "The Champion" there is a never-ending line of fun that captures every audience. Charlie is a "White Hope" and will be for

Four Days

Starting Today at the

LIBERTY

The Biggest Picture House on Pacific Avenue.

Pacific Avenue Near Ninth

Chaplin's 1915 comedy drew fans to the Liberty   TPL

of the building constructed in 1887. This started an accordion-like movement as that space soon morphed into two show houses, the **Circuit Theater** and the **Scenic Theater,** which would operate in tandem until 1913 when another remodel combined the viewing spaces into the **Melbourne Theater,** which would become the **Strand Theater** from 1918 to 1921, at which point the building got out of show business and became a butcher shop before being demolished in 1939.

Across South 11th St, still on the west side of the street at 1110-16 Pacific, the California Block Building had been constructed in 1899 as an architectural brick and stone gem. From 1904 to 1906 the **Empire Theater** operated there before giving way to the **Exhibit Amusement Company** which offered movies and an arcade in 1907 before closing. The storefront was remodeled for clothing stores, a use that lasted until 1930 when the building was demolished for the nine-story Z System Parking Garage.

Farther down the block at 1128 Pacific, the **Palace Theater** opened in 1910. It was remodeled in 1928, but closed in the same year. Its glory (gory?) years seemed to have come early. In September of 1914 the Palace showed a beating heart on screen that, well let the *Tacoma Daily Ledger* explain: "X-ray motion photography, the latest triumph of moving picture producers, has scored one of its greatest hits in a picture coming to the Palace Theater today for three days only, ending Thursday night. A living human torso was placed before the camera and while the crank was turning each tiny film was picturing the beating heart and the flowing blood through the body."

Two months later with the outbreak of World War I, newspaper accounts related the Palace would be showing the "first movie films of actual fighting in Europe…. Antwerp's brave defense is graphically told in pictures taken right in that city. In addition to the British defense of Antwerp even civilians helped and the film shows thousands of them digging trenches for the soldiers. The retreat of the British is then shown, and the oncoming victorious Germans can be seen in the distance."

In 1941, a month before the attack on Pearl Harbor would plunge the United States into World War II, the space previously occupied by the Palace was remodeled into a 400 seat house named the **Cameo Theater.** During the war operator Vito Cuttone donated space in the building for the Red Cross. The Cameo closed in 1959.

The films were X-rated by the time the Cameo closed in the 1980s and the oldest existing brick building in the city was demolished ⦿ TPL

Before there had been the Palace Theater, there had been the Palace Hotel. An elaborate Turkish bath was discovered when the building was demolished in 1960 to make way for a project called the Escalade. The project must have seemed like a good idea at the time, but the moving stairs would take out a popular theater on Broadway.

Another block south at 1314-16 Pacific, the **Arcade Theater** was open for one year in 1911. Virtually next door at 1318-20 Pacific the **Lyric Theater** operated 1910–1914, then came the **Shell Theater** from 1916 all the way until 1960. The relocated **Cameo Theater** followed in 1961 and lasted until 1986, at which time the billings were X-rated and what was regarded as the city's oldest brick building (1883) was demolished in an effort to "clean up seedy Lower Pacific Avenue."

Across the street at 1321-25, a string of vaudeville houses operated beginning with the **Haymarket Theater** 1892–1895 followed by the **Columbia Theater** in 1896 followed by the **Owl Theater** 1897–1904 followed by the **Phenix Theater** 1905–1906.

Back on the west side of the street at 1340-42 Pacific the **Coast Vaudeville Theater** ran from 1908 to 1911. As noted above, this area was long regarded as

Tacoma's "tenderloin" district, vice problems related to "audience participation" at the theaters were often reported. Peter Sandberg "the King of 14th Street" controlled much of the red light district. The Milwaukee Café, which had occupied the old Coast Vaudeville space since the Forties, didn't need to change character when it was used as a set for a down and dingy bar in the shooting of the movie *The Prodigal* in 1982. Four years later it fell before the wrecking ball.

Along Broadway

The City of Tacoma didn't change the name from C Street to Broadway until 1915 and that was motivated by a business faction who felt the street had become the corridor of commerce and needed a more dignified name. Of course, with the Pantages and Theater on the Square currently situated on the street – and the ghosts of the Tacoma and a string of other show houses – Broadway now resonates as Theater Row in Tacoma.

As mentioned earlier, Murray Morgan related the saga of the Savoy Theater at 708-712 Broadway. The other show place that fronted Broadway north of 9th Street was the **Mecca Theater**. The 1908 building, 755-59 Broadway, had been the Stothart Hotel followed by activities ranging from an auto parts store to a book-store to the popular Sherman Clay music store to a clothing store before what was referred to as the Mecca Adult Theater opened in 1972. For all the tug of wars between the ribald and the respectable forms of entertainment that had been waged since the first box house doors swung open, this was arguably the last stand for the seamy side of show business in Tacoma.

The controversial film *Deep Throat* was seized by police during a showing at the Mecca in March 1974, but the seizure was overruled by court order. When the theater closed in 2006 it was described as an end to "a tawdry chapter in Tacoma's history," but the Gintz Group kept a sense of that history when they converted the building into residential units as the Mecca Condominiums.

Across 9th, the Pantages wasn't the first theater to occupy the site where it sits today. When the Gross Brothers built their grand department store in 1888 with its clock tower, they helped define 9th and Broadway as the architectural trophy case of Tacoma when paired with the construction of the Tacoma Theater a year later. With the death of Abe Gross in 1895, the store became the Jones Block when William Jones purchased it. Amid the mix of uses in the five-story building were two small theaters, the **Majestic Theater** which operated from 1909 to 1910 and the **Dream Theater** 1912 to 1916 – the latter disappearing in the rubble as the store went down and the Pantages Theater would rise.

Murray Morgan has covered the importance of the Tacoma Theater which opened in 1890, but we shouldn't forget the tiny **Malan-Magrath Theater** that operated in 1905 in the southernmost storefront of the Tacoma – as if hiding in the skirts of the queen show palace. On the other side of the wall, a wall that still stands facing a parking lot, a sequence of movie houses would occupy the space.

In 1914 the 420-seat **Colonial Theater,** located at 916-18 Broadway, was the first building in Tacoma constructed exclusively for motion pictures. Two years later it became the first theater in Tacoma with air conditioning. It opened with the motion picture *Tillie's Punctured Romance* starring Charlie Chaplin and Marie Dressler.

After the Colonial closed in 1930, the concrete structure was renamed the Keyes Builidng in 1931, a black vitrolite tile with silver trim was applied to the façade and the theater space was converted to retail until

1934. At that point Mike Barovic took over the property and converted it to the **Beverly Theater,** named for his daughter. From 1945 to 1946 the venue was named the **Telenews Theater** with an emphasis on newsreels. From 1949 to 1951 the **Broadway** was on the marquee, the name having come available after the theater next door became the Music Box. By 1968 a charm school, jewelers and fabric store had come and gone, at which point the Court C Coffeehouse and Court C Artist's Mall opened off the alley. Having closed in 1975, the place was remembered at the time of its demolition in 1988 as "peace, love, funky Court C."

We will come back to the Theater on the Square, which was built directly across the street from the Colonial site in 1993. To make way for that theater and the open gathering space immediately south, half a dozen buildings were demolished. Among those was a structure at 924-26 built in 1890 by the Tacoma Land Company and designed by Pickles & Sutton, who were the architects for the Savoy Theater among other distinctive structures in the Richardson Romanesque style. For the years 1904–1905 the **Orpheum Theater** presented vaudeville there.

Moving south across 11th at 1105-17 Broadway, the **Bijou Theater** opened in 1908 offering a mix of vaudeville and motion pictures. Immediately above the theater was the gymnasium for the YWCA where

Newsreels and movies shared billing at the Telenews
 TPL

the girls' basketball and gymnastics "played havoc with the delicate machinery which threw the reflection of the reels on the screen that produced grotesque effects in the picture dramas." Another problem was the girls' dining room could not "be made to fulfill modern ideas of dining room cheer and prettiness" and they moved on. So did the movie house, closing in 1914 and opening a new **Bijou Theater** at 1109 Broadway in 1915 where the shows were shown without gymnastic jolts until 1932.

Back across the street at 1110 Broadway, the **Standard Theater** opened as a vaudeville house in 1896. Peter Sandberg, regarded as a vice king bigger than Harry Morgan, bought out the aforementioned Haymarket Theater on Pacific and consolidated his operation – which included his theater band playing out front before each show, acts that changed weekly in a house that offered private boxes and a "large stock of wines, liquors and cigars." Despite the hardcore "snack bar" the Standard closed in 1898. The **Royal Theater** took over the space a decade later, operating 1910–1911.

Next door at 1112 Broadway the **Vaudette Theater** operated for 1907. In a building at 1312 Broadway the **World Theater** showed "first class photo plays" 1919–1920. In the Fifties, night clubs occupied the building in a manner that got them busted for bootlegging.

Built as an 800-seat theater at 1131-33 Broadway in 1914, the **Apollo Theater** opened as "a handsome new movie house," added a new organ in 1921 and almost simultaneously closed. Along came John Hamrick, a name that would dominate Tacoma's theater operations for decades, to open the doors in 1922 as the **Blue Mouse Theater.** Five years later he remodeled the theater and introduced the "Vitaphone" sound system that would deliver the "talkie" era to movie audiences.

The Blue Mouse was the first theater in Tacoma to show a "talkie" when *The Jazz Singer* opened in January 1928. Starring Al Jolson the film was considered the first commercial feature to mark the transformation from the silent screen era to movies that synchronized sound and image in a manner that could be heard in a large theater.

Jolson had made several personal appearances in Tacoma, the first at the Grand in 1904. He also played the Tacoma Theatre in *Roberson Crusoe, Jr.* in 1916, a show so popular that ticket prices doubled. The

Blue Mouse had standing room only for the run of the *Jazz Singer* and, like audiences across the nation, Tacomans cheered when Jolson in one of the recorded patches of dialogue, uttered the prophetic phrase "Wait a minute, wait a minute, you ain't heard nothing yet."

The talking movies proved so popular Hamrick closed the theater for another remodel at the end of 1928. The theater underwent another remodel in 1934 and still another makeover came in 1949. The Blue Mouse closed in 1957 following Hamrick's death a year earlier. In 1960 the closed theater was demolished to make way for the uphill terminus of the Escalade moving sidewalk that would extend from Broadway to Commerce Street where another section would connect to Pacific Avenue – at a site that required demolishing the building where the Palace and Cameo theaters had been located.

The Blue Mouse showed the first "talkies" in Tacoma ⦿ TPL

All of this brings us to the **Theatre on the Square**, built in 1993 at 915 Broadway. Where to begin? … When the Blue Mouse building was demolished in 1960, that set in motion a set of ventures intended as urban upgrades that pretty much put the urban core in jeopardy for the next quarter century.

There were four escalades, moving steel surfaced sidewalks, built by the City of Tacoma with the stated intention of lessening the burden of climbing the hills between Pacific and Broadway. As noted above, one went where the Blue Mouse had been and dropped travelers at Commerce where they could cross and then proceed onto the next moving ramp to Pacific. The other set connected mid-block between Ninth and Eleventh, Broadway to Commerce to Pacific.

Steph Farber, who along with Phyllis Harrison, owns LeRoy Jewelers on Broadway, reflected on the influence of the topography on the urban core. "One of the challenges downtown Tacoma had always faced was the way it was laid out with long, fairly level avenues running north and south, but with steep hill climbs on the blocks connecting them – Enter the Escalade!"

Today you can experience the the lower part of the northern pathway on the stairs under the Park Plaza North Garage and the route from the Blue Mouse to the Cameo can be traveled on stairs that, according to a plaque on Broadway, were built in 1987. Of course, that signals that the moving sidewalks, even though they were celebrated as the "first in the nation" when built, didn't survive. One problem was a budget-devastating amount of vandalism to the machinery and portals. Another problem was that in 1974 the City decided the best way to counteract the flight of retail and its customers to the Tacoma Mall, which had opened in 1965, as well as the impact of suburbia in general, was to create a mall downtown. "A pedestrian only mall," noted Farber, "blocked off to vehicles, made no sense in a city where, as one restaurateur noted in that era, 'If Tacomans can't drive to the bathroom, they just won't go.'"

Broadway, which had been one of the busiest streets in town, was blocked off to vehicular traffic from Ninth to 13th. Streetscape enhancements were installed, including aggregate and brick surfaces, canopies and fountains – one of which still sits on the corner of 13th. There was even talk of bringing in an old-fashioned electric trolley to roll up and down the four-block stretch.

Meanwhile, as if the plot needed thickening, a promot-er named Stanley Harris out of Portland had secured a World Trade Center franchise and said he wanted to build two towers on the site adjacent to the Pantages. He took up options on at least half a dozen buildings and gave tenants 60-days notice to vacate. This pretty much drove off the already staggering retailers, a lone exception being LeRoy Jewelers, which moved across the street to its present location and continued on its way to what is now a 75-year-old business.

By the time Harris' folly had played out, ownerships in most of the buildings he had optioned were so complex and the buildings had so badly deteriorated from neglect, eight buildings were demolished in December 1980. Among those, as mentioned above, was the former home of the Orpheum Theater. The Jones Building, which housed the Roxy at the time, narrowly escaped that fate, and Harris went to McNeil Island Federal Penitentiary for tax evasion.

It took four more years for the City to abandon the plaza and escalades and reopen Broadway to traffic. The Music Box had burned down in 1963 and other than a smattering of porno shows, the Roxy and Rialto were the only theaters left out of all the playhouses that had occupied downtown. In this most dire of settings, community leaders had the vision and drive to set forth on the mission to restore the Pantages Theater and re-establish Tacoma's cultural heartbeat at Ninth and Broadway.

At this time, the **Heilig Theater,** built in 1927 at 47 St. Helens and renamed the **Temple Theater** in 1931, was converted to the Saint Helens Convention Center before settling in as the Landmark Convention Center in 1995. **The Grand Cinema** would open at 602 Fawcett Avenue in 1995. Profiles on these theaters are treated separately in this chapter.

The $12 million public-private funded Broadway Center for the Performing Arts produced the 300-seat Theatre on the Square, a new rehearsal hall and open public space all situated adjacent to the Pantages Theater. The Theater on the Square was designated as a new home for the Tacoma Actors Guild, the group having presented its first production in 1979 at the Temple Theater, then calling St. Leo's School on Yakima Avenue its performance home for the next dozen years before the new theater with its distinctive corrugated metal walls opened in October 1993. That relationship ended with the closing of TAG in 2007.

As if to prove the Theater District still held its century-long spell on entrepreneurs seeking to make a mark conducting show business, yet another major scheme emerged in the 1990s. This time it was to be a 320,000-square-foot megaplex of retail and residential uses anchored by a 16-screen movie theater. The City of Tacoma negotiated with developers to build an 800-vehicle garage at the north end of the complex that would be constructed along Broadway from 7th to 9th. After a series of developers made unsuccessful runs at acquiring the old Elks Temple and stumbled over other challenges the plan faded away.

From where the multiplex might have been it is an easy walk to The Grand Cinema, the Rialto, the Theatre on the Square and the Pantages. Considering the drama that has played out since Smith's Place, the Alpha Opera House and the Theatre Comique beckoned folks to come inside in the 1880s, Tacoma's treasured venues are well positioned for many encores.

BCPA

(Below) In the early 1980s, six buildings have been demolished on the site between Commerce and Broadway, adjacent to the Pantages Theater, shown on the right. The shell of one of the infamous escalades is visible on the far left. Pierce Transit built a bus garage on this site in the early 1990s, above which the Theatre on the Square and open plaza were built in 1993. Plans are being developed to transform the plaza into a prominent gathering place and outdoor performance venue.

BCPA

TPL

TACOMA'S DOWNTOWN THEATERS

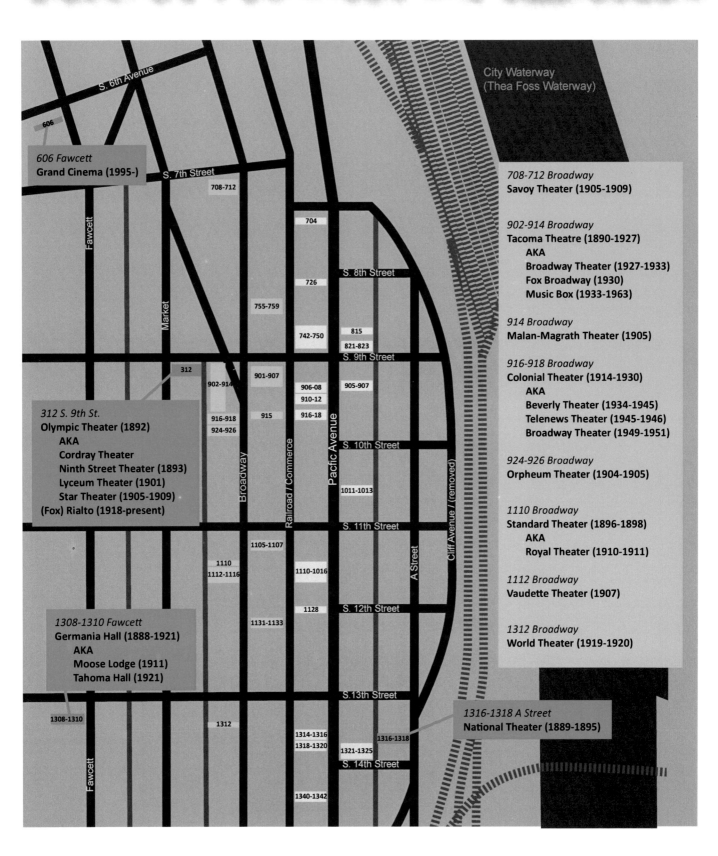

City Waterway
(Thea Foss Waterway)

606

606 Fawcett
Grand Cinema (1995-)

S. 6th Avenue

S. 7th Street

708-712

704

S. 8th Street

726

755-759

742-750

815
821-823

S. 9th Street

312

901-907

902-914

906-08
910-12

905-907

312 S. 9th St.
Olympic Theater (1892)
AKA
Cordray Theater
Ninth Street Theater (1893)
Lyceum Theater (1901)
Star Theater (1905-1909)
(Fox) Rialto (1918-present)

916-918
924-926

915

916-18

S. 10th Street

1011-1013

S. 11th Street

1105-1107

1110
1112-1116

1110-1016

1128

S. 12th Street

1131-1133

1308-1310 Fawcett
Germania Hall (1888-1921)
AKA
Moose Lodge (1911)
Tahoma Hall (1921)

S.13th Street

1308-1310

1312

1314-1316
1318-1320

1321-1325

1316-1318

1316-1318 A Street
National Theater (1889-1895)

S. 14th Street

1340-1342

708-712 Broadway
Savoy Theater (1905-1909)

902-914 Broadway
Tacoma Theatre (1890-1927)
AKA
Broadway Theater (1927-1933)
Fox Broadway (1930)
Music Box (1933-1963)

914 Broadway
Malan-Magrath Theater (1905)

916-918 Broadway
Colonial Theater (1914-1930)
AKA
Beverly Theater (1934-1945)
Telenews Theater (1945-1946)
Broadway Theater (1949-1951)

924-926 Broadway
Orpheum Theater (1904-1905)

1110 Broadway
Standard Theater (1896-1898)
AKA
Royal Theater (1910-1911)

1112 Broadway
Vaudette Theater (1907)

1312 Broadway
World Theater (1919-1920)

Fawcett

Market

Broadway

Railroad / Commerce

Pacific Avenue

A Street

Cliff Avenue / (removed)

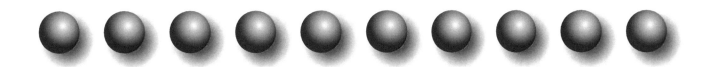

704 Pacific
Smith's Place (1877-1882)

726 Pacific
Casino Theater (1888)

742-750 Pacific (in Donnelly Hotel)
Searchlight Movie Palace (1897)

906-908 Pacific
Princess Theater (1912-1914)
   AKA
   Liberty Theater (1915-1928)
   Riviera Theater (1929-1950)
   Capri Theater (1964-1968)

910-912 Pacific
Crystal Theater (1904-1907)
   AKA
   Pantages (1908-1918)
   Oak Theater (1918)
   Columbia Theater (1918)
   Victory Theater (1918-1923)

916-918 Pacific
Nicolodeum Theater (1908)
   AKA
   Circuit Theater and
      Scenic Theater (1908-1913)
   Melbourne Theater (1913-1918)
   Strand Theater (1918 -1921)

1110-1116 Pacific
Empire Theater (1904-1906)
   AKA
   Exhibit Amusement Company (1907)

1128 Pacific
Palace Theater (1910-1928)
   AKA
   Cameo Theater (1941-1959)

1314-1316 Pacific
Arcade Theater (1911)

1318-1320 Pacific
Lyric Theater (1910-1914)
   AKA
   Shell Theater (1916-1960)
   Cameo Theater (1961-1986)

1340-1342 Pacific
Coast Vaudeville Theater (1908-1911)

815 Pacific
Theatre Comique (1887-1892)

821-823 Pacific
Grand Theater (1905-1910)
   AKA
   Majestic Theater (1911-1912)
   Empress Theater (1913-1914)
   Hippodrome Theater (1915, 1918-1920)
   Regent Theater (1916-1917)
   American Theater (1921)

905-907 Pacific
Shaw Brothers Movies (1893)

1011-1013 Pacific
Alpha Opera House (1882-1890)

1321-25 Pacific
Haymarket Theater (1892-1895)
   AKA
   Columbia Theater (1896)
   Owl Theater (1897-1904)
   Phenix Theater (1905-1906)

755-759 Broadway
Mecca Theater (1972-2006)

901-907 Broadway
Majestic Theater (1909-1910)
Dream Theater (1912-1916)
Pantages Theater (1918-present)
   AKA
   RKO Pantages (1929-1930)
   RKO Orpheum (1930-1932)
   Roxy Theater (1932-1983)

915 Broadway
Theater on the Square (1993-present)

1105-1107 Broadway
Bijou Theater (1908-1914, relocated to 1109 Broadway, 1915-1932)

1131-1133 Broadway
Apollo Theater (1914-1921)
   AKA
   Blue Mouse Theater (1922-1957)

Map designed
by Chris Fiala Erlich

Babe's Recollections of Movie-going in Tacoma

Months before her passing in 2015, Griselda "Babe" Lehrer recalled her childhood experiences attending the Mickey Mouse Club program at the Temple Theater.

"The Mickey Mouse Club was held every Saturday at the Temple Theater. We would be dropped off at 9 a.m. and picked up at 6 p.m. The show was 10 cents and popcorn was five cents. We usually brought our own lunch. The day would start with a band rehears-

al, then they would play for everyone. There would be an amateur hour with local kids performing on stage. There would be prizes provided by merchants. Mickey Mouse would appear on the screen and lead us all in the Mickey Mouse song. Then the films would start with coming attractions, then a serial that was always a cliff-hanger to get us to come back for more next week. Then there would be the Pathé Newsreel, Mickey Mouse cartoon and then the main movie, which were often Westerns. They never presented the same show, it was always something new.

"Will Conner, who operated the theater, was in charge. He would get up on stage and MC the show. The place was almost always packed, kids ranged in age from about eight to 15. Everyone was pretty well behaved. I guess this kind of phased out as television became more popular in the 1950s."

In the 1983 75th anniversary program for the Pantages and Rialto theaters, Babe related her memories of movie-going dates with her husband-to-be, Herman Lehrer:

"It was very special. In the 40s you would wear white gloves to go to the theater on Saturday afternoon, and then have ice cream at the Cave Restaurant afterwards. Movie houses filled up after the annual Daffodil Parade as spectators looked first for lunch, then for a movie when the parade left downtown. Sundays and movies went hand in hand. Sometimes we'd make a day of it, starting with movie at the Rialto, then another at the Music Box and wind up at the Roxy.'"

Kisses and Chores in the Family Theater Business

The 1934 opening of the Beverly had a personal touch TPL

Eighty-three years after the grand opening of theater that was named for her, Beverly (Barovic) Foley has clear memories of that event – which is pretty remarkable considering she was only four years old and had the lead role in the welcoming of its first customers. But, first, a bit of background on how that came to be.

In the 1920s, Beverly's grandfather Dominic Constanti, began showing silent films at the Slovanian Hall, 2306 North 30th St., in Old Town. With Beverly's father, Mike Barovic, they developed the Liberty Theater in Puyallup, the Avalon Theater in Bellingham, the Fife Drive-in, the Riviera Theater in Sumner and the Riviera Theater in downtown Tacoma. The latter, opened in 1929 as a modern 600-seat house located at 906-908 Pacific Avenue, immediately next door to where Alexander Pantages had opened his first Tacoma theater. The Beverly Theater was at 916-18 Broadway.

As to the opening of the Beverly on August 20, 1934, the Barovics displayed their acumen for promotion. Here was a cute four-year-old standing on a stool in the lobby on opening day of a theater named for her, handing out flowers – Roses for the ladies, carnations for the men. "So many ladies kissed me my mother had a hard time getting all the lipstick off my face." And, how savvy to have the young girl showcased when the opening movie was *Little Miss Marker* starring Shirley Temple in her first major motion picture at age six, only two years older than Beverly.

And, we can't resist digressing into a bit of nostalgia for the fun of cinema in the Thirties as portrayed in this plot summation courtesy of Wikipedia(CC-BY-SA).

The film tells the story of "Marky" (Shirley Temple), whose father gives her to a gangster-run gambling operation as a "marker" (collateral) for a bet. When he loses his bet and commits suicide, the gangsters are left with her on their hands. They decide to keep her temporarily and use her to help pull off one of their fixed races, naming her the owner of the horse to be used in the race.

Marky is sent to live with bookie Sorrowful Jones (Adolphe Menjou). Initially upset about being forced to look after her, he eventually begins to develop a father-daughter relationship with her. His fellow gangsters become fond of her and begin to fill the roles of her extended family. Bangles (Dorothy Dell) – girlfriend of gang kingpin Big Steve (Charles Bickford), who has gone to Chicago to place bets on the horse – also begins to care for Marky, and to fall in love with Sorrowful, whose own concern for Marky shows he has a warm heart beneath his hard-man persona. Sorrowful, encouraged by Bangles and Marky, gets a bigger apartment, buys Marky new clothes and himself a better cut of suit, reads her bedtime stories, and shows her how to pray.

However, being around the gang has a somewhat bad influence on Marky, and she begins to develop a cynical nature and a wide vocabulary of gambling terminology and slang. Bangles and Sorrowful, worried that she acquired bad-girl attitude means she won't get adopted by a "good family," put on a party with gangsters dressed up as knights-of-the-round-table, to rekindle her former sweetness. She is unimpressed until they bring in the horse and parade her around on its back. Big Steve, returning to New York, frightens it which throws her and she is taken to the hospital.

Big Steve goes there to pay back Sorrowful for trying to steal Bangles, but is roped into giving Marky the direct blood transfusion she needs for her life-saving operation. Sorrowful, praying for her survival, destroys the drug which, administered to the horse, would have helped it win the race but killed it soon after. Big Steve, told he has "good blood," and pleased to have given life for a change, forgives Bangles and Sorrowful. They plan to marry and adopt Marky.

The Barovics obviously knew how to market a good story and three years after their daughter made her welcoming gestures on a stool in the lobby of the Beverly they had a family photo-op astride horses and costumes in front of the Riviera to promote the movie *Checkers*.

As Beverly grew older she would often accompany her mother and father to Seattle on Tuesdays and Thursdays to select films. "There was what was known as 'Film Row' on Second Avenue where all the major studios had their offices – MGM, Paramount, United Artists and so on – and the theater operators would negotiate what films they wanted and the terms, first run, second run. While my father was doing that Mother and I would go shopping and have lunch. The Rendezvous Restaurant was where all the theater operators would meet after the film negotiations were over, have a drink and talk about business before everyone headed back to their theaters. There was a small screen theater in the back of the restaurant and we would sometimes watch a film there." The restaurant still exists with what is now called the Jewelbox Theater offering a mix of live entertainment and film virtually every night.

Between the fun outings, Beverly knew first hand the chores that went with running the facility, including cleaning the theater. "It was particularly bad after Saturday matinees when kids would pee on the floor so they wouldn't miss anything on the screen." She would have preferred to be handing out roses and carnations.

The Barovics made promotions a family affair　📷 TPL

A Daffodil Parade float passes the Riviera in 1939　📷 TPL

The Blue Mouse and the Vitaphone

By Deborah Freedman

John Hamrick's 1927 remodel of Tacoma's downtown Blue Mouse included installation of a Vitaphone system. Developed from telephone technologies by Bell Laboratories and Western Electric, the new method played accompanying audio from a 33-1/3 record placed on a turntable coupled to the projection motor. The film operator placed a needle in the center of the disc and the record played outward. Warner Brothers' first major success with this technology was the 1926 premiere of *Don Juan* starring John Barrymore, which featured a synchronized musical soundtrack, but no dialog.

The following year *The Jazz Singer* with Al Jolson added dialog before several musical selections, a key event in the transition of silent films to talkies. The film debuted in New York in October of 1927 and premiered in Tacoma at the Blue Mouse Theater in January of 1928.

One of the three film operators at the Blue Mouse was Roy Kneeland, whose career spanned nearly forty years. Kneeland worked at the Blue Mouse until about 1932, then at the Music Box for more than twenty-five years before finishing his career at the Rialto in the early Sixties. (His uncle, William H. Kneeland, was one of the founders of the town of Shelton.)

However the Vitaphone system, like many innovative technologies, was short-lived. Equipment was expensive and cumbersome, and susceptible to synchronization errors. The discs' physical condition deteriorated so quickly that a chart was printed on the labels to note the number of times played. After two dozen uses the disc had to be discarded.

Most importantly, the recording method made film editing nearly impossible. The Vitaphone system was soon replaced by technologies that recorded sound directly on the movie film. By the early 1930s theater owners were forced to again convert their equipment, in a pattern that has continued for nearly a century.

Present

VITAPHONE

— AND —

JOHN BARRYMORE
in "Don Juan"

THS

PROPERTY OF
ELECTRICAL RESEARCH PRODUCTS, INC.

OPERATING INSTRUCTIONS
FOR WESTERN ELECTRIC
SOUND PROJECTOR SYSTEM

THIS IS COPY No. 318

ISSUED TO

THS

THS

Vitaphone Said to Be Greeted by Popularity

Vitaphone is taking the Pacific-Northwest by storm, according to John Hamrick, theater owner in that section of the country. Hamrick installed Vitaphone equipment in his Portland Blue Mouse Theater and a little later in his Seattle theater.

According to Sam L. Warner, in charge of all Vitaphone activities, both theaters have played to capacity audiences since the Vitaphone installations, the sight-sound innovation becoming more popular as its entertaining qualities were advertised by word of mouth by pleased patrons Hamrick, who is noted among theater men for his showmanship, has just ordered Vitaphone equipment for installation in his Blue Mouse Theater in Tacoma, Wash., thus giving the three biggest cities in the Northwest each a Vitaphone equipped theater. In connection with these houses Hamrick has also booked complete programs of Warner Brothers pictures.

THS

TPL

Hamrick and Conner – Maestros of Tacoma Theaters

John Hamrick is recognized as the first Tacoma theater owner to show a talking picture when he presented the *Jazz Singer* at his Blue Mouse Theater on Broadway in 1928. As with any pioneer breaking new ground, he had positioned himself with visionary preparation.

Will Conner 📷 **TPL**

After purchasing and remodeling the Apollo Theater in 1922, he renamed it the Blue Mouse Theater – a name he reportedly adopted from a theater of the same name he discovered while in Paris. Translating the name from original "souris bleue" played to American sensibilities and installing a synchronized image-sound system called Vitaphone set Hamrick on course to deliver the era of "talkies" to audiences in the collection of theaters he owned from Seattle to Portland.

With a Blue Mouse theater in each city, he was doubled up in Tacoma with the Blue Mouse "Junior," as the Proctor theater was affectionately known. He would take over the Helig Theater in 1932 and rename it Hamrick's Temple Theater, a name proclaimed on the largest vertical sign in the city.

Hamrick, known to invest in upgrades and patron-pleasing amenities at his theaters, was born in Kansas in 1876 and acted on his belief in the emerging silent film medium by opening the first motion picture theater in Kansas City, Missouri. His involvement in Tacoma's mainstream theaters expanded to the Music Box and the Roxy, the latter coming into his stable in 1935 at the time Ned Edris, a longtime employee, became his partner.

He was described as "an abstemious man who had a flair for organization and ability to give the people, movie-wise, what they liked."

His devout religious beliefs engaging his business role could be witnessed in the early Thirties when the Music Box showed the provocative Mae West in *She Done Him Wrong* with the advertisement noting "Of No Interest To Children Under 16." This was in the pre-censorship era, but Hamrick filled out the bill with an "Extra Special – Hear Pope Pius XI Speak for the first time on the talking screen," and the announcement that coming soon would be Cecil B. DeMille's *Sign of the Cross.*

At the time of his death in 1956 at the age of 80 in New York City, he was president of Hamrick Theaters, which was then operating more than a dozen theaters in the Northwest. Nine year's later, as fire and smoke engulfed the former Tacoma Theater, the marquee read, "John Hamrick's Music Box."

While Hamrick's name was on the marquee, it was Will Conner who had the keys to the burned building. He also had the keys to the Roxy across the street and, as one who had built a career in the theater business and knew the show must go on, he grabbed the film for *The Birds* from the Music Box, ran an ad for the change in venue and popped the film in the Roxy cameras the next night.

Conner, who had acquired control of Hamrick's operations along the way, was operating the Roxy, the Proctor (Blue Mouse Junior), Music Box, Temple, Rialto and Narrows in Tacoma as well as theaters in Seattle and Portland. His career in theater started when, as a high school student in Auburn, he learned how to be a

John Hamrick, left, and Ned Edris, who have purchased the Roxy theater at 9th and Broadway. Edris today became a partner in Hamrick's local theaters, which include the Music Box, Blue Mouse and Temple theaters.

* * *

Hamrick And Edris Take Over Theater

Will Operate House at 9th and Broadway As Well as Music Box, Blue Mouse And Temple; Conner at Roxy

📷 TPL

projectionist showing silent films and creating promotional materials for movies and vaudeville acts.

While working for the Fox Theater Company in Centralia, he was loaned to the Disney Company at the personal request of Walt Disney to start Mickey Mouse Clubs. A few years later, he would be found on stage leading a house full of kids when the Mickey Mouse Club would meet every Saturday at 1 p.m. at the Temple Theater. The afternoon ritual included Disney cartoons and films, including a serial that would make sure they couldn't wait to get back the next week.

> "Who's the leader of the club
> That's made for you and me?
> M-I-C-K-E-Y M-O-you-S-E!"

Conner joined the Hamrick theater chain in 1932 at a time when the Blue Mouse was the only theater operating downtown in the depths of the Depression. They reopened theaters in subsequent years and, because the idea of concession stands inside theaters was still a number of years off, he and Edris set up a popcorn wagon across the street from the Temple Theater. In time Edris sold his shares and Hamrick passed away, leaving the Conner Theater Corporation as the premier independent operator in the area, a position he held until retiring in 1974. He held ownership in the

Rialto building until 1990 when a purchase was facilitated on behalf of the City of Tacoma.

In addition to displaying movies, Conner had promoted vaudeville and musical performances at the Temple. He talked of the appeal of live appearances of celebrities, such as boxing champions. "Guys like Dempsey and Tunney used to just skip rope or punch a bag, then do an exhibition against some local tough guy. As acts, they weren't much, but the people would stand in line for hours just to see them," Conner reminisced years after retiring. "W.C. Fields was originally a juggler and he was as funny off stage as on. He'd juggle cigar boxes and go through his patter. That's how he found out he was funny."

In a letter sent to Murray Morgan in 1993, Conner related the formula on which Pantages vaudeville had been built.

"Vaudeville was formatted usually with five acts. There would be a pit orchestra of eight to 10 members directed by Max Frolic, later a Tacoma restaurant owner. Each of the first four acts would be 15 minutes long and the final act 30 minutes. There was usually a matinee at 2 p.m. and evening performances at 7 and 9 p.m.

"The first act, in vaudeville terms, was an action act. Usually it was jugglers, sword swallowers, something like that. The second act was usually a song and dance couple with comedy patter. By that time the audience was settled enough from the action act. The third act was what we call artistic, usually classical dancers, singers or instrumentalists. Or maybe a portrait painter who would do yours in 90 seconds. The fourth

Conner and Edris operated a popcorn wagon in front of the Temple TPL

act was almost always comedy routines. Rural comedy was big.

"The last act was what we called the flash act, a zinger. These were the high priced acts, the escape artists like Harry Houdini who played the Pantages every year. He would pack 'em in. Or magician Alexander the Great, who invented sawing women in half. Or Russian Cossack dancers with swords and all. Mind readers, fire eaters and throwers, animal acts, Siamese twins saxophone players... toward the end, it would be maybe a stage band with a noted singer – but that was more popular in the unit shows of the 1930s.

"The curtain rolled up from the bottom and had little boxes on it with advertisement. The pit orchestra would entertain between acts and Frolic was a violinist and quite a showman. He stood on a chair so he was three-feet higher than the rest of the guys. He'd wave his bow around and the like. He was like an act in himself."

"Everything moved quickly between acts, as soon as the act took its applause, the curtain came down and the props and set for the next act was moved on stage and the curtain went back up. Everything was very precise. They would announce the acts with cards inserted into a lighted frame on each side of the proscenium arch. Later girls in cute costumes carried the card across the stage. Master of ceremonies came later after the Pantages era.

"RKO vaudeville introduced a 20-minute motion picture program consisting of a news reel and an eight-minute subject called Aesop's Fables just before the vaudeville acts went on. They also increased the number of acts from five to six. When motion pictures came on the scene it was the death knell for vaudeville. The acts could make more money in pictures and save the expense of traveling from city to city."

Conner, who passed away in 1996, and Hamrick represented a half century of innovative and high quality entertainment through their operation of theaters. Service was important to them. On the passing of the era when ushers would direct people to their seats with little flashlights and hush those who were disruptive, Conner once lamented, "Now people could fall over and die in the aisle and no one would know for weeks." The words of a man who had used a smile and fine touch to prevail in a turbulent business.

Mae West in *She Done Him Wrong*

In answer to a segment in the March 2017 issue of *The Atlantic*, which asked "What was the most influential film in history?" Anna Biler, filmmaker, answered:

"Mae West's witty dialogue, revealing gowns, purring voice, and sexual innuendos in *She Done Him Wrong* (1933) made her an icon of a type of frank female sexuality that would define the early 1930s and the pre-censorship era, and would inspire concepts of high camp and female sexual independence in cinema for decades to come."

The Heilig/Temple Theater

By Murray Morgan

Cal Heilig had symbolized the best in theater in Tacoma since 1891 when he resigned as secretary to the mayor and replaced John Hanna as manager of the Tacoma Theatre. Thus, Tacomans were saddened in 1925 when Calvin Heilig, in a deal front-paged in the News Tribune as "the largest single property transaction in the history of Tacoma," sold the Tacoma Theatre to Henry A. Rhodes. The new owner paid $325,000 in cash and assumed a mortgage of $125,000 on the building.

Cal later went on to build a Western chain of show houses, including The Heilig in downtown Portland. He maintained a residence called "Shorehouse" on American Lake and saw an opportunity to create a new live theater venue when the Tacoma Theatre was converted primarily into a motion picture palace and renamed The Broadway in 1927.

A Mason, he was aware that the Masonic organizations of Tacoma planned to build a 10-story temple at South Second Street between St. Helens and Broadway. It was intended to provide meeting space for the 18 Masonic bodies in Pierce County, as well as offices for the Grand Lodge of Washington, library and vault storage, a soundproof room for band practice, a rooftop area large enough to allow the Shrine Patrol and the Knights Templar drill teams to practice formation marching, a banquet hall designed to seat 1,500 as well as several small dining facilities. Teaming with another prominent Mason, Scott Z. Henderson, Heilig persuaded the building committee to include a 2,000 seat theater, which they promised to lease.

Ambrose J. Russell was the architect chosen to design the Masonic Temple. Born in India in 1857 to Scottish missionary parents, Russell had been educated at the University of Glasgow and at l'Encole des Beaux Arts in Paris before migrating to America in 1892. He was associated with architectural firms in Boston, Kansas City and St. Louis before coming to Tacoma in 1892 – just in time to experience the collapse of the building boom during the Panic of '93.

His early work was largely residential, but after the return of prosperity following the discovery of gold in the Yukon and the shipping boom occasioned by the American takeover of the Philippines after the Spanish-American war, Russell received numerous commissions for public buildings.

He designed the Governor's Mansion in Olympia, the First Baptist Church in Seattle, the Tacoma Armory, the Perkins Building and two versions of the Tacoma

The Temple Theater was known as The Helig when the theater opened in 1927

PSTOS

Country Club, after the first structure burned. Among the residences he designed was the Rust Mansion. By 1927, when assigned to design the Masonic Temple, he was generally acknowledged as Tacoma's leading architect.

Familiar as he was with big buildings, Russell had no experience with theater design. His closest encounter was a design sketch he had drawn for the girls' gymnasium built in the 1890s alongside the first Annie Wright Seminary northeast of Wright Park – a wood-frame building that many years later was converted into the Tacoma Little Theatre on the present site of Stadium Thriftway.

Despite inexperience, Russell was able to nestle a 2,000-seat theater, commodious and comfortable, into the Masonic Temple without doing violence to the desired Second Renaissance Revival style – a combination of classical details and form with flat and restrained decoration – which was then much in vogue for institutional buildings.

The theater Russell conceived held seats for 1,200 on the main level, another 800 in the balcony. By cantilevering the balcony from a six-foot steel beam that ran the width of the Temple, Russell was able to eliminate support posts, thus improving sight lines and adding seating capacity. A Kimball pipe organ, "costing more than $20,000," was built into the theater and has survived as originally installed.

The Temple stage – 47-feet deep, 87-feet wide with a proscenium 47½ feet at apex, was inevitably described as the "largest north of San Francisco." Below and back of the stage were 14 dressing rooms and, a new luxury, several shower rooms. The seven-story fly loft, one of the largest hemp (rope-suspended) lofts in the nation, allowed for up to 42 separate sets three-stories tall, to be flown.

The asbestos fire curtain, painted by Edward Misener of Portland in association with Bert Straight of Tacoma, portrayed the ruins of an ancient city on the Nile against a background of desert vastness. Taylor Moses, who created the Temple of Minerva curtain for the Tacoma Theatre in 1890, came to look at it and pronounced it superb. Moses' own curtain was eventually transferred from the Tacoma Theatre to the Temple, where it hung in the fly loft until it disintegrated in 1994.

Décor in the theater was described as "Art Deco Egyptian" in colors of rose, muted blue and golden brown. Tacomans were happy that for the first time a local firm was commissioned to furnish the local showplace. McCormack Brothers supplied vast yardage of brown velour which was used not only for the stage

Live performances and movies shared billing during the years John Hamrick operated the Temple

TPL

curtain but along the entire length of both sides of the house, along the outer aisles, over the windows and doorways, at the dividers between orchestra and parquet sections, and around the boxes and balcony. It was boasted that there was four times more velour in the Temple than in all Seattle.

As agreed before construction began, Heilig leased the theater for five years. He called it the Heilig Temple Theater, but locally it was known simply as The Heilig. He booked shows that were touring his Western circuit of theaters. To open the new house on October 27, 1927 he brought in *The Madcap,* an inconsequential operatic confection that had been whipped up to fit the talents of Magedela (Mitzi) Hajos, a 36-year-old Hungarian charmer, who for more than two decades had been doing variations on her first big hit, the operetta *Sari.* She appeared previously in Tacoma in a 1920 production of *Head over Heels* and in 1924 *The Magic Ring.*

Among those treading the Heilig boards with her were Sidney Greenstreet, who at the age of 48 was still 14 years away from his film debut as the sinister Kasper Guttman in *The Maltese Falcon*, and the urbane Authur Treacher, later to dignify the screen as the perfect butler in films ranging from *Magnificent Obsession* to *Mary Poppins.*

Mitzi was followed to the Heilig by the 31-year-old Metropolitan Opera baritone Lawrence Tibbett who was paying his first visit to the Pacific Northwest. Tibbett's voice filled the theater, applause thundered back. On his first appearance here, as on his last 30 years later, his final encore was *On the Road to Mandalay.* Decades later, it reverberates in the memories of those who heard him.

Tibbett, too, was soon drawn to Hollywood by the advent of sound. He was nominated for an Oscar in 1930 for his role in *The Desert Rogue Song.* The first impact of sound was being felt in Tacoma when Mitzi and Tibbett made their appearances here. The canned voices of the Six Original Brown Brothers could be heard scratchily on a Vitaphone short at John Hamrick's Blue Mouse then blocks south on Broadway.

Months later Tacomans could both see and hear Al Jolson in the partial talkie *The Jazz Singer.*

The silent films died quickly. The talkies, in conjunction with the Depression that followed the 1929 stock market crash, also killed the national vaudeville circuits, crippled the national companies that took

Broadway successes on tour, and put at risk most resident stock companies. When Heilig's five-year lease on the theater in the Temple expired in 1932 he made no attempt to renew it.

The theater was then leased to the veteran Northwest showman John Hamrick, who appointed Will Conner as manager. Conner, who became a movie projectionist while in high school in Auburn, ran John Hamrick's Temple Theatre as an employee until 1948 when he became a partner in the business.

Under Conner's guidance, the Temple continued to present touring plays and international concert artists when available. The Temple remained the place where one dressed for the theater and where a new generation was introduced to opera by the San Carlo, to ballet by the Ballet Russe, and to Broadway by the occasional national touring company.

The theater was remodeled in 1948 to make it more suitable for movies. The loge sections on the main floor were removed, all the original seats were replaced with new ones with semi-reclining backs and automatic lifts. An experimental movie screen, somewhat similar to the one that in 1953 was introduced nationally as CinemaScope, was installed to eliminate distortion. Conner operated the Temple until 1974 when he retired. The theater was then leased to Maurice Mullendore of Auburn. It was dormant during much of the 1980s before undergoing another renovation and emerging as the Saint Helens Convention Center in 1992. In 1995 the facility took on its current name as the Landmark Convention Center.

Theater Ads

January 4, 1918   **April 19, 1963**

AMUSEMENTS

TACOMA THEATER.
Afternoon and evening—Italian Battlefront Pictures.

PANTAGES THEATER.
Vaudeville.

HIPPODROME THEATER.
Vaudeville.

MELBOURNE.
Jane Caprice in "Every Girl's Dream;" the great Halifax disaster; "The Battle of the Aine;" Famous Frolickers comedy.

LIBERTY.
Charley Chaplin in "The Champion."

PARK THEATER.
"Fighting Trail, Mon's Prey No. 7;" "John Tom Little Bear," "Sidetracked Slugger," Hard Times comedy.

ROSE.
"The Bowstring," second episode of "The Seven Pearls," featuring Mollie King; "The Ringer," with Grace Darling, and a cartoon comedy.

LINCOLN.
Last series of "Stingaree;" first episode of "The Fighting Trail," and two comedies.

VAUDETTE.
High class photo plays.

ALOHA.
High class photo plays.

IDLE HOUR THEATER.
"The Millionaire Vagrant," with Charles Ray, and a comedy.

February 27, 1918

January 6, 1918

March 5, 1928

August 25, 1918

SHIPYARD ACTIVITIES

Conference Sept. 4 to Consider Best Means for Prevention of Shipyard Accidents

A meeting which is expected to be of great interest to shipyard workers and employers will be held Sept. 4 at an early in the assembly room of the Chamber of Commerce. The purpose of this conference will be to discuss the coordination working of the industrial insurance law and to consider the best methods of operating under it to secure the greatest results in accident prevention work.

While accidents are increasing that lateness, it is pointed out, would be vastly greater than it is now were it not for the fact that quite a number of employers of the state have succeeded in greatly reducing the accidents in their plant by establishing and maintaining a very high standard of accident prevention work. A few of these have engaged in this work so intensively that they have reduced their accident cost to almost nothing. What these men have done can be done by others and the communities feels it is said that it is entirely possible to devise means to bring this fact to the attention periodically all employers of the state and to that way enlist their cooperation. It is stated that by united effort a million or more dollars can be saved annually to the employees of the state.

St. Paul Veterans Pleased With Wright Yard Gavel

Some weeks ago the boys at the Wright yard made a gavel from wood entering into the construction of the Tahoma and sent it to the Worth Eagles Camp No. 2 United Spanish-American war veterans at St. Paul. The following, in reply to the gift, has been received by M. A. Hodges, of the Wright yards.

Loyal Comrade:

"Last night, although one of the hottest we have had, brought out a good attendance at camp meeting, and as you have guessed, Charlie Hodges was there, although a little late this time, coming in after the meeting had started.

Imagine the pleasant surprise that was given to us from you all, through Charlie That gavel. I assure you, all be used at all meetings from now on.

"It is hard for me to express the appreciation that the comrades have for this historic gift, made from material used in the good ship Yakima, may she remain safe during the war while sailing up to swing the ships. You saved you enabled by all the comrades. You and the comrades at the Wright yards who assisted in making it may have cause to be proud. Comrade, we wish to have you extend the sincere appreciation of the camp to the comrades who helped you in the making of this gavel. The unanimous sentiment of the men was "May you all live long and prosper!"

"Again thanking you on behalf of the

Sincerely and fraternally,
G. L. BLAKER, Commander."

Seen at the Vaudeville Houses

CRAMER, BARTON & STARLING
PANTAGES

PHYLLIS GORDON
IN "UNDER THE TOP"
HIPPODROME

Three Stars on Pin; Tears in His Eyes

The "buds" of the Foundation yards had a flag service Friday afternoon and put up a flag with 141 stars on it. The yard band was present, the soldiers were there and also the fathers of the boys at the front. Then there was the interested observer and spectator. The ceremony was pretty and impressive, the observer thought, and he was impressed especially at the close as the colors came down and the bugler played the "Star Spangled Banner."

The observer and spectator watched and the call of the bugle made war and neat to the workings of both. The observer got his eyes centered on a little grey mustached man in the uniform of one of the yard workers. The little man's hat was drawn over his eyes and as the observer listened to the bugle call he noticed that the chin of the little man began to twist, like the chin of little and nervous old men and women will. It seemed incongruous to the observer that the chin of the little old man should move. Then a tear and an other set, a damp trail down the little old man's cheek. The observer stared harder with his spectator and then the observer, allowed for some reason, his glance to slip down and then he understood. The lapel of the little old man's coat carried three tiny service stars.

The flag was down and the little old man stopped over to make sure that the name was on the list of fathers there while the spectator cheered to the observer, as he brushed his eyes, that it was such men as the little old man in

RUSSIANS REPLY TO WILSON'S NOTE

Bolsheviki Contend Czecho-Slovaks Counter Revolutionary

AMSTERDAM, Aug. 24—The Russian Bolshevik government has replied to the Japanese-American message to the Russian people, explaining the motives of intervention in Siberia. The version of the Russian reply appearing in the Tageblatt of Berlin, as telegraphed from Stockholm under date of August 23 says:

"The American and Japanese governments have addressed a message to the Russian people in connection with the landing of their armed forces on Russian territory. Both governments declare their armed intervention was dictated by the desire to come to the aid of the Czecho-Slovaks, who, it is said, are menaced by Germans and Austrians.

Says Hang Defend Revolution

"The statement made by the American and Japanese governments is not based on accurate information. The German-Austrian agents who are now menaced by either Germans or Austrians...

Victory Theater Signs for Fox Productions

Announcement was made last night by Edwin J. Myers, manager of the Victory theater, that he had signed a contract for the year for all playing and special productions produced by the Fox Film company...

PRICES FIXED FOR COAST SALMON

NO BOOSTING OF HOTEL RATES STATE FAIR WEEK

MEN OF 46 TO 56 NOW ACCEPTED IN ARMY

Tacoma Theater

Continuous 1 to 11 | Continuous 1 to 11

Another Big Double Bill

Starting Sunday Aug. 25

This Week We Offer to Our Patrons Two of Their Favorite Screen Stars.

Norma Talmadge

Any Seat
Any Time
20c
Children 10c.
Tax Included.

Two Shows for the Price of One

Norma Talmadge

—IN—

"The Social Secretary"

ONE OF HER GREATEST HITS.

The Biggest and Best Show in Town for the Money

Send the Children in the Afternoons

Douglas Fairbanks and Bessie Love in Triangle Play, "The Good Bad Man."

Two Hours of Splendid Entertainment

Remember Any Seat
20c
Children 10c.
War Tax Included.

Douglas Fairbanks

SUPPORTED BY BESSIE LOVE AND A SPLENDID COMPANY

—In—

"The Good Bad Man"

One of Fairbanks' Best Comedies.

APOLLO

ALWAYS A GOOD SHOW

4 Days Starting Today

WALLACE REID

Supported by ANN LITTLE

in

WALLACE REID In "Believe Me, Xantippe" A Paramount Picture

"Believe Me, Xantippe"

(A Paramount) Picture

WE RECOMMEND IT TO YOUR NOTICE BECAUSE it is a superior photoplay attraction. It contains all the elements that please the eye, the taste, the emotions. The story is dramatic, the photography unusually fine and in every other way it will appeal to you forcibly.

ADDED ATTRACTIONS

"Our Allies, the Tanks"	Animated News-Weekly	Rollin-Pathe Comedy
One of the Most Interesting Features of the War.	And Official War Pictures.	A Side Splitting Farce.

Artistic Plaque Designed By Wright Yard Men

In addition to patriotic work and in prosecution of their task of making the war the Wright yards as a unit further by way of making their each creation a testament. As a sample, a plaque in the form of a plaque on heavy guide oak, artistically finished and measuring 24 to 26 inches, will depreciate the point.

First Aid Station At Wright Shipyards

Safety and first aid has made another noble addition at the Wright shipyards.

CARPENTERS LEAVE COMMITTEE OF 25

Local Union Opposed to 7-Cent Fare and Withdraws Representative

The Carpenters' union of Tacoma has requested its business agent, J. Sterling Parsons, to withdraw from the committee of 25 which is considering the street car situation...

NEW STRAND TO OPEN VERY SOON

Everything will be finished in the new Strand theater, formerly the Melbourne, when it reopens...

76 Neighborhood Theaters in Review

When they struck up a conversation at the **Sunset Theater** on a Friday evening in 1955, they were teenage boys hanging around the concession stand in the lobby. They had come mainly to see if they could make a connection with the girls who had come without dates.

For teenagers, the neighborhood theaters tended to be as much a social scene as interest in what was being shown on the silver screen. At the Sunset the squirming teenagers were on the left side of the center aisle and the adults were on the right actually trying to watch the movie. By curious circumstance, on this particular evening the movie was the pop icon *Blackboard Jungle* – a film about juvenile delinquents that caused parents to associate rock n' roll with teenage transgressions.

Bill Engelhart didn't need the movie to goad him into transgressions, he needed rock n' roll. He had come to the Sunset that

evening with Frank Dutra. As they stood in the lobby Buck Ormsby and Lassie Aanes approached them. They were all students at Jason Lee Junior High, but had what might be described as a nodding acquaintance. That changed when the topic of music came up.

"Buck played the steel guitar, Lassie played drums, Frank played the sax. I played the guitar and we started talking about getting together and practicing in my dad's garage. We got together the next morning at Hoyt's Café to kick around some ideas. Out of that conversation we formed a band that we called the Blue Notes, a name that I picked up from a group of older Black blues musicians that I had jammed with," Engelhart recalled decades later.

"It's been over 60 years since that time, but as I think back about us starting a band I can still feel the excitement that was running through my body. God, if only I could find that feeling again. I still get excited about events in my life, but not with the same passion as a teenager about to embark on the ride of his life." Engelhart would become a Northwest musical icon with Little Bill and the Blue Notes. Ormsby would break away several years after that evening at the Sunset Theater to form the legendary rock band The Fabulous Wailers.

The Sunset, located at 2502-04 Sixth Avenue, had been built with seating for 600 in 1919 in the silent film era, played its first talkie 10 years later, was remodeled twice, bombed once, became the **Guild Sixth Avenue Theater** in 1962 and was sold to a glass retailer in 1975.

About the bombing: On October 6, 1930, George James Carroll (alias George O'Beirne, alias George Dawson and alias George Smith), who had served time in Walla

The Sunset Theater opened in 1919 TPL

The Community Theater after 1930 bombing TPL

This was the Community World Theater in 1987–88 ⊚ TPL

Walla State Penitentiary for stealing a fur coat in Tacoma and had previously served time at Folsom Prison, bombed the Sunset and the **Community Theater.**

At first the police thought the after-hours bombings were related to a labor dispute involving the projectionists union, but after two years of major police work, it was determined this was the act of a parolee with a bad attitude. Carroll's motive for the bombings was to create mayhem for his own entertainment.

Police were positive that Carroll was responsible for the two bombings, but apparently he was into reruns since he was actually convicted for a second bombing at the Community Theater on September 7, 1932. When he confessed, he said he always waited until after midnight before bombing to make sure that the building would be empty of people. He was sentenced to two to five years.

The Community Theater, built in 1924 at 5441 South M Street, promoted the installation of a Perfectone sound system in early 1930. Eight months later Carroll tossed his first bomb at the theater, blowing away the entry and lobby, then struck again 15 months later before being arrested. The action settled down to what was on the screen until the theater closed in 1966.

It reopened for a while as a porno theater, then closed. As if the place couldn't stand the quiet, it was reopened in 1987 as the **Community World Theater** to serve as a mecca for the grunge and punk music scene. In April of that year, Kurt Cobain and Krist Novoselic performed their first concert as Nirvana. While they would go onto legendary international acclaim, many other bands contributed to making what was known as CWT a magnet for fans from throughout the Northwest. But, by mid-year 1988, the old theater was done with show business.

Spreading Out

In the Teens and early Twenties, as vaudeville shows first began to share billing with silent movies then gave way to the screen at the downtown theaters, venues started popping up in the neighborhoods. Located within walking or easy street car distance, these theaters tended to be smaller in seating capacity, often tucked into buildings built for a different purpose and unlikely to be recognized as a theater today, if still standing.

Ironically, one that was actually built as a theater might be the hardest to envision having once served that purpose. That would be the long, single story white building at 2701 N. 21st. Built in 1914 as the **Bungalow Photo-Play Theater** by Charles Henriot. the theater opened on April Fools Day and stated the place was constructed "to resemble the home as much as possible," but with a "commodious foyer" and featured "our beautiful Pianola Player" to accompany the silent films. The operators proclaimed "You'll Remember Us" in their opening night ad, but the Bungalow closed within two years.

The former Bungalow Theater on North 21st ⊚ BJ

People remember theater-going experiences for the shows, for the socializing, for the connections that were made – as recalled by Bill Englehart at the Sunset. Sometimes those memories can hurt in their purity. In the early 1990s, the owner of a shop in the building that had been the Bungalow Theater, found an elderly man sitting on the front steps crying. He said his wife, who he first met at the theater, had recently died. "You'll Remember Us," indeed.

The Rex Theater, located at 3805 Yakima Avenue South, opened in 1912 on Christmas Eve with campstool seating for 150. Perhaps that wasn't the only creature comfort lacking, because the doors were closed six years later. But, all was not lost as the reincarnation of The Rex was built by S.H. McKowan at 3809-11 Yakima Avenue South in 1919. This time seating capacity was up to 650 and nicely appointed, including a nursery

In 1937, a new Rex marquee replaced original sign 📷 TPL

where the movie could be watched without disturbing other patrons.

The Rex lasted until 1957 before giving way to a higher calling as the Tacoma Calvary Temple. But, the show business heroine was to be rescued once again, or at least there was a lady in the plot as The Rex revealed itself once again as a theater in 1980 – this time showing porno movies, sometimes under the stage name **Playtime Theater.** That proved to be somewhat of a tease as The Rex finally turned off the dim lights in 1986. As if the building just couldn't decide whether it was supposed to play or pray, it was occupied by New Restoration Christian Ministries in 2005.

Theater names changed at the same location, theaters kept the name and moved, all of which was a reflection of the fast-changing genre from vaudeville to silent films to talkies to color film to competition with television and beyond. One gets the impression that those making the marquee signs and newspaper display ads were doing better than the folks trying to get seats filled in front of movie screens.

Hans Torkelson built the **Park Theater** at 3510 McKinley Avenue in 1913. He must have felt it too small, because eight years later he built a new theater next door that seated 250. Sold in 1926, the Park endured a burglar who came in through the coal chute in 1954 before closing its doors in 1961.

At 2212 North 30th, a person identified as S. Popovich took out a permit to operate a moving picture show under the name **Crown Theater** from 1912 to 1915.

The Park Theater offered vaudeville in 1913 📷 TPL

The name changed to the **American Theater** in 1916 before closing in 1918. This later would be the site of Old Town Photo owned by Ron Karabaich.

Down the block, in 1915 the **Zelinski Theater** and store operated at 2118-20 North 30th St. in Old Town, across the street from the Spar Tavern. The Zelinski gave way to **My Favorite Theater** (aka **Favorite Theater**) for a few months in 1920. A new venture called the **Hollywood Theater** tried to make it go in 1922, but didn't last the year.

In a building constructed in 1888, where a child was born in 1893 in what was then Davidson's Drug Store, the **Rose Theater** opened in 1911 after being purchased by Robert McKinnell. The theater, located at 953-57 Tacoma Avenue South, closed in 1918, but McKinnell was not done with theaters. In 1920 he built a new theater at 514-16 South 11th and adapted the former name to create the **New Rose Theater** for this operation that would last until 1937.

Six decades after the screen had gone dark, the former theater was in the hands of jazz legend Red Kelly,

The New Rose Theater lasted until 1937 📷 TPL

whose jazz club was in an adjacent building on the corner of South 11th and Tacoma Avenue. The former Rose was in rough shape and draining Kelley's resources to the extent that hanging onto his club was in jeopardy. Fellow musicians held a fund-raising event and Kelly's club would survive, but the Rose building fell to the wrecking ball a month later.

In 1923, while operating the second version of the Rose, the McKinnell Brothers built the **Paramount** at 3816 North 26th St. The theater, which featured a Photoplay organ, opened with *Back Home and Broke* and lasted 10 years, despite having the patrons flee from a stink bomb in 1930 and suffering an arson fire in 1932. The **Orion Theater** had been the first theater in the Proctor District, occupying the corner site at 2602 North Proctor St. from 1914 to 1916.

While these houses were short-lived, longevity has reached historic proportions at the **Blue Mouse Theater** which was started in 1923. It was affectionately referred to as the **Blue Mouse Junior** at times to distinguish it from the Blue Mouse located downtown on Broadway. After circling through the names **Proctor Street Blue Mouse** (1925–27) **Proctor Theater** (1928–1978) and **Bijou Theater** (1978–1993) the cinema became the **Blue Mouse Theater** again in 1994. Read more about one of the longest continuously operating theaters in the country in a separate article in this chapter.

Moving to the south end, **The Movie** was built at 5042-46 Yakima Avenue in 1921. A year later, Inez B. Lyons purchased the theater and changed the name to **The Lyric**. With a seating for 250, the theater was run by Inez until it closed in 1927.

The emergence of movies attracted a wave of entrepreneurs, but many soon learned operating a theater was a tough business as witnessed by these houses

that didn't last more than a year. The **Isis Theater** at 3737 South Park Avenue (1915), the **Fern Theater** at 8401 South Park Avenue (1914), the **Bell Theater** at 4538 South M Street (1914), the **Ryan and Wooden Moving Picture Theater** at 3201 Portland Avenue (1913), the **Nickelodeon Theater** at 2305-07 Pacific Avenue (1913) and the **Majestic Theater** at the same address (1914). The **Gem Theater** made it a bit longer with a run from 1914 to 1915 at 3010 Portland Avenue.

At 4801-05 Yakima Avenue, the **Mission Theater** opened with seating for 500 on June 27, 1924. Five months later the theater was leased to Henry Berglund. A month later the name was changed to **Victory Theater.** Three years later the theater was sold and a pipe organ was installed at a cost of $15,000. In 1936 the name was changed to the **Capitol Theater.** In 1951 a bandit robbed the theater. After a 38-year run, the screen went dark for good in 1962.

In the 5400 block along South Tacoma Way there were a string of early theaters beginning with **Star Moving Picture Theater** in 1909 operated by John H. Marks. From 1910 to 1912 Radner R. Pratsch operated the **Idle Hour Theater.** In 1913 George W. Sauriol began a six-year run of the **Orpheum Theater** before converting the building to retail and apartments that bore his name into the mid-Seventies. The **Realart Theater**

This was the Paramount Theater 1923–33

The Realart Theater operated from 1919 to 1960

had the staying power others in that block lacked, opening in 1919 with seating for 488 and a nursery. It lasted until 1960.

Although the movie industry was still in the silent era and tame by almost any standards, there was concern among some factions that "clean pictures" were difficult to find. One such group organized themselves as the **Tacoma Educational & Amusement Co.** and opened up what was billed as "the first educational moving picture theatre in the United States" in July 1912. According to *The Tacoma Tribune*, the theater, located at 2711 Sixth Avenue, would show "a selection of educational, scientific and 'approved' photoplays, the latter running to comedy. No more *Dick Derringer's Defeat* or the *Boy Murderer's Revenge* sort of picture will be offered." Admission was five cents. In 1915 the "coming to the neighborhood of another show house forced the theater out of business for the want of sufficient patronage to pay expenses." As a religious-oriented entity, the theater was closed on Sundays, posing a further competitive disadvantage.

The new arrivals in the neighborhood played on Sunday, but were hardly more successful:

The **Royal Theater** occupied 2717 Sixth Avenue 1912–1913, then after a gap, its doors opened again as the **Lyceum Theater** 1915–1916 before giving way to a drug store and sanitarium. A block away at 2606 Sixth Avenue the **Washington Theater** operated 1913–1914 before a name change to the **Sunset Theater** 1915–1919, which was relinquished to **Everybody's Theater** 1920–1925 and a final effort was made in the name of the **Capitol Theater** with an emphasis on musical comedies 1926–1929. And yes, for those of you who have been paying attention, you correctly observed the Capitol name re-emerged in 1936 on Yakima Avenue and Bill Englehart's eventual hangout the Sunset would adopt that name in 1919. The aforementioned Victory Theater name would reappear at a downtown location, as would the Lyceum.

K Street, now Martin Luther King Jr. Way, featured a vibrant commercial district, including a number of early show houses. The **Thannhaeuser Theater** had a one-year run in 1911 at 1020 K Street. The **Aloha Theater** operated at 1010-12 K Street from 1914 to 1918. The **Vaudette Theater,** operated by Bert Bertleson, seated 225 and operated at 1110-12 K Street from 1911 to 1925. Several blocks south, at 1518-20 K St., the **Lincoln Theater** operated by Hans Torkelson (who also had the Park Theater) had

The Kay St. Theatre opened in 1924   ⊚ TPL

Crowd in front of renamed K St. Theatre in 1940   ⊚ TPL

seating for 300 from 1916 to 1931. **The New Lincoln Theater** opened in 1942 and was gone by 1945. The K Street Tabernacle took up residence for two years before **V-Deo Theater** opened in 1950, but was gone by 1953. A grocery store held forth until a 1977 fire took what was described as and "historic silent-films theater."

Farther south at 1821 K Street the **Alhambra** ran from 1915 to 1917. Beyond that, at 2152 K Street, the **Emerald Theater** had lasted only the year of 1914.

Back up on the corner of what is now 11th and MLK, the **Kay Street Theatre** opened in 1924 with the organist composing *The K Street March* for the event. With ample seating for 700 the theater showed its first "talkie" in 1929, by which time the name had been changed to the **K St. Theatre.** The theater endured a holdup in 1936. (It's a wonder any of these places survived for the robbers, bombers and firebugs that preyed on them.) The K St. Theater made it until 1955 – after having provided a backdrop for one of the great street gatherings in Tacoma history, when on July 3, 1940, thousands jammed K Street to celebrate the openings of both the first Narrows Bridge and McChord Field.

Post World War II era

In the years immediately following World War II, housing development surged westward and theater development followed. In 1949 the modern 600-seat **Narrows Theater** opened at 7116 Sixth Avenue with a twin bill, "Northwest Stampede" and "Give My Regards to Broadway." Twelve years after the Narrows closed in 1984, the songs of Broadway returned when **Tacoma Musical Playhouse** took up residence in 1996, then purchased the building in 2002. The relighting of the '40s era marquee provided a signal of survival rare for Tacoma's theaters.

Tacoma Little Theatre, which celebrates its 100th anniversary in 2018, has not wandered far from the site of its first productions. Known initially as the Tacoma Drama League, the community theater began in the Annie Wright Seminary gymnasium on a site now occupied by Stadium Thriftway in the triangle between North Sixth Avenue and Division. An early venue was the First Congregational Church at 209 South J Street. The home they now call their own was created from a converted automobile repair shop at 210 North I Street the organization acquired in 1940 and then expanded in 1950.

In what turned out to be a one-year run, the **Image Theater** occupied the former Defiance Grocery at 5102 North Pearl St., in 1971. The programming was an offering of film classics under the operation of Paul Doyle.

Drive-ins

Postwar America revolved around the automobile, and the theater-going experience would expectedly include doing so in a vehicle – whether it be a station wagon full of kids, a pickup backed up to the screen with viewers wrapped in blankets or those who were not concerned that they couldn't view the screen through steamed-up windows. The sequence of those scenarios more likely played out in reverse order.

Billed as "Tacoma's New Miracle of Entertainment," The **Star-Lite Park-in Theater** opened in 1948 at 8301 South Tacoma Way. The first twin-bill featured *Golden Earrings* starring Ray Milland and Marlene Dietrich and *Adventure Island* starring Rory Calhoun and Rhonda Fleming. Between a robbery in 1950 that netted $2,000 and another in 1963 that took $1,500 out of the coffers, the theater hosted drive-in sunrise services. The good and bad played out on and off the screen until 1996 when the theater closed, giving way to a swap meet that still occupies the site 20 years later.

Three nearby drive-ins that attracted motorized movie fans included: The **Tacoma Auto-View Drive-In,** located at 9901 South Tacoma Way, which opened in 1947 with *A Night in Casablanca* starring the Marx Brothers, and was destroyed by fire in 1948. The **Fife Drive-In Theater**, located at 1601 Goldau Rd., East, was built in 1950 by Mike Bavoric and W.R. Forman on 15 acres with a capacity of 600 cars. It closed in the mid-80s and was demolished in the early 90s to make way for an apartment complex. The **One Hundreth & Twelfth Drive-In Theater** opened in 1971 at 112th St. E. in Parkland and was demolished after closing in 1989.

The **Auto View Drive-in Theater** opened in 1950 on 15 acres at 1202 North Pearl St. and closed in 1986 so the land could be developed for condominiums. As we have witnessed, theaters seem to have been strangely vulnerable to robberies and other forms of damage. An incident in 1951 was bizarre and, considering the culprit being nine-years old, maybe the most poignant.

After escaping from Remann Hall detention center where he was being held for setting fires, the boy made his way to the Auto View on a Sunday afternoon and smashed windows at the ticket booth and projection room. He unreeled several hundred feet of film, but fortunately did not set the film on fire. That evening police nabbed him after he set two small fires on the fairways at Highlands Golf Club. He had stolen $6.50 from the change box at the theater. When caught, the money was recovered except for the 40 cents the nine-year-old had spent on candy and a soda at the golf club.

Multi-Screens

Before we circle back 15 years to acknowledge a theater that holds a special place in Tacoma's cinema history, the emergence of the multi-screen venues needs to be acknowledged. **Tacoma West Cinema,** located at 1802 South Mildred St., was the first up when Sterling Recreation Organization (SRO) built a three-screen theater with total seating for 1,000 in 1983. Five years later, the theater expanded to seven screens. By 1998 there were not enough collective faces in front of all those screens and James Center was without a movie house.

Concurrent with the Tacoma West Cinema, SRO launched a five-screen multiplex in 1983 called the **Tacoma South Cinema** at the Oak Plaza Shopping Center, 7601 South Hosmer St. The lights went out in 2002, but it passed along a bit of its legacy, donating

Like a ghost of the multiplex era, the closed theater looms over the vacant parking lot on South Mildred St. **BJ**

450 seats (blue, of course) to the Blue Mouse Theater in Proctor.

In 1988 the **Lincoln Plaza Cinema** opened with eight screens at 31 Montana Avenue. Four years later two robbers tied up workers and took off with the cash. Eight years after that the place was closed.

In what would become a sort of death spiral for mainstream movie houses in Tacoma, several multi-screen theaters swirled through venues and name changes before the musical chairs stopped and Tacoma had no houses showing first-run corporate releases.

In the Tacoma Central Shopping Center at 3102 South 23rd Street, Cineplex Odeon Theaters built a six-plex in 1990 called **Tacoma Central Theater.** With seating for 200 to 290 per screen the theater had a capacity of 1,500. In 2001 the theater was dark. A year later, **Galaxy 6** took over operation of the building. In 2009, this theater was closed and the Galaxy 6 moved to 2208 Mildred St. West, (the former home of the **Narrows Plaza 8 Theater,** built in 1983), changed its

name to the **Galaxy Narrows Theater** and closed in early 2013.

Now back to what was expected to be the future of theater-going when **Tacoma Mall Theater** opened in 1968 at 4302 Tacoma Mall Boulevard. Designed by architect George T. Nowak for Forman United Theaters, Inc., this would be the last single-screen theater built in Tacoma. It cost $1 million and it showed. Billed as "Elegance in Entertainment," its expansive lobby featured a contoured 72-foot-long walnut paneled snack bar – the longest on the West Coast – Belgian glass mirrored walls and four $6,000 imported, custom-made crystal chandeliers, each containing 3,250 clear crystal pendants. Plush red carpet covered the floor and, high above, recessed lighting gave off the illusion of stars.

Inside the auditorium 2,000 yards of red draw curtains lined the walls surrounding the 1,200 seats that were deeply upholstered and staggered so that every patron would have a clear view of the wall-to-wall, floor-to-ceiling screen. An opening night the likes of

The Tacoma Mall Theater opened in 1968 **TPL**

The spacious lobby featured crystal chandeliers **TPL**

which Tacoma hadn't seen in the 40 years since the Broadway Theater opened in the remodeled Tacoma Theatre, drew a sellout crowd and featured celebrities in evening dress. And yet, six years later the auditorium was divided to accommodate a second screen and the name was changed to the **Tacoma Mall Twin.** In 2002 the theater was demolished to make way for a store devoted to selling Krispy Kreme doughnuts.

When the Galaxy Narrows Theater closed in 2013 only two independent houses remained – The Blue Mouse in the Proctor District and the Grand Cinema downtown. Tacoma was without a mainstream movie theater for the first time in over 100 years.

The reappearance of a corporate theater chain in Tacoma came in 2015 when the Cinemark opened **Century Point Ruston and XD Theatre** as a nine-screen multiplex at Point Ruston – a $1 billion mixed-use development on the former Asarco copper smelter site. Each screen is viewed from steeply banked rows of plush reclining seats in auditoriums served with bright digital images and sound systems. Cinemark hopes the state-of-art sensory indulgences will make the theater-going experience competitive with all the entertainment gadgets people have in their own homes. And, as a century of our history has shown,

going to the movies opens up all sorts of possibilities – like meeting your future spouse or finding partners to start a rock n' roll band.

September 1, 1957

The Century opened at Point Ruston in 2015 BJ

The Blue Mouse

By Bill Evans

"You're kidding. They named a movie theater after a Mouse?" Yes, they sure did… a Blue Mouse!

On Tuesday evening, November 13, 1923, a prominent theater operator named John Hamrick did just that. It was on that date that Hamrick's Blue Mouse Theater had its Grand Opening at 2611 North Proctor Street. Other than for restoration or repairs the Blue Mouse has remained open every single evening since 1923. That's over 34,000 evenings! It is no wonder that the Proctor District Blue Mouse Theatre is one of the very oldest continuously operating movie theaters in the United States. Another interesting fact is that the theater is believed to have been named after one in Paris, France that Hamrick attended in 1919. Also, Hamrick had the great good fortune to meet up with an architect from London by the most unique and memorable name, Fitzherbert Leather. It was he who designed the "garden style arts and crafts" building which was constructed at a cost of $20,000.

Hamrick sold the Blue Mouse to Will Conner, another prominent theater operator, in 1927 and the name was changed to the Proctor Theater. Thirty-three years after having dedicated the Proctor district

Blue Mouse, John Hamrick died on November 30, 1956. Following another sale in 1978, the name was then changed to the Bijou Theater. In 1988 a woman named Shirley Mayo purchased the theater and ran it successfully until failing health, severe rheumatoid arthritis, forced her to sell the movie house in 1993. Understandably, Shirley wanted to return home to be with family in Arkansas. One local developer approached Mayo. He wanted to purchase the building, add a second floor and convert the property into office space. To her great credit, Shirley refused to let that happen. A plan of action was put together by several merchants, persuading a group of 17 friends to raise enough money, $140,000, to purchase the theater and then to refurbish it to its original 1923 charm.

That plan saved the theater, which regained the original Blue Mouse name in February 1994.

One other very fortunate reality for the Blue Mouse is that it is part of a walkable community, an urban village. Just the other evening, I made my way to Metropolitan Market from our apartment at Proctor Station. I passed by Rudy's, Walla Walla Clothing, Colors and the Pacific Northwest Shop before crossing North 27th Street, the Saturday home of the Proctor Farmers Market. I then passed Teaching Toys, the North End Tavern and La Fondita before my attention was drawn to the 25 Blue neon Mice scurrying across the marquee of the historic theater. They, also, have a story to tell. At the time of the community effort to save the Blue Mouse, I had asked friend and world renowned

The popular Proctor District venue was the Bijou Theater (1978-1993) before it reclaimed the Blue Mouse Theater name in 1994　TPL

Famed glass artist Dale Chihuly created the scampering blue "mouses" for the marquee

glass artist, Dale Chihuly, if he would make a signature piece of art for the theater. He came up with not one but 25 "signature pieces." Dale's first "public neon"!

In 2015, the manager of the theater, Sue Evans, came to the realization that she would have to take the theater into a new era, the digital age. "Go digital or go dark." The switchover was absolutely necessary but very expensive. Sue arranged with Kickstarter to manage a campaign to try to raise $75,000. To her great satisfaction, over 1,000 backers pledged over $84,000.

Many very good and interesting things continue to happen both at the theater and in the community of which the theater is a huge part. For example, on January 13, 2010 the Blue Mouse was placed on the National Register of Historic Places. Then there's every 2nd and 4th Saturday evening of the month when the Blue Mouse plays host, at midnight, to the crazy but entertaining Rocky Horror Picture Show. Concerts are also common. Students from a local high school,

Wilson, entertain the community with their "Show Choir! Jazz Choir! Soloists! Concerts." This building signifies living history and the beloved "Blue Mouse" continues on with sights set on its "just around the corner" hundredth birthday in 2023.

– Bill Evans has been a Proctor merchant for over 40 years and is a former Tacoma City Councilmember and Past-President of the Proctor District Association.

O n the evening of April 18, 2017, a caring cadre representing The Grand Cinema family – which consists of devoted patrons, administrative staff and volunteers – celebrated in the lower lobby of the theater located at 606 Fawcett Avenue in the Merlino Arts Center.

The celebration was for the 20th anniversary of the non-profit theater, an occasion acknowledged by the Tacoma City Council's issuance of a proclamation declaring "The Grand Cinema Day" and by a letter from Washington State Governor Jay Inslee citing the Grand's contribution to the community.

The Grand Cinema has firmly established itself as the South Sound's non-profit home for independent, foreign and local film – having drawn over two million customers through its red doors during the past 20 years. When its predecessor, a commercial theater named "Grand Cinema Theater" failed due to financial problems, The Grand Cinema was established as a non-profit organization legally defined as Grand Tacoma Cine Club.

The success has been built by a small group of community organizers and a large band of volunteers who, since 2006, have functioned under the leadership of Executive Director Philip Cowan. In that year, The Grand Cinema held its first annual Tacoma Film Festival and 72 Hour Film Festival.

The theater opened as a one-screen operation and soon expanded to three screens, then added a fourth screen in 2009. This growth came from sizable community donations and through even more extensive community support in 2013 when the Grand met the significant challenge of converting from 35mm print film to digital projection. Acoustical and aesthetic upgrades have been added to enhance the theater-going experience for regular movie patrons as well as those participating in film clubs and camps, educational programs, special night film series, awards parties and a variety of film festivals. The Grand Cinema proudly proclaims this unique programming is augmented by what is billed as the best popcorn in town, whose secret ingredient is rumored to be love.

The non-profit theater has attracted over two million customers as it celebrates its 20th anniversary　◎ BJ

Greetings from the Governor

April 18, 2017

I am pleased to extend warm greetings to all of those celebrating the Grand Cinema's 20 anniversary. Congratulations on this exciting milestone!

The Grand Cinema's 20th anniversary drew acknowledgements from the governor and City of Tacoma

A View Behind the Screen at The Grand Cinema

Philip Cowan, executive director of The Grand Cinema, provides insights into the operation of the independent non-profit art house as it celebrated its 20th anniversary in 2017.

Q: As an independent theater, what is the process for selecting films that you want to show at The Grand? How do you become aware of what films are available? Are all films screened before selection?

Philip Cowan

For the 10 years I've been at The Grand, I'm pretty much been the sole person to select films. In the first year I leaned a lot on others as I learned the industry (I was brought over because of my ability to run a business rather than for my knowledge of the film industry). Over time I learned how to compare what I like versus what the Grand audiences like. Mostly they are the same, but I'm trying to please them more than myself, though I do like to bring in films that push our audiences beyond their usual comfort zone from time to time.

I follow the industry in many different ways:

• A high percentage (maybe 80%?) of our films play at major film festivals before they hit cinemas theatrically. That gives me a chance to read their reviews and gauge audience reactions. In the case of the Sundance Film Festival, I attend that annually so I get to see about 40 new films each January via that.

• Reviews. There are reviews from film festivals, then later reviews from when they open theatrically. Because most of the films we play don't open across the nation all on one day as the biggest studio releases do, that gives some lead time to both read reviews (*Rotten Tomatoes* is the best aggregator of reviews), but it also gives us a chance to see attendance when a film opens in New York and Los Angeles. It is surprisingly accurate. If a film bombs with attendance in New York/Los Angles in week one, Tacoma also isn't likely to be interested in the film. I try to focus on films that get better than a 70% rating on *Rotten Tomatoes*.

• Every Friday I read the reviews of new films in the *New York Times*. Since most films open there first, it gives me a chance to learn about a film the moment it comes out. Films can often take a month to go from NY/LA to Tacoma, so there is some time to search for additional reviews when a film of interest pops up.

• Distributors (more later on that too): Distributors have track records and if a film gets sold to one of our top distributors like Sony Pictures Classics, Roadside or Fox Searchlight, I can bet that it is both a quality film and likely fits our audience. If I've never heard of the distributor, there is probably a reason the bigger distributors passed on the film, though I still look into it if it seems interesting.

• I listen to a podcast on *Indiewire* that talks about Independent films. *Film Comment* is a good source for films that debut abroad at International Festivals.

• I also see a few dozen films at the Seattle International Film Festival each spring.

Overall I probably only see about a third of our films before we play them. There are just too many films to see, and if I can read enough about a film, that is a quicker process than watching them. You have to remember that for every film we play at The Grand, there were probably three I saw that I chose not to play, so it can be quite labor intensive. Most theaters our size have someone with a higher percentage of their job dedicated to film selection, but for me as executive director, it is just one piece of a much bigger role, so I can't see them all. Honestly, the bigger the film is, the less likely I'll have seen it – those films are often obvious to play. It is the smaller films that don't have a strong distributor behind a marketing campaign that need more care and attention in the decision-making.

For the films I do screen ahead of time, most are via a secured link online. Larger releases have pre-screenings for cinemas in Seattle so I go up there maybe once a month to see a film that is on the bubble of whether or not to play.

Q: Once you have identified films that you want to show, do you have to bid on them? How do other theaters in the marketplace impact the selection process?

For the most part, The Grand has a strong enough reputation so that if we want a film, we get it. The trickier part is getting the timing to line up between The Grand and the distributor. I may have an opening one week, but not the following week. The distributor may not be ready to give it to us until the following week, but we may already be committed to another film then. Booking films is like a big jigsaw puzzle. Generally films open in New York/Los Angeles on day one, then come to Seattle one or two weeks later. Sometimes we can open the same date as Seattle, but more frequently we are one or two weeks behind them. Distributors for smaller films roll out their films slowly because they hope for strong word of mouth. They don't have the money to market them equally in New York to Seattle to Tacoma, so strong reaction out of Seattle or on radio (NPR stories help us a great deal) help the film open stronger here.

A few years ago when the multiplexes in central Tacoma were open, there was an industry standard that between the three of us, a film could only play at one location. That meant in the films that overlapped markets, we'd compete for a film. Because of that, I often didn't try to get a film from a big distributor because I know we were likely to lose out. Once they went under, however, things changed. For several years we were the only first-run cinema in Tacoma so we could get anything we wanted. We still didn't go after big mainstream films, but films that fit The Grand like *The King's Speech* were much easier to get. Before that I'd be sweating out decisions by distributors. Now with the new waterfront cinema, there is no rule that relegates films to only one cinema at a time. Part of that is just changes within the film industry. There have been lawsuits in other states where cinemas took distributors to court over exclusive agreements with the larger cinema chains. It was proven to be anti-competitive to completely shut out independent theaters so now distributors are much more willing to play films at nearby locations.

Overall, we know what our audience likes so we go after those films. We don't need to play *Star Wars* because our audience can easily see that at other theaters. Most of the other films we play, if we didn't play them, they would bypass Tacoma completely so we just let some films pass on to them so we can play other limited releases.

Q: Do you look for a certain mix of styles in the shows that you want to present at any given time? For example, do you look for a mix of lighter and more serious films among the four or five films being offered each week?

A lot of the timing on films is predetermined by when the film is available. Ideally I'd like to have a diverse set of films at any given time, but sometimes we need to take a film at precise dates or risk never playing it at all. We do try not to open two foreign films on the same day or two documentaries. They'd compete

against each other too much and neither would do as well as if we opened them in separate weeks. So ideally yes, we do try to get a good mix, but sometimes the timing isn't as precise as we'd like it.

Q: There have been favorite films that have run for weeks. What determines how long a film will run? Do you have to rebid to keep a film each week?

Films throughout the cinema world stay in a cinema as long as they are doing well. Every Monday morning we rank the films from the Friday–Sunday weekend from highest grossing to lowest grossing film. There is a rough threshold of about $2,000 gross for a film that provides a guideline. A film that grosses above $2,500 is definitely going to stay for another week. One that grosses $1,600 or less is pretty likely to leave. Films in between could go either way depending on what our other commitments are in the coming week. So when we schedule films weeks in advance, we don't always know what film they will replace, just that they'll replace something.

Sometimes we get to a Monday morning only to realize that, for example, all our films did great but we are also committed to open a new film on Friday. Depending on the films involved, we might try to push back the film one more week. Or we might keep all the current films but on an adjusted number of screenings so that the new film can come in. Distributors count on reliability on timing so it isn't good practice to change dates on films if we can help it.

So if a film comes and goes after only one week, that means no one came to see it. I try to keep films a second week when at all possible, but if the attendance isn't there in the first week, it is only going to go down from there in week two.

The industry standard is that if a film is doing well, you don't drop it. That makes sense for both us and the distributor. We don't want to drop a film that people want to see, and the distributor wants us to keep a film as long as we are making them money. To drop a film too early is to jeopardize our relationship with a distributor and would most definitely hurt us the next time we ask for a film.

Q: How do you decide what films to show for the one-time events, such as Tuesday nights?

This is both an issue of film popularity and timing. Some films just don't have an audience to support them for an entire week. That is the prime reason for starting the Tuesday Film series because it allows us to bring in so many films that otherwise wouldn't have played in Tacoma. On the other side of it, sometimes, particularly during "Awards Season" in December to February, we may want to play a film for a week, but the other films are so strong that there isn't room to open another film. The Tuesday series provides an outlet to at least play the film for a day so we didn't have to pass on it completely.

Q: From a logistical standpoint, what is the difference between the film and digital eras? How many canister reels were used in the film era versus the current use of DVDs? If there were multiple reels, how did the film move from one projector to the next without a break in the action?

In days of 35mm prints, the logistics of getting films were much tougher. A small film might only have 50 prints to go around the country so you had to wait in line to get it. Now a distributor can just copy the film on a hard drive and ship it wherever they want. They still have an expense involved to do so, but it is nothing like the cost of thousands of dollars to strike an additional 35mm print.

35mm prints generally came in two huge canisters, or more for a really long film. Projectionists would then take each of these and build it into the full film. Simplistically, we would load the films onto big platters, then tape (splice) each film segment together to make one long string of 35mm images. Nowadays, we get the hard drive, copy it onto each projector and we are pretty close to being ready to go.

Within the industry most films come to us encrypted so that if one is intercepted, a film pirate won't end up with a playable version of a big film like *Star Wars* before it comes out. Each theater gets a digital key that opens a precise film for a precise set of dates on only that theater's projectors. Without the key, you can't watch the film. And even with the key, it won't work on projectors other than the one for which it is issued.

We try to prescreen all of our films a day or two before they open so we make sure they work properly. Sometimes we have to wait for the encrypted key to open before doing the test screening. For example, we may be opening a film on Friday, but the key doesn't activate until Friday morning at midnight. That doesn't give us long to problem-solve if something doesn't work, but luckily such problems are rare.

Q: What significant changes have occurred in the business in your experience, and what changes do you anticipate in the operation of The Grand?

Easily the biggest issue in my tenure was the switch to digital. Very small theaters in rural America often couldn't afford the $70k cost to upgrade each screen. The looming problem is the question of how long our digital projectors, which are essentially computers, will last. People can type away on a personal computer for a decade if everything goes well, but sometimes they die a few years after purchase. Having to go through another $70k per screen fundraising campaign every decade is kind of a nightmare scenario if you have to do it for eternity. The old 35mm projectors were like old cars: you had to do maintenance and they'd break down occasionally, but if you put a few new parts in, the engine could more or less function like new. Computers don't work the same way.

Threats to The Grand would come from mainstream theaters that had a lot of screens. Every screen a cinema adds increases the likelihood that they'll be playing art-house fare. If they have nine screens, Hollywood big releases can keep them full. If they go up to 15 screens, they start spreading themselves thinner and they'd be dipping into more "Grand" type films. So my hope for the future of The Grand is to not have another big chain move into Tacoma. Our big 5 to 10 films a year provide the revenue to support all the smaller films we play. If we didn't have as much attendance from those top films, the entire art-house cinema model would quickly be in jeopardy.

Philip Cowan profile

Philip Cowan, with a degree in finance and a masters in international management, transitioned from a business career in his native Texas to an eight-year management position with the Tacoma Rainiers. Stints as a volunteer and a board member led to his position as executive director at the Grand in 2006.

"I was hired for my business background, but learning how to select films that fit our audiences is easily the most rewarding part of my job."

U.S. MILITARY TOURNAMENT
TACOMA STADIUM JULY 24-30

TWO THOUSAND PICKED
UNITED STATES REGULARS

4 U.S. MILITARY BANDS

BROADSWORD & MOUNTED
COMBATS - WALL SCALING

THRILLING FEATS
OF HORSEMANSHIP

THOUSANDS OF DOLLARS
IN CASH PRIZES

TACOMA HIGH SCHOOL AND ONLY PUBLIC SCHOOL STADIUM
IN THE WORLD. SEATING CAPACITY 30.000

This poster (1910) and one on page 160 (1911) promoted events at what would be named Stadium Bowl WSHS

D RATES ON ALL RAILROADS

UNDER AUSPICES TACOMA CHAMBER OF COMMERCE

Other Venues in Review

When it came to people gathering in Tacoma, the biggest crowds and some of the most significant civic and entertainment events have occurred in venues outside the theaters. More than 150 names are represented in Tacoma's historic theater scene and fewer than half a dozen remain active today. By contrast, of the 20 or so notable venues reviewed here, nearly all of them are still attracting people through their doors and turnstiles.

In separate articles, we cover the **Elks Temple,** located at Broadway & South 7th, built in 1916; the **Washington National Guard Armory,** built in 1909 at South 11th & Yakima; the **Stadium Bowl,** dedicated as Tacoma Stadium in 1910, located adjacent to Stadium High School at Stadium Way; **Lincoln Bowl,** first built as Lincoln Field in 1920, rebuilt as Lincoln Bowl in 1948 and further renovated in 2011, located at 701 South 36th St., and **University of Puget Sound Memorial Fieldhouse,** built in 1949, located at 3326 North 11th St., and the **Auditorium Building,** built in 1922 at 1308-10 Fawcett Avenue.

The **Masonic Temple,** built in 1927, located at 47 St. Helens, followed the First Masonic Temple, for which President Theodore Roosevelt laid the cornerstone at 734-36 St. Helens in May, 1903. It was demolished in 1929 to make way for the new Medical Arts Tower (now the Tacoma Municipal Building). After wearing the names of the Helig Theater, the Temple Theater and the Saint Helens Convention Center, the Masonic Temple is now the Landmark Convention Center.

Here is a review of other venues, some long gone, some converted to other uses, some the centerpieces of Tacoma's entertainment scene.

Aside from Stadium Bowl in its prime, the **Tacoma Dome** can gather the most people for the widest variety of events among all Tacoma venues. Able to seat up to 23,000 for concerts, it is the largest wooden dome structure by capacity in the world. Designed by architects McGranahan and Messenger, the Dome opened in April 1983 and has since hosted events ranging from concerts to basketball, hockey and soccer to motocross to figure skating to wrestling. Owned by the City of Tacoma and located adjacent to I-5 at 2727 East D St., the Tacoma Dome is a distinctive landmark on the Tacoma skyline. Inside, the neon sculpture designed by Stephen Antonakos survives as a reminder of how a community can pretty much tear itself apart over a work of art. The installation remains despite petitions and efforts to recall City Council members in a 1984 effort to have it removed.

Cheney Stadium was constructed in 42 days in response to an offer by the San Francisco Giants to move their Triple-A affiliate to Tacoma if the city could open the stadium for the beginning of the 1960 baseball season. Wooden grandstand seats from Seals Stadium in San Francisco were moved to Tacoma. With seating for 6,000, the stadium, located at 2502 S. Tyler St., has hosted Pacific Coast League teams since its opening, many of those decades under the general management of indomitable promoter Stan Naccarato. The stadium is named for Ben Cheney, a prominent businessman who was another strong supporter of Tacoma sports. In 2009 the City of Tacoma invested in a $30 million renovation of the ballpark which hosted the Pacific Coast League All-Star game in 2017.

Cheney Stadium was remodeled in 2009   BJ

The **Greenwich Coliseum** was built in 1926 at 407 South 13th St. In the 1930s, the the arena and ballroom offered a wide variety of activities with wrestling on Monday, boxing on Thursday, dancing on Friday and Saturday. In 1940, the structure became the **Coliseum Bowling Palace** and hosted decades of bowlers until closing in 1972. The building was demolished in 1975 and is now the site of the Downtown YMCA.

For five years, from 1890 to 1895, the **Tacoma Speeding Park** was the center of horse racing in the region. The park was also occasionally used for the County Fair and other activities but horse racing was by far the most popular event. The site was also known as the Tacoma Driving Park, or simply the North End Race Track.

The race track sat on 80 acres, from N. 14th St. to N. 28th St., from N. Union Ave. to N. Monroe St. The grandstand was located at North 25th and North Washington Streets. The track was a one-mile-long oval and 60-feet wide. The grandstand could hold 4,000 spectators. The notorious Harry Morgan leased the site, which was designated as "School Land," from the state of Washington.

Morgan, Tacoma's boss gambler and all-around vice king, owned the Theatre Comique on Pacific Avenue. He began construction of the race track in 1890. He financed the project to replace the Tacoma Driving Park in Tacoma's South End, which closed in 1888. The project cost Morgan more than $200,000. Historian Herbert Hunt noted that "Morgan had made much money but he also had spent it." The cost of the race track was one of the reasons that Morgan's fortune was not as large as expected when he died in 1890.

Morgan never got to see the new track in operation. He died on April 26th and the track opened July 1, 1890, presenting four days of racing to celebrate the Fourth of July. Martin Dillon, a Morgan crony and the chief of

Metro Parks – Crowd-pleasing Activities and Solitude

The City of Tacoma established a parks district as part of the 1880 charter and, in 1907, formed a separate entity that is now known as Metro Parks Tacoma. The organization owns and operates nearly 200 parks and recreation facilities extending from Browns Point in Northeast Tacoma to Northwest Trek Wildlife Park in Eatonville. No other venues offer such a range of activities, from team sports to large crowd events to family picnics to concerts to playtime to quiet strolls.

As the founding force in Tacoma's development, the Tacoma Land Company donated sites for the key elements it felt would make Tacoma a great city in the West. Wright Park, named for the TLC president, is a 29-acre site located at 6th Avenue and I Street that fits that goal – an arboretum of over 700 mature trees, surrounding a lake, play area and a Victorian-style conservatory built in 1907. Established in 1886, the park has attracted crowds for concerts and festivals while as serving a green oasis for quiet escape from the bustling area surrounding it.

Heading west straight across town on 6th Avenue, Titlow Beach park was established in the 1920s on the site of a former resort hotel. In 1955, a large pool

was installed that was the site for swimming competitions as well as recreation for thousands of Tacomans until it was closed in 2013 and turned into a sprayground site. In 1963, 111 contestants were drawn to the park for a world octopus wrestling event. Extremely low tides draw hundreds of people to probe the exposed tide pools.

While the two parks noted above are among many of Metro Parks' recreational assets, Point Defiance Park and Zoo is rated as one of the finest urban parks in the country. Originally a military reservation, the 702-acre site is situated on the Northwest tip of Tacoma. The park is lined with beaches, covered with forest through which trails and Five Mile Drive weave, and features ornamental gardens and the Japanese style Pagoda – which, beginning in 1914, was the streetcar station. The zoo was founded in 1905 and the aquarium followed 20 years later.

Festivals have attracted throngs to the park, be it Zoolights during the winter holidays or events such as shown in the above picture when an estimated crowd of 30,000 turned out on July 16, 1939 to watch the Golden Jubilee Water Carnival.

police, took over the lease from Morgan's estate. He named it Morgan's Memorial Speeding Park in his honor, but the name did not last.

The lease passed to a group of local racing fans who formed the Tacoma Speeding & Exhibition Association. Local real estate investors John S. Baker and Stuart Rice were key players as was smelter owner William R. Rust.

Grand plans were made to make the track an important West Coast venue, and some improvements were made. However, it too could not make it through the financial crisis of the mid 1890s. The last major races were held in 1895. The 1896 Sanborn Map of Tacoma shows the race track as abandoned and "seldom used."

The Tacoma Speeding Park was no more by 1899. The state of Washington decided that the School Land Second Addition was no longer in a rural area. The land was platted and put up for sale. Soon the land was covered with housing in the growing North End.

The **King Roller Rink,** also know as the **King Arena,** was built at 2707-13 Pacific Ave. in 1931. With a white maple flooring, there were over 800 pairs of skates available for renting. The Arena Athletic Club presented wrestling and boxing matches on a weekly basis. The building is now a warehouse with the address 2705 Pacific Ave.

The **Tacoma Ice Palace,** built at 3801 South Union Ave., in 1946 featured cream colored concrete blocks and a bowstring roof span of 162 feet, which was the second-largest in the Northwest at the time. An estimated 15 to 18 tons of what was called "Pele's hair" (rock wool) was spun from Tacoma Smelter slag to insulate the sub-floor beneath the ice. This provided 14,400 square feet of skating area, ample room for 500 skating couples.

The first Tacoma Rockets pro hockey team of the Pacific Coast League played its first game at the arena on October 19, 1946. The team folded in May 1953. Professional wrestling was a regular feature. (See Bill Baarsma's memories of the big 1952 showdown between Tacoma's Frank Stojack and the Masked Marvel.) In 1955, the facility was renamed the Acme Storage Co., and used for grain storage. That operation ended with a fire later that year. By 1962 the expansive site was used as a go-kart track.

Another conversion took place in 1963 when it was renamed the **Tacoma Sports Arena.** With a brand-new dance floor, roller derby and professional short-track indoor motorcycle racing were part of the entertainment menu along with rock n' roll shows that included The Wailers, a Battle of the Bands between the Sonics and the Galaxies and an appearance in 1965 by James Brown and the Flames. In 1982 the arena became the Players & Spectators video gaming center, an operation that closed in 1986 after a partial roof collapse. The building still exists and is in commercial use.

The decorative expo structure lasted from 1891–98   ⊙ **TPL**

The **Exposition Building** opened in 1941 at 1616-32 East 26th Street and was used as a Boeing plant during World War II. It was named for the original **Western Washington Industrial Exposition Building** that opened at 714 North Tacoma Avenue in 1891 and was destroyed by fire in 1898.

The **Bicentennial Building** opened a week before the Fourth of July in 1976. It was the only building on the West Coast built in honor of the nation's Bicentennial. Renamed the **Tacoma Convention Center** in 1992, it was purchased from the City of Tacoma by the adjacent Hotel Murano in 2010. By then, the City of Tacoma had built the new **Convention Center** at 1500 Broadway in 2004.

One of the busiest venues for entertainment is the Puyallup Tribe's **Emerald Queen Casino**, built adjacent to I-5 between Tacoma and Fife in 2004. The new entertainment center replaced the original casino built in 1996, located in a paddle-wheel riverboat and adjacent land-based structure on the Blair Waterway at the Port of Tacoma.

Nearly a century earlier, large crowds of Tacomans had ridden the street car to Point Defiance to watch events ranging from rowing races to beauty contests. Archival photos show people swarming over the Point Defiance Boathouse & Pavilion as far back as 1903. That structure was demolished in 1933. A second pavilion was built in units between 1919 and 1925 next to the original pavilion. Converted into an aquarium in 1935, that structure was burned by arson in 1974. A third pavilion opened in 1940 and in 1984 was also burned by arson. The current pavilion opened in 1988.

The **Scottish Rite Cathedral** built in 1922 was designed to "follow closely the ancient architecture of King Solomon." A number of concerts, balls and conventions were held in the facility located at 5 South G Street, but its most notable event was the appearance in June 1923 by Sir Arthur Conan Doyle, a writer and physician who created the character Sherlock Holmes. Billed as a "spiritualist lecturer" and criminologist, Doyle arrived at a time when Tacoma authorities wondered if he might be able to solve the mysterious disappearance of a married couple. He said that was outside his skill set, but might have gotten story ideas when the vanished wife was believed to have been disposed of in the kitchen stove and the husband had vanished without a trace. Doyle did dispel rumors of the time that Sherlock Holmes was dead as a fictional character. On the contrary he proclaimed, "It is the only means I have of making a living" and he was continuing to write stories about the famous sleuth and his assistant, Dr. Watson. "No, Sherlock Holmes is not dead." So true, nearly a century later.

Other Fraternal Venues

In the early part of the last century, a number of venues were built as social and entertainment centers for various fraternal and ethnic groups. These include **Normanna Hall,** built in 1923 at 1502 Martin Luther King Jr. Way to serve the Norwegian community. The name of the winner of the Lutefisk Eating Contest in October 1940 is now a mystery.

Slavonian Hall, located at 2306 North 30th St., was dedicated in 1907. *A Fish Story*, the sculpture by Larry Anderson that stands in front of the hall celebrates the Croatian immigrant community that was prominent in Old Town. The hall was home to the **Tacoma Little Theater** group from 1933–39, before that acting company found a permanent home at 210-12 North I St.

Valhalla Hall was dedicated in 1922 to serve the Swedish community at 1216 (now) Martin Luther King Jr. Way. Booker T. Washington and Dr. W.E.B. DuBois addressed the local NAACP in 1913.

Swiss Hall, located at 1902-04 Jefferson and dedicated in 1913, was sold to the University of Washington

Tacoma in 1992. A year later, Gayl Bertagni, Bob Hill and Jack McQuade leased the first level and created The Swiss Restaurant and Pub. Known affectionately as "The Swiss," the venue remains as one of the most significant music scenes in the South Sound. Tacoma artist Dale Chihuly left a Venetian Glass exhibit at the Swiss in 1994, where it is still on display as "a permanent loan."

When it was built in 1908, the **Eagles Lodge,** located at 1305-07 Fawcett Avenue, was directly across the street from the Germania Hall. After that venue burned down in 1922, the Auditorium replaced it. The Eagles Lodge was expanded in 1957, but, in an abandoned state, was demolished in 2007 after the roof collapsed.

The **Odd Fellows Hall** was built at 602 Fawcett Avenue in 1925. Singers Paul Robeson (1948) and Fats Domino (1956) performed in the hall many years before Paul Merlino purchased the building in 1983 and renamed the building the Merlino Art Center in honor of his parents. The Grand Cinema opened in 1995 on the Fawcett entrance and Tacoma City Ballet occupies the classically appointed Jan Collum Ballroom on the Sixth Avenue level.

The Pythian Temple, built at 924-26 Broadway in 1907 as the Knights of Pythias, Commencement Lodge No. 7, replaced the first Pythian Temple which was built on the same site in 1884. Designed by Frederick Heath, the Temple features an ornate stonework façade and a two-story meeting hall highly decorated in original woodwork, plaster and murals. The exterior north wall has ghost images of advertisement murals dating back to the building's first years. The plaque on the sidewalk in front of the building commemorates George Francis Train's famous around-the-world adventure that began and ended at this site in 1890.

The original ornate meeting hall has survived for 110 years TPL/TSC

1

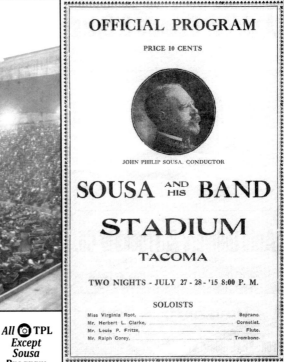

OFFICIAL PROGRAM

PRICE 10 CENTS

JOHN PHILIP SOUSA, CONDUCTOR

SOUSA AND HIS BAND

STADIUM

TACOMA

TWO NIGHTS - JULY 27 - 28 - '15 8:00 P. M.

SOLOISTS

Miss Virginia Root, _____ Soprano.
Mr. Herbert L. Clarke, _____ Cornetist.
Mr. Louis P. Fritze, _____ Flute.
Mr. Ralph Corey, _____ Trombone.

2   TSC

1&2) Cars encircled the field when Sousa performed at Stadium Bowl in 1915; 3) 1925 concept to cover Stadium Bowl; 4) Western singer and movie actor Gene Autry and his horse Champion at UPS Memorial Fieldhouse in 1949; 5) L-R: President John Kennedy, PLU President Robert Mortvedt, Senator Warren Magnuson and Senator Henry Jackson. A crowd of 25,000 jammed into Cheney Stadium to hear the president on September 27, 1963

THE TACOMA NEWS T

Would Convert Stadium Into Greatest Auditorium

3

5

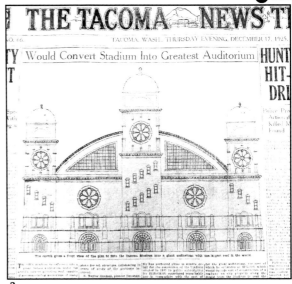

4

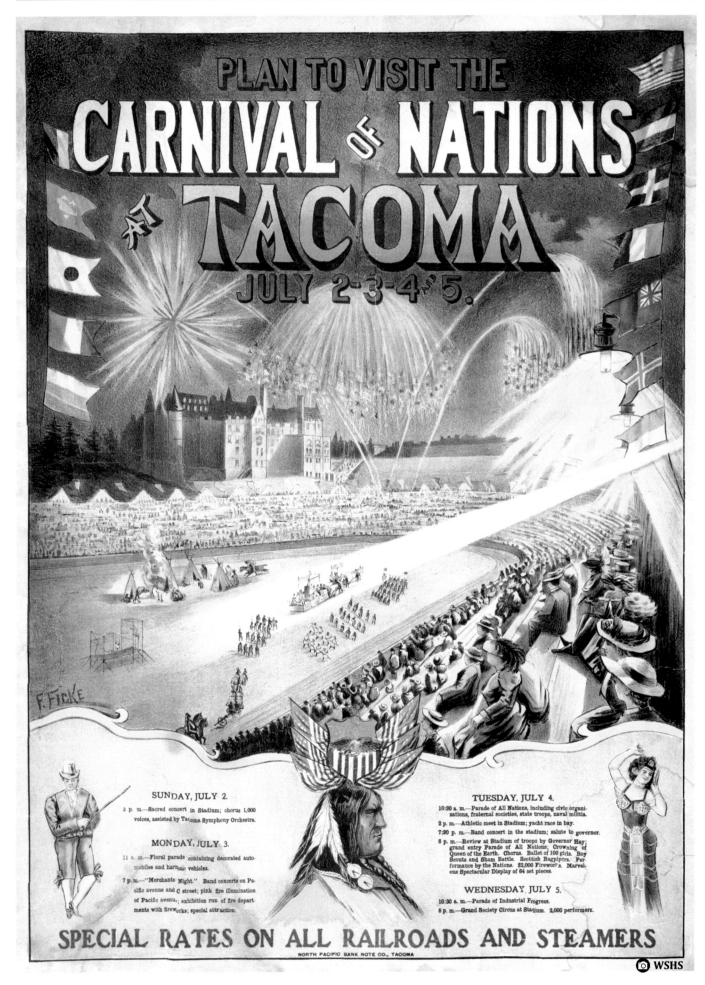

Legendary Duty for The Armory

If a building could earn medals for varied service, the brick façade of the Washington National Guard Armory would be as emblazoned as a career general's chest. With the stature of a fortress crowned with crenelated parapets and a tower the likes of which could allow a king to survey his domain, the Armory has posed proudly on the corner of Yakima Avenue and South Eleventh Street since it was dedicated on January 1, 1909.

Designed by Ambrose Russell and Everett Babcock, the Armory stood back to back with the Pierce County Court House for 50 years, presenting as striking a dynamic architectural pairing as any site in Tacoma's history. After the Court House (built in 1893) was demolished in 1959 (historians' heartbreak), the Armory soldiered on with its distinctive street presence and hosted a vast array of activities inside its ornate brick walls.

Over a span of 100 years, the facility was operated with a curious mix of building management. The Armory served as a military facility complete with cannons and munitions at the ready for generations of National Guard members drilling to deal with civil disorder and, periodically, to be called up for war. All the while, the widest range of community related activities drew Tacomans into the expansive drill hall.

The parade of events and uses for which it has been used span from rose shows to temporary jail facilities. In between were home shows, high school dances and graduations, rock n' roll concerts, dog shows, auto shows, Golden Gloves boxing championships, religious revivals, wrestling matches, weddings, roller derbies, orchestra and theatrical performances and speeches that filled the place to the rafters by presidents William Howard Taft, Woodrow Wilson, Harry Truman, Richard Nixon, and the Crown Prince of Norway.

The building went through periodic remodels, including the removal of a drop ceiling to expose an intricate steel truss system holding up the vaulted roof 40 feet above 20,000 square feet of polished hardwood drill hall space. The horse stables had long ago been abandoned, the military equipment and uniforms changed over the decades and in 2011 the National Guard determined they were done with their home after 102 years and put it on the market. Two years later, the Guard found a buyer in Fred Roberson, a prominent redeveloper of historic Tacoma properties. It was as if the the cavalry bearing an historic preservation banner had arrived to save the day – or, in this case, to save one of Tacoma's most distinctive venues.

The Armory and the Pierce County Courthouse formed this imposing streetscape image until the latter was demolished in 1959   ⊙ TPL

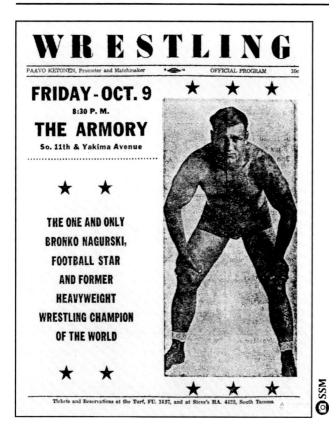

WRESTLING

PAAVO KETONEN, Promoter and Matchmaker   OFFICIAL PROGRAM   10c

FRIDAY - OCT. 9
8:30 P. M.

THE ARMORY
So. 11th & Yakima Avenue

★   ★

THE ONE AND ONLY
BRONKO NAGURSKI,
FOOTBALL STAR
AND FORMER
HEAVYWEIGHT
WRESTLING CHAMPION
OF THE WORLD

★   ★

Tickets and Reservations at the Turf, FU. 1437, and at Steve's HA. 4423, South Tacoma

SSM

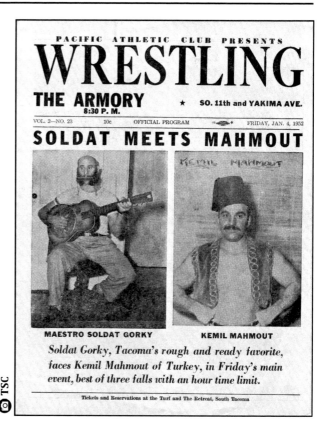

PACIFIC ATHLETIC CLUB PRESENTS

WRESTLING

THE ARMORY   ★   SO. 11th and YAKIMA AVE.
8:30 P. M.

VOL. 2—NO. 23   10c   OFFICIAL PROGRAM   FRIDAY, JAN. 4, 1952

SOLDAT MEETS MAHMOUT

MAESTRO SOLDAT GORKY   **KEMIL MAHMOUT**

Soldat Gorky, Tacoma's rough and ready favorite, faces Kemil Mahmout of Turkey, in Friday's main event, best of three falls with an hour time limit.

Tickets and Reservations at the Turf and The Retreat, South Tacoma

TSC

A 1947 Veterans Day ceremony was part of the military activities at the Armory

Richards Studio, Tacoma

TPL

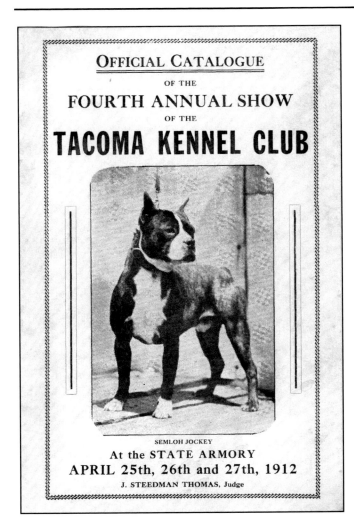

OFFICIAL CATALOGUE

OF THE

FOURTH ANNUAL SHOW

OF THE

TACOMA KENNEL CLUB

SEMLOH JOCKEY

At the STATE ARMORY

APRIL 25th, 26th and 27th, 1912

J. STEEDMAN THOMAS, Judge

1955   25c

OFFICIAL PROGRAM

Tacoma Athletic Commission

GOLDEN GLOVES

7th Annual   **Tacoma Armory**

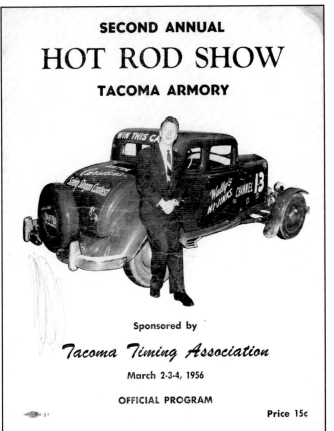

SECOND ANNUAL

HOT ROD SHOW

TACOMA ARMORY

Sponsored by

Tacoma Timing Association

March 2-3-4, 1956

OFFICIAL PROGRAM

Price 15¢

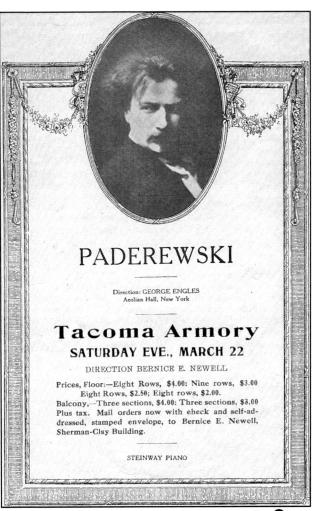

PADEREWSKI

Direction: GEORGE ENGLES
Aeolian Hall, New York

Tacoma Armory

SATURDAY EVE., MARCH 22

DIRECTION BERNICE E. NEWELL

Prices, Floor:—Eight Rows, $4.00; Nine rows, $3.00
Eight Rows, $2.50; Eight rows, $2.00.
Balcony,—Three sections, $4.00: Three sections, $3.00
Plus tax. Mail orders now with check and self-ad-
dressed, stamped envelope, to Bernice E. Newell,
Sherman-Clay Building.

STEINWAY PIANO

The array of programs indicates the wide range of events that have been held in the past 100 years   *All* ⊚ **TSC**

Roberson Brings New Life to the Old Armory

Fred Roberson was first drawn to the century old Armory by its iconic architecture. Looking at its arrow slit windows, parapets, and projecting bartizans he proclaimed, "Doesn't every man want to own a castle?"

Beyond such romantic notions, Fred's real attraction to this building is that it possessed everything that draws him to a project: historic relevance, robust engineering, and understandably, a compelling price. It was too tempting and unique of a challenge for him to pass up when he worked out a deal with the state of Washington for $950,000 in July, 2013. But ultimately, at his core, Fred saw this as a further opportunity to preserve and improve the city he loves, Tacoma. One of his primary agendas for the building is to develop a museum component featuring both significant American military ventures and Tacoma historical artifacts.

Fred has likely further invested more than twice what he paid for the landmark building. He has replaced the bulk of the old plumbing (which includes all of the radiators in the building), and the majority of the wiring. Every ceiling on the commercial level will be demolished and resurfaced. A saving grace is that the building's seismic and fire-suppression systems have been updated. A lot of the work is reclaiming order from the labyrinth of rooms that were created over the past 100 years. Brick walls have been exposed, wood floors have been discovered under commercial vinyl tile. Fred also created a 3,000-square-foot event space (the Roosevelt Room) for weddings, fundraisers, auctions, and other gatherings of up to 200 people. As he has done for decades, Fred's imaginative adaptive re-use of historic properties is being applied to the Armory and the community is the benefactor.

As he recalled his personal event experiences in the building, dating back years, he realized that a primary goal would have to be to preserve the community's availability to the expansive drill hall. The Broadway Center for the Performing Arts was the ideal partner to manage such events and that relationship has grown to the extent he will eventually gift the building to that organization.

In BCPA's hands his grandchildren's kids might go see the silent speed of inline skaters racing on the 20,000-square-feet of polished hardwood floors, or a concert or an exhibition or any activity that can draw community together.

Fred Roberson views the expansive drill hall 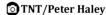 TNT/Peter Haley

The distinctive architectural features remain in good condition, while an interior space has been converted into the Roosevelt Room event space

Tacoma Elks Lodge

By Tim Hills

The historic Tacoma Elks Lodge, at Broadway and South 7th Street, has always been a showpiece. From its debut in 1916, it was meant to impress all who encountered it, inside and out. Even in its recent abandoned, decomposing state, the building still retains much of its glory; the graffiti throughout its interior only adds to its epic quality. Long a Tacoma landmark, the Elks Lodge's significance and the fond memories it conjures up rightly center on the fraternal group for which it was built. But it has had other notable lives, too, and soon will begin yet another.

With its beautiful, classic halls, auditoriums and other gathering spaces, the Elks Lodge has been the scene of many entertaining events, both for private and public audiences. It is certainly worth noting that the original founders of the national Elks organization were a small, convivial group of New York City actors, musicians, composers and producers working in the theaters of Broadway and off-Broadway during the mid-1860s. In 1867, these men, who dubbed themselves the Jolly Corks, soon were meeting with regularity on Sundays – which by New York law were meant to be dry – to enjoy one another's company, as well as some beer they had stashed the night before. In the months following, more serious, civic-minded professionals joined the ranks and reshaped the loose arrangement into the Benevolent and Protective Order of Elks in February 1868. As part of this process, the original "Corks" were summarily drummed out (though the Cork's leader would later be posthumously reinstated and recognized as founder).

Here in Tacoma, the city's first Elks Lodge (No. 174), was established in 1890, 22 years after the formation of the national Elks organization. The prominence of both Tacoma and the local Elks lodge rose dramatically over the next two decades, and by 1910, the Elks had purchased land and were making plans to erect a monumental new home in what was becoming the premiere part of town.

Seattle architect, Edouard Frere Champney, a native of France who trained at École des Beaux Arts, was selected to design the new Elks Lodge. His vision, informed by his work on recent world's fair buildings and grounds, was to create a stunning, iconic four-story Elks Lodge that visually connected with two commanding, highly important Tacoma buildings, City Hall and the Northern Pacific Railroad headquarters. Champney achieved this by adding another component to the construction: the Spanish Steps, based on the famous Roman staircase of the same name. Tacoma's steps were built so that they fluidly cascaded alongside the Elks Lodge, from the busy commercial Broadway corridor to the point of power at City Hall and the NPRR building.

When ceremoniously opened on February 19, 1916, the new lodge and Spanish Steps were heralded as "a revelation in architecture and furnishings." And for the next half century, the Tacoma Elks remained a highly regarded and respected part of the community. Into the 1960s, the Elks Lodge was hailed as *the* place to go for dances and entertainment. And of course, a primary mission of the fraternal group was always service to the community, sponsoring and organizing countless fundraisers, sports teams, parades and other civic activities.

Its membership included modest wage earners on up to some of the city's elite, including captains of indus-

(L) Bands from regional Elks Lodges filled the Spanish Steps for the dedication in 1916. (R) A formal ball with dance band on stage ⊙TPL

try, legal eagles, mayors and even a Washington State lieutenant governor. The latter, Emmett Anderson, also had the distinction of serving as exalted ruler of the national Elks. It's said, too, that war-hero and future president, Dwight D. Eisenhower paid a visit to the Elks Lodge in the late 1940s.

Even after the Elks relocated to a new building in the mid-1960s, the old lodge remained important for lots of Tacomans. Well into the '70s, it was the scene of many varied private and public events. Here, for a time, the annual Red Rose Cotillions were put on by and for the city's African American high school students. Here, too, was where the gay community's annual coronation event was staged at least once. And in between, many a company party and class reunion was held within these hallowed walls. Then there are the persistent rumors of underground concerts staged here in the '90s. And when a key was no longer need-ed for entrance, graffiti artists gloriously ran amuck, leaving wonderfully vivid dreams and imagery on the towering walls.

It would seem that the Jolly Corks of old had taken up residency, brimming with revelry and energized by an opportunity to make up for lost time! And such is the spirit in which this grand, old lodge leaps into its new incarnation.

– *Tim Hills is Historian for McMenamins Pubs, Breweries & Hotels.*

Everything from community youth events to... **TPL**

...fraternal "old-timers nights" regularly filled the Elks **TPL**

The Elks Club, Tacoma, U. S. A.

The Spanish Steps remain an integral part of the Elks Building architecture **TPL/TSC**

McMenamins – Tacoma Elks Temple

By Tim Hills

Tacoma's 1916 Elks Lodge was built as an extraordinary gathering place with an unflinching devotion to the community at large. These are qualities that attracted and resonated with Portland-based McMenamins Pubs, Breweries & Hotels. Since 1983, McMenamins has had great fun connecting with communities through good music, food, art, craft beer, history, and events, all within comfortable, creative environs, ranging from the 150-square-foot White Shed Pub to the 72-acre Edgefield Manor.

We are thrilled and inspired by the amazing opportunities present at the Elks Lodge, and within Tacoma's historical and vibrant Theater District. Our restoration of the old lodge's beauty and fraternal ambiance will be accompanied with an infusion of artfulness and irreverence reminiscent of the Jolly Corks, those Gotham friends and theater-types who fell in together to form what became the Benevolent and Protective Order of Elks.

Highlights of McMenamins Elks Lodge will include sweeping views of Commencement Bay, a fine restaurant serving well-prepared Pacific Northwest fare, a craft brewery, live music in the grand ballroom (which opens onto the Spanish Steps), and five small bars, including one with a South Seas-theme and waterfall feature. There will be 46 lodging rooms, most of which will be creatively housed in the 28-foot-high top-floor, formerly the ceremonial lodge room, along with trees and an edible garden. Throughout will be artwork, photos, and events celebrating the past, present and future of this remarkable place and the city around it. *Estimated opening is late 2018.*

Musings from a Former Mayor

Bill Baarsma reflects on notable sporting events that drew large crowds and delivered timeless memories at Tacoma's iconic venues.

The Tacoma Stadium and Big Time Football

When finally finished in 1910, the Tacoma Stadium was truly something to behold. Built in large measure through the sale of commemorative stamps by school kids and season tickets for events not yet scheduled, the Stadium was simply the largest publicly owned venue of its kind in the entire country. Former President Theodore Roosevelt spoke there on April 5 1911 and proclaimed: "I have visited, I think, most of the great cities of the world, and there is not one of them which has a stadium such as this, situated with such an outlook as this... you have done something... which must have a very marked effect upon all other cities in the union." And TR was right!

Frederick Heath, the Stadium's architect, declared the venue as "one of the most remarkable structures ever built" and a "poem in masonry." School district leaders referred to the vast concrete amphitheater as a "great community center" able to hold 35,000 to 40,000 spectators comfortably. With completion of the Stadium, Tacoma was truly ready for "ShowTime" and especially big-time sports.

Famous performers, politicians and celebrities came from far and wide to this one-of-a-kind venue. John Phillip Sousa's band played "El Capitan" among its many selections before a crowd of 22,000, the largest seated audience in the band's history. Presidents Woodrow Wilson and Warren Harding as well as

The game at Stadium Bowl was the big news the morning of December 7, 1941. The next morning's newspaper announced that we were at war.

Upton Sinclair, Babe Ruth, General John Pershing, William Jennings Bryan, Louis Armstrong and Bob Hope were among the many luminaries who included the Tacoma Stadium on their itinerary. But the stadium was also the site of truly the biggest of big-time college athletics and because of that, it became known as the Stadium "Bowl."

One would have to list the University of Southern California Trojans, Texas A&M Aggies, Penn State Nittany Lions, Washington Huskies, Washington State Cougars and Oregon State Beavers as premier college football programs. Football teams from each of those schools competed before thousands of fans in the "Bowl." In fact, the USC Trojans team played its first game outside of California and its first against Oregon State on Thanksgiving Day in 1914 in the Stadium. OSU (known then as the Oregon Agricultural College) eagerly agreed to move the game from Corvallis to Tacoma to play in the largest venue in the Western United States. (The undefeated but once-tied University of Washington "Sun Dodgers" turned down an opportunity to play the OSU squad in a rematch.) With the outbreak of World War I, the game was billed as a benefit for the Belgium Relief Fund. Local boosters paid for the teams' travel and accommodations, but they arrived without fans, cheerleaders, marching bands or a local following. The meager turnout was a disaster for the city promoters. OSU won 38-6.

Local civic leaders waited nearly three decades before trying to organize another Stadium contest between two big-time college football powers. In the interim, the UW Huskies came to town to play the overmatched College of Puget Sound Loggers. There were seven games played in the Bowl between the two teams during the 1920s and 1930s – including the first night game in the Northwest under the lights. Thousands of local fans turned out hoping for a miracle Puget Sound win that was not to be. But the local fans did see arguably two of the greatest All-American Husky running backs to ever play the game, in the Bowl, during the 1920s – record setters George "Wildcat" Wilson (1923–25) and Chuck Carroll (1926–28). In 1940, the Tacoma Stadium became the site of the first-ever Lumber Bowl, pitting the underdog Pacific Lutheran College Gladiators, led by the "Marvelous Marvs" Tommervik and Harshman, against the football powerhouse and undefeated Gonzaga Bulldogs – the self-styled "Fighting Irish" of the Northwest. In an upset that captured the fancy of sports writers throughout the country, Pacific Lutheran scored on a last-minute Harshman field goal to prevail 16-13 before 15,000 stunned, then wildly cheering fans.

When other, larger venues opened up across the country, local boosters in 1925 promoted the idea of covering the Tacoma Stadium with a dome making it "the greatest auditorium the world has ever known." E. Taylor Gardner, local architect and engineer, drew up the plans and a fundraising effort began. That effort ran out of steam, but in 1941 civic leaders led by Mayor Harry P. Cain came up with another idea: A postseason, big-time football bowl game featuring the Washington State Cougars and a nationally ranked opponent. Thus, came the first Evergreen Bowl game at the Stadium, pitting the Cougars against the fifth-ranked Texas A&M Aggies.

Unlike the 1914 promotional disaster, the Evergreen Bowl featured a winning state team, Washington State College, and with it thousands of local fans, cheerleaders and a marching band. The Aggies brought a cadre of boosters from the Lone Star State. Special accommodations were made for the many national sports writers present to cover the game. The matchup was played before over 25,000 fans on December 6, 1941. The Aggies won the hard-fought contest 7-0. The next day, the country was at war with Japan. That ended, for the time being, the Evergreen Bowl.

After the war's end, The Evergreen Bowl returned to the Tacoma Stadium on November 27, 1948. The game pitted the powerful Penn State Nittany Lions against the Cougars, led by their All-Conference star Don Paul, in a rematch from a game played the prior year. Again, the Cougars fought hard, this time in the rain and mud, but lost 7-0. Nearly 20,000 fans attended despite the inclement weather. (Films of the two games are available on the Internet.) In April of 1949 a 7.1 earthquake shook the Stadium from its foundation, leading to its condemnation. That ended big-time football in Tacoma. (Later, Stadium restoration efforts took place in 1960, 1980 and 1985. The horseshoe end of the bowl as well as sections nearest the bay were removed reducing its current capacity to 15,000.)

The Tacoma Armory and the Big Game

The Tacoma Armory was the site of what local sports fans called the "Big Game" on December 22, 1948, when a very good University of Washington basketball team visited Tacoma to play what it termed an "exhibition" against the College of Puget Sound. The visit was to celebrate the grand opening of the Puget Sound Memorial Fieldhouse on campus. But bad weather delayed the opening until the spring of the following year, so another venue was needed. The Armory, a site for boxing and wrestling matches, was the obvious choice. When the Huskies stepped onto the court they were greeted by a raucous, standing-room crowd of over 3,000 rabid Logger fans and a towering CPS team that featured three players standing 6'7" (true giants for the era). Led by the dominant rebounding of center Rod Gibbs and the deadeye shooting of guard Bob Fincham, the Loggers prevailed by a 48-41 score. The Tacoma team's upset win over the favored quintet from the big city to the north was the subject of conversations at local watering holes for years to come.

Lincoln Bowl and Big-Time Boxing

Over the decades, the Lincoln Bowl (first built as Lincoln Field in 1920) was the site of hard-fought crosstown high school football games pitting the Stadium Tigers and Lincoln Abes. There were times when the two teams came to battle undefeated and untied with major city bragging rights at stake. But the biggest show in the Bowl came when Lincoln graduate "Irish" Pat McMurtry took his campaign to be heavyweight champion in the ring before 11,000-plus adoring fans in two 1956 matches. He had all the tools to be champion – awesome punching power and elite boxing athleticism. Those qualities were on display in Lincoln Bowl on July 13 when Pat defeated, by decision, former heavyweight champion Ezzard Charles. Two months later, an overly trained and underweight McMurtry lost a disputed decision to light heavyweight champion Willie Pastrano. Tacoma fight fans were convinced that Irish Pat could become the champion with the right training and management. But his career careened from big wins to shocking defeats and ended in 1959 with a stunning first-round knockout loss in Portland.

Cheney Stadium and Willie Mays

After a 50-year absence, Triple-A minor-league baseball returned to Tacoma in 1960 when the Phoenix Giants team were lured to the city after the completion of the Ben Cheney Stadium. The Giants, affiliated with the major-league San Francisco team of the same name, played five seasons in Tacoma before leaving for Tucson. The Tacoma Cubs, Twins, Yankees, Tugs, Tigers and Rainiers followed (four of the affiliations were under the stellar leadership of franchise manager Stan "The Man" Naccarato who successfully fought to keep minor-league baseball in Tacoma). Many of Tacoma's players moved up to the major leagues. Some, like Juan Marichal of the Giants, made it to the Baseball Hall of Fame. The biggest all-time thrill for

Willie Mays and Ben Cheney in 1964 📷 **TPL**

local baseball fans, however, had to be when the San Francisco Giants arrived in town to play exhibition games against their minor-league counterparts. It was during those unforgettable games that the great Willie Mays played in centerfield at Cheney Stadium. Local baseball fans queued up for autographs and Willie and his teammates gladly obliged.

Puget Sound Memorial Fieldhouse and Bill Russell

The University of Puget Sound Memorial Fieldhouse was completed in the spring of 1949 and became the class of the state's small-college basketball venues. During the 1970s the Puget Sound Loggers played winning games against major college foes on the Fieldhouse court including: Gonzaga, Nevada Las Vegas, Seattle, Boise State, Portland State, Portland, Idaho and Montana. In 1976 the Loggers became the first university from the state to go on to win an NCAA small-college basketball championship after defeating the University of North Dakota at the Fieldhouse before 5,000 fans. But lost in the pages of history was the most remarkable game ever played in the Fieldhouse. That game, played on April 22, 1958, featured the greatest basketball players in the world. Somehow, someway, local sports promoter Clay Huntington convinced the National Basketball Association All-Stars to play an unscheduled contest in Tacoma during a barnstorming tour after season's end. The East All Stars, led by the league champion Boston Celtics players Bill Russell, Bob Cousy and Bill Sharman defeated the West All-Stars in the Fieldhouse by a record-setting score of 149-136. Twelve players who stepped on the court that evening are now enshrined in the Naismith Memorial Basketball Hall of Fame.

The Tacoma Dome and the Sonics

Under a campaign led by the irrepressible duo and legendary home town sports promoters Stan Naccarato and Doug McArthur, Tacoma voters approved by a resounding vote the construction of their "Dome of Our Own" in 1983. With that, the city finally had a premier venue suitable for big-time sports of every kind. In 1987, the Tacoma Stars made a run for the championship of the Major Indoor Soccer League title before losing a heartbreaking match to the Dallas Sidekicks before a record-setting crowd of 21,728 fans. The NCAA Women's Final-Four basketball championship was played in the Tacoma Dome in 1988 and 1989. Professional ice hockey was also featured with the Tacoma Rockets and, later, Sabercats. But big-time sports really arrived in the City of Destiny when the Seattle Super Sonics played the entire 1994–95 season in the Dome while Key Arena was being remodeled. The team was led by NBA all-stars Shawn Kemp, Gary Payton and Detlef Schremp and finished second in the Pacific Division. Hopes for a championship run were dashed, however, when the team lost to the Los Angeles Lakers in the first round of the playoffs.

Some Final Thoughts

Arguably the three most accomplished Tacoma athletes (all women) did not compete in the big local arenas but set Olympic and world records on the world stage. Wilson High School grad Kaye Hall Greff set a women's world swimming record in the 100-yard backstroke (the first woman to ever break the one minute barrier) and garnered two gold medals and a bronze in the 1968 Olympics. Kaye went on to represent the University of Puget Sound at the World University Games in Italy where she won more golds.

Gretchen Kunigk Fraser, who also studied at Puget Sound, was the first American skier – man or woman– to win a gold medal in the winter Olympics (1948). She garnered the gold in the women's slalom and captured a silver in the women's downhill (also an American first).

And finally, Jeanne Naccarato, a Midwest transplant and spouse of the late Stan Naccarato, set a women's world professional bowling record in 1986 with 40 straight strikes and a three-game set of 300, 300 and 264. The 864 series is one of the highest in recorded history regardless of gender.

– William (Bill) Baarsma served two terms as Mayor of Tacoma (2002–2009) and on the Tacoma City Council (1992–1999), was a tenured professor of business and public administration for 33 years at the University of Puget Sound and is president of Tacoma Historical Society.

The Pantages local baseball team posed with a poster behind the first Tacoma Pantages Theater that was located on Pacific Avenue in 1911

WSHS

Showtime Wrestling in Tacoma

By Bill Baarsma

Professional wrestling was always a part of Tacoma's "Showtime" in the 1950s. Each match played out with a plot, three acts, villains, heroes and a dramatic ending – after much rehearsing. The local stages could be found at the Tacoma Armory and the Tacoma Sports Arena, and the performances were always scheduled on Friday and Saturday nights.

Big-time professional wrestling in Tacoma was, to a large degree, all about its champion and home town hero Frank Stojack. He graduated from Lincoln High School, earning an astonishing 13 varsity letters, academic scholarships and, after graduation, going on to be an All-Coast player on the Washington State College football team. He was undefeated as a collegiate wrestler. He later played in the East-West College All-Star Game, squaring off across the line of scrimmage against future president Gerald Ford. He competed in over 4,000 matches during his illustrious professional wrestling career and even spent a year in the National Football League.

After his football playing days ended, he began a career as a professional wrestler. Frank became known far and wide – from Chicago to Los Angeles – as a scientific and skilled grappler and was always one of the good guys in the dramas played out in the ring. The people in Tacoma loved him for it.

In December of 1951 Tacoma's wrestling fans were stunned to read in the *News Tribune* that Frank had lost his Pacific Coast heavyweight title to the villainous and mysterious Masked Marvel (Buddy Knox) in a match at the Eagles Auditorium in Seattle. A rematch in Tacoma, and revenge, was in order and local promoter Paavo Ketonen made the arrangements for the biggest wrestling event in city history at the Sports Arena. Emma Stojack, Frank's spouse and a long-time family friend, provided my Dad (Clarence), Mom (Connie) and me, as a nine-year-old, front-row arena seats to root Frank on and to see the Masked Marvel get his comeuppance. The show was set for Friday, January 11, 1952 and it was a sellout with a packed house of 6,000 rabid fans.

The Airplane Didn't Spin

Frank was ready to go that January evening. Before a roaring crowd, he moved in to maneuver the masked man into his signature wrestling hold – the airplane spin. It was truly a unique and renowned hold, and

in it Stojack would hoist his opponent shoulder high and spin him around and around. He would then body slam the dizzy and disoriented foe and get the three count. But the Marvel was a cunning opponent and had a counter move with every effort Frank would make. The match had a one-hour time limit, and as the minutes went by, the crowd urged its hero to spin the man of mystery to victory. Frank tried and then tried again but he fell short of the winning fall as the bell rang. It was a draw and that meant that the Masked Marvel would retain his title – for the time being. After the match an exhausted Stojack, still in his athletic robe, came back from the dressing room to greet my folks and shake my hand. It was a thrill of a lifetime.

Afterwards, Dad, Mom and I headed out to the parking lot to find our car and head on home. Much to our shock, we saw an obviously inebriated man standing by our 1949 Ford apparently relieving himself on the back tire. I then saw my dad remove his wire rimmed glasses and give them to Mom. I was convinced in my mind that I would now see Dad perform the Stojack airplane spin and body slam the guy right there in the arena parking lot. Dad sternly marched up to the man, put his hands his hips and said: "Sir, would you please step aside so that we might get into our car." "Sure, pal," the man said as he staggered off. Not a word

PACIFIC ATHLETIC CLUB PRESENTS

WRESTLING

THE ARENA
8:30 P. M.

★ SO. 38th and UNION AVE.

VOL. 2—NO. 24   10c   OFFICIAL PROGRAM   FRIDAY, JAN. 11, 1952

PACIFIC COAST TITLE BATTLE ★

VS.

FRANK STOJACK
Challenger

MASKED MARVEL
The Champion

Frank Stojack of Tacoma will attempt to regain the coast junior heavyweight title in a best of three falls match with the Masked Marvel, present title holder.

Tickets and Reservations at the Turf and The Retreat, South Tacoma

SSM

about the incident was said as Dad drove us home. I was deeply disappointed but did, in the end, learn a lesson. Once we got back to our house on North Anderson Street, and as Dad hosed off the car, I asked him why he didn't body-slam the man or at least punch him in the nose. His reply: "Bill, no one was hurt and we all got home safe and sound. Remember that."

Tacoma's Wrestling Politician

In 1953, Frank easily won a seat on the first nine-member council elected under Tacoma's new city manager form of government. He continued wrestling and won the world light heavyweight championship and was proclaimed the "King of Northwest Wrestlers." (You can view, on the Internet, Tacoma's wrestling politician square off against the villainous Dutch Hefner in a match held at the Chicago International Amphitheatre on May 7, 1954.)

Ironically, despite his many accomplishments in the classroom, on the playing field and in the ring, Stojack was roundly criticized, laughed at and denigrated as a City Council candidate. His political response was to take on the elites and the establishment with a populist message. A newspaper ad, designed and written by his brother Pete, showed a picture of Frank's hands with the words: "These are the hands of Frank Stojack. Yes, Stojack. Construction worker, wrestler. But these hands stand for thousands like them – hands of workers, of people who use their hands for a living…. There are those who say that a man who works with his hands is not qualified for public service. You, the voters, have an opportunity to refute that statement at the polls by electing Frank Stojack to the new council." The ad resonated with the electorate and Frank finished ahead of the pack with far more votes than any other candidate. Most Tacomans, particularly those living in the South End, believed that Frank deserved to be selected mayor by the council (mayors were not directly elected in Tacoma until 1958). But the council majority passed him over explaining that it would be unseemly for the city's mayor to be a professional wrestler on the side. Frank's supporters were furious – and they would reward his popularity by electing him Pierce County Sheriff in 1958.

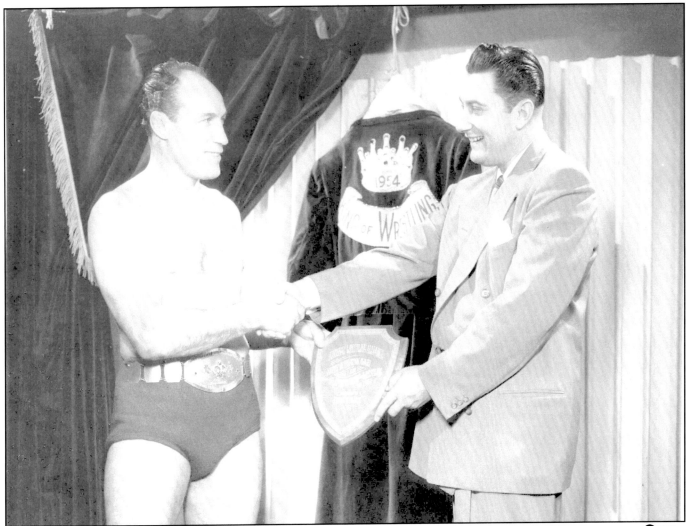

One of the Tacoma's most dynamic athletes, Frank Stojack, left, celebrates a wrestling title with his brother, Pete, in 1954 TPL

Tacoma Speedway

In 1912, three years after the Indianapolis Motor Speedway was built, the Tacoma Speedway was laid out on a five-mile dirt track that ran along Lakewood streets now known as Steilacoom Blvd, Gravely Lake Drive, 112th St., and Lakeview Avenue. The stands, seating 16,000, stretched a third of a mile along Lakeview.

While *Showtime in Tacoma* has focused on where people have gathered within the city limits, the Tacoma Speedway not only carried the name, but that name represented the most prominent auto racing facility in the Western United States at its time. Besides, the track probably kept every lumber mill in Tacoma busy when the track, which had been reduced to three and one-half miles in 1913, was laid out on a two-mile course in 1914 and surfaced with 2x4s set on the narrow edge. That amounted to over two million board feet of lumber, held together with 15 tons of 20-penny nails.

As a further effort to keep Tacoma ranked as the Lumber Capital of the World, when the grandstands burned down in 1916, they were replaced with seating for 16,000 – the largest wood grandstands in the world at that time. With turns banked 18-feet high, the speedway was known as "Indy of the West" and attracted some of the nation's biggest names in motor racing.

Race days were huge events, attracting throngs from around the region. On July 4, 1916, in addition to auto races and a band concert, the big promotion was a planned train wreck. A mile long stretch of rail was laid down, two locomotives, one named "Seattle" and the other "Tacoma," were sent roaring toward each other at over 20 miles per hour. Newspaper accounts described the scene: "There was a clash and explosion as the engines telescoped and the wreck was hid by dense clouds of steam and smoke." The locomotive named "Seattle" stayed on the tracks, "Tacoma" didn't and everyone seemed to think it was a pretty wild and crazy event nonetheless.

Thrills didn't equate to adequate revenue, however, and on another Fourth of July, this one in 1922, the speedway held its final big race before closing later that year. The grand finale was all about big time racing with an overflow crowd of 30,000 on hand for the 250-mile race. Jimmy Murphy pulled ahead in the last few laps and edged out Tommy Milton in a record time of 2:33:55 with an average speed of 97.6 miles per hour – picking up the winner's share of the $25,000 purse.

At the wheel of the pace car that started the race was legendary race driver Barney Oldfield. In 1903 he had been the first auto racer to break the mile-a-minute (60 mph) barrier. He parlayed his fame into starring roles in Broadway musicals and motion pictures. In the 1913 silent film *Barney Oldfield's Race for a Life* the plot pioneered the theme of a villain tying a damsel in distress to train tracks and the hero (Barney) racing in his car in hopes of reaching her before the train.

Barney Oldfield

Oldfield prepares to drive pace car for start of big race on July 4, 1922 Both TPL

NOW PLAYING

Theater District

Reviving the Heartbeat

Tacoma wouldn't be a fully formed city without the Theater District. It would have commerce, houses and apartments, hotels and offices, schools and hospitals, businesses large and small, governmental and social services, a mix of entertainment and recreational facilities, all the things that make for a generally workable municipal organism. It would be, in essence, a functioning body – but, lacking a heart.

The heart, as it is located, emanates from a radius centered at 9th and Broadway. Within the vicinity of several blocks, virtually all the important institutions were established – the Northern Pacific Railroad headquarters, Old City Hall, the Tacoma Hotel, the built-up commercial "main street" along Pacific Avenue, the first venues of public assembly in bars, theaters and churches, up the hill to the county court house and the Armory, and later the city government offices. That geographical orientation was established by the vision of Theodore Hosmer to relocate the Tacoma Land Company office so the Tacoma Theatre could be built on that site.

Throughout this book we have explored the saga of Tacoma's entertainment history. The city founders believed that their aspirations for Tacoma to become a great city called them to make a statement with a grand theater. The architectural character of what they built in 1890 supported their aspirations, which they proudly promoted as "The Temple of Drama and Opera."

The evolution of the many dozens of theaters that followed, highlighted by the Pantages and Rialto theaters, created a dynamic entertainment era. Historian Michael Sullivan envisioned a street scene looking down 9th from Broadway when he reflected on the Theater District of the 1920s: "There's a good chance that many of the fashionable people in this image work in the entertainment district and are headed to one of 19 'ticket' theaters located within a few blocks of each other on this late wet afternoon. The nearby boarding houses, apartment buildings and hotels were home to hundreds of stagehands, musicians, ushers, promoters, theatrical agents and ticket office management staff that trafficked the streets and alleys day and night. On any one of those given nights there were 10,000 theater seats to be filled in Tacoma's legitimate movie and vaudeville houses, burlesque and music halls, and the many downtown jazz clubs and brown spots. As evening approached, all the marquee lights would come on, ticket boxes would open and Tacoma's Theater District would blaze into the high life. I can hear the music."

The Theater District was the Gathering Place and crowds assembled by the thousands for parades, political rallies, fraternal assemblies, and a wide variety of street events – ranging from dare-devil stunts to labor riots. The first automobile dealership in the state and first automobile in Tacoma were on these streets. Wright Park was established on donated land. An Irish immigrant and Civil War veteran named Ros-

© TPL

(L) An iconic image of the Rialto, Broadway and Orpheum theaters with lights on for an evening in the 1930s. (R) Military parade fills Broadway in 1949.

sell O'Brien initiated the practice of standing for the national anthem when he rose during a meeting at the Bostwick Hotel on October 18, 1893. The rest, as we stand in unison, is history.

The Theater District even influenced the design of the First Baptist Church (now Urban Grace Church), constructed at 9th and Market in 1924. The building's foundation was designed to support five additional stories if the structure was ever converted to a theater and the sanctuary was designed for the presentation of concerts. The likes of opera star Tussi Bjoerling and bluegrass bands have called the acoustics among the best they have ever experienced.

The concentration of assets in the Theater District peaked in the decade after World War II. What followed was the writing of rather desperate chapters in the saga of the Theater District extending into the 90s. As we discussed in the Downtown Theaters chapter, there were efforts in the name of urban renewal to stem the tide of commercial flight when the Tacoma Mall opened in 1965. Drug gangs, prostitution and blight crowded out mainstream Tacoma's desire to patronize downtown. A number of family friendly movie houses went to porno shows to demolition. Perhaps it was a dose of bad karma that caused an underground fire to smolder for years at the Northeast Tacoma disposal site where so many of Tacoma's demolished architecturally attractive buildings were buried. The great city Hosmer and Company had envisioned a century earlier was fading into another example of suburban sentiments causing a community to abandon its urban core. The heart was breaking.

As we explored in the chapter on the Pantages Theater, a group of visionaries saw hope amid the bleak-

ness and believed restoring the iconic theater would make an important cultural statement. Their efforts have paid significant dividends for the community.

Over the past quarter-century, a very encouraging array of investments has been made in downtown, including nine museums, the University of Washington Tacoma campus, cafes, brewpubs, artist studios as well as residential and recreational entities. Much of this has been achieved in restored historic properties. There are non-profit groups promoting activities and aesthetics in the area, including SpaceWorks, which fills vacant storefronts with art and creative enterprise. Theater District Associates presents the First Night New Years Eve celebration. The Theater District Association raised funds for such public amenities as Ben Gilbert Park and the tile mural depicting a throng of fans filling Ledger Square to receive World Series results. A section of Court C was renamed Opera Alley and an identity that once was notorious now represents a site where wedding pictures and car commercials are made. In 2015, the Tacoma City Council passed a resolution celebrating the unique attributes of the Theater District. The historic Daffodil Parade has been joined by Tacoma Pride and Ethnic festivals as annual events. A two-block stretch of Broadway is blocked every Thursday for the summer Farmers Market. As this is written, the Broadway Center and Pierce Transit are exploring ideas to transform the Theatre Square area on Broadway into Tacoma's most appealing gathering space.

The New Urbanism movement which promotes a vibrant, walkable, culturally diverse environment plays to the trend lines for the Theater District. The resurrection of aspirations for Tacoma's greatness as a city are carried forward with a promising heartbeat.

(L) Women line up for a 1946 Roxy corset and bra fashion show. (R) Pantages, Broadway and Colonial theaters frame busy Broadway scene in 1927.

1

2

1) *Eleanor Roosevelt left the Union Club on Broadway a week after Pearl Harbor.*
2) *Six months later, a group of men were sworn into military service in a ceremony at 9th and Broadway.* 3) *The City's 1930 Christmas Tree was in the middle of Broadway, next to the streetcar lines.*
4) *In 1974, Broadway was converted to a no-vehicle plaza from 9th to 13th in an attempt to compete with the Tacoma Mall that had decimated downtown retail when it opened in 1965.* 5) *Mayor Ben Hanson rode the escalade from Commerce to Broadway in 1961. The moving sidewalks were abandoned by the mid-1980s when Broadway was reopened to vehicles.*

All ◉ *TPL*

3

5

4

1

2

3

1) *Charlie Chaplin lookalikes line up in Court C in a 1921 promotional contest for* The Kid *showing at the Rialto.*
2) *Over $500,000 in war bonds were sold when a 1942 Labor Day crowd of over 8,000 gathered at 10th and Pacific.*
3) *The Los Angeles Newsboys appeared for a week at the Rialto on their cross-country singing tour in 1924.*
4) *Protestors against three-time presidential candidate Robert Taft march in front of the Temple Theater in 1947.*
5) *National Guardsmen confront striking lumber mill workers at 11th and A Street in 1935.*

All TPL

4

5

1

2

3

4

1) Urban Grace Church, built as the First Baptist Church, has anchored the Southwest corner of 9th and Market since 1925. 2) The church sanctuary has been praised for its acoustics by classical musicians and bluegrass singers, alike. 3) In the midst of WWII in 1942, no new tires were available for the parking-meter collection cart, so it remained stuck in front of the Roxy Theater. 4) Broadway from 9th to 7th was Tacoma's first Auto Row. As those dealerships moved out, this became Antique Row. 5) The only surviving theater building from the 1800s, the former Casino Theater still shows off its ornamentation at 726 Pacific Avenue.

All ⊙ TPL
except #2 ⊙ TPL/TSC

5

Street Performance

1

4

2

3

1) Harry Kahne, the "Upside-down Man," performed on the side of the Broadway Theater in 1930. 2) With a firm bite, performer Jack Nerbuda pulled a new 1925 Chandler and five passengers up hill on Broadway from 13th to 7th. 3) An even more bizarre stunt had occurred in 1909 in front of the first Pantages Theater on Pacific, when a man let a loaded Cadillac roll over him. He travelled the country betting he could survive such a stunt, but his luck ran out several years later when he was crushed to death. 4) Betty and Benny Fox performed acrobatics atop a platform on the roof of the Winthrop Hotel for 31 straight hours in 1934.

All ⊙ TPL

Tacoma Presidential Visits

One of Tacoma's most memorable historical images depicts the huge crowd gathered at 9th and Broadway for a speech by United States President Benjamin Harrison on May 6, 1891. The future site of the Pantages Theater provided a dramatic scene from the bunting-draped façade of the Gross Brothers department store to men climbing on telephone poles. Harrison was popular because he had signed the bill for Washington to become a state two years earlier.

Harrison would be one of 13 U.S. Presidents to visit Tacoma on a total of 18 different occasions. Each visit brought capacity crowds to various venues, including street gatherings that blocked 9th and Broadway for political rallies.

Rutherford B. Hayes (1877–81)
October 14, 1880

Benjamin Harrison (1889–93)
May 6, 1891

Theodore Roosevelt (1901–09)
May 22, 1903

William Howard Taft (1909–13)
October 1, 1909, October 10, 1911

Woodrow Wilson (1913–21)
September 13, 1919

Warren G. Harding (1921–23)
July 5, 1923*

Franklin D. Roosevelt (1933–45)
October 1, 1937, September 22, 1942

Harry S. Truman (1945–53)
June 23-25 1945, June 10, 1948, October 3, 1952

Dwight D. Eisenhower (1953–61)
October 16-18, 1956, November 9, 1958

John F. Kennedy (1961–63)
September 27, 1963**

Jimmy Carter (1977–81)
September 23, 1980

Ronald Reagan (1981–89)
April 19, 1984

Bill Clinton (1993–2001)
September 19, 1996

* Harding died of a heart attack 28 days
    later in San Francisco
** Kennedy was killed 56 days later in Dallas

Under a sea of umbrellas, thousands turned out for Harrison in 1891

(L) President Truman, (M) Mayor Val Fawcett, (R) Gov. Mon Wallgren

Jimmy Carter rode down Pacific Avenue on the roof of his car in 1980

All TPL

In one of Tacoma's most spectacular parades, sailors from the visiting Great White Fleet marched down Pacific Avenue on May 30, 1908

The Bostwick Building

The sentinel. That's an apt description for the role the Bostwick Building has played in the Theater District for well more than a century. Built as the Bostwick Hotel in 1889, the triangle-shaped building has witnessed the pageantry of cultural events as they have played out at the 9th and Broadway/St. Helens intersection.

Huge crowds have gathered in front of the building for parades, political rallies, and street stunts. Theater marquees have changed names, theaters themselves have come and gone. The street-level retail has included jewelry and hat stores, cafes, malt and coffee shops. The space was used as a fictitious pizza joint in the 1990 movie *I Love You to Death*, starring Kevin Kline and Tracey Ullman.

Not only has the Bostwick been a witness to historical happenings, it can stand up and take a bow for making history for, well, starting the custom of standing for the National Anthem. Rossell G. O'Brien originated the custom of standing for the playing of the *Star Spangled Banner* while attending a meeting at the Bostwick Building in 1893. There is a plaque on the Broadway side acknowledging this event.

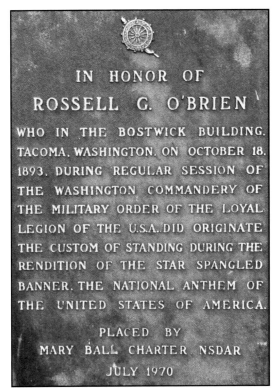

IN HONOR OF ROSSELL G. O'BRIEN WHO IN THE BOSTWICK BUILDING, TACOMA, WASHINGTON, ON OCTOBER 18, 1893, DURING REGULAR SESSION OF THE WASHINGTON COMMANDERY OF THE MILITARY ORDER OF THE LOYAL LEGION OF THE U.S.A. DID ORIGINATE THE CUSTOM OF STANDING DURING THE RENDITION OF THE STAR SPANGLED BANNER, THE NATIONAL ANTHEM OF THE UNITED STATES OF AMERICA.

PLACED BY MARY BALL CHARTER, NSDAR JULY 1970

 BJ

TPL

 TPL

TPL

The Tacoma Hotel

Soon after it opened on August 8, 1884, the Tacoma Hotel gained the reputation as the grandest hotel north of San Francisco. That was the intention of the Tacoma Land Company when it commissioned famed architect Stanford White to design the 185-room hotel, which was perched on a bluff overlooking Mount Rainier and the, then unblemished, tideflats of Commencement Bay.

The brick and stone structure occupied a full block on A Street from South 9th to 10th and featured a 200-foot long veranda and spacious grounds. Presidents and celebrities stayed at the hotel, along with Jack the Bear (see adjacent story). The 85-foot totem pole was erected in 1903 and narrowly escaped being destroyed when the hotel burned in 1935. The totem pole was later moved to its current site in Fireman's Park.

The hotel was destroyed by fire on October 17, 1935

The spacious foyer was typical of the hotel's grandeur

Jack the Bear
& Other Animal Celebrities

By Deborah Freedman

Not all performers are human. As long as there have been traveling shows and circuses, audiences have been entertained by trained animals – from domestic to exotic, from four-legged to reptilian. In Tacoma we have observed the actions of beloved creatures in the Point Defiance Zoo & Aquarium, including E.T. the walrus, Dub-Dub the seal, and Cindy the elephant. Yet other animals have not been given such professional care and handling, or suitable environments.

Earl Irwin, owner of the B & I Circus Store shopping center, purchased a pair of baby gorillas from the Congo in 1964. Burma died shortly after she arrived in Tacoma, but her brother Ivan survived. He lived at first in the Irwin's home, and later in a concrete and glass enclosure near the pet shop at the shopping center. Many Tacoma children grew up regularly visiting Ivan, who lived at the B & I for over twenty-five years. In 1994, after a civic outcry, Ivan's owners gave him to Seattle's Woodland Park Zoo. Ivan found a new home at Zoo Atlanta, where he was successfully integrated with other adult gorillas. He died there in 2012. He is now memorialized by a bronze statue at the entrance to the Point Defiance Zoo.

However, 80 years before Ivan's birth, Tacoma's residents and visitors were entertained by the antics of Jack the Bear. Orphaned as a cub by an unknowing hunter, Jack also had a twin sister, Jennie. The two were raised as pets in a cabin south of Tacoma, where they learned to take a bottle and rock themselves to sleep in a rocking chair. However, they quickly outgrew the cabin and became too clever to be kept any longer as farm pets.

Jennie's fate is unknown, but it's unlikely that she was returned to her natural environment. Jack was sold in 1883 to the owners of the Tacoma Hotel, still under construction. He, too, was given a home of his own – an area surrounded by a low wooden fence, complete with spring water and an overhanging tree. Yet, raised as a pet, Jack was comfortable around humans and occasionally climbed over his fence to visit the tourists on the long porches of the hotel on the bluff. Hotel staff would use brooms to shoo him back into his home. Later they attached a chain to his collar to keep him from escaping.

Jack's trainer and companion was Frank B. Reilly, who spent time with Jack and taught him to hold a glass mug in his front paws and drink beer. Jack became the hotel's mascot – featured in their publicity materials and known widely as Jack the Beer Bear. However, Jack learned to slip out of his collar and began exploring the nearby streets of Tacoma. In 1892 he was shot and killed by a police officer, surprised by the sight of an 800-pound black bear coming around a dark street corner.

The Tacoma Hotel suddenly lost one of its featured attractions. Not to be deterred, hotel management called in taxidermist Edwards and had Jack's body stuffed and put on display in the hotel lobby. There he stayed for another thirty-five years, and somehow came through the 1935 fire that destroyed the hotel. His deteriorating body was kept at the Washington State History Museum until 1958. The area where Jack lived is now the southeast edge of Fireman's Park in downtown Tacoma.

JACK TACOMAS PET BEAR

Worthington W. Pickerill

The Theater District has been a magnet for drama in many realms, including the excitement generated by the very first car to roll across the city's unpaved streets. In 1899, Worthington W. Pickerill posed in a four-horse-power "Locomobile" – the first automobile in Tacoma. The vehicle cost $750 and was an immediate attraction on the street, gathering crowds to inspect "the wagon that ran without horses." He later became president of the Washington Automobile Co., the city's first auto dealership, located at 710-12 Pacific Avenue.

In the new vehicle, Pickerill can be seen below in front of the W.W. Pickerill & Co. Music House, located at 901-03 Pacific Avenue. He had organized music clubs featuring mandolin and guitar and, after outgrowing his original store, moved to 946 Pacific and opened Tacoma's first roof-top garden where nightly song and band music could be heard and ice cream and sodas enjoyed. He also operated a tiny performance hall called the Princess Theater at 906 Pacific Avenue, next to the first Pantages Theater. In 1912, for a short period, he took over the Majestic Theater at 821-23 Pacific.

Pickerill didn't have all the "firsts" in Tacoma's early auto history. The State of Washington decided in 1905 to issue license plates and No. 1 went to Sydney Albert (Sam) Perkins, who owned the *Tacoma Daily* and *Sunday Ledger* and the Perkins Building on the corner of 11th and A Street. In 1911 Perkins won the *El Primero* yacht in a dice game from Chester Thorne (Thorne Castle, Lakewood) and left the vessel to his heirs upon his death in 1955. Restoration efforts are being pursued for the vessel, considered one of the most luxurious yachts ever in West Coast waters and worthy of transporting no fewer than four United States presidents.

Tacoma's first automobile dealership offers 1906 Fords  TPL

In 1899, Pickerill drew attention with Tacoma's first automobile. Note wood-planked street. TPL

George Francis Train – A Promoter Out of Time

By Deborah Freedman

George Francis Train was likely the greatest promoter to ever draw a crowd in the young city of Tacoma. His stated mission was to make Tacoma the most prominent city in the West, proclaiming that he could do so by stirring up global publicity by racing around the world in record time.

The plaque in the sidewalk in front of the Pythian Temple at 924-26 Broadway marks the site where George Francis Train began and ended his 1890 trip around the world. Train suggested the publicity stunt, and the crowd-funding method of financing it – selling tickets to a lecture at the brand new Tacoma Theatre before his journey. R. F. Radebaugh, owner of the *Tacoma Daily Ledger,* took him up on his offer. Prominent residents of Tacoma, including J.W. Sprague, Isaac Anderson and Allen C. Mason, bid for the honor of purchasing the first box seats.

When he arrived in town in a pure white suit to promote his adventure, he proceeded from the train station to the Tacoma Hotel in a carriage followed by "the biggest band ever assembled on the West Coast." After the preamble of fund-raising he was ready to make history. At daybreak on March 18th, cannon fire boomed from the bluffs and reportedly every church bell in town clanged farewell as Train leapt into a waiting carriage in front of the offices of the *Ledger* and dashed down streets lined with supporters to board the chartered steamer *Olympia* and head off onto his journey.

Determined that his record-setting trip be documented for posterity, Train was accompanied by Sam W. Wall, a reporter with the *Ledger,* who brought along a new Kodak camera. Train's promotional style was more suited to today's blogs and social media posts, as his frequent telegraph dispatches were printed in newspapers across the nation. Train's goal was to complete the westward trip in just 60 days, breaking the record of 70 days set by Boston reporter Nellie Bly the year before.

However, Train had a deeper motivation. He himself had previously made several trips around the world, and in 1870 accomplished the journey in just 80 days. Author Jules Verne developed the concept in a children's fiction book, (as Train said, "wrote fiction of my fact,") but never credited Train as his inspiration. As further insult, Nellie Bly's trip was promoted to demonstrate that a living woman could overcome a fictitious man, Phileas Fogg, again with no mention of Train. Mrs. Radebaugh happened to be in Boston and in communication with Train when Nellie Bly returned from her trip and the scheme was born.

George Francis Train TPL

Compounding Train's frustration, the actual trip took longer than planned due to holiday schedules, missed connections and passport requirements. Train expected the Northern Pacific Railroad to have a special train waiting for him upon his arrival in New York, ready to whisk him back to Tacoma in just three days. However, Radebaugh's request was refused by NP land agent Paul Schulze and Train had to travel on regular routes along the Union Pacific. Cheering crowds lined a parade route to greet Train upon his return to Tacoma on May 24, 1890. He had completed the journey in 67 days and 13 hours, a world record at the time, but was fuming over the NP snub.

Train's history with the Northern Pacific Railroad was a long one. He was present at Promontory Point, Utah, in May of 1869 when the last sections of the transcontinental railroad were linked. Two weeks later he was lecturing in San Francisco, proposing that a trip around the world could be completed in 90 days. He arrived in Portland, Oregon at the end of June and was featured in several lectures during the July Fourth festivities.

Also in Portland at the time were six members of a Northern Pacific engineering team – Moorhead, Johnson, Roberts, Claxton, Canfield and Wilkeson. Their job was to inspect proposed railroad routes and locations. Somehow Train persuaded the team to allow him to join them. The group left Portland and arrived in Tacoma on July 8, 1869, then traveled on to Seattle, Whatcom and Victoria, before returning to Portland. (Train, long a supporter of Irish independence, was not popular in British Victoria and nearly caused an incident.)

Train fell in love with the site of Tacoma, and afterwards claimed that he had convinced the group then and there to select Tacoma as the terminus of their new transcontinental railroad route. He became Tacoma's earliest promoter, likely devising the phrase "Tacoma: City of Destiny," paired with "Seattle, Seattle, Death Rattle, Death Rattle."

However, Train's personality was so eccentric that he gained a reputation bordering on insanity, inviting scorn and ridicule. He wore a long bright blue coat with gold buttons and signed hotel registers in brightly colored ink, in a time when black was the norm. Yet Train was far ahead of his time in choosing to become a vegetarian, supporting women's rights, and refusing to shake hands in avoidance of germs. (His parents and sisters died during a yellow fever epidemic when he was four.) He eventually was considered little more than a crank (a term he coined to describe his mental machinery) spending his latter days in parks feeding birds and speaking only with children. The editor of the *Louisville Journal* once described him as having "the brains of 20 men in his head, all pulling in different directions."

His erratic personal style clearly caused history to overlook his business accomplishments. A brief timeline of his early activities indicates a man perhaps simply far ahead of his time.

> 1853 – Followed the gold rush to Melbourne, Australia, where he helped develop port facilities while serving as a correspondent to several American newspapers.

> 1860/1861 – Established the first rail routes between Liverpool and London.

> 1862 – Assisted the Union Pacific Railroad in western expansion through a new method of financing known as Credit Mobilier (although it later sunk into scandal) and developing over 500 lots in Omaha.

> 1864 – Unsuccessfully ran for U.S. president as an independent, and again in 1872.

> 1867 – Canvassed with Susan B. Anthony and Elizabeth Cady Stanton in support of enfranchising women with voting rights.

> 1868 – Gave a lecture in Portland urging the development of salmon canning.

> 1869 – Lectured San Francisco audiences to embrace hard-working Chinese laborers.

George Francis Train: Born March 29, 1829 in Boston, died January 19, 1904 in New York.

Topeka Daily Capital, May 23, 1890, "It cost Tacoma a good deal to get rid of George Francis Train for sixty-five days, and now he is back again. Tacomans must feel discouraged."

Plaque embedded in sidewalk at 924 Broadway　　TPL

For the first half of the 20th century, the most popular genre for movies was the Western, often set in the latter half of the 19th century. *The Great Train Robbery* (1903) is considered the first Western and was followed out of the silent film era by the likes of *Stagecoach* in 1939, making John Wayne into a star. *Riders of the Purple Sage* was a big hit in 1918.　TPL

City of Tacoma Theater District Resolution

Req #14-1159   Amended 2-10-15

RESOLUTION NO. 39113

BY REQUEST OF COUNCIL MEMBER THOMS

A RESOLUTION relating to community and economic development; directing the City Manager to work with staff to incorporate the "Theater District" label and brand in its future community and economic development efforts, as described in the North Downtown Subarea Plan of the City's Comprehensive Plan.

1   WHEREAS the North Downtown Subarea Plan identifies the core of
2
3 Tacoma's Theater District as being located in the vicinity of South 9th and
4
5 Broadway Streets, and
6
7   WHEREAS organizations within and in proximity to the Theater District
8
9 create a cultural footprint, and include the Pantages and Rialto Theaters, the
10
11 Broadway Center for the Performing Arts, Theatre on the Square, Tacoma Youth
12
13 Theater, Grand Cinema, Pythian Temple, Urban Grace Church, Temple Theater,
14
15 and Tacoma Historical Society Museum, and
16
17   WHEREAS the Theater District is home to the City's core performing arts
18
19 organizations, including the Northwest Sinfonietta, Puget Sound Revels, Tacoma
20
21 City Ballet, Tacoma Little Theater, Tacoma Concert Band, Tacoma Opera, Tacoma
22
23 Philharmonic, Tacoma Symphony Orchestra, and Tacoma Youth Symphony
24
25 Association, and

  WHEREAS the Theater District has, for the past 125 years, served a vital

role as the public gathering place for cultural and civic events, including the

Broadway Farmers' Market, First Night celebration, annual Christmas Tree

Lighting, Brew Five Three/Tacoma's Beer & Blues Festival, Daffodil Parade,

-1-

Res14-1159amend.doc-JH/Ctok-bn

Tacoma Pride Festival, and multiple other events that draw thousands to the heart

of Downtown Tacoma, and

  WHEREAS the Theater District Association brings together the collective

efforts of neighborhood residents, arts organizations, business and property

owners, churches, and social services dedicated to the development and

promotion of one of Tacoma's most dynamic mixed-use neighborhoods, and the

non-profit organizations that are located within and support the Theater District

generate $18 million in economic impact annually, and

  WHEREAS, over the past ten years, neighborhood activism has promoted

the development of the following projects: Opera Alley, Antique Row, Broadway

Local Improvement District, Spanish Steps, Tacoma-Kitakyushu Japan Sister City

Commemorative Garden, Spirit of Sarah Bernhardt Statue, Rialto Theater Art Wall,

the Crane mural, Ben Gilbert Park, historic photo mural and Gateway/Goddess

project, and

  WHEREAS the culture and charm of the Theater District serves visitors,

residents and merchants alike, offering a variety of restaurants, live entertainment

venues, coffee shops, pubs, bookstores, antique shops, boutiques, art galleries,

spas, and professional services tucked within a variety of living spaces, and

  WHEREAS the North Downtown Subarea Plan calls for the use of the

"Theater District" as a specific branding mechanism that is easily understood by

locals and tourists alike as a description of a vibrant and appealing area in

downtown Tacoma, and

-2-

Res14-1159amend.doc-JH/Ctok-bn

  WHEREAS the City Council desires to incorporate the Theater District label

and brand in future community and economic development and marketing efforts,

to promote and convey the Theater District's entertainment attractions and cultural

vibrancy; Now, Therefore,

BE IT RESOLVED BY THE COUNCIL OF THE CITY OF TACOMA:

  That the City Council hereby directs the City Manager to work with staff to

incorporate the "Theater District" label and brand in its future community and

economic development efforts, as described in the North Downtown Subarea Plan

of the City's Comprehensive Plan.

Adopted   FEB 1 0 2015

                          Mayor

Attest:

_____
City Clerk

Approved as to form:

_____
Deputy City Attorney

-3-

Res14-1159amend.doc-JH/Ctok-bn

Ledger Square Law
Salutes

Arts and culture are key components to the economic and social vitality of a community and the Theater District has been the center of Tacoma's cultural heritage for over a century. Serving as Tacoma's gathering place, the Theater District has long witnessed the intersection of culture, politics and commerce. After a long and storied history, the Theater District is now home to vibrant options in restaurants, housing and small businesses, all anchored by notable cultural amenities. Ledger Square Law, a boutique business law firm serving a diverse South Sound clientele, was eager to become a contributing player in the revitalized Theater District when it chose the location of its new home. The attorneys and staff at Ledger Square Law salute *Showtime in Tacoma* for celebrating our rich history and endorsing the value of a community working together for an even brighter future.

THE LEDGER SQUARE LAW PARTNERS
STUART C. MORGAN • CLEMENCIA CASTRO-WOOLERY
L. CLAY SELBY • JASON M. WHALEN
253.327.1900 • LEDGERSQUARELAW.COM

The Distinguished Dozen

Twelve performance organizations have played varied but impactful roles on Tacoma's cultural landscape extending back well into the last century. These profiles, composed by representatives of the organizations, provide historical perspectives on institutions that collectively represent hundreds of years of distinguished live performances. Organization names have changed, at least two entities no longer operate independently, one is nearing its 100th anniversary and others have existed for more than half a century.

Symphony Tacoma
By Andy Buelow

SYMPHONY
TACOMA

The orchestra that Tacoma grew has called the Pantages Theater its home venue for much of its adult life. This has been a key factor shaping Symphony Tacoma's artistic personality.

Built as a theater, not a concert hall, the Pantages features sharply raked seating and crisp, clear acoustics. This creates a sense of immediacy and accessibility; almost the feel of a chamber performance – "like having an orchestra in your living room," as one patron puts it.

The resulting sound contrasts with many purpose-built concert halls where – to borrow a phrase from composer and critic Virgil Thomson – "the surface becomes so shiny that nothing else can be perceived."

At a Pantages concert, one can almost reach out and feel the brush strokes on the musical canvas – or "touch the sound," as Symphony Tacoma describes it in its current branding tagline. Decades of shaping and honing the orchestra within this environment has created a concert experience that is pure Tacoma.

The orchestra known today as Symphony Tacoma predates by nearly 40 years the 1983 renovation of the Pantages as a performing arts venue. It was founded in 1946 as the College of Puget Sound Symphony by conductor Raymond Vaught, and gained its early footing as a "town-and-gown" orchestra.

In 1959, University of Puget Sound music professor Edward Seferian was hired as music director, a position he held for 35 years. Under his guidance, the ensemble blossomed, gradually transitioning out of its affiliation with

Early years at the Temple Theatre JS

ST

Edward Seferian ⊙ JS

Harvey Felder ⊙ ST

Sarah Ioannides ⊙ ST

the university into the stand-alone Tacoma Symphony Orchestra. It retained its community focus, utilizing local volunteer musicians while presenting world-renowned artists in concerts with the symphony. For many years concerts were offered free of charge in such diverse settings as Life Center and the Landmark (Temple) Theater.

The reopening of the Pantages in 1983 gave the orchestra a stable home in the heart of the Theater District. Sometime during the ensuing decade it began charging admission, as well as providing honorariums to its core players. However, it remained a largely volunteer, community-based organization.

Ten years later, the hiring of Harvey Felder as music director began the ensemble's transformation into a professional orchestra. Felder expanded the season, hired new musicians, established a volunteer resident chorus, instigated education programs and concerts for young people, and continued to present top-drawer guest artists for concerto appearances. Under his leadership, the symphony grew in artistic quality, season length and community impact.

In 2014, the symphony welcomed new music director Sarah Ioannides, whom the *Los Angeles Times* called

"one of six female conductors breaking the glass podium." Ioannides' welcoming personality, dynamic podium presence, and creative programming caused a surge in attendance and garnered high critical acclaim. The orchestra's artistic quality soared with every concert cycle, as she re-forged the ensemble into a tight, cohesive instrument.

Programmatically, Symphony Tacoma presents five main-series classical concerts, holiday pops and springtime cabaret pops, and a series of classical choral programs. In addition to the Pantages, the orchestra performs several times annually in the jewel-box Rialto Theater, generally featuring classical repertoire for which the smaller venue's acoustics are particularly well suited. A growing menu of community engagement activities includes Mini Maestros, an interactive series for children ages 2–8; Simply Symphonic, an educational series for fourth and fifth graders; a string instrument coaching program in under-served Tacoma high schools; and master classes for the Tacoma Youth Symphony. The orchestra makes frequent appearances at the Washington State Fair and the Tacoma Dome accompanying such celebrity artists as Chris Botti, Patti LaBelle and Chicago.

With a vibrant artistic personality and dynamic leadership, the organization is cultivating a dedicated, supportive musical community that gathers frequently to experience great music together. In an age where home entertainment systems, iPods and MP3s dominate, Symphony Tacoma is keeping performance alive – Tacoma-style – in the heart of the Theater District.

– Andy Buelow is executive director of Symphony Tacoma.

Tacoma Little Theatre
Compiled by Judith Cullen

The years surrounding World War I were times of great changes across all societal and cultural strata, and the stage was not immune from this great shift. While the successes of vaudeville, melodramas, touring theatricals of the 19th Century, and the emerging new media of cinema battled to define entertainment in the new century; more locally created performing art was coming to life through the Little Theatre Movement. Little Theatres can be seen as a precursor to the Off-Broadway movement of the 1950s, and may also be viewed as the birthplace of community theater in America.

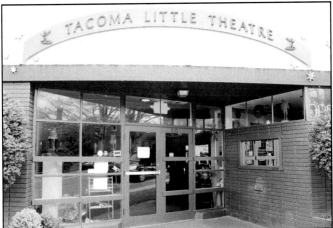

TLT home at 210 North I Street since 1940 TLT

A 1936 Tacoma Drama League play TLT

Nearing a century of dramatic performances TLT

The Little Theatre Movement was a result of young theatre actors, directors, technicians, and designers who were influenced by European Theatre and the ideas of German director Max Reinhardt, the designing techniques of Adolphe Appia and Edward Gordon Craig, and the staging methods at the Théâtre-Libre in Paris, the Freie Bühne in Berlin, and the Moscow Art Theatre. The Movement sought to provide experimental centers for the dramatic arts, distinct from prominent commercial theatres of the day.

In October of 1918, a group of civic-minded community members founded the Tacoma Chapter of the Drama League of America (known as the "Tacoma Drama League" or sometimes as the "Civic Drama League"). The Drama League of America sought to promote theater and the study of theatrical literature and culture as a means of community building and individual enrichment. The Tacoma Chapter was comprised of the Civic Drama School and the Tacoma Little Theatre. The Drama League provided oversight, governance, and promoted the two operational wings. 1918 to 1919 saw classes, play readings, study groups, and the first fully realized production in December of 1919, a production of George Bernard Shaw's *You Never Can Tell.* While some gaps may be found in its production history for various reasons including the Great Depression and World War II, records show that organizational activity has never ceased since those early days in 1918.

The Civic Drama League found a home in the "New" Gymnasium of Annie Wright Seminary, then located on the block bounded by Division Avenue, North 1st Street, and Tacoma Avenue. Productions ranged from an annual melodrama and classical plays, to contemporary works including Eugene O'Neill's controversial *Emperor Jones,* an early twentieth century indictment of slavery and enslavement.

After Annie Wright moved to its current home and sold its North 1st Street area properties, the Civic Drama League performed at the Slovenian Hall at 2306 North 30th St., from 1933 to 1939. In 1940, the acting company found a permanent home for its operations when it purchased the former site of Tacoma Motors, built originally in 1913 as an auto repair shop. The first performance at the 210 North I St., location was Maxwell Anderson's *Knickerbocker Holiday,* which was also the first of many musical productions presented in the decades to come.

In 1950 the lot immediately to the north of the theater space was purchased, the auditorium enlarged and an adjacent structure was built to include a spacious lobby, offices, and expanded bathrooms with plans for further amenities in the future.

Today, Tacoma Little Theatre (TLT) is the surviving entity of the original three. TLT is governed by a volunteer Board of Directors, and is managed by a small professional staff. TLT hires directors and contracts designers and other production leadership positions from among those with professional or other significant experience. The actors, crew, ushers, and all other theater functions are accomplished by over 250 volunteers from a four-county area giving over 10,000 volunteer hours a year to provide their friends, family, neighbors, co-workers and community with some of the best community created theater this area has to offer.

– Ms. Cullen served Tacoma Little Theatre from 1993 to 2006, first as production manager, and then as producing artistic director. Today she consults on special projects, assisting the current staff with new initiatives.

Tacoma City Ballet

In 1955, Miss Jan Collum founded The Jan Collum School of Classical Ballet and The Concert Ballet Group of Tacoma. By 1965, The Concert Ballet Group of Tacoma was renamed BALLETACOMA, a 501(c)(3) non-profit corporation, and a ballet company of six dancers had blossomed into thirty. BALLETACOMA, under the astute artistic direction of Miss Collum, forged a local, regional, and national reputation for excellence in the instruction and performance of classical ballet. In 1995, BALLETACOMA was re-christened Tacoma City Ballet and both the school and company were amalgamated under the same 501(c)(3) non-profit corporation.

Having relocated from 124 North I Street in 1983, today both the ballet school and company remain housed in The Merlino Art Center. The school features The Jan Collum Ballroom, which is one of the historic crown jewels of our city. The ballroom's 6,000 square feet of clear-span space, 20-foot ceiling height, Palladian windows, decorative plaster moldings gilded in 24-carat gold, and sprung hardwood floors create the perfect residence for a ballet school and company. Here, in beautiful spacious old-world elegance, thousands of dancers have studied, rehearsed, and performed the art of classical ballet.

In 1983 the City of Tacoma opened the doors of its newly renovated Pantages Theater, which was intended to specifically house the community's performing arts organizations. In that opening year, BALLETACOMA was invited to perform *The Nutcracker* accompanied by the Tacoma Symphony Orchestra. For BALLETACOMA, who had been presenting an annual performance season since 1955 in various tiny theaters and high school venues, this was a milestone. The Pantages Theater became the ballet company's performing home, and not only was *The Nutcracker* performed there annually, but countless other ballet productions as well. In 2016, Tacoma City Ballet finished its final and 33rd consecutive performance of *The Nutcracker* in the Pantages Theater.

Miss Erin Ceragioli is the current Executive/Artistic Director of Tacoma City Ballet and the Director of Tacoma City Ballet School. She began her primary study of classical ballet under Miss Archalee Correll, and continued her advance study under the tutelage of stellar teachers Harold Christensen, Lew Christensen, William Christensen, Benjamin Harkarvy, Robert Joffrey, Janet Reed, Patricia Stander, and Maria Tallchief. After a short professional career as a dancer, Miss Ceragioli chose to teach classical ballet, and studied the syllabi of the Danish, English, French,

Performances of The Nutcracker have been a Tacoma City Ballet holiday tradition for more than 30 years

TCiB

Italian, and Russian Schools of Ballet, earning her certifications. In 1987, she accepted a position on the faculty of The Jan Collum School of Classical Ballet at the request of Miss Collum. In 1990, after four years of teaching in the school and serving the company as ballet mistress and assistant artistic director, Miss Jan Collum appointed Miss Ceragioli as co-artistic director of BALLETACOMA.

In 2009 Tacoma City Ballet created a performance space, The Jan Collum Ballroom Theater in The Merlino Art Center, which afforded the company the opportunity to present small-scale annual productions. After eight successful seasons, The Jan Collum Ballroom Theater was fully equipped with professional stage accouterments in 2016, and now has the capacity to house an audience of 300. While The Jan Collum Ballroom Theater is a wonderful additional performing venue, Tacoma City Ballet will still continue to produce and present annual favorite ballets, and create new and innovative large-scale productions each season for the grand theatrical stage.

The 2017–2018 Season adds yet another milestone to Tacoma City Ballet's history, as the company becomes the Resident Dance Company of the new Federal Way Performing Arts and Event Center. Henceforward, Tacoma City Ballet will be performing its ever-favorite annual production of *The Nutcracker* and full-length classical ballet productions there as well.

In 2017–2018, Tacoma City Ballet celebrates its 62nd Performance Season, and proudly continues to preserve and perpetuate a legacy filled with a rich history that has touched thousands of hearts, minds, and souls with the beauty of the classical art of ballet.

– Composition provided by Tacoma City Ballet.

The Second City Chamber Series

The history and tradition of chamber music reaches back over 300 years, beginning with early Baroque composers such as Rameau, Telemann and Bach. It flourished in the 18th–19th centuries, while the 20th century brought growing experimentation with more unusual combinations of instruments. Some of history's greatest composers chose chamber music as the medium in

which to express their most profound and intimate musical thoughts.

The usual definition of chamber music is music performed in an intimate setting and written for a small instrumental ensemble, one player per part. Chamber music stresses personal expression and conversation among players, rather than virtuosic display or leadership by a conductor. Each member is responsible for a close musical dialogue with the rest of the ensemble. It is the ultimate in collaboration.

The Second City Chamber Series – Tacoma's own award-winning producer of professional chamber music concerts – has been dedicated to the quality performance of chamber music masterworks both old and new since its founding by pianists Willa and William Doppmann in 1977.

Unlike many classical music organizations that present traveling artists (who may play the same concert in Seattle, Spokane, New York, and Tacoma), the Second City Chamber Series has a tradition of producing concerts that are individually developed for Tacoma audiences.

Each year since, the Second City Chamber Series has brought together many of the finest musicians of the Northwest and beyond to perform interesting, challenging, and entertaining chamber music in an artfully assembled series of chamber music programs for audiences around Pierce County, and with a visibility that extends throughout the Puget Sound. Since its inception, the Series has performed at the Great Hall at Annie Wright School, but has since expanded its operation to include a summer series at Lakewold Gardens, a recital series at First Lutheran Church in Tacoma, and a youth program, open to middle-school and high-school students throughout Pierce County, known as the Young Chamber Players.

Svend Rønning SCC

SCC

Nurtured by its longtime Artistic Director Jerry Kracht from 1982 to 2007, Second City Chamber Series concerts often combine well-known works of the classical masters with the lesser-known works from cultures and traditions around the world. This deliberate, artistic combination of the old and the new creates a unique programming tradition that is well-known by audiences in the region and respected by critics. Artistic Director Svend Rønning (2007–present) has continued these traditions, while also creating thematic programming, designed to educate and to entertain.

By promoting awareness and appreciation of chamber music for its listeners and providing a convenient and ready forum for its performers, Second City has truly become first for chamber music in Tacoma.

– *Composition provided by Second City Chamber Series*

Tacoma Youth Symphony

By Kristina Thomas

In the summer of 1963 the Tacoma Arts for Youth Council held a two-week-long arts festival at Pacific Lutheran University. One of the musical offerings was a string orchestra. The 28 students who participated enjoyed the experience so much that they asked if they could continue on Saturdays during the school year. The first Tacoma Youth Symphony consisted of 80 junior high and high school students. In the fall of 1964, a second orchestra was added, the Tacoma Junior Symphony. Rehearsals were held in the new University of Puget Sound music building and concerts were held at PLU's Eastvold Auditorium and local schools. Dr. Paul Oncley was the first conductor and Virginia Morrison led the organization. Over the years TYS has

been conducted by C. Irvin Wright, Stanley Chappel, Steve Amundson and Harry Davidson and is currently conducted by Dr. Paul-Elliott Cobbs.

TYSA has expanded over the years to meet the needs of the students it serves. Currently the Tacoma Youth Symphony Association is comprised of six orchestras with an enrollment of nearly 400 students ages 7–21 from all over the greater Puget Sound area. Current TYSA conductors include Mr. Dale Johnson, who has been with TYSA since 1979, Mrs. Karla Epperson and Ms. Elizabeth Ward.

Over TYSA's history the Tacoma Youth Symphony has performed in Switzerland, Scotland, England, Holland, France, Austria and Germany. In 2000 TYS was chosen to perform in Carnegie Hall after a rigorous application process and returned to Carnegie Hall in 2005. The Tacoma Youth Symphony represented Washington State at the 2008 Festival of the States in Washington, D.C., the 2013 Festival of the States in Boston and performed at the National Festival of States in Los Angeles in May 2017.

Part of what makes TYSA so unique and so successful is the nurturing, family like environment that the staff endeavors to create. While setting the bar high musically, TYSA also teaches students leadership skills and teamwork and, in doing so, prepares students to meet

TYSA

The organization will celebrate its 55th anniversary in 2018 ⊙TYSA

the challenges they will face throughout their lives. Those who have gone through our programs have gone on to be leaders in their chosen fields, whether the field is music, law, medicine, business, education, etc. TYSA plays a positive role in the lives of its students.

The orchestras of the Tacoma Youth Symphony Association perform 11 public concerts each year at Urban Grace Church and the Rialto Theater. In addition, there is an annual Chamber Music Concert, performances at Festival of Trees and a Victorian Country Christmas, Education Concerts for fourth-graders from schools all over Pierce and Southern King Counties, school concerts, performances in retirement homes and string quartets that perform for events in the community. For over 50 years, TYSA has developed into one of the premier youth orchestras in the country while continuing to enhance its position as an educational and performance organization home-based in the heart of Tacoma's Theater District.

– *Kristina Thomas is marketing director for Tacoma Youth Symphony*

Northwest Sinfonietta

I n the fall of 1991, harpsichordist and Pacific Lutheran University lecturer Kathryn Habedank conceived of a chamber orchestra performance in Tacoma to commemorate the 200th anniversary of the death of Mozart. To lead this one-time event, she contacted friend and conductor Christophe Chagnard, whom she had met during their time at the New England Conservatory. From the success of this first performance

NORTHWEST Sinfonietta

grew the Northwest Sinfonietta – a chamber orchestra designed to complement the existing classical music community while invigorating the concert experience. With their perseverance, the Sinfonietta was quickly established as one of the premier professional ensembles in the Pacific Northwest.

During this initial period of growth, the orchestra began branching out and serving many different communities throughout the region. In these formative years, the orchestra also recorded a critically-acclaimed CD of Mozart Symphonies, and held an annual Youth Concerto Competition for young musicians.

As the organization grew, the Sinfonietta began establishing educational initiatives to broaden the reach of classical music. These included the Heart Strings audience-building effort; the Orchestra at Work student education program; and Music off the Record, a free music appreciation lecture series. By 2008, Northwest

Over a quarter century of celebrated performances ⊙NWS

Sinfonietta was named Resident Chamber Orchestra of Benaroya Hall; two years later, with the support of community leaders and city government, the orchestra began regular concerts at Puyallup's Pioneer Park Pavilion.

In 2012, Northwest Sinfonietta became only the third professional U.S. orchestra to visit and perform in Cuba since the 1959 revolution. A visit from Cuban musicians that season also marked the Sinfonietta's debut in the S. Mark Taper Auditorium in Benaroya Hall, with a side-by-side performance in October 2012.

A major change came in 2014 as Christophe marked the end of his acclaimed 24-year tenure as Northwest Sinfonietta Music Director and the organization announced its intention to become the fifth orchestra in the world to adopt an Artistic Partner model of operations. This approach emboldens musicians to actively participate in the artistic identity of the organization while exploring collaborations with world-renowned conductors.

The 2015–16 Season celebrated the 25th anniversary of the Sinfonietta and welcomed the three inaugural Artistic Partners to the region. In advance of the season opening, the orchestra was honored to receive the Governor's Arts and Heritage Award for twenty-five years of excellence in the arts.

As the orchestra looks towards its 30th anniversary season and beyond, it remains rooted in the core values on which it was founded: the passion and collaborative spirit of its musicians; the excitement of innovative, classically-based concerts; and the desire to share amazing works of art with communities throughout the Pacific Northwest Region.

"The 12-year-old Northwest Sinfonietta, based in Tacoma under the direction of conductor Christophe Chagnard, has developed into an ensemble that can hold its own among the best classical-music organizations in the Northwest."
– *The Seattle Times, September 2002*

"Hearing a Northwest Sinfonietta concert is like drinking a great young wine: enjoyable, with both tangy notes and occasional flashes of stunning perfection."
– *The News Tribune, October 2006*

"In all, the concert that thoroughly deserved its lengthy ovation, and which exemplifies the best of what a contemporary chamber orchestra should be."
– *The News Tribune, November 17, 2014*

– Composition provided by the Northwest Sinfonietta and Co-Founders: Christophe Chagnard and Kathryn Habedank

Tacoma Musical Playhouse

Tacoma Musical Playhouse (TMP) was founded by Jon Douglas Rake in January 1994 to fulfill a need in Tacoma for a theater company that specializes in the uniquely American art form of musical theater. Mr. Rake's artistic leadership of the company, supported by a need in the  community and an availability of excellent local talent, are the driving forces behind its success. The primary artistic team of Jon Douglas Rake, Artistic Director and Jeffrey Stvrtecky, Music Director, provide stability to the productions at TMP. This stability has assured a level of quality that is maintained from production to production and anticipated by an ever-growing, musical-theater-loving audience.

TMP's mission is "Enriching lives through the art form of musical theater," with the belief that people's lives are enriched by high-quality entertainment. Sometimes that entertainment challenges people to think about life issues; other times it offers opportunities for hilarity; and still other times it offers moments for tears. In all cases, however, the experiences move people's emotions and take them to a new place in their thinking. TMP has enriched people with productions such as *Into the Woods, The Music Man, The Sound of Music, Oklahoma, Disney's Beauty and the Beast, Thoroughly Modern Millie* and *West Side Story.*

TMP is the fastest-growing arts organization in the Puget Sound region. From its modest beginning at Annie Wright Kemper Center and then to a church basement, TMP has rapidly expanded. TMP moved into the 380-seat Narrows Theatre in 1995, then bought the playhouse and its surrounding Narrows Shopping Center in 2002.

A $1.2 millon renovation was finished in 2012 that included creating an orchestra loft, a new stage with new theatrical lighting and sound and up-grading the building to be ADA compliant.

The TMP season includes six main stage shows which run four or five weekends each and regularly books its performers for specialty shows throughout the

Cast of Cats   ⊙TMP/KD

James and the Giant Peach   ⊙TMP/KD

Former Narrows Theater is now TMP home   ⊙TMP/KD

community. TMP has also been a presenting organization, hosting the Seattle hit comedy show *Late Nite Catechism, Marni Nixon, The Voice of Hollywood,* and *A Tribute to Red Skelton,* and various regional jazz artists in the Narrows Theatre. In the 2006–07 season, we launched the TMP Family Theater program. Five productions for children, presented by adults, are offered each season.

Education is a priority for the organization. Initially, a Summer Musical Theater Youth Camp trained a group of talented and eager young performers, culminating in a fully-staged public production. A Winter Break

Youth Camp, an After School Academy, and a Summer Honor Camp were added to the educational programs ensuring nearly year-round activities for young people at TMP.

TMP has a positive economic impact on the West End neighborhood demonstrated by the fact that it is likely that the Narrows Theatre would not have survived if TMP had not purchased the property . As a result, the purchase of the building ensures the continued availability of arts programs in the West End that are easily accessible to Central and North Tacoma, University Place, Fircrest and Lakewood. As attendance continues to reach near-capacity for our main stage productions, we will continue to evaluate the need to potentially offer additional performances. We are grateful that the support of our patrons provides us with opportunities for even greater growth.

– Profile provided by Tacoma Musical Playhouse

Tacoma Concert Band
By Mark Reutlinger

The Tacoma Concert Band was the creation of Robert Musser, a Professor of Music at the University of Puget Sound. He was an active professional musician in the area, and in the summer of 1981 he decided to form a professional quality community band, something that did not yet exist in the Puget Sound region. He asked all the best musicians he knew in the area if they would join, and all agreed. The all-volunteer TCB thus began in the fall of 1981, playing at Tacoma's Stadium High School, and in 1986 it moved to the Pantages Theater in downtown Tacoma.

The TCB's mission is to provide the Puget Sound community with a professional-quality wind ensemble performing the very finest symphonic band music; to offer a high-quality performance opportunity to local wind and percussion musicians; to support and encourage the region's school band programs; and to reaffirm the community concert band's position in American music. In furtherance of its mission, it performs both a series of four subscription concerts each season and free Concerts in the Parks in the summer. Approximately sixty volunteer musicians perform with the TCB at each concert.

Performing a wide variety of music, Tacoma Concert Band has been recognized locally and internationally   ⊙ **TCoB**

The TCB has become the premier community symphonic band in the region, having also earned an international reputation through its several European tours. It has received awards of excellence from, among others, the Tacoma Arts Commission and the John Philip Sousa Foundation. The band programs a wide variety of music and draws a very diverse audience. It has produced CDs and DVDs of its music and has been featured in the local print and broadcast media. In support of music education, the band sponsors an annual student solo competition, invites outstanding student musicians to play with the band, and has performed special concerts for local grade school children.

By virtue of the type of music it plays, the diversity of the audience it draws, and the number of local musicians it serves, the TCB is able to provide a cultural experience different from, and complementary to, other music ensembles in the region. With a solid foundation and the support of its members and patrons, the Tacoma Concert Band plans to continue to provide Tacoma and the Puget Sound region with the highest quality symphonic band music well into the future.

– Mark Reutlinger is Executive Director of the Tacoma Concert Band

Tacoma Opera

Tacoma Opera was founded in 1968 as the Tacoma Opera Society and presented its first production, *Die Fledermaus* by Johann Strauss, Jr. at the Eastvold Auditorium on the Pacific Lutheran University campus. In 1981, with the help of Dr. Hans Wolf, then director of community outreach for Seattle Opera, the company turned professional and changed its name to the Tacoma

Opera Association. Wolf became the new director of the company and a production of *Die Fledermaus* was again successfully staged that year. Under Dr. Wolf's leadership and along with the organizational guidance of long-time executive director, Anne Farrell, the company produced many operettas and grand operas over the next several years. The company also produced numerous premieres including the West Coast premiere of Jacques Offenbach's *Christopher Columbus* and the world premiere of a brand-new opera, *The Pied Piper of Hamelin,* by Seattle composer Carol Sams.

In the late 1990s, Both Wolf and Farrell retired from their positions and Rod Gideons became the executive director of the company and David Bartholomew the artistic director. During their time, the company continued to expand by producing larger scale mainstream operas. Kathryn Smith came to the company in 2003 as general director, extending the continued growth of the company until the economic downturn of 2008, after which she successfully shepherded the company through some very difficult financial times. She left Tacoma Opera in June of 2011 to take a position as general director of Madison Opera in Madison, Wisconsin. Dr. Noel Koran joined the company as general director after Ms. Smith's departure and comes to Tacoma Opera from a long background in opera, having been a singer, stage director, producer, educator and arts administrator in a career spanning nearly 40 years.

Tacoma Opera, which will celebrate its 50th anniversary in 2018, has grown from a small,

TACOMA OPERA SOCIETY

PRESENTS

DIE FLEDERMAUS
BY JOHANN STRAUSS

February 8 and 10, 1968

EASTVOLD AUDITORIUM
PACIFIC LUTHERAN UNIVERSITY

First production program 1968 TO

SOTA
By Elizabeth Hirschl

The Tacoma School of the Arts (SOTA) was first conceived in 1999 as a way to make use of community arts resources for educating students. Rather than having students sit inside a theater, music, or art class confined within a more traditional high school structure, this innovative educational concept would occur in the midst of the museums and theaters that punctuate the downtown corridor. SOTA's first group of sophomores entered the school in fall 2001, located primarily in a building on the corner of South 21st and Pacific Avenue. In the fall of 2003, the performing arts classes moved into the Theater District with a remodel of the former Ted Brown Music building in the 1100 block of Broadway.

By expanding to the Theater District, not only were students more connected to the inner workings of the performance arts, but as clusters of students walked 10 city blocks between the two main locations they represented a form of lively performance themselves. This fostered a sense of camaraderie between the students and the downtown businesses, helped to energize Downtown Tacoma, and taught students a sense of social responsibility.

SOTA has now grown to include 9th graders and now serves 650 students from across Tacoma. Through a Tacoma School District equity-focused admission process and a lottery to determine acceptance, SOTA's student body reflects the greater Tacoma community

2018 will mark 50 years of dramatic performances TO

amateur based company, little-known outside of the city of Tacoma, into a vibrant regional opera company attracting audiences from all over the Pacific Northwest and beyond. The company has solidified its position as a cultural icon for the South Puget Sound region and has exciting plans for the future. The company has discovered over the years that there is great value in presenting opera in an intimate performance environment so that audiences can connect more directly with the music, the story and the performers in operas we present. For centuries, opera has been associated with grandiose, large scale and expensive productions that focus on spectacle, but the art form has unfortunately become financially inaccessible to the everyday general population as presented in the larger opera houses in America. Tacoma Opera is intent on redefining opera in this country as an intimate and accessible art form that allows audiences to experience opera in a uniquely personal way, touching the heart and stimulating the mind. This is our philosophy and it is with this philosophy as our guiding light that we will continue into our next 50 years presenting opera up close and personal. It's been a great journey so far and we, at Tacoma Opera, look forward to the next 50 years of serving the South Sound region with exciting, intimate and accessible opera productions.

– Profile provided by Tacoma Opera

Students bring vibrancy to Theater District street scene BJ

Student artistic expression takes many forms ⊙ SOTA/DP

in terms of race & ethnicity, socioeconomic status, and neighborhood orientation. The school continues to partner with organizations in the Theater District, including the Broadway Center for the Performing Arts. Many technical theater students get their start in the professional world by working in these alliances.

The non-profit Elements of Education Partners funds an Adjunct Instructor Program which brings professional artists into the classroom at SOTA. The adjunct instructors make it possible for SOTA to offer a variety of classes and for students to form relationships with professional artists. These relationships have integrated the school into the fabric of the performing arts community in a way that stimulates learning and provides a richer texture to the environment in which SOTA operates.

There are plans for SOTA to become even more ingrained in the Theater District with the the school district's purchase and remodel of the building that sits on the site of the former historic Tacoma Theater at 9th and Broadway. Initially, this space will house humanities and language departments. As of spring 2017, the plan is to renovate the space to include seminar rooms and performing arts spaces that can be used by the school as well as the greater community.

– Elizabeth Hirschl, a 2006 SOTA graduate, is Development Director for Elements of Education Partners

Tacoma Actors Guild
By Nan Peele

While the Tacoma Actors Guild has been gone for nearly a decade, the distinctive role it played during its existence as Tacoma's only professional theater company and the emotions conveyed during its demise provide insight into the passion and dedication arts organizations can evoke in the culture of a community.

When I joined the board of the Tacoma Actors Guild in the early 2000s, I had only been in the Northwest a few years and had been exploring the area's arts venues. My first introduction to local theatre came a few weeks after arriving when a new friend introduced me to Tacoma Little Theatre. As I became more involved in the community my appreciation of Tacoma's arts evolved into a pledge of loyalty and support. When TAG closed its doors in 2007, and was forced to lay off its 24 employees, it was one of hundreds of theatres, some in our region (e.g., The Empty Space Theatre), that faced the same fate. With the ensuing recession, as families struggled to pay mortgages and bills, an evening at the theatre was not among their options. Foundations reduced budgets and donations dwindled.

It was a sad ending to a 29-year run for the organization that was founded in 1978 by University of Puget Sound professor Rick Tutor and William Becvar, a professor of drama at Pacific Lutheran University. A four-show run of *Guys and Dolls* at the Temple Theater was an encouraging success. In 1979 TAG began its first full season in St. Leo's School, which would serve as its home for 10 years.

When the City of Tacoma, with support from the arts and business community, built Theatre on the Square adjacent to the Pantages Theater, TAG had its performance home from 1993 until the end in 2007. In all, TAG produced over 180 plays seen by nearly one million people. The range of productions from classic to contemporary, serious drama to comedy, were always presented with the highest quality in performance and presentation.

Though it remains painful that we couldn't save TAG, many memories of that time are inspiring due to the teamwork, dedication, kindness, and generosity demonstrated by so many. Following the sad announcement to the executive director, Pat Patton, in

Six plays were presented in 2004–05 season   ⊙ TPL

February 2007, that funds were not sufficient to meet the next payroll and staff must be laid off immediately in accordance with law, the announcement in the morning's paper provoked generous offerings from the community. Creditors were eventually paid except for a few who generously forgave the debt, and TAG did not declare bankruptcy.

One board member, a local banker, offered his downtown bank's meeting room to call ticket holders... focusing first on those scheduled for the upcoming canceled performances. Several board members also stood outside Theater on the Square the nights of the cancelled performances to meet ticket holders and apologize if we'd been unsuccessful in notifying them. The phone calls continued for days and became conversations of thanks for pleasant memories as well as suggestions for change if we found a way to survive. But perhaps the most memorable calls were those incoming from our fellow theatres who wanted to help. Lakewood Playhouse, Tacoma Little Theatre, and Tacoma Musical Playhouse all offered to honor TAG tickets to any of their upcoming performances and asked what else they could do.

Though, TAG is no more despite such dedicated effort, it is warmly remembered by many... among them some young adults who experience arts with more passion as Star Camp alumni. The teamwork demon-

strated by our local community theaters in 2007 is still in place and apparent in their current collaborations. They, and other arts organizations such as our Broadway Center for the Performing Arts and Symphony Tacoma, have set a Tacoma standard to continually strengthen efforts that make the arts accessible and inclusive to everyone in our city.

– Nan Peele was former Board President of the Tacoma Actors Guild

Tacoma Philharmonic

In 1933, 21-year-old Eugene Linden hitchhiked from his Portland home to Tacoma with the desire to start an orchestra. The first rehearsal was of historical significance: three musicians responded. Mr. Linden was satisfied, "No musicians would have been a failure, three was a beginning."

In a few short months Mr. Linden brought together 65 musicians. Rehearsals were held in many Tacoma locations: Ted Brown Music Company and the Winthrop Hotel were the first. Hosted every Sunday, the first regular rehearsal hall was the basement of the State Armory. Once interest in the orchestra project developed, rehearsals were transferred to the Scottish Rite Cathedral, where the company remained until the first concert in March 1934.

During the first two years there was not any pay for musicians. Linden gave his time freely to form the orchestra and commuted each week from Portland. Mrs. Belle Hodges Fletcher, a Tacoma resident since 1884, generously extended Linden an invitation to make her home his headquarters during his time building the orchestra.

The first concert was on March 17, 1934, at Jason Lee Intermediate School with an attendance of 800 music lovers. The second concert followed on June 5, 1934. The organization developed a constitution, by-laws, incorporated and officially adopted the name Tacoma Phil-

Founder Eugene Linden   ⊙ TPL

harmonic in 1936. In the 1940s, Tacoma Philharmonic performed for servicemen locally many times.

Nearly a decade later in 1947, Tacoma Philharmonic merged with the Seattle Symphony to create the short-lived Pacific Northwest Symphony Orchestra, with Maestro Linden as the combined orchestra's Music Director. In 1951, due to rising orchestra costs, the Tacoma Philharmonic's Board of Directors made the monumental decision to become a presenting organization rather than a performing group. Since then, the Tacoma Philharmonic made it their mission to present the finest orchestras, chamber ensembles and solo artists in classical music.

As of May 1, 2012, the non-profit structure of the Tacoma Philharmonic was folded into the non-profit structure of the Broadway Center. Thus the deep connection to this community and commitment to present classical music and education will live on through the Tacoma Philharmonic Endowment Fund held in trust by the Broadway Center. This fund will underwrite approximately 30% of all future activities. Future programs will include: four annual concerts, new educational classical music services at K–12 campuses and The Beatrice Herrmann Young Artist Competition. The competition, named in honor of the Tacoma Philharmonic's long-time benefactor, will continue to promote excellence in musical performance, encourage young musicians in their pursuit of high artistic standards, and to foster a love for the performing arts in the community and throughout the Puget Sound.

– Source information by the Broadway Center for the Performing Arts

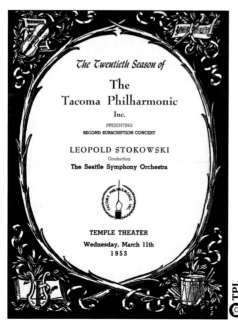

Program from 1953 concert at Temple Theater

Performers

(Top) With a mirror to show off her skills, Selika Pettiford performed on an electric organ with two keyboards at the Olympus Hotel in 1948. She could sing in more than six languages.
(Middle) Esther Stayner poses at the Broadway Theater organ. She was also the organist for the Rialto Theater in the 1920s.
(Bottom) A group of performers believed to be the Fanchon & Marco's Road Show No. 1 from Los Angeles posed outside the Broadway Theater in 1928. TPL

NOW PLAYING

Bold Sounds/ Dark Rooms

A Tacoma Musical Medley

From brass bands drawing patrons into box houses to the pure voices of world-class soloists on concert hall stages, from booming spectacles in the Tacoma Dome before 23,000 fans to jazz trios in a quiet bar, from rock and grunge legends to theater organists in the silent film era, from classical music concerts to bluegrass, from places where blacks couldn't get served to clubs where black musicians played all night, from vaudeville performers to church choirs, from ethnic music in fraternal halls to all-city dances at the Armory, from bands marching along parade routes to dance contests at the Winthrop Hotel, from country & western music to psychedelic shows, from Sousa in Stadium Bowl to Elvis in Lincoln Bowl, from serving as the birthplace of Bing Crosby to being adopted by jazz legends Art Mineo and Red Kelly, from 80-piece orchestras soaring symphonically to heavy metal dances busted by the cops, from big jazz bands in ballrooms to R&B bands in blues bars, from the dance bands at the Top of the Ocean to theater musicians in the orchestra pit, from country and folk music fiddlers to mosh pit divers, from music in the parks to open mic nights, from the days before Tacoma was a city to the present, the widest diversity imaginable in music has filled our ears, moved our feet and stirred our emotions.

As has been presented throughout this book, music has played a dominant role in drawing people to gather in every venue built for entertainment and some that weren't. The range of diversity in the types of music is a reflection of what has been popular in a particular era and how those trends in taste can ebb and flow through the decades. Tacoma has drawn many of the legendary names in music to its venues and many home-grown talents have gained global stature.

The sounds need not be loud to be bold in their appeal. The venues need not be dark, but it seems better that way as the audience experience ranges from weekend dances to once-in-a-lifetime concert memories. In this chapter we offer a taste of Tacoma's popular music scene and its music makers.

Brown Spots

As teacher, historian and advocate for historical causes, Michael Sullivan is particularly adept at prowling the nuances in Tacoma's character. In the process he can provide insights that in mainstream research might otherwise remain obscure. Which brings us to the Brown Spots. "These were African-American after-hours clubs that flourished downtown from the '20s through the '50s. Called "Brown Spots" by black and white people alike, the clubs attracted the cream of jazz performers of that era, artists like Ella Fitzgerald and Louis Armstrong. Booked into nightclubs in Seattle, they'd do their last act at one or two o'clock in the morning and then they'd get on a night train and go to Tacoma," he said. "They'd find a Brown Spot downtown and they would smoke weed and play jazz through the night. In the morning, they'd catch the train (and some sleep) en route to Portland, and by eight o'clock the next night they were back on stage. And, of course, the pattern would be reversed for those heading from Portland to Seattle, Vancouver, Chicago, etc."

3 a.m. on September 6, 1930 at the Little Harlem Rondivoo TPL

Bing Crosby

Harry "Bing" Crosby was born on May 2, 1903 in a house his father built at 1112 North J Street. Considering he moved to Spokane when he was three years old, Tacoma can at least take credit for providing the setting for his first words. That voice would become a bass-baritone so appealing it made him the most prolific recording artist of the 20th century. For a quarter-century beginning in the early 30s he was the leader in record sales, radio ratings and cinema earnings. It must have been the Tacoma water that set his talents in motion.

Pat O'Day

Although he would become a regional rock and roll powerhouse rather than the international star that Bing Crosby was, **Pat O'Day** is another who drew his first breath in Tacoma (1934). According to rock historian Peter Blecha: O'Day was born as Paul Berg, the son of a preacher who ran a radio ministry on KMO radio. Raised in Bremerton, he attended radio school in Tacoma and in 1959 he was on the air at legendary rock station KJR. When he hired the **Wailers** to play at the famed **Spanish Castle** he began building an empire that would eventually involve presenting over 58 separate teen-dances a week throughout the state. O'Day increased the interest in Northwest music around the nation to a level that wouldn't again be attained (and surpassed) until Seattle's grunge rock movement of the 1990s.

Elvis at Lincoln Bowl

On the afternoon of September 1, 1957, **Elvis Presley** shook, swiveled, shimmied, and rolled out what 6,000 fans came to see from the most iconic figure in rock history. Performing on a makeshift stage erected on the **Lincoln Bowl** field, Presley's appearance came almost exactly one year after his debut on the

Ed Sullivan TV show in which cameras refused to show him below his wiggling waist. The Tacoma crowd did not encounter any such censorship and fans scooped his footprints out of the dirt after he leapt off the stage and escaped into a waiting limousine. He was headed to Seattle for an evening concert before 16,000 fans at **Sicks Stadium.**

Kent Morrill was enjoying plenty of adulation as a member of **The Fabulous Wailers,** a rock n' roll sensation in Tacoma and on the verge of being credited as perhaps America's first garage band. He wanted to see The King, but his ego prevented him from buying a ticket. "I was in high school. We wouldn't go see Elvis because all the girls were crazy over him and we were jealous," he recalled years later. "So, we climbed up in trees across the field and watched the show with binoculars."

Eric Burdon

Forty-seven years after sparking a riot in his concert at **Cheney Stadium, Eric Burdon** returned to Tacoma for a concert at the **Pantages Theater.** Maybe it was a mellowing with age or respect for the setting, but there was none of the rock throwing and responding tear gas from police that had filled the evening in 1970 when Burdon tried to invite a couple thousand fans sitting on "Tightwad Hill" to join the paying customers inside the stadium.

Auditorium/Crescent Ballroom

Out of the ashes of the Germania Hall, the **Auditorium** was constructed in 1922 at 1308-10 Fawcett Avenue. Designed by Roland Borhek, the building's façade still bears the name "AUDITORIUM," although that use has long since given way to commercial uses. The likes of Rudolph Valentino appeared there in 1923. Eight years later the property was combined with the adjacent building, a Ford dealership built in 1918, and renamed the **Crescent Ballroom**.

Big dance bands, political conventions, and eventually rock n' roll shows made this a popular venue

Crescent Ballroom restored as commercial use   ⊚ BKJ

through the middle of the 20th century. Among the bands that played the Crescent were the **Wailers, Green River, The Fleetwoods, Butthole Surfers, Paul Revere and the Raiders and Sugarloaf.** By the 80s the place was closed and at risk of demolition. A revival was launched as the **Legends Auditorium** in 1990, and **Nirvana** and the **Melvins** packed the place as the home of Tacoma's grunge scene. By the turn of the century the shows were over, the mirrored ball that had sparkled in the ballroom disappeared before turning up at the South Park Community Center –

where, we might presume, seniors could reminisce about the days when they danced the night away to some of Tacoma's most memorable bands.

Jerry Miller

Born in Tacoma (1943) and eventually back in his hometown after establishing himself as one of the most highly regarded guitarists of all time, Jerry Miller got his first career break while playing at the Crescent Ballroom. "In 1962, after I left high school, a guy named Larry Thompson from Tacoma who was playing drums with **Bobby Fuller,** heard me playing at the Crescent Ballroom. Within two days I jumped on the Greyhound for El Paso where I moved in with Bobby and his parents. At that time, it wasn't known as the **Bobby Fuller Four,** just Bobby Fuller, with his brother, Randall, and Larry and myself. I recorded four tracks with them including the original *I Fought the Law.*" He was a founding member of the 60s Bay Area band **Moby Grape.** *Rolling Stone* ranked Miller 68th on its list of the 100 greatest guitarists of all time and the 1967 album *Moby Grape* was ranked 124 on its list of the 500 greatest albums of all time. Miller performs as a solo artist and with the **Jerry Miller Band.**

The **Jimi Hendrix** song *Spanish Castle Magic* reflected on his experiences playing with Miller and other Northwest musicians at the famed dance hall.

Traveling North, Traveling South

To follow S*howtime in Tacoma* sometimes meant traveling old Highway 99 north and south to experience some of the greatest music acts in the history of the Northwest. The **Spanish Castle,** an architectural statement that fit its name, was located midway between Tacoma and Seattle. The **Evergreen Ballroom,** located just north of Olympia, resembled a cross between a barn and an airplane hangar. It's what happened inside that established these two venues as showcases for virtually every great performer to tour the country and for bands based in Tacoma.

Both were built in 1931 as dance halls to serve the big-band era and hosted everything from country to soul acts, but found their most glorious nights in the rock 'n' roll era of the late 50s, early 60s. The Wailers could draw a couple thousand teenagers for dances at the Castle and Tacoma bands could pack in the crowds at the Evergreen amid the likes of **Count Basie, James Brown, Johnny Cash, Bill Haley & The Comets, Janis Joplin, Buck Owens, Chuck Berry, Charlie Parker, Ike & Tina Turner** and **Hank Williams.** As the rock scene faded, the Spanish Castle lost its draw-

ing power and was bulldozed in 1968. At virtually the same time, Interstate 5 opened, drawing traffic off Highway 99, and the Evergreen Ballroom was never quite the same – burning to the ground in 2000.

Century Ballroom

Closer to home, the distinctive **Century Ballroom,** located on Highway 99 at 54th East in Fife, packed every bit the dance hall power of the Castle or Evergreen. Built in 1934 by Rocco Manza and James Zarelli, the domed ballroom was designed by Bert Smyser, who had designed the distinctive Java Jive five years earlier (see below.) With 20,000 square feet of floor space, the Century booked all the big names of the era, including **Tommy Dorsey, Kay Kyser, Guy Lombardo, Bob Wills and his Texas Playboys, Gene Krupa, Duke Ellington, Count Basie, Nat King Cole, Hank Williams, and Lionel Hampton.** During World War II the ballroom ran two shifts of dancing with the second starting at 1:30 a.m. to serve the swing shift workers at the nearby defense plants. Dance marathons could go on for days.

The Century and the Hotel & Restaurant Employees Union promoted the annual "Cooks, Waiters and Bartenders Tray Derby" in which dozens of men and women restaurant and hotel employees would each be given a tray of food and beverages at the starting spot of Ninth and Broadway and challenged to cover the five miles to the dance hall without spilling a drop. Nineteen women and 25 men competed in the 1938 race with the winner clocking in at 55 minutes, 15 seconds and the top female less than a minute behind him. The ballroom closed in 1955 and was converted to a shopping mall before burning in 1964.

(Lower Left)1938 winners pose: Frances Taylor, Mondau's Tugboat (L); Stanley Johnson, Pappy's Cabin (R) 📷 TPL

Old-Time Fiddlers

TPL

In February 1930, RKO Pantages Theater and the *Tacoma News Tribune* sponsored a five-day contest to choose the best "Old-Time Fiddler" in Tacoma/Pierce County. All contestants would appear on a Pathe News Weekly sound newsreel to be shown throughout the United States. Charles Kahana of the Puyallup Tribe (shown standing, second from left) won the first place prize of $25 and received special recognition on the newsreel. Joined by the Pathe cameraman and sound technician on the right, the fiddlers posed for this picture on February 14th in Wright Park.

Alas *Wintergrass*

It felt personal from the start, kind of a barstool romance where everyone knew what this was all about. Bluegrass, music that should feel at home in Tacoma with all its lyrics of longing, lost opportunities, doin' time for doin' wrong, hopes for salvation, promises undone and revenge taken – carried by high harmonizing voices delivered over offerings of fiddles, banjos, bass and guitar. Bluegrass music from its roots in Appalachia to the streets of Tacoma, that's what felt so right when *Wintergrass*, billed as a mid-winter bluegrass festival, was launched in 1994. The founders, Rob Folsom, Patrice O'Neill, Earla Harding and Charlee Glock-Jackson, brought in the "Father of Bluegrass" Bill Monroe for the very first three-day event. Over the next 16 years the festival grew to four days, played on

stages at the Bicentennial Pavilion, several lounges and the temple of sound, Urban Grace Church. Many fiddlers and pickers came to town and never went to see performances because they were having too much fun jamming around the clock in nooks and lobbies of the Sheraton Hotel. The legends of the genre and international groups with their own interpretations came each year to eventually establish *Wintergrass* as one of the very top music festivals anywhere. It was as if Tacoma had finally found another anthem for its spirit.

Alas, as with any romance things can start to drift. As we should have expected from all those songs, when a partner starts looking at options, you better hope she doesn't catch the eye of someone rich, handsome and motivated. The Bellevue Hyatt was all three and, despite some last-gasp efforts by Tacoma officials, *Wintergrass* up and moved to Bellevue. Bellevue! How could she leave for some place that lacks even a little bit of soul in its stride or gravel in its voice? Whew, that one hurt and even worse, we hear that the festival is doing better than ever since we were left staring at the bottom of our glass and wondering. As the late Leonard Cohen tells us, "It's partner found, it's partner lost and hell to pay when the fiddler stops." Alas, *Wintergrass*.

Music and Mayhem at the Tacoma Dome

Amid an abundance of the good, there has been the bad and the ugly as concert-goers have filled the Tacoma Dome to its wooden rafters to hear some of the greatest performers in world of music. As noted in the adjoining list of headliner shows, **Bruce Springsteen** has performed five times at the Dome. Maybe it's his New Jersey tenacity, but he came back four times after his first visit in 1984 at which time he said the "Tacoma Aroma" made him and his band sick. Not only has the air gotten significantly more pleasant in Tacoma over the past 30-some years, but the tragedy and mayhem of early Dome concerts has also been avoided.

An incident in the first year of operation could have taken the roof off and did end festival-style seating ever since. A Fort Lewis soldier set fire to the Dome roof with a military flare that caused $20,000 in damage at an **AC/DC** concert. A Seattle man was stabbed to death during a 1986 **Judas Priest** concert and a man died of an overdose during a 1988 **Motley Crue** concert. That is the same year singer **Michael Jackson** canceled three sold-out shows, leading to a lawsuit by ticketholders against Ticketmaster. There were mixed reviews about the quality of singing in the showers when the **Seattle Sonics** played their 1994–95 season in the Dome.

Blues Vespers

One of the undercurrents of the music scene in Tacoma is the **Blues Vespers** program that bubbles to the surface the third Sunday evening of each month at **Immanuel Presbyterian Church**, located at 901 North J Street. **Reverend David R. Brown** developed a love of the blues as a youth growing up in Greenwich Village. When he came to Tacoma in 2005 Rev. Brown established what could be characterized as a melding of church and a state-of-mind about the music. "Blues music and its cousin, gospel music, often expresses in its words and music human joy, longing, passion and pain. Why shouldn't this music be in church along with poetry and prayer?" According to the response from the community, it fits well. "This has lifted off, exploded over the years," Brown added. "We've had just about every major blues group in the Northwest." **Little Bill Engelhart** plays at the Blues Vespers twice a year.

Rev. Brown is involved with the Broadway Center for the Performing Arts and other organizations in the promotion of music programs and other forums for community discussion. "These programs are what might be considered religious neutral, aimed at bringing forward topics like justice and human rights." Rev. Brown has received national and international recognition for his Blues Vespers program. While attending a **Big Joe Lewis and His Blues Kings** concert in London, the British musician called out to the "Blues Reverend" from the stage. **Chad & Jeremy,** British folk rockers from the 60s, performed the last concert of their touring careers, by performing at Blues Vespers. "I believe music is best as a communal experience," Rev. Brown commented. "Too often music is treated as a sound track as people go about their lives, rather than a shared experience. I think that's why people find something fulfilling at our concerts."

Dining and Dancing

In the 1920s into the 1960s there were nightclubs, restaurants and cocktail lounges sprinkled throughout Tacoma that provided varying styles of music for dancing.

Some were dives, some were classy. In their heyday, and each of them had its own, these four establishments were highly popular for those wanting to eat and move their feet. Each place offered its own style of entertainment, be it dance orchestras, can can girls, dance contests or country swing, they each attracted many Tacomans out for a night of fun.

The **Top of the Ocean Restaurant,** built to look like a ship, was constructed on pilings along Ruston Way in 1946 by owners Allen Rau and Bert Sundgren at a cost of $262,000. The restaurant had four dining rooms and a private suite for the Tacoma Athletic Club, which bought the restaurant in 1948. The popular dance and dining spot could seat up to 700 and had a floating dock that could accommodate 20 yachts. **Louie Grenier and his Orchestra** provided dance music at the waterfront site for 27 years. The unique venue was destroyed by arson in 1977, but a bronze sculpture marks its location just west of the fish store on Ruston Way.

Top of the Ocean Restaurant 📷 TPL

Steve's Gay 90's 📷 TPL

Another entertainment landmark ended its fun run in 1977 when **Steve's Gay 90's** closed. Opened in 1941 by Steve Pease and John Stanley, its distinctive right-angle sign was a familiar sight at 5238 South Tacoma Way. A newspaper ad pretty much told the story: "Gay 90's Revue. Can Can Girls Dancing. Smorgasbord noon to midnight. Old Time Vaudeville Acts. Open 24 hours, 7 days a week. Phone MA4-1590. Old Highway 99."

Now known as **Bob's Java Jive,** this Tacoma icon has been about everything imaginable as an entertainment spot, currently sharing stage time between grunge bands and karaoke, and its best hope to celebrate its 100th anniversary in a dozen years is simple momentum. In 1929, veterinarian Otis G. Button teamed up with architect/contractor Bert Smyser to build the **Coffee Pot Restaurant** – constructing it in pre-fabricated sections on the Tideflats and bolting it together onsite at 2102 South Tacoma Way. Bob Radonich purchased the property in 1955 and his wife, Lylabell, renamed it the Java Jive after a song by the **Inkspots.** The distinctive coffee pot structure earned acclaim as one of America's cool Roadside Attractions and was placed on the National Register of Historic Places in 2014.

When it opened in 1926 the **Winthrop Hotel** was considered the gem of downtown hotels for travelers and a glamourous social setting for Tacomans. Located between Broadway and Commerce at South Ninth, the 12-story hotel struck a handsome pose on the city skyline. The grand Crystal Ballroom featured four crystal chandeliers above a 4,500-square-foot dance floor. Two large dining rooms could seat up to 500 diners and accommodated many community groups for meetings and events.

TPL

Ruth DuCharme and Orville Fuller pose in front of Bill Winder (far left) and his Hotel Winthrop Orchestra in January of 1926. The pair won the Southwest Washington Championship Ho-down Ballroom Charleston competition, a contest title befitting the four-week event, which was sponsored by the Rialto Theater and the Winthrop Hotel.

Never able to thrive financially, the Winthrop was converted to subsidized housing in the early 70s. The chandeliers are still in place and new owners plan to eventually reopen the Crystal Ballroom for social events.

Jelly Roll Morton

Ferdinand LaMothe, born in 1890 to a mother who ran a bordello in New Orleans, transformed himself into **Jelly Roll Morton** and claimed to be the inventor of jazz. Even skeptics, turned off by his arrogant self-promotion, struggled to find evidence to dispute his claims or to deny his pioneering influence as a composer and early jazz pianist. It is believed Morton took his talents on the keys in clubs around Tacoma during a period of 1917–20 when he and his wife, Anita, owned a "rooming house" in Ponders Corner – no doubt engaging in practices learned from his mother's establishment.

Jazz Players

In the era of big bands and jazz combos there were jazz musicians so talented those on the dance floor might be compelled to stand back and marvel at the artistic expressiveness of these players. Tacoman **Corky Corcoran** was so good so early that he was adopted by the great Harry James and his wife (actress Betty Grable) so Corcoran, still a minor, could tour as saxophonist for the legendary **Harry James Band.** **Bill Ramsey** was born in Centralia and taught himself to play the sax while stationed at Fort Lewis during World War II. He spent years on the road as **Count Basie's** sax player before returning to Tacoma where he often played for the **New Yorker Orchestra** under the direction of bass player **Art Mineo.** Mineo, along with **Red Kelly,** join Corcoran and Ramsey as the biggest jazz figures to find a home in Tacoma. Mineo and Kelly came from elsewhere, both played the bass, both are jazz legends.

Bill Ramsey   TPL   *Corky Corcoran*   TPL

Art Mineo at the New Yorker

The New Yorker Café opened as a nightclub at 1501 Sixth Avenue in 1946 with the Long Island Coffee Shop, the Staten Island Room, the Coney Island Room

Art Mineo and friends perform in the legendary jam session at the New Yorker in 1951 TPL

that would seat 350 people around a dance floor and the Manhattan Room – the latter was the main lounge and featured a huge replica of the New York skyline made from wood blocks. To bring all this to life it seems only appropriate that the man who would direct the **New Yorker Orchestra** for 28 years was Art Mineo, born in Brooklyn in 1918.

His Sicilian mother taught him to love opera and he would compose operas later in his life, but his passion was jazz and he became a highly regarded bassist. He would compose space music to be played for the **Bubbleator** at the 1962 **Seattle World's Fair** and, along with his musician wife, Toni, would compose arrangements for the 10-piece house orchestra – highly regarded musicians in their own right, and often enhanced when jazz legend friends of Mineo would sit in.

Beyond his musical talents, Mineo used his business savvy to help get the rock scene rolling in the 50s. He helped the **Ventures** get started and was the original manager of the **Wailers** – a group he guided into creating their own record label, the first owned by a rock band. Mineo passed away in 2010.

The night before the remodeled New Yorker was to

open to the public in November 1951, there was an invitation-only event at the restaurant. Art Mineo's house orchestra was scheduled to play, but three of his good friends – who happened to be among the greatest jazz musicians in the world – had a night off while on tour in Seattle. That's how Tacoma drummer Dick Moorehead and Art, on bass, ended up jamming with Joe "Flip" Phillips on tenor saxophone, Oscar Peterson on piano and Bill Harris on trombone. It might have been the best jazz group to ever play in Tacoma.

Red Kelly

How global was the reach of **Red Kelly's** reputation? Thirteen years after he died (2004) Tacoma Public Library received an email from a man in China trying to reach Kelly in hopes of getting his signature "as my birthday gift." He went on to add: "…he was, he is and will always be the best! I thank him, he taught what is strong and carry on!"

When Red Kelly closed **Kelly's Restaurant** and Lounge at 11th and Tacoma Avenue in 2003, the memorabilia and autographed pictures covering the walls drew the attention of the Smithsonian Institution. (Tacoma Public Library acquired the collection.) The club had been operating for 20 years, but the pictures represented over 50 years of jazz history that Kelly had been making along with all the greats. The wall is like a who's who of who's ever been among the greats in jazz.

Kelly, born in Montana in 1927, picked a "big old bass fiddle that no one played" while at Queen Anne High School in Seattle in the early 40s. He fell in love with big band music the first time he heard it. "That was the end of it for me. I couldn't finish school or anything." At 16 he joined a local band, but was soon in New York and on to a career in which he played with the likes of **Stan Kenton, Woody Herman, Harry James**. "I've had a fascinating life. I've been all over the world doing what I love. Not bad for a guy who never finished his sophomore year in high school."

Kelly played with the greats, but he didn't include Elvis among them. "I played with Elvis Presley for a week. It was the most boring thing in the world and he was the most untalented person I've ever seen. I've played with the best – **Billie Holiday, Ella Fitzgerald, Billy Eckstine, Frank Sinatra.** Give me a break! Elvis Presley?" Elvis' picture was not on the Wall of Fame.

As part of his research for a class paper while a student at the University of Washington Tacoma 20 years ago, Doug Prather spent time interviewing Red and his wife, Donna, at Kelly's Jazz Club. Kelly provided him with a reflection about what it is like when the great ones get it absolutely right:

"When we said 'We saw the big man tonight' that meant that you got into that thing where it was so powerful that you don't even know what your name is or what the tune is. It's just one big instrument, it's not a bunch of guys there. 'We saw the big man tonight.' Now once you do that, you spend the rest of your life trying to do it again. And, you do, maybe once or twice a year. If there's a religion, that's mine."

It is that level of transcendent experience that performers and patrons hope to find when it's *Showtime in Tacoma*.

Three jazz legends: Red Kelly on bass, Harry James on trumpet and Buddy Rich on drums

TPL

Gettin' Down
on Lower Broadway

Two careers that have extended beyond 60 years rose out of an area of downtown that was in fast decline in the 1950s. The area, generally south of 13th Street, was known as Lower Broadway and was punctuated with buildings that had been built in Tacoma's boom times at the turn of the century, but had become filled with drab bars as a precursor to demolition. The blighted setting didn't stop Fred Roberson and Little Bill Engelhart from engaging this neighborhood with their compatible, if not directly interactive quests.

Fred Roberson

Before Fred Roberson would embark on more than half a century of historic restoration projects in downtown Tacoma, he owned a bar that was on the frontlines of racial prejudice in Tacoma. "In 1953 I bought a bar called the 'Kennel' at 1347 Broadway (now in the area of the Murano Hotel). It had been a hillbilly bar playing country music and I changed the name to the Tiki and switched to blues bands. This was an area known as Lower Broadway where blacks could be served on the west side of the street, but not on the east side where my place was. When I started serving blacks in the Tiki the soldiers from the Deep South didn't like that and there were a lot of fights, some of them I got caught up in trying to keep order.

"I had a hard time getting a dance license, because the authorities didn't like blacks and whites dancing together. There was this thing called the 'Police Morals Squad' that was headed up by a guy named 'Honest

John' Hickey. This was right after the City had gone to a City Manager form of government after all the corruption scandals. I thought I'd have to be paying on the side to be able to operate, but Honest John said, 'You don't have to give me anything, just run the place right.' I was selling real estate during the day and working the bar at night and, after six years, I decided to stick to real estate. Unfortunately, there was a lot of prejudice being practiced in the community where blacks and other minorities could not buy a house in Tacoma. It took a long time get things where everyone had a fair shake."

The Seaport Tavern in 1950s TPL

Little Bill Engelhart

From his first steps into what became a legendary career as a rock and blues musician, Little Bill Engelhart was driven to immerse himself in the environment where he could tap the roots of that music scene in Tacoma – which drew him to Lower Broadway.

"I do remember the music. There were three places that stand out in my memory. The Tiki, The El Paso and The Congo Cafe. The Tiki had live music six nights a week. I played there several times. I think it paid $10 each. The Seaport was on Commerce Street. The crowd was over-age hookers and way-into-it alcoholics. We played there for sandwiches and drinks. I'm not sure why but we seemed bent on living the hardest life we could.

The Tiki Tavern in 1950s TPL

Little Bill Engelhart at the Swiss in 2017 📷 Alex Brikoff

Broadway Record Store after it closed in 1960s 📷 TPL

"All of these places had their own personality. Especially The Congo Cafe. The guy in charge was Hamp. He never smiled and nobody gave him any trouble. I heard some great music at the Congo. One that stands out was The Master Sounds – Monk Montgomery on bass and Buddy Montgomery on piano. They were brothers of one of the most famous guitar players in the world, Wes Montgomery! The local musicians will always be a big part of my Lower Broadway day dreams. Atlas Cole, Preacher Jimmy Ellis, Roland Green, Johnny Morre and so many others. I'm proud to be able to say that for a time, I was one of the Broadway musicians.

"The Broadway Record store was a place where, as teenagers, we found all those Rhythm and Blues 45s that Bob Summerise was playing on the radio in Tacoma. The guy that owned the place was Beaver*. He had a speaker right outside the door where he played non-stop R & B all day long. It was also where Rockin' Robin Roberts found the recording of *Louie Louie* by Richard Berry. After all these years Lower Broadway still stands out as the street where I became who I am today – the people, the attitude and most of all the music."

*Fitzgerald "Eager" Beaver was a disc jockey. In 1961 he moved to Seattle and founded The Facts *newspaper – Seattle's most important African American publication.*

Top National Record Store Sales Jan. 1958

1 – AT THE HOP – Danny and the Juniors
2 – GREAT BALLS OF FIRE – Jerry Lee Lewis
3 – APRIL LOVE – Pat Boone
4 – PEGGY SUE – Buddy Holly
5 – STOOD UP – Ricky Nelson
6 – JINGLE BELL ROCK – Bobby Helms
7 – JAILHOUSE ROCK – Elvis Presley
8 – YOU SEND ME – Sam Cooke
9 – KISSES SWEETER THAN WINE – Jimmie Rodgers
10 – RAUNCHY – Bill Justis & His Orchestra

Source: Weekly Top 40, www.weeklytop40.wordpress.com

Top National Rhythm & Blues Sales 1958

1 – WHAT AM I LIVING FOR – Chuck Willis
2 – ROCK-IN' ROBIN – Bobby Day
3 – DON'T/I BEG OF YOU – Elvis Presley
4 – LOOKING BACK/DO I LIKE IT – Nat King Cole
5 – ALL I HAVE TO DO IS DREAM – Everly Brothers
6 – IT'S ALL IN THE GAME – Tommy Edwards
7 – JUST A DREAM – Jimmy Clanton
8 – YAKETY YAK – Coasters
9 – WITCH DOCTOR – David Seville
10 – LITTLE STAR – Elegants

When Rock Ruled

Peter Blecha, unquestionably the most informative guide into the Northwest rock 'n' roll scene, was the founding senior curator with Seattle's music museum, the Experience Music Project (EMP) and has written extensively on the bands and venues that made music history in Tacoma and the region. Today he runs the Northwest Music Archives website. These EXCERPTS from a number of his articles on **HistoryLink.org** *are provided with his permission and our eager encouragement for readers to explore these pieces more fully.*

The Barons – Tacoma's Doo-Wop Pioneers

"A half-decade prior to the Pacific Northwest's great rock 'n' roll eruption of 1959–1960 – a period that saw a series of teenage groups (including the **Fleetwoods, Frantics, Shades, Gallahads, Wailers, Ron Holden and the Thunderbirds, and Little Bill and the Bluenotes)** all suddenly burst onto the national scene with hit records – yet another local group blazed that same trail. Tacoma's talented doo-wop singers, the **Barons,** were signed to one of America's most esteemed independent labels, the Los Angeles-based Imperial Records, and scored a series of promising hits. Unfortunately, the group was a bit ahead of its time – the Northwest didn't even have an organized teen-dance scene yet – and the Barons disbanded before they were able to make the most of their remarkable success.

"The Pacific Northwest – although never considered a hotbed of hard-core 1950s rhythm & blues music – certainly could boast a number of African American a capella doo-wop groups. ... Tacoma had the **Four Pearls**, **Skylarks, Cool Breezers, Parking Meters, Chantz –** and the most accomplished of them all, the Barons... The founding members of that group – William Gold (lead), Sterling 'Stokey' Wilford (tenor), Carl Charles (baritone), and Malcolm Parks (bass) – grew up in Tacoma's Eastside housing projects and met while singing together in the choir at the old Bethlehem Baptist Church (1721 South I Street). Later while attending Lincoln High School and Stadium High School they began rehearsing at each other's homes and that's when they adopted the Barons as a name and began singing rhythm & blues tunes – including a batch written by Gold... Before long some of the guys'

religiously strict parents disapproved of the R&B lifestyle and such pressures were a factor in causing the Barons to dissolve."

The Teen Scene

"The rock 'n' roll scene in the Pacific Northwest had been bubbling for a couple years already when it got a major kick-start in 1959. During that year several area bands saw their debut records leap, almost simultaneously, from local radio playlists to national and even international, hit status. That string of successes began with Olympia's Fleetwoods, went to Tacoma's Little Bill and the Bluenotes, then to Seattle's Frantics, and finally to Tacoma's Wailers. The action continued into 1960 when Tacoma's **Ventures,** Seattle's Gallahads, and Ron Holden and the Thunderbirds scored national hits.

The Ventures **TPL**
(L-R) Howie Johnson, Don Wilson, Bob Bogle, Nokie Edwards

"One cumulative result of all that was the forging of a recognized 'Northwest Sound' – and a general realization that the region had developed a vibrant teenage rock 'n' roll scene based on weekly dances, successful recording studios and record companies, and supportive radio stations. That scene's signature song came to be the then-obscure 1956 rhythm and blues tune, *Louie Louie* by Los Angeles's Richard Berry (1935–1997). *Louie Louie* was popular as a dance tune and most every Northwest band (including the Gallahads and Thunderbirds) performed its own version – and a number chose to record it. In 1961 the Wailers scored a huge radio hit with their influential rendition and Little Bill Engelhart (b. 1939) and the **Adventurers** released theirs as well. Over the following years the Ventures, **Kingsmen, Viceroys,** and **Sonics** followed suit.

"Time raced on, and the culture, music, and teen-scene evolved. By about 1970 the original scene was but a memory as all the pioneering bands (except the never-say-die Ventures), record companies, and recording studios were defunct. But a keen fondness for the old sounds remained and a new "supergroup" of veteran players emerged with a new oldies-focused band, **Jr. Cadillac.** Composed of members of the Wailers, Frantics, Sonics, and other vintage bands, Jr. Cadillac would go on to become the single biggest regional nightclub draw over the following two decades. The group would also be appreciated as the living torchbearer of the Northwest Sound – and it would play a central role in various 'scene reunion' gigs in the upcoming years."

The Ventures

"Not long after the demise of the Barons, the Ventures were formed, going on to become the top-selling instrumental band of all time, and to be inducted into the Rock 'n' Roll Hall of Fame. It is difficult to overstate the influence The Ventures had on modern music, with affectionate testimonials from a lengthy list of celebrities. The tense cool of The Wailers and The Sonics could have never existed without the blisteringly catchy surf rock The Ventures pioneered."

The Sonics

"The Wailers had some chart successes, but weren't willing to endure the hustle of the East Coast recording industry, which may have sealed their fate as regional legends. As local heavyweights, they quickly inspired another famous Northwest Band – The Sonics. This irrepressible band burst on the Tacoma music scene with *The Witch* in 1964, a song of sexual

The Sonics pioneered the punk movement ⊚ PBC

warning that effectively serves as a recommendation. Their most influential song, *Strychnine*, came from the same record, *Here Are The Sonics…*. Monoliths of modern rock such as Kurt Cobain and Jack White have effusively stated their admiration of this signature Northwest band, citing their unconventional recording techniques and forceful punk approach. Again – Tacoma.

"The improbable 'career' arc of Tacoma's Sonics is that of a teen combo who pounded their way to the top ranks of Northwest rock bands by 1965 – and then crumbled in the psychedelic musical aftermath of 1967's Summer of Love. Like countless other American garage-bands of the era, the Sonics might have faded into total obscurity. They had, however, managed to forge a particularly brutal style that went on to earn them legendary status as pioneers of the entire subsequent punk rock movement.

"The Sonics' saga is also one of a raw band who went from playing modest roller-rinks, to headlining the area's major halls like the Spanish Castle Ballroom, to opening for major touring acts at the Seattle Coliseum. But even with a caustic sound that limited their ability to garner widespread radio airplay – and thus, they failed to ever score a national hit – the Sonics would ultimately be hailed for having heralded the subsequent emergence of punk rock in the 1970s. Indeed, their unique contributions were never forgotten, and in the decades hence the Sonics' post-mortem fanbase grew into a global phenomenon that demanded – and was finally rewarded with – a triumphant international reunion concert tour between 2007 and 2008."

Rockin' Robin Roberts

"A founding father of Northwest rock 'n' roll, Tacoma's 'Rockin' Robin' Roberts (1940–1967) initially sang with that town's trailblazing 1950s white rhythm & blues combo, the Blue Notes. But in mid-1959 he was lured away by their crosstown rivals, the Wailers, who had mainly been known for their role in helping define the original Northwest rock sound, which consisted largely of instrumental tunes. His addition to their lineup proved to be a wise move: Roberts's energetic manner, riveting voice, and deep knowledge of R&B music all combined to make him as charismatic a front man as the Pacific Northwest would ever produce.

"Ever ambitious, Roberts was a key instigator in pushing his fellow band members to form their own record company, an unprecedented move for a teenaged group. Etiquette Records' debut release – the earliest garage-rock version of *Louie Louie*, and one that featured Roberts's electrifying vocals – became a number one, region-wide radio hit in 1961 (and again in 1962), and can be credited with inspiring legions of later bands. Sadly, though, Roberts – who more than any other individual embodied the frenetic spirit of the early Northwest rock scene – would die far too young. (While working as a chemist in San Francisco in 1967, Roberts was killed when the car he was riding in as a passenger crashed going the wrong way on a freeway.)"

The Wailers & Etiquette Records

"Etiquette Records – a trail-blazing firm formed by three young Tacoma musicians in 1961 – was an enterprise that broke *all* the old rules. Despite its polite and classy sounding name – not to mention that of its sister company, Valet Publishing – Etiquette quickly came to rule the Pacific Northwest's rock 'n' roll roost by producing and promoting raucous and gritty music that came to be favored by teenaged bands and their fans in the region.

"Founded as a partnership by three members of Tacoma's top band, the Wailers – 'Rockin' Robin' Roberts (vocals), Kent Morrill (piano/vocals), and John "Buck" Ormsby (bass) – Etiquette issued a grand total of 26 45s and eight LPs between 1961 and 1967. But it was not quantity so much as quality that made the company successful and influential. Etiquette initially erupted with the world's first garage-rock version of *Louie Louie* – and went on to issue the classic Wailers *At the Castle* LP, the Sonics' proto-punk radio hits *The Witch* and *Psycho* and their long-play masterpieces, *Here Are the Sonics* and *Sonics Boom*, among many other revered '60s classics.

The Wailers (L-R) Rich Dangel, Mike Burk, Mark Marsh, Kent Morrill, John Greek TPL

The Boys from Tacoma

"It was 1959 when Clark Galehouse of New York's Golden Crest record company signed Tacoma's pioneering rock combo, the Wailers – or rather (according to the band's founder and original rhythm guitarist, John Greek) as the only member over the age of 18, he signed the five-year exclusive contract as the band's official leader. The Wailers originally formed as an instrumental-oriented combo that featured Greek, Morrill, lead guitarist Rich Dangel (1942–2002), saxophonist Mark Marush, and drummer Mike Burk. Their association with Golden Crest initially resulted in two instrumental radio hits – *Tall Cool One* and *Mau Mau* – that summer and a classic LP, *The Fabulous Wailers*, which was released in December 1959.

"But by then tensions between the band and the label had surfaced: Golden Crest had wanted the high-school-aged guys to move to the East Coast where their career could be better managed. But the high-school-aged musicians rejected that plan, which resulted in a drop-off of corporate interest in promoting the band's discs or recording any new ones. Meanwhile big changes were already underway. Back in August they'd lured singer, Lawrence F. 'Rockin' Robin' Roberts (1940–1967), away from his teen-R&B group, Little Bill and the Bluenotes, and also added a 13-year-old powerhouse girl singer named Gail Harris... .

"... With their formerly friendly relationship with Golden Crest strained to the point of a standoff, the Wailers felt stymied in their desire to cut more hits.

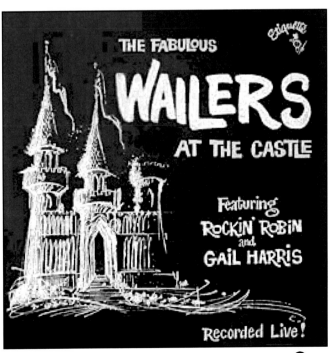

PBC

But with those concerns over contractual complexities weighing heavily on their minds – in fact discussions were held about disbanding the group – it was while sitting at Tacoma's New Yorker restaurant one day that Roberts, Morrill and Ormsby hit upon the idea of the guys forming their *own* label. It was an audacious notion that was supported by only 50 percent of a band that had lingering worries about what Golden Crest's reaction might be. ...

"... Still, they inched forward by booking time in Seattle at Joe Boles's (1904–1962) home studio (3550 Admiral Way), which had already been the site of hit recording sessions in 1959 for Olympia's Fleetwoods, and Seattle's Frantics – and even Little Bill and the Bluenotes. After a successful day there, the band emerged with two songs in the can: *Louie Louie* and a blistering romp through Ray Charles' *Maryann.* The Wailers knew that they had produced something hot, but they proceeded to waste the following half-year bickering about who would get the label credit: The Wailers or Rockin' Robin.

Etiquette Emerges

"But then fate stepped in and forced the Wailers' hand. It was in March 1961 that Ormsby happened by Seattle's Northwest Recorders where his former bandmate, Little Bill Engelhart, was completing a session with a new band, the Adventurers, and audio engineer Kearney Barton. Shocked that the song being cut was none other than *Louie Louie*, the record exec-wannabe bolted out of the studio and rushed an already pressed (but label-less) 45 of his band's *Louie Louie* right over to KJR radio where the kingpin DJ, Pat O'Day, put it on the air and an instant hit was born.

"Perhaps Tacoma may not be home to massive icons of Western culture. But this town certainly produced music that other musicians listened to and were inspired by, leaving an impression on rock's history that is difficult to measure. But when was rock music ever about measurement or clarity?"

Excerpts were sourced from these essays by Peter Blecha on www.HistoryLink.org:

Barons, The: The Northwest's First Hit-making '50s Teen Rock 'n' Roll Group
By Peter Blecha Posted 11/18/2009 • HistoryLink.org/File/9207

Etiquette Rules! The Northwest's Reigning '60s Garage-Rock Record Company
By Peter Blecha Posted 4/10/2009 • HistoryLink.org/File/8947

Louie Louie – the Saga of a Pacific Northwest Hit Song
By Peter Blecha Posted 2/15/2003 • HistoryLink.org/File/5206

O'Day, Pat (b. 1934) – Godfather of Northwest Rock?
By Peter Blecha Posted 4/03/2001 • HistoryLink.org/File/3130

Roberts, "Rockin' Robin" (1940–1967)
By Peter Blecha Posted 11/29/2009 • HistoryLink.org/File/9217

Sonics, The: Tacoma's '60s Garage-Rock Teen Titans
By Peter Blecha Posted 12/14/2008 • HistoryLink.org/File/8844

"The Great Northwest Rock 'n' Roll Show" reunion gig of early local rockers kicks off on July 20, 1980
By Peter Blecha Posted 4/14/2013 • HistoryLink.org/File/10375

Out of the Legacy of Loud

By Rev. Adam McKinney

The bumper sticker version of the story of rock and roll in Tacoma goes something like this: due to the city's proximity to McChord Field, planes flying overhead would tend to drown out the music. Our music needed to be louder, and that loudness planted its roots in the scene, fostering bands like the **Sonics** and **The Fabulous Wailers** and, later on, generations of garage rock acts and a culture of punk and metal bands.

It's an easy act to mythologize your hometown. In actuality, Tacoma's growth – as well as its setbacks – as a musical town, are more complex and multifaceted than the tall tale of loud music being born under the thumb of military noise. Known as the City of Destiny, Tacoma was once thought to be the cultural hub of Washington. Seattle eventually snatched that title and Tacoma was forever relegated to the position of underdog, striving musically and economically to match its outsized rival. Making things worse, Tacoma sits in a place besieged by so-called blackout clauses, limiting touring bands playing in Seattle from playing in certain nearby areas, necessitating their skipping Tacoma.

In many ways, this has cast a pall over Tacoma, but it is well reflected in how its music scene has evolved. Following developments in the '60s with very influential bands, Tacoma would then suffer from laws enacted in the '70s and '80s – as well as perceptions of Tacoma's crime rate – that would result in bands tending to play in Seattle and Olympia, instead of visiting the city in between. One of the main drawbacks to getting the general public to come out to Tacoma shows – in particular the effect this had on all-ages shows – was this tendency of none but the bold willing to show up. In speaking with **Bon Von Wheelie,** drummer for Tacoma garage rock institution *Girl Trouble*, we find how limiting the Tacoma music scene was in the '80s.

"I'm of the opinion that nobody wanted kids to get together and play music here, which always seemed nuts to me," says Von Wheelie. "The only real all-ages show at a venue was when Jim May put on a hardcore show at the **Tacoma Odd Fellows** hall in 1982 (now **the Merlino Arts Center** at Sixth & Fawcett) and the Tacoma Police showed up at that one in riot gear. I

mean full-on riot gear to stop some kids from going wild and playing music. ... There were many shows, including Community World, that would post giant 'no dancing' banners, since there was now a distinction between a concert and a dance. It was mostly meant as another way to stop young people from playing music and going to shows. Times were pretty grim, especially in Tacoma. It was definitely not a music-friendly town. All-ages venues had a very short life span."

Von Wheelie refers to the **Community World Theater** (5441 South M Street), which was the first all-ages rock venue in Tacoma (in the way that we currently understand an all-ages rock venue to be). Formed by **Jim May**, the Community World Theater was an establishment that attracted a lot of outstanding acts in a short timeframe (1987–88) including a number that would come to be widely known, such as **Beat Happening**, **Camper Van Beethoven**, **Fugazi**, **NOFX**, **NoMeansNo**, **Screaming Trees –** and the first concert **Kurt Cobain** and **Krist Novoselic** performed as **Nirvana.**

"It was amazing he could keep it open for the year that he did," says Von Wheelie of May's handling of the

Community World Theater. "Community World was like watching a really great reality show before reality shows were popular. ... I'll never forget hanging in the lobby at one of the shows and somebody out front started puking. Without missing a beat, Jim told the workers at the 'concession stand' (which consisted of a popcorn machine Jim had scored) to pass him the 30-foot hose that was curled up there. He took the hose, pointed it at the sidewalk and then hollered, "Turn it on!" People on the sidewalk backed away and Jim quickly sprayed it off. By the way everybody immediately snapped into action, it was obvious this was a nightly occurrence."

The Community World Theater would last a relatively short time, but it managed to set a standard for the quality of bands that were willing to come to Tacoma. It also established a format for all-ages venues to begin popping up and bolstering Tacoma's new generation of musical stability – setting up a standard for all-ages shows aided in bringing bands to Tacoma that might otherwise have stayed away. All-ages shows tap into a demographic that is frequently eschewed, with teenagers so often driving music's popularity and visibility. The tragic downside to this obvious synergy is the absurd difficulty of all-ages venues to stay afloat.

There are many unfortunate venues that have closed in Tacoma, but the largest portion goes to those that include all ages. Chief among these (though there are many others) are **Hell's Kitchen** (3829 Sixth Avenue) and **The Viaduct** (5412 South Tacoma Way.) Situated on South Tacoma Way, The Viaduct was home to a steady stream of hardcore bands, providing an alcohol and drug-free venue for under-agers to get involved in the music scene. Hell's Kitchen, located on Proctor and Sixth Avenue, functioned both as a bar and as an all-ages venue. This was the venue that truly served as the follow-up to the Community World Theater, as it drew in people like the **Melvins, Dick Dale, Macklemore,** and other acts that otherwise wouldn't have found a reason to come through Tacoma.

Hell's Kitchen took advantage of the repeal of laws allowing venues with bars being able to hold all-ages shows. Unfortunately, they would also eventually fall victim to restrictions about fire codes, having to shutter their doors and find a 21+ location downtown, which would also end up closing. The sprinkler ordinances would affect assorted other burgeoning downtown venues, such as **The Warehouse** and **The Peabody Waldorf.** Growing concern in the City of Tacoma would make it increasingly difficult to keep an all-ages venue running.

With the difficulty of up-and-coming venues to keep their viability, other music heavyweights dug their feet into the soil and maintained their standing. **Bob's Java Jive** (2102 South Tacoma Way), always a standard for dive-bar efficacy and charming dinge, has

Java Jive has maintained a standard for "dive-bar efficacy" while reaching for its 100th anniversary

long attracted a wide array of bands that don't mind performing in a bar that features a bathroom where one can pee while high-fiving a guy that's sitting on the john. The Jive has hosted a murderer's row of acts over nearly a century of its coffee-pot-shaped existence, including bands like the **Ventures** and various luminaries of the grunge era.

Jazzbones (2803 Sixth Avenue) meanwhile, has shaped itself over the years to resemble very little of its jazz-influenced beginnings. Initially known as the Victory Club, featuring open mic talent and emerging artists, Jazzbones has since become established as one of the most frenzied venues in town. Nowadays, Jazzbones busies itself with rap, reggae, and Top 40 cover bands, making it the premier meat market and meeting place for college graduates on the prowl. Its history as a center for jazz greats has largely shifted, though the spirits of those outstanding acts linger.

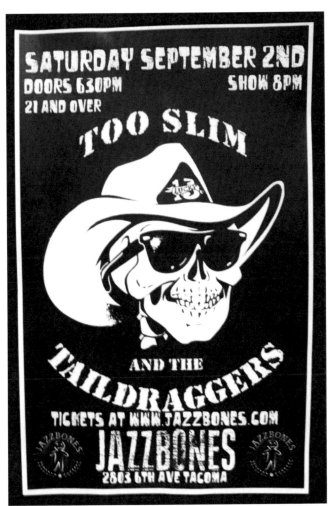

The spirit of outstanding acts lingers at Jazzbones RJB

Entering into a climate of venues opening and closing with increasing frequency, some places have managed to pass the test of time and maintain their stability. The first venue to accomplish this was the **New**

Frontier Lounge (301 East 25th), which is nearing its 10-year anniversary. The New Frontier initially established its relevance through a consistent booking of shows that highlighted indie rock, among other forms of music that didn't get wide recognition in Tacoma's widespread punk and metal leanings.

The Valley (1206 Puyallup Avenue) has also proven to be a haven of diverse offerings, frequently providing the most musical options per week, under a wide umbrella of genres. Their habit of hosting shows that only charge by donation situates them firmly in the Tacoma DIY tradition of function over profit. As for all-ages, the scene that Von Wheelie and others might say is the reason for Tacoma's existing perseverance as a music-friendly town, **Real Art** (5412 South Tacoma Way) – in the old Viaduct building, no less – is doing its level best to bring high-quality shows to the underage crowd.

"Tacoma has always been a nuts and bolts type of town," says Bon Von Wheelie. "This has been going on since the Wailers, Sonics, and **Little Bill** were playing dances at the **Armory, Red Carpet,** and **Crescent Ballroom**. It's a working class town, and the bands who come from Tacoma reflect that. In Seattle, they have everything brought to them. The big shows normally came to Seattle and skipped Tacoma. So people had to make their own music here and perform for each other. It's a real DIY type of city. We all know each other. When we play in Tacoma, we feel like the family is coming over for dinner. We support each other's bands. It's been that way since we started out. I know touring bands who have told us that playing Tacoma shows is really fun. We aren't afraid to get excited."

Being afraid of optimism has long been Tacoma's bag. When it comes to venues, and their relative longevity, a bit of skepticism comes with the territory. What we never lack, though, is the ability to create and reinvent. We may all be underdogs, but starting low can only project an upward trajectory. And as long as those planes stay loud, we'll match their volume.

– Rev. Adam McKinney has been writing professionally about music since 2009. In addition to writing about pop culture ephemera for The Weekly Volcano *and* Oly Arts, *he runs a five-day indie music festival in Tacoma called* Squeak and Squawk

Music Shows Under the Dome

A list of the headliners who have played concerts at the Tacoma Dome, including some who have appeared multiple times.

1983 – Rick Nelson (played at the Grand Opening), David Bowie, Neil Diamond, Sammy Davis, Jr., AC/DC.

1984 – Billy Joel, Alabama, Elton John, Kenny Rogers, Judas Priest, Rod Stewart, Bruce Springsteen

1985 – Merle Haggard, Bryan Adams, Rick Springfield, Tina Turner, Huey Lewis & the News, Amy Grant, Prince

1986 – Frank Sinatra (senior), Bob Dylan, Tom Petty & the Heartbreakers

1987 – Boston

1988 – Crosby, Stills & Nash, Chicago, George Michael, AC/DC, Eric Clapton, Bruce Springsteen

1989 – The Who

1990 – ZZ Top, M.C. Hammer, New Kids on the Block, Phil Collins, Janet Jackson

1991 – Guns N' Roses, Paul Simon, The Judds

1992 – Garth Brooks, Bruce Springsteen

1993 – Alan Jackson, Reba McEntire

1994 – Vince Gill, Whitney Houston

1998 – Jimmy Buffett, Shania Twain, Spice Girls

2000 – Iron Maiden, Bruce Springsteen

2002 – Paul McCartney & Wings, Rolling Stones, Sheryl Crow, Aerosmith, Bruce Springsteen

2003 – Toby Keith, Santana

2004 – Louie Louie Fest

2011 – Ozzy Osbourne, Taylor Swift

2012 – Van Halen

2013 – Fleetwood Mac

2014 – Miley Cyrus, The Eagles, Katy Perry

2015 – Miranda Lambert, Motley Crue

2016 – Black Sabbath, Def Leppard, Brad Paisley

2017 – Blake Shelton, Tim McGraw & Faith Hill, Lady Gaga, Bruno Mars, Ed Sheeran, Kendrick Lamar

Ⓞ BJ

The Notable Nine

Nine significant museums line Tacoma's downtown core to form an impressive and distinct district showcasing some of the world's best collections and unique artwork. Discover creative culture, exquisite glass, timeless history in many formats, classic automobiles, family fun and maritime heritage in Tacoma's Museum District.

LeMay – America's Car Museum
2702 East D Street, Tacoma, WA 98421

Grand opening 6/2/2012

Alan Grant/Grant Price (Los Angeles) architect

The largest car museum in North America and rated among the top car museums in the world, celebrates America's love affair with the automobile.
www.americascarmuseum.org

Tacoma Art Museum
1701 Pacific Avenue, Tacoma, WA 98402

Opened 5/3/2003

Antoine Predock (Albuquerque, New Mexico), architect

Haub Family Wing of Western Art grand opening 11/15/2014

Benaroya Collection Wing being developed in 2017

Founded in 1935 by the Tacoma Art Association

The 81-year-old organization features collections of glass art, studio art jewelry, Japanese woodblock prints and Western American art.
www.tacomaartmuseum.org

Museum of Glass
1801 Dock St, Tacoma, WA 98402

Grand opening 7/3/2002

Arthur Erickson (Vancouver, BC), architect

90-foot cone houses glass hot shop

Dale Chihuly Bridge of Glass connects the museum with the Washington State History Museum.

Dedicated to the Studio Glass movement through exhibits, programs and the hands-on studio in the cone-shaped Hot Shop. **www.museumofglass.org**

Foss Waterway Seaport
705 Dock Street, Tacoma, WA 98402

Dedicated 2/25/1995

Housed in the former Balfour Dock wheat warehouse, built in 1900

Grand reopening after renovation and remodeling 5/11/2013

Celebrating Tacoma's rich maritime history through interpretation, education, events and exhibits.
www.fosswaterwayseaport.org

Washington State Historical Museum
1911 Pacific Avenue, Tacoma, WA 98402

Dedicated 8/10/1996

Charles Moore (Austin, Texas), architect

$40.8 million project used 350,000 bricks and 13 poured-in-place concrete arches

Founded in 1891 as the Washington State Historical Society

Sharing the stories of Washington's vibrant past and making connections with today through permanent and rotating exhibits. **www.washingtonhistory.org**

Shanaman Sports Museum
2727 East D Street, Tacoma, WA 98421

Opened 1994 at the Tacoma Dome, completed in 1983

Recreating and chronicling the history of sports in Tacoma-Pierce County through written and visual display. **www.tacomasportsmuseum.com**

Tacoma Historical Society Museum
919 Pacific Avenue, Tacoma, WA 98402

Founded in 1990

Opened 3/2014 in the Provident Building, built in 1903

Tacoma Historical Society preserves, presents, and promotes stories of the city's past.
www.tacomahistory.org

Children's Museum of Tacoma
1501 Pacific Avenue, Tacoma, WA 98402

Established by local parents in 1985

Grand opening 1/14/2012 in the Sprague Building, built in 1890

Celebrating the power of play while nurturing growth and development for children and parents.
www.playtacoma.org

Karpeles Manuscript Library Museum
407 South G Street, Tacoma, WA 98405

Opened 6/25/1991

Housed in the former Edward B. Rhodes Post, American Legion, built in 1930.

The world's largest private holding of important original manuscripts and documents.
www.rain.org/~karpeles

Theater Name	Address	Dates of Operation
Alhambra	1821 K Street	1915–1917
Aloha Theater	1010-1012 K Street	1914–1918
Alpha Opera House	1011-1013 Pacific Avenue	1882–1890
American Theater	2212 North 30th	1916–1918
American Theater	821-823 Pacific Avenue	1921
Apollo Theater	1131-1133 Broadway	1914–1921
Arcade Theater	1314-1316 Pacific Avenue	1911
Auto View Drive-in Theater	1202 North Pearl	1950–1986
Bell Theater	4538 South M Street	1914
Beverly Theater	916-918 Broadway	1934–1944
Bijou Theater	1105-1107 Broadway	1908–1914
Bijou Theater	1109 Broadway	1915–1932
Bijou Theater	2611 North Proctor	1978–1993
Blue Mouse	1131-1133 Broadway	1922–1957
Blue Mouse Theater (Jr.)	2611 North Proctor	1923–1924
Blue Mouse Theater	2611 North Proctor	1994–present
Broadway Theater	902-914 Broadway	1927–1929, 1931–1932
Broadway Theater	916-918 Broadway	1949–1951
Bungalow Photo-Play Theater	2701 North 21st Street	1914–1916
Cameo Theater	1128 Pacific Avenue	1941–1959
Cameo Theater	1318-1320 Pacific Avenue	1961–1986
Capitol Theater	2606 Sixth Avenue	1926–1929
Capitol Theater	4801-4805 Yakima Avenue	1936–1962
Capri Theater	906-908 Pacific Avenue	1964–1968
Casino Theater	726 Pacific Avenue	1888
Century Point Ruston & XD Theatre	Point Ruston	2015–present
Circuit & Scenic Theater	916-918 Pacific Avenue	1909–1913
Coast Vaudeville Theater	1340-1342 Pacific Avenue	1908–1911
Cogswell's Hall	8th and Pacific Avenue	1881–1882
Colonial Theater	916-918 Broadway	1914–1930
Columbia Theater	1321-1325 Pacific Avenue	1896
Columbia Theater	910-912 Pacific Avenue	1918 (few months)
Community Theater	5441 South M Street	1924–1966
Community World Theater	5441 South M Street	1987–1988
Cordray Theater	(9th Street Theater)	
Crown Theater	2212 North 30th	1912–1915
Crystal Theater	910-912 Pacific Avenue	1904–1907
Dream Theater	901-907 Broadway	1912–1916
Edison Theatre	914 Broadway	1903–1904
Emerald Theater	2152 K Street	1914
Empire Theater	1110-1116 Pacific Avenue	1904–1906
Empress Theater	821-823 Pacific Avenue	1913–1914

Everybody's Theater	2606 Sixth Avenue	1920–1925
Exhibit Amusement Company	1110-1116 Pacific Avenue	1907
Favorite Theater	(My Favorite Theater)	
Fern Theater	8401 South Park Avenue	1914
Fife Drive-In Theater	1601 Goldau Road E	1950–1985
Fox Broadway	902-914 Broadway	1930
Fox Rialto	(Rialto Theater)	
Galaxy 6	3012 South 23rd	2002–2009
Galaxy Narrows Theater	2208 Mildred Street West	2010–2013
Gem Theater	3010 Portland Avenue	1914–1915
Germania Hall	1308-1310 Fawcett Avenue	1888–1921
Grand Cinema	606 Fawcett	1995–present
Grand Theater	821-823 Pacific Avenue	1905–1910
Guild Sixth Avenue	2502-2504 Sixth Avenue	1962–1975
Haymarket Theater	1321-1325 Pacific Avenue	1892–1895
Heilig Theater	47 Saint Helens Avenue	1927–1931
Hippodrome Theater	821-823 Pacific Avenue	1915, 1918–1920
Hollywood Theater	2118-2120 North 30th	1922
Idle Hour Theater	5400 block South Tacoma Way	1910–1912
Image Theater	5102 North Pearl	1971
Isis Theater	3737 South Park Avenue	1915
Jewell Theatre	1318-1320 Pacific Avenue	1915
K Street Theater	Corner 11th & MLK	1924–1955
Liberty Theater	906-908 Pacific Avenue	1915–1928
Lighthouse Theater	3809-3811 Yakima Avenue South	1974
Lincoln Plaza Cinema	31 Montana Avenue	1988–2000
Lincoln Theater	1518-1520 K Street	1916–1931
Lyceum Theater	312 South 9th	1901–1904
Lyceum Theater	2717 Sixth Avenue	1915–1916
Lyric Theater	1318-1320 Pacific Avenue	1910–1914
Lyric Theater	5042-5046 Yakima Avenue	1922–1927
Majestic Theater	901-907 Broadway	1909–1910
Majestic Theater	821-823 Pacific Avenue	1911–1912
Majestic Theater	2305-2307 Pacific Avenue	1914
Malan-Magrath Theater	914 Broadway	1905
Mecca Theater	755-759 Broadway	1972–2006
Melbourne Theater	916-918 Pacific Avenue	1914–1918
Mission Theater	4801-4805 Yakima Avenue	1924
Movie	5042-5046 Yakima Avenue	1921
Music Box	902-914 Broadway	1933–1963
My Favorite Theater	2118-2120 North 30th	1920
Narrows Plaza 8 Theater	2208 Mildred Street West	1983–2009
Narrows Theater	7116 Sixth Avenue	1949–1984
National Theater	1316-1318 A Street	1889–1895

New Lincoln Theater	1518-1520 K Street	1942–1945
New Rose Theater	514-516 South 11th	1920–1937
Nickelodeon Theater	2305-2307 Pacific Avenue	1913
Nicolodeum Theater	916-918 Pacific Avenue	1908
Ninth Street Theater	312 South 9th	1893–1900
Oak Theater	910-912 Pacific Avenue	1918 (few months)
Olympic Theater/Cordray	312 South 9th	1892
One Hundred & Twelfth Drive-In Theater	401 112th Street East	1971–1989
Orion Theater	2602 North Proctor	1914–1916
Orpheum Theater	924-926 Broadway	1904–1905
Orpheum Theater	5400 block South Tacoma Way	1913–1918
Owl Theater	1321-1325 Pacific Avenue	1897–1904
Palace Theater	1128 Pacific Avenue	1910–1928
Pantages Theater	910-912 Pacific Avenue	1908–1918
Pantages Theater	901-907 Broadway	1918–1928, 1983–present
Paramount	3816 North 26th	1923–1933
Park Theater	3510 McKinley Avenue	1913–1921
Park Theater	3508 McKinley Avenue	1922–1961
Phenix Theater	1321-1325 Pacific Avenue	1905–1906
Playtime Theate	3809-3811 Yakima Avenue South	1981
Princess Theater	906-908 Pacific Avenue	1912–1914
Proctor Street Blue Mouse	2611 North Proctor	1925–1927
Proctor Theater	2611 North Proctor	1928–1977
Realart Theater	5400 block South Tacoma Way	1919–1960
Regent Theater	821-823 Pacific Avenue	1916–1917
Rex Theater	3805 Yakima Avenue South	1912–1918
Rex Theater	3809-3811 Yakima Avenue South	1919–1957
Rex Theater/Playtime Theater	3809-3811 Yakima Avenue South	1980–1986
Rialto (Fox)	312 South 9th	1918–present
Riviera Theater	906-908 Pacific Avenue	1929–1950
RKO Orpheum	901-907 Broadway	1931–1932
RKO Pantages	901-907 Broadway	1929–1930
Rose Theater	953-957 Tacoma Avenue South	1911–1918
Rose Theater	514-516 South 11th	1920–1937
Roxy Theater	901-907 Broadway	1933–1983
Royal Theater	1110 Broadway	1910–1911
Royal Theater	2717 Sixth Avenue	1912–1913
Ryan & Wooden Moving Picture Theater	3201 Portland Avenue	1913
Savoy Theater	708-712 Broadway	1905–1909
Scenic Theater	(Circuit Theater)	
Searchlight Movie Palace	742-750 Pacific Avenue	1897
Shaw Brothers Movies	905-907 Pacific Avenue	1893
Shell Theater	1318-1320 Pacific Avenue	1916–1960
Smith's Place	704 Pacific Avenue	1877–1882

Standard Theater	1110 Broadway	1896–1898
Star Moving Picture Theater	5400 block South Tacoma Way	1909
Star Theater	312 South 9th	1905–1909
Star-Lite Park-in Theater	8301 South Tacoma Way	1948–1996
Strand Theater	916-918 Pacific Avenue	1919–1921
Sunset	2502-2504 Sixth Avenue	1919–1961
Sunset Theater	2606 Sixth Avenue	1915–1919
Tacoma Auto-View Drive-In	9901 South Tacoma Way	1947–1948
Tacoma Central Theater	3102 South 23rd	1990–2001
Tacoma Education & Amusement Co.	2711 Sixth Avenue	1912–1915
Tacoma Little Theatre	210 North I Street	1940–present
Tacoma Mall Theater	4302 Tacoma Mall Boulevard	1968–1973
Tacoma Mall Twin	4302 Tacoma Mall Boulevard	1974–2002
Tacoma Musical Playhouse	7116 Sixth Avenue	1996–present
Tacoma South Cinema	7601 South Hosmer	1983–2002
Tacoma Theatre	902-914 Broadway	1890–1926
Tacoma West Cinema	1802 South Mildred	1983–1998
Tahoma Hall	(Germania Hall)	
Telenews Theater	916-918 Broadway	1945–1946
Temple Theater	47 Saint Helens Avenue	1932–1991
Thannhaeuser Theater	1020 K Street	1911
Theater on the Square	915 Broadway	1993–present
Theatre Comique	815 Pacific Avenue	1887–1892
Vaudette Theater	1110-1112 K Street	1911–1925
Vaudette Theater	1112 Broadway	1907
V-Deo Theater	1518-1520 K Street	1950–1953
Victory Theater	4801-4805 Yakima Avenue	1925–1935
Victory Theater	910-912 Pacific Avenue	1919–1923
Warwick Theatre	1110-1112 MLK Jr Way	1919
Washington Theater	2606 Sixth Avenue	1913–1914
World Theater	1313 Broadway	1919–1920
Zelinski Theater	2118-2120 North 30th	1915–1919

Tacoma Theaters By The Year

Table and graph developed by Deborah Freedman

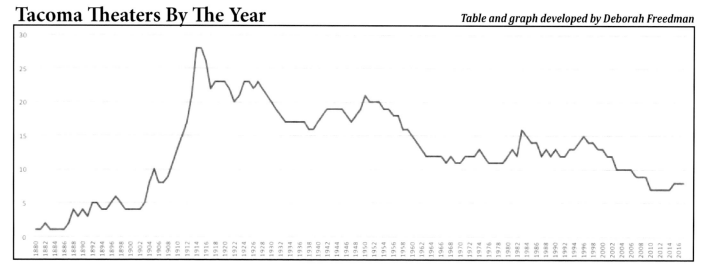

The Northwest's First Movie?

By Deborah Freedman

There's an inherent risk in attaching the word "first" to a pioneering event or endeavor. However, the management of Tacoma's Apollo Theater did just that in July of 1916. Their newspaper ad for the motion picture *Gog-Gle-Hi-Te* (Where Land and Water Meet) proclaimed it was the "first real motion picture feature every produced in the northwest." The key word was "feature," as several short documentary pieces had been recorded earlier during the 1909 Alaska-Yukon-Pacific exposition.

The movie was filmed in and around Tacoma, and produced by the Pacific Coast Motion Picture Company, "a Tacoma corporation." (Four years earlier the same company had operated briefly in San Francisco, publishing sheet music.) The motion picture portrayed pioneer days and Indian lore and prominently featured "our mountain," just as the struggle over the name of Mt. Tacoma vs. Mt. Rainier was coming to a head.

The "five big reels of unsurpassed scenic grandeur" featured an entire cast of Tacoma talent, including leading man Grattan Guerin as Napoleon Despar. Guerin, previously a featured organist at the Colonial, conveniently also served as the musical director at the Apollo. He composed music for the film and conducted the orchestra during the five-day engagement. That summer Guerin (1890–1986) filed a copyright for the song *I Adore You, Dear Old Washington* before moving on to California, where he continued his musical career.

The 1916 motion picture was produced and directed by Lionel Dobell, an English actor recently arrived from London. By August he was reportedly in rehearsals for the starring role in *The God and the Woman* at the company's studios in the Tacoma building. Dobell (1871–1947) married and moved on to Seattle, where he made films for the Red Cross during World War One and later performed in radio.

Movies Made in Tacoma

Title	Year	Genre
10 Things I Hate About You	1999	Comedy, Drama, Romance
99 and 44/100% Dead	1974	Action, Adventure, Comedy
Ad Around Us	2017	Documentary
Atilla a Love Story	2012	Drama
Battleground	1949	Action, War, Drama
Beautiful Brit Baker	2012	Crime
Becoming Icizzle	2009	Documentary, Biography, Comedy
Bible Quiz	2013	Documentary
Black Circle Boys	1997	Drama, Horror, Thriller
Black Top Dreams	2006	Drama
Blue Caprice	2013	Biography, Crime, Drama
Born to Be Wild	1995	Adventure, Comedy, Drama
Born to Fight	2011	Action, Family
Chihuly in the Hotshop	2008	Documentary
Chips, the War Dog	1990	Adventure, Drama, Family
Chrome	2017	Adventure, Sci-Fi
Cinderella Liberty	1973	Drama, Romance
Come See the Paradise	1990	Drama, Romance, War
Commencement	2013	Drama
Countdown	1996	Crime, Mystery, Thriller
Cult Killer: The Story of Rick Rodriguez	2006	Documentary

Title	Year	Genre
Demon Hunters	1999	Comedy, Horror
Diary of Ellen Rimbauer	2003	Drama, Horror, Mystery
Eleanor and Franklin	1975	Biography, Drama, Romance
Enough	2002	Crime, Drama, Thriller
Eyes of the Totem	1927	Drama
Flaming Forest	1926	Action, Drama
Frivolous Sal	1924	Western
Game On II	2016	Comedy, Drama
Gamers: Dorkness Rising	2008	Action, Adventure, Comedy
Gamers: Natural One	2013	Comedy, Fantasy
Get Carter	2000	Action, Crime, Drama
Girl Who Wasn't Wanted	1930	Adventure, Western
Gog-Gle-Hi-Te	1916	Western
Go-Kustom TV	2017	Documentary
Golden Bed	1924	Drama
Half Empty III	2011	Drama
Hand That Rocks the Cradle	1992	Drama, Thriller
Heart of the Game	2005	Documentary, Sport
Heart of the Yukon	1927	Adventure
Hearts and Fists	1926	Drama
Holmes University 4: Origins of the Fall	2016	Crime
House Rulez	2014	Comedy
I Love You to Death	1990	Comedy, Crime
Jack Boyz	2016	Crime
Jacqueline Bouvier Kennedy	1981	Biography, Drama
Khane Black	2012	Thriller
Last Seen in Idaho	2017	Crime, Mystery, Thriller
Late Autumn	2010	Drama
Lemonheads	2017	Comedy, Drama, Thriller
Les Copains	1965	Comedy
Limbo	2008	Comedy
McNeil Island	2018	Drama
Montgomery House: the Perfect Haunting	2010	Documentary
Officer and a Gentleman	1982	Drama, Romance
Patent Leather Kid	1927	Drama, Romance, Sport
Powder River	1921	Western
Prefontaine	1997	Biography, Drama, Romance
Preston Tylk/Bad Seed	2000	Mystery, Thriller
Pride is Forever	2012	Documentary
Punk Band	2018	Documentary
Recoil	2011	Action
Say Anything	1989	Comedy, Drama, Romance
Sentenced Home	2006	Documentary
Simple Creature	2016	Sci-Fi, Thriller
Stay Awake	2017	Thriller
Stephen King's Rose Red	2002	Horror, Mystery, Thriller
Sweet Revenge	1976	Comedy, Crime, Drama
Tammytown	2007	Comedy
The Prodigal	1982	Drama
Thin Ice	1937	Comedy, Musical, Romance
Three Fugitives	1989	Action, Comedy
To Hell and Back	1955	Action, Biography, Drama
Toxic Lullaby/Gone with the Dead the Movie	2017	Action, Horror
Traveling in Olympia	2001	Drama
Tugboat Annie	1933	Comedy, Drama
Tugboat Annie Sails Again	1940	Comedy, Drama, Romance
Turning Points Stories of Life and Change in the Church	2005	Documentary
Waiting for the Light	1990	Comedy
War Games	1983	Sci-Fi, Thriller
When the Door Opened	1925	Drama
Winds of War	1983	Drama, Romance, War
Windy City Incident	2005	Comedy
Wings of the Storm	1927	Drama
You Can't Win	2016	Drama

Sourced by Ilona Perry
This list of movies made in Tacoma does not include shorts (there were many), reality TV show episodes or video games.

NOW PLAYING

Author Profiles

Murray Morgan

More than a quarter century ago, Murray Morgan proposed a collection of stories about the history of Tacoma's theaters. "It would be a social history told in narrative style with emphasis on individual personalities, rather like *Skid Road* and *Puget's Sound,* but with more illustrative material.

"With vast lack of modesty, I feel I am uniquely qualified for this book. I'm well acquainted with the history of the town. I reviewed plays as a sideline for nearly 30 years. I enjoy telling history through the interplay of colorful personalities, of whom there was no lack in Tacoma." It was a project he pursued with passion,

but was left as a work in progress at the time of his passing in the year 2000.

Lane Morgan, the daughter of Murray and Rosa, holds all rights to her father's works, published and otherwise assembled as manuscript drafts and notes. Through her generosity, boxes of materials were made available and specific rights were granted for the authors to develop the many essays that are featured in *Showtime in Tacoma* under Murray's byline. While a number of the books he authored in his 84 years remain in print, it is particularly satisfying that his rich storytelling about Tacoma's historic theaters now becomes available to new audiences through these essays.

Lane recalls his approach to the theater reviews: "I think what made Murray's reviews valuable for many was that he was knowledgeable and interested, but not a theater-world insider. He wasn't writing to impress other critics but to help other audience members, and he didn't really care about the prestige of any particular venue, cast, or playwright. He judged the works on their merits – using his own writer's criteria for making characters come alive through their interactions. Not surprisingly, he also liked to research and present the play's historical context. His reviews often included vignettes about the playwright or the earliest critical responses.

Murray and Rosa in the Murray Morgan Room of Tacoma Public Library Main Branch

© UWSC/Mary Randlett

"Several times in junior high and high school he let me bring friends along to productions he was reviewing. Later some of them told me it was their first chance to see live theater, that a new world opened up. He would have been so pleased to see his granddaughter Deshanna on stage in Tacoma."

Murray, a graduate of Stadium High School and the University of Washington, studied journalism at Columbia University. "I was going to school and applying all over New York for jobs," he recalled years later." When Pearl Harbor was attacked, I got offered every single job I'd applied for and I took them all." He worked for *Time* during the day, for CBS nights and for the *Herald-Tribune* on weekends.

When Murray married Rosa in 1939, they spent their honeymoon on a kayak trip down the Danube River and eventually made their home in a cabin in Auburn that had previously been the Trout Lake Dance Hall. As they shared life together she was his editor as he wrote books, newspaper columns and theater reviews. Before he died he began donating his research materials to the Tacoma Public Library, followed by his entire research collection, comprising more than 3,000 volumes, after his death. The special collections at the Tacoma Public Library are held in the Murray and Rosa Morgan Room.

He wrote *Skid Road,* his best-known book, in the late 40s while working as a tender on the 11th Street Bridge at night and teaching writing at the College of Puget Sound during the day. The historic structure was renamed the Murray Morgan Bridge in 1997. He also was a radio commentator with the courage to lead crusades against corruption and political misbehavior.

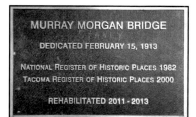

Lane Morgan (L) and Mayor Strickland at bridge dedication 📷 BJ

The late Caroline Gallacci, a prominent local historian, once reflected on Murray's influence: "Writing a history is an awesome task, especially for us living in Tacoma and Pierce County who have Murray Morgan's shoes to fill... Murray was always a beacon for us stumbling through historical unknowns, and a person that any of us could call upon when our research led us to documentary dead ends. He was a true teacher

– a one of a kind – who could so easily resurrect the past in ways beyond belief."

Ron Magden, a renowned historian and teacher in his own right, taught for many years alongside Murray at Tacoma Community College. "Murray always said he was a better writer than a teacher. The thousands of students he taught would never agree with that self-assessment. A magnetic spark ignited when he began to lecture. You felt you were physically present at the great moments of Pacific Northwest history. It was not uncommon that students would give him a standing ovation at the end of the course term."

After working with his words throughout this project, the authors of *Showtime in Tacoma* are inspired to offer a standing ovation for Murray's enduring legacy as a historian, teacher and compelling storyteller.

Deborah Freedman

Deborah Freedman has a detective's shrewdness for tracking down historic facts about people, places and events and, with uncovered information in hand, she has a story tellers' touch to bring said information to life. Those skills are exhibited in a number of pieces she provided for *Showtime in Tacoma*, both the book and accompanying exhibit at the Tacoma Historical Society museum.

Photo by Patrick Igo

Deb Freedman is retired from twenty years with the Tacoma Public Library, where she learned to enjoy doing research and storytelling. Those skills have helped her in her second career as a volunteer, researcher, writer and presenter. An award-winning teacher and author, Deb previously created two titles in Tacoma Historical Society's series of *21 Tales* books for elementary students. In 2015 Deb received the prestigious City of Destiny Award from the City of Tacoma in recognition of her work as a volunteer for Tacoma Historical Society during its transition to a new facility. Deb lives in Gig Harbor, Washington.

Deb has been a regular presenter for the Jewish Genealogical Society of Washington State since the organization's creation, offering genealogy tips for beginners. Drawing on her storytelling skills, Deb has become a popular speaker at synagogues, retirement centers and genealogy and historical societies throughout Western Washington and Oregon. She has participated as a teacher in Pacific Lutheran University's Learning Is For Ever program. Most recently Deb Freedman has created an interactive Jeopardy-style game of Tacoma history.

Deb Freedman's special interest is researching the previously-undocumented Jewish community of the nineteenth century in Tacoma, Washington. (In fact, she can claim to be the world's leading expert on the subject, since she's likely the only one.) Her book entitled *Tacoma's Dry Goods and Wet Goods: Nineteenth Century Jewish Pioneers*, was published by Tacoma Historical Society Press in July of 2016. She was also the curator of the Society's exhibit of the same name, which ran July 26–November 26, 2016.

Steph Farber & Phyllis Harrison, PhD

Steph Farber (Lowell, Jason Lee, Stadium) and Phyllis Harrison (Wainwright, Hunt, Wilson) are both third-generation Tacomans with strong ties to the Theater District. Steph's father opened LeRoy Jewelers in 1941 at 950 Broadway. The store – now a national award-winning destination for custom jewelry design – has for the past 75 years been a South Sound destination, always on Broadway, always between South 9th and South 13th. Steph spent much of his youth in the store and, a few years after graduating from the University of Washington and Pacific Lutheran University, joined the business as bench jeweler and designer. Phyllis migrated to other parts of

BJ

the country after high school. After attaining degrees from Washington State University and Colorado State University, Phyllis earned her Doctorate at the Folklore Institute at Indiana University. After working in Colorado and Nebraska, she returned to Tacoma in 1988. In 1995 she, along with master shipwright Mike Vlahovich, founded The Commencement Bay Maritime Center, now the Foss Waterway Seaport.

Phyllis and Steph met through the Broadway Center for the Performing Arts. Dedicated both to the arts and to downtown Tacoma, the Farber family supported the restoration of the Pantages Theater in the early 80s and Steph served as a dedicated member of the board through the tumultuous early days on into the development of the Theater District. Phyllis worked at the Broadway Center for several years. In 1993 the pair researched and wrote an anniversary program documenting the history of the Pantages and Rialto theaters and the development of Tacoma's Theater District. Their extensive involvement with the Theater District, through research and personal experiences, provided the basis for a number of insightful articles in *Showtime in Tacoma*.

Phyllis left the Broadway Center to launch The Art Stop, a national award-winning gallery of contemporary American Craft which now shares space with LeRoy Jewelers. Steph and Phyllis married in 2001 and have continued their support of the arts and downtown Tacoma – just as the arts and downtown have supported them and the entire community.

Marshall L. Johnson

The image titled "Theatre Row circa 1930" that adorns the front cover of *Showtime in Tacoma* is representative of many of Marshall Lysander Johnson's paintings of Tacoma and the Northwest. The artist's color sense shows his wide diversity. His distinctive style is reflected in vibrant colors, expressive use of palette knife and strong brush-work for bold statements and, at times, soft colors for subtle moods. His primary medium is oil on canvas. Other works include watercolors and reproductions of his art such as limited edition serigraphs, giclées, and lithographs.

Marshall was born in Bellingham, Washington. He began painting at a very early age. Later, he earned fine art degrees from both the University of Washington in Seattle and the Art Center College of Design in Los Angeles. Marshall continued to paint while working in the corporate world. In 1978, he left his position as art director for a major Washington corporation and became a full-time artist. Marshall's paintings are found in private and corporate collections worldwide. He is a Life Member of the Northwest Watercolor Society (NWWS) and a Signature Member of the American Society of Marine Artists (ASMA). Among many projects for organizations, he designed the logo for the Tacoma Historical Society. The artist and his wife Bonnie have a studio and home on Orcas Island.

Blaine Johnson

Throughout his adventuresome career, Blaine Johnson identifies two themes that are woven through his varied pursuits – working with words and working with wood. These themes overlay roles he has performed in writing, real estate and community development, construction and management. Many of those activities have been the motivation to co-author *Showtime in Tacoma* with Brian Kamens.

The "words" started professionally with stints at the *Seattle Post-Intelligencer* covering the Seattle Sonics and then as Sports Editor. He authored two books from that era, *What's Happenin'? A Revealing Journey Through the World of Professional Basketball*, published by Prentice-Hall and *Calling the Shots*, published by Simon & Schuster. His writing has been recognized with national and regional awards.

He held two positions in the horse racing industry, first as Publicity Director for Longacres Race Track and then as Executive Director for the Washington State Horse Racing Commission. This was followed with a position as Director of Port Relations for the Port of Tacoma. While performing in the latter role, Blaine served on committees and interacted with business and community leaders who were trying to resurrect the Downtown sector during this mid-80s timeframe. When McClatchy purchased the *Tacoma News Tribune* in 1986, Blaine moved into a position as Assistant Managing Editor, furthering his engagement with the community.

Throughout his roles in the realm of "words," Blaine restored old houses and commercial buildings. In 1992 he left the TNT to pursue the realm of "wood" fulltime, which led to the building of townhomes in west Tacoma and partnership endeavors to restore the former Savoy Theater on Broadway and convert it into commercial use. This led to the creation of Opera Alley between South 7th and St. Helens. Blaine joined with other partners to convert the former YMCA on Market Street into a residential condominium called the Vintage Y and to construct a mixed-use building next door called the Roberson on Ledger Square.

Blaine was the founding president of the Theater District Association, a neighborhood group that raised funds and politically promoted the Broadway LID to develop streetscape enhancements that included Ledger Square and the Ben Gilbert Park on St. Helens. He served on the Asarco Development Strategy Team, negotiated on behalf of the City of Tacoma in the purchase of properties for the Thea Foss Waterway development and serves on the Business Improvement Area (BIA) board. The only time he has worked away from Tacoma in the past three decades was a stint as Chief Executive Officer for the Law Offices of Scott Warmuth in San Gabriel, California.

"I was raised primarily in Seattle. I've lived in New York City and Los Angeles and a handful of places in between. I've been in all 50 states and 49 countries. I travel to explore and learn. I made Tacoma my home when I married my wife, Catherine, 35 years ago. Informed by my experiences elsewhere, I was intrigued by the possibilities I discovered in Tacoma and, more importantly, I was inspired to invest emotionally, financially and strategically in trying to make a difference here.

"I believe in the New Urbanism concepts of developing a culturally diverse, walkable, architecturally appealing, artistically vibrant, historically rooted community. That's why I am committed to being here and why I wanted to write this book."

Witness to a Renaissance

A Personal Prospective By Scott Warmuth

My insights into Tacoma were informed through my friendship with Blaine Johnson, who moved from Seattle (where I grew up) to Tacoma in the early 1980s.

I had left Seattle to live in New York, Los Angeles, Washington D.C. and other places throughout the world, and after Blaine moved to Tacoma I would make many visits back home to the Northwest. In the 1980s, visits to Tacoma to meet Blaine usually involved walks through downtown and along Ruston Way. Frankly, things looked bleak and without prospects. Blaine kept telling me Tacoma had real potential and deep historical roots. He has been proven right, and the roots are colorfully portrayed in *Showtime in Tacoma.* The potential has been realized in ways I simply could not have imagined back in my early visits, but I see Tacoma now as a vibrant, attractive city that exhibits many of the qualities of the world-class cities I have lived in throughout my life.

The rehabilitation by Blaine and his partners of the 1889 building that once had been the Savoy Theater and the development of Opera Alley gave me a sense of what dynamic things could actually happen in Downtown Tacoma. This was followed by more projects, market rate residences and offices, new cafes, stores and brew pubs, parks and new streetscapes.

I saw the University of Washington campus emerge, the Foss Waterway develop from an industrial wasteland, the opening of all the new museums, the amazing transformation of the former Asarco smelter site and so much more. The clientele in my law office in Los Angeles is comprised almost exclusively of the Chinese diaspora. I am impressed how Tacoma has committed to the Chinese Reconciliation Project on Ruston Way.

My son, Anthony, graduated in 2012 from the University of Puget Sound, which enhanced my involvement with Tacoma. He has followed up his positive school experiences with investment in Tacoma real estate. All those who have had the vision and taken action to make all these positive things happen should be proud of what has been achieved in the past 20 or 30 years. As an outsider who has been able to witness these impressive developments, I applaud all that has been accomplished and am eager to see the next acts in Tacoma's renaissance.

– Scott Warmuth makes his home in Pasadena, California. He founded the Law Offices of Scott Warmuth, a leading litigation and immigration firm, in 1984.

Scott Warmuth   **Anthony Warmuth**

Court C (S. 7th to St. Helens) was transformed into Opera Alley

S. 7th, Market and St. Helens transformed into Ledger Square

Former Savoy Theater transformed into the Passages Building

Ben Gilbert Park was transformed from a weed patch

Tacoma Historical Society

Tacoma Historical Society is a community-supported volunteer-driven 501(c)(3) charitable, nonprofit corporation, and is dedicated to the preservation, promotion and presentation of the history of the City of Tacoma and its people. Tacoma Historical Society works to forge connections between past and present generations, fostering an appreciation of the past and a sense of place within our community's history. The Tacoma Historical Society Museum and research center is located at 919 Pacific Avenue. **www.tacomahistory.org**

Brian Kamens

If life's work should be interesting, pursued with passion and meaningful to others, Brian Kamens' life's work has and continues to achieve just such a satisfying status. The product of that work has provided a truly remarkable depth of knowledge of Tacoma's historical character and is the foundation for the stories and details presented in *Showtime in Tacoma.*

A native of Plymouth, Connecticut, Brian discovered Tacoma while touring the country in 1976 and soon found employment at the Tacoma Public Library, an institution he regards as "a great library system in a fascinating city."

Brian's "life's work" began as a lunch-hour hobby. Library patrons would often ask about the history of their home, but unless they lived in a well-known mansion there was little information to be found. Brian ran across an article in the 1901 *Tacoma Daily Ledger* with pictures of more than 50 local homes. This inspired him to begin indexing the local papers for house and building news by address.

The research was first entered on 3-by-5 cards which led to a typed version. As popularity for the information grew, the research became part of his regular library activities. As the Internet grew, it was a perfect match for putting the building index online, eventually including links to the library's photograph collection.

In compiling the index, Brian read every Sunday newspaper and scanned every daily newspaper from 1883 to 1966. He continues to add information to the Pierce County Buildings Index, which has reached nearly 70,000 individual addresses and has become an important resource for researchers of all kinds. In developing this resource, Brian offers, "It has been an honor and a privilege to watch the history of the City of Destiny unfold before me in the pages of our local newspapers."

His activities expand well beyond the dusty bound volumes of yellowed newspapers. Brian was a founder and the first secretary when the Tacoma Historical Society was formed in 1990. He served as the society's program chair for several years, conducts walking tours and has been in charge of research for the society's popular annual Historic Homes of Tacoma Tour.

In 2001, Brian was awarded the Tacoma Historical Society's Murray Morgan Award. In 2003, the American Library Association's *Library Journal* named him a national Library Mover and Shaker. In the same year, the Washington State Historic Preservation Office honored him with the Award for Outstanding Achievement in Historic Preservation Education. He is the author of several reports and bibliographies. In 1989, the year of the Washington State Centennial, he was co-author of *To Live in Dignity; Pierce County Labor, 1883–1989.*

Brian currently serves as the Supervisor of the Tacoma Public Library Northwest Room and Special Collections.

Brian's List of Lost Architectural Gems

Arguably, no one is more familiar with the buildings that have occupied the Tacoma landscape than Brian Kamens. Many buildings have provided a showtime presence on Tacoma's streetscapes. This is his list of the most architecturally significant properties that have been lost to time through neglect, fire or someone's idea there was a better use for the site – often resulting in parking lots where architectural gems once stood.

TACOMA HOTEL, 913 A St

TACOMA THEATRE, 902-14 Broadway

HOTEL FIFE/DONNELLY HOTEL, 742-50 Pacific Ave

GROSS BROTHERS DEPARTMENT STORE,
901 Broadway

TOP OF THE OCEAN, 2217 Ruston Way

MUNICIPAL DOCK, 1025 Dock St

JAPANESE LANGUAGE SCHOOL, 1715 Tacoma Ave S

WEAVER STUDIOS, 1600 Titlow Rd

CRYSTAL PALACE MARKET, 1101-13 Market St

HOTEL ROCHESTER/BONNEVILLE HOTEL,
109 Tacoma Ave S

LUZON BLDG., 1302-04 Pacific Ave

WASHINGTON INDUSTRIAL EXPOSITION BUILDING,
714 Tacoma Ave N

COLONIAL THEATER, 916-18 Broadway

WALKER'S CASTLE OF MUSIC, 1023 N Oakes St

Residences

ALLEN C. MASON RES., 4301 N Stevens St

WALTER SUTTER RES., 2600 N Carr St

Continued List of Lost Gems with Photos: *All Photos* ⊙TPL

ANNIE WRIGHT SEMINARY, 611 Division Ave

CALIFORNIA BLOCK BUILDING, 1110-16 Pacific Ave

PIERCE COUNTY COURT HOUSE, 1012 S G St

NELSON BENNETT RES., 505 Broadway

FIDELITY BLDG., 949-55 Broadway

CENTRAL SCHOOL, 1114 S Altheimer St

SAMSON HOTEL, 1152-56 Fawcett Ave

HENRY HEWITT, JR. RES., 501 N 4th St

ANTON HUTH RES., 504 N 3rd St

FIRST METHODIST CHURCH,
423 Martin Luther King, Jr. Way

WILLIAM F. SHEARD RES, 509 N Yakima Ave

NOW PLAYING

Acknowledgments

This project, covering an extensive span of local history across an eclectic range of topics within the realm of Tacoma entertainment, involves many people deserving salutes of gratitude from the authors. Essays by Murray Morgan are a significant component of *Showtime in Tacoma*. We are honored that his daughter, **Lane Morgan,** trusted us to develop these stories and provided us with boxes of notes, drafts and various compositions which are showcased in the resulting essays... Five years ago, the authors embarked on a plan to develop this book as a partner project with **Babe Lehrer's** biography of Alexander Pantages. Since Babe's passing two years ago, her family has committed to bringing her book to publication. We appreciate the coordination provided by Babe's sons **Michael** and **Bradley** as well as writer **Ethan Yarborough.** Babe's passionate support for the arts was shared by another force of community leadership, **Dawn Lucien.** Before her recent passing, she shared many hours of insight related to the restoration of the Pantages Theater and other community projects. We applaud the Broadway Center for planning to honor both of these inspiring women as part of the upgrades being conducted for the Theatre on the Square... BPCA Executive Director **David Fischer's** commitment of support has helped considerably to bring both this book and Babe's to publication. As conveyed in the Foreword, his vision for management and development of the Broadway Center has allowed us to write a much more encouraging story about the future of arts and culture in Tacoma... Which was evidenced in Tacoma Mayor **Marilyn Strickland's** much-appreciated message expressing that civic optimism.

We are grateful for the opportunity to publish this book in partnership with Tacoma Historical Society Press. There are roles large and larger that make a book like this happen. **Deborah Freedman** has the title of Tacoma Historical Society treasurer, but her roles in authoring a number of pieces in this book, editing, guiding research and developing the *Showtime in Tacoma* exhibit at the THS museum place her in a rare category the authors acknowledge with deep-felt gratitude... In the same THS camp, we thank president **Bill Baarsma** for his efforts to bring to us tales of Tacoma's major sports events... (articles for which **Marc Blau** of the Shanaman Sports Museum provided historic photos.)... We take comfort in the fact THS vice president **Dale Wirsing** applied his editor's eye, honed by a long newspaper career, to our copy... **Brendan Balaam** provided another level of editing and research as part of the THS team... The authors and everyone involved with THS Press are very grateful that artist **Marshall Lysander Johnson** honored *Showtime in Tacoma* by donating use of his iconic painting "Theatre Row Circa 1930" for our cover.

Contributions from writers representing specialized perspectives enrich this book with their insights. We applaud the efforts by **Steph Farber and Phyllis Harrison** as they resurrected previous research and personal experiences to provide several pieces relating to the saga of the Pantages Theater restoration and the renaissance of the Theater District... Former City Council Member **Bill Evans** dug through his memories to relate the resurrection of the Blue Mouse Theater... We thank **Lauren Hoogkamer** and **Mick Flaaen** for telling us about the rediscovery of the film *Eyes of the Totem* and providing the piece on Weaver Studios... We offer thanks to **Beverly Foley** for sharing her experiences of growing up in the family theater business and to **Philip Whitt** for revisiting memories of a bygone era of the film industry including his days as an early manager of The Grand Cinema... That theater is now under the management of **Philip Cowan** and we are grateful for his participation in our extensive Q&A related to the film selection process... We are grateful for these insightful contributions pertaining to various aspects of the music arena: **Syd Newell's** piece on her impresaria grandmother, **Peter Blecha's** offerings on Tacoma's rock 'n' roll history, **Rev. Adam McKinney's** piece on the more contemporary music scene, and **Little Bill Engelhart's** stories about his music memories from junior high school to today's Blues Vespers at Immanuel Presbyterian Church, a program **Rev. David Brown** took the time to discuss with us... We thank **Tom Blackwell** of the Puget Sound Theater Organ Society for providing us use of materials on that organization's informative website and offer thanks to **Wayne Keyser** for use of information on his vaudeville history website.

We are appreciative of the time and effort behind the profiles provided by each of the dozen performance organizations featured in this book, as well as permissions to use images representing their groups.

We thank each museum profiled for similar access to images. Those performance organization profiles were provided by:

Andy Buelow, Symphony Tacoma; **Judith Cullen,** Tacoma Little Theatre; **Erin Ceragioli,** Tacoma City Ballet; **Sven Rønning,** Second City Chamber Series; **Kristina Thomas,** Tacoma Youth Symphony Association; **Christophe Chagnard** and **Kathryn Habedank,** Northwest Sinfonietta; **Mark Reutlinger,** Tacoma Concert Band; **Noel Koran,** Tacoma Opera; **Jon Douglas Rake,** Tacoma Musical Playhouse; **Elizabeth Hirschl,** SOTA; **Nan Peele,** Tacoma Actors Guild;

Those who roam deeply in the realm of local history serve as valuable guides and we thank four individuals who have made valuable contributions over the years to the development of this book – **Ron Magden, Michael Sullivan, Ron Karabaich** and **Thomas R. Stenger.** Many images in this book come from the pictures and artifacts T.R. and Ron K have collected over the decades.

There are people whose role it is to facilitate access to information. We are grateful to the following for performing this role in such a supportive manner: Tacoma Public Library staff **Jean Fisher, Christine Bassett, Jody Gripp,** and **Ilona Perry** – who sourced the list of movies made in Tacoma; **Nicolette Bromberg,** University of Washington/Special Collections Division; **Eileen Price,** Washington State Historical Society/Reference; **Holly Klindt, Jared Wigert,** Broadway Center; **Jennifer Dean,** Urban Grace Church; the Terryville CT Public Library; and **Donna Kamens.**

Ultimately, the words and pictures need to become a book. We chose the Tacoma-based firm LaserWriting to make that happen and, after many weeks of shared endeavor, are most appreciative of the design/layout/production skills provided by **David Petersen** and owner **John Leach.**

Personal note from Blaine
While Brian and I have written as a unified voice, I want to take this opportunity to acknowledge his role as a partner. Over the past five-plus years, we have been developing the ingredients that are presented in this book. I am most appreciative of the passion, patience and sincere commitment to accuracy that Brian has dedicated to our story telling... And, as anyone who has taken on such consuming endeavors knows, a lot of one's life goes on hold during the process. I thank my wife, Catherine, for graciously supporting me with the time to work and for applying a keen "reader's eye" as materials were developed.

Sponsors

For all the collaborative efforts to create this book, it would still be sitting in a digital file awaiting the means to start the presses if it wasn't for the generosity of five sponsors. With their belief this book will encourage an appreciation and support for art and culture in Tacoma, these sponsors have underwritten the production and printing costs. With deep gratitude for their support, we thank **Fred Roberson** and **Mat Shaw,** Tacoma historic property developers; **Scott Warmuth** of the Warmuth Foundation, Pasadena, California; **Mike McMenamin** and historian **Tim Hills** of McMenamins, which owns historic hotels and theater pubs based in Portland, Oregon; **Jason Whalen, Clemencia Castro-Woolery, Stuart Morgan** and **Clay Selby,** partners in Ledger Square Law, Tacoma; and **Team Totem** (in alliance with **Tacoma Historical Society)** saviors and promoters of the historic film *Eyes of the Totem.*

The Dollar Value of "Arts/Culture"

A national consulting organization has calculated that the nonprofit arts and culture sector is a significant industry for greater Tacoma's marketplace. Americans for the Arts in its most recent Prosperity 5 study finds that $137.2 million in economic activity is generated from spending by arts and culture organizations ($74.6 million) and event-related spending ($62.6 million) by their audiences, not including cost of event admission.

This sector supports 3,656 full-time equivalent jobs, generates $86 million in household incomes, and delivers $14 million in local and state government revenues.

"Tacoma's nonprofit arts and cultural organizations are integral to our commercial ecosystem," said City of Tacoma Arts Administrator Amy McBride. "They directly support a wide array of occupations spanning many industries."

"This study demonstrates that the arts are an economic and employment powerhouse both locally and across the nation," said Robert L. Lynch, president and CEO of Americans for the Arts.

Additional information is available at **www.cityoftacoma.org/aep**

Photo & Use Credits/Permissions

All photos and other images are authorized for use in *Showtime in Tacoma*. The codes adjacent to each photo corresponds with the list below.

BCPA –	Broadway Center for the Performing Arts
BCPA/LM –	BCPA/ Lisa Monet Photography
BCPA/CVGP –	BCPA/Chip Van Gilder Photography
BCPA/Act –	BCPA/Act Photography
BLC –	Babe Lehrer Collection
BJ –	Blaine Johnson
JS –	Jan Seferian
JB/RH –	Jazzbones/Rachel Hogan
LOC –	Library of Congress (1)
McM –	McMenamins renderings
NWS –	Northwest Sinfonietta
PBC –	Peter Blecha Collection
PSTOS –	Puget Sound Theatre Organ Society
RBC –	Roberson Building Corp
RKC –	Ron Karabaich Collection
SCC –	Second City Chamber
SOTA/DP –	School of the Arts/Drew Perine
SSM –	Shanaman Sports Museum of Tacoma-Pierce County
ST –	Symphony Tacoma
TCiB –	Tacoma City Ballet
TCoB –	Tacoma Concert Band
THS –	Tacoma Historical Society
TLT –	Tacoma Little Theatre
TMP/KD –	Tacoma Musical Playhouse/ Kat Dollarhide
TNT –	Tacoma News Tribune
TNT/PH –	Tacoma News Tribune/Peter Haley
TO –	Tacoma Opera
TPL –	Tacoma Public Library
TPL/TSC –	Tacoma Public Library/Thomas R. Stenger Collection (4)
TSC –	Thomas R. Stenger Collection
TYSA –	Tacoma Youth Symphony Association
UW/SC –	University of Washington Special Collections (2)
WSHS –	Washington State Historical Society (3)

(1) LOC – Library of Congress, Prints & Photographs Division, [LC-USZC4-3653] Sarah Bernhardt poster

(2) University of Washington Libraries, Special Collections, Waite 198, UW35520, UW35519, UW38004 – Mary Randlett Photograph Collection

(3) Washington State Historical Society (Tacoma, Washington) Catalog numbers: 2017.0.9, 2017.0.4, 2017.0.210, 2000.0.26, 2000.0.6, 2014.0.490

(4) Thomas R. Stenger donated over 2,000 historic postcards to the Tacoma Public Library archives.

With the exception of University of Washington Special Collections and Washington State Historical Society, which were compensated and permissions for use were granted, all compositions, interviews, photos and other images were provided as courtesy donations to this project.

CC-BY-SA - Creative Commons Attribution ShareAlike license, https://en.wikipedia.org/wiki/Little_Miss_Marker

Use of museum images were authorized by each organization.

Encore

Given the theatrical context of our journey through *Showtime in Tacoma*, we thought a brief summation might be viewed as a three-act play. In Act One, the transcontinental railroad arrives in the 1870s and the heroes are introduced – civic leaders who want to make Tacoma the great city of the West, led by Theodore Hosmer and the Tacoma Land Company. While the envisioned greatness is not fully achieved, much of the next 80 years passes with Tacoma functioning as a commercially viable, culturally active community. Until, Act Two, when downtown retail collapses with the opening of the Tacoma Mall in the mid-60s. By the late 70s, a distressed downtown and residential core has been left to perish on the side of the road to suburbia. Civic pride has disintegrated to the point it's "in" to brag about staying out of downtown.

But, then, Act Three opens with the arrival of another cast of heroes who have the vision and guts to make a stand against downtown's dismal demise. Channeling the original founders who built the Tacoma Theatre in 1890 as a statement of civic greatness, the Pantages Theater restoration 90 years later marks the climatic turning point for downtown Tacoma. This resolution sets in motion many valuable contributions, including University of Washington Tacoma, museums, and the current mission to further enhance the Broadway Center theaters. This current act is Now Playing, open-ended as to its possibilities, depending on the vision and resolve of the current cast of players in Tacoma's ongoing drama.

 WSHS
 RKC

Top Left: *In this 1873 image of what would become 7th and Pacific, the larger building is believed to be Ira Cogswell's livery stable, the first place of community gathering. Note persons standing next to foreground stump.* **Top Right:** *This image was taken in 1888 from the Northern Pacific Railroad headquarters building. One year later the Savoy Theater building would be constructed on Broadway to the left of the church. Old City Hall would be built in the lower right corner.* **Bottom:** *In 1885, Hosmer's house (white building in center) faced St Helens. It would be turned to face 9th – where it sits today as the oldest house in Tacoma. The larger structure at right would become the site of the Tacoma Theatre four years later. Note undeveloped tideflats.* TPL

1

2

3

4

1) This image of the 1950 Daffodil Parade illustrates the vibrancy of downtown at mid-century with throngs of viewers amid a backdrop of stores and theaters. 2) One of the more bizarre cultural-political convergences was this scene in 1924 when Irvings Imperial Midgets European Theatrical Troupe took time out between their three daily shows at the Pantages to participate in the Pierce County Sheriff's annual demolition of seized liquor stills during prohibition. 3) The 1886 Waddell Building at 15th and Pacific had lost a floor, was painted pea green and had trees growing out of it in 1979. 4) After a 2004 restoration, it is now home to the upscale Pacific Grill Restaurant, flanked by the Marriot Hotel and Greater Tacoma Convention and Trade Center.

1) A street-art expression of Tacoma's century old mantra beckons us to the future. 2) Crows wearing opera glasses gaze from a Theater District mural by artist Natalie Oswald. 3) In addition to theatrical shows, community gatherings, including a variety of annual festivals, are drawing people back downtown to lively events, such as this Theater District block party in Opera Alley. 4) Built in 1875, Theodore Hosmer's house, currently perched at 309 9th, has seen the rise, fall and resurrection of the Theater District. 5) Weary from marching in a 1931 pet parade, young Bobby David plunked down in front of the Rialto Theater. His dog, Rags, leaves us with the reminder: It's always Showtime in Tacoma.